16 $\frac{50}{01}$ EL

NEW ITALIAN WRITERS

AN ANTHOLOGY OF

NEW ITALIAN WRITERS

EDITED BY MARGUERITE CAETANI
AND SELECTED FROM THE PAGES OF THE
REVIEW BOTTEGHE OSCURE

GREENWOOD PRESS, PUBLISHERS
WESTPORT, CONNECTICUT

Originally published in 1950
by New Directions, New York,
in the form of selections from the periodical *Botteghe Oscure*

Reprinted with the permission
of Lelia Caetani Howard, Rome, Italy
through her attorney, Philip W. Amram, Washington, D.C.

First Greenwood Reprinting 1970

Library of Congress Catalogue Card Number 72-110822

SBN 8371-3211-8

Printed in the United States of America

CONTENTS

Mario Soldati   *The window*   9

Giorgio Bassani   *Poems*   91

Tommaso Landolfi   *Cancroregina*   95

Attilio Bertolucci   *From « The indian hut »*   157

Giuseppe Dessí   *Angel Island*   161

Giorgio Caproni   *The funicular*   181

Joyce Lussu   *Two short stories*   188

Franco Fortini   *Poems*   197

Vasco Pratolini   *The girls of Sanfrediano*   201

Alfonso Gatto   *Novel 1917*   303

Giorgio Bassani   *Love story*   307

Antonio Rinaldi   *Poems*   345

Roberto Roversi   *Poems for a print-collector*   348

Guglielmo Petroni   *The house is moving*   355

Notes on contributors   475

THE WINDOW

BY

MARIO SOLDATI

I

— or not to be

Coming back to London after twenty years, and after a war, such a war, a *war between us*; walking about once more in Piccadilly at night, after saying good-bye to all that forever; seeing my darling Twinkle again, at last! Although by now her hair has gone white, certainly has been, and will remain, the greatest joy of my old age.

Twinkle's eyes had not changed. I was still unable to give a name to their colour, so intensely did they sparkle; I could still, with absolute justification, call her *Twinkle*. And in her emaciated face, the skin was still fresh and pink as of old. And when I embraced her, at Victoria Station, I realised that her body, in spite of the passing of the years, was still what it had been: sinewy, athletic, vibrant. She had changed her clothes, but not the style of them: now she dressed in the fashion of twenty years ago, exactly as twenty years ago she had dressed in the fashion of another twenty years before that. As I clasped her in my arms, I suddenly felt young and filled with faith and with the enthusiasm of an Alfieri. What was Twinkle other than England itself, the England I loved, grown old, indeed, but younger than ever?

9

And, just as there had been in the past, at every desultory resumption of our friendship, now again there was a sudden exchange of confidences, from her to me, from me to her; of questions, answers, affectionate irony, eager reminiscences, programmes; but the programmes were all on her part.

Let me make myself quite clear: I am a lover of order, and a most orderly man myself. I have always organised my work in programmes of absolute precision. But I never dreamed of using the method for my holiday periods, for my hours of pleasure. My imitation, based on admiration, of English ways had won for me, in professional circles, a reputation for precision and correctness utterly un-Italian; but in my off-time, I always preserve my national characteristics.

Inversely, Twinkle, although she was generous, impulsive, a rebel against Anglo-Saxon conventionality, averse to any regular occupation, flinging herself continually into absurdly altruistic activities, tolerated in her own country for her « eccentricities », and forgiven as being the victim of too-prolonged visits to the Continent, had never given up her sky-blue note-books, in which English people write down days, and sometimes months, ahead, at what time, where, and with whom they will have lunch, tea, cocktails or dinner.

This time once more, a few minutes after our first youthful embrace, while the taxi was taking us from Victoria Station to my old hotel, miraculously unscarred, opposite the Green Park, there arose the inevitable disagreement.

« This is what I've been planning for you », said Twinkle; « this morning a rest, lunch at the hotel, then more rest until four; at four I will call for you and we will go for a walk in Hyde Park; at half-past five you will come to my place for tea,... » whereupon, seeing that this prospect of my future, minute for minute, had saddened me, she broke off: « Of course you loathe programmes. Forgive me, it comes so naturally to me, I had quite forgotten. We will do just as you like, of course ». She swallowed hard, then with an effort, and with all the amiability at her disposal, which was great, she wound up in Italian: « *Faremo quello che capita, così. Va bene?* » [1]

So it turned out that towards three c'clock we left the hotel and started to stroll down St. James's Street. It was an April afternoon, and windy; great white and black clouds raced over the sky, pierced every now and then by the early sun. You sensed the sea that surrounded England on all sides, and, hovering over the sea, Spring time. I reminded Twinkle of the lines:

> Oh, how this spring of love resembleth
> The uncertain glory of an April day,
> Which now shows all the beauty of the sun
> And by and by a cloud takes all away

Twinkle smiled sadly, and I attempted to translate the lines into Italian.

We were at that moment passing in front of Burlington House, and we stopped, unconsciously, before the poster of the exhibition that takes place, every spring, on its premises.

« Twenty years ago we came here too », I said to Twinkle; I had been to London then also at the same time of year. Didn't she remember? Twinkle had grown sad and silent. I took her gently by the arm.

« Wouldn't you like us to go to see the Exhibition again, just as we did then? »

« Yes », she replied. But I could see that she was thinking of something else; and that her thoughts were not cheerful.

« Perhaps you wouldn't like that? Would you prefer a little walk in the Park? »

« No, let's go in », she answered *sotto voce*, as though she shrank from rejecting, if she spoke too loud, the mournful thought that had come over her. « But it won't be the same as it was then ».

« Why not? As long as I'm with you, I don't feel as though anything were changed ».

---

[1] We will do whatever turns up, is that all right?

« Thank you », she said, climbing the stairs so slowly, that for the first time I suddenly remembered her age. « You are too sweet for words. But don't you see, I'm like this. Everything is always fine. But when the past, the past of those days comes back to my mind with some unforeseen contrast, as in this case, I feel... not exactly old, old is putting it feebly, I feel as though I were dead and buried ». I looked at her. And once more, just as in the past, just as always, I respected her silence. I had loved Twinkle, now I can say it. I had been fonder of her perhaps than of any other woman I have ever known. For a man like me, who has never run after phantoms, who has always preferred what he has had or was able to get to what he didn't have or couldn't get, it was undoubtedly a great, long, exceptional but unhappy passion. For her it was, only and always, friendship. She never concealed it from me. Even if she did not explain the reasons of her refusal, but simply declared that her feelings towards me were based on a vigorous friendship, not on a vigorous or a feeble love, she never fooled me. Until, during my long exile in America, I gradually succeeded in convincing myself that I had to believe her. There was no secret behind her pure forehead, no mistery behind the sparkling laughter of her eyes. When we met, Twinkle had already lost her first love: her husband, who had left her a widow in her early youth. That was all. And so I succeeded, at a distance, with my longing for her and the very need that I felt for corresponding with her by mail, in overcoming my Latin materialism and coming around to her Anglo-Saxon spiritualism: after all, friendship, between man and woman, *was* possible. In one word, I succeeded in transforming even my love into friendship.

The tender affection that I experienced, now, as I felt her arm resting on mine while we slowly walked from one room to the next past the rows of pictures, was akin to that which I should have experienced with a sister, a mother, a daughter: perhaps it was an affection that partook of all these three kinds, and in addition of something exquisite and uncorruptible, because we were not linked together by blood, by memories and by heritage, but by a free choice, a spiritual sympathy. What else, if not this, is friendship between man and man? We had many memories in common, Twinkle and I! So many happy days, in Rome, in Venice, in London, in Paris, on the Swiss lakes, on the Italian riviera. And if I had not lost the memory of my desire and of my hopes, yet this memory was rendered ironic by my final renunciation which by now was longer, in separation, than that desire and those hopes; so that it did not trouble my present tenderness, but almost coloured it with a cheerful tinge. During the last few years we had been able even to write about it. And to-day we were able even to talk about it. When I had arrived at the hotel, for instance, I had asked for a suite, so that she could come up and keep me company at breakfast. We were standing in front of the reception-clerk, and could hardly refrain from laughing: looking at one another, both of us had remembered the days of old, and my comic, insistent and equally vain attempts, every morning, to embrace and kiss her, at breakfast, more than she cared to allow. Dear old Twinkle!

Unexpectedly, I felt the increased pressure of her arm on mine. Then, all at once, her body faltered. If I had not hastened to hold her up, I truly believe she would have fallen. She looked towards a distant spot in the hall and said:

« Do you see that picture, that picture over there? »

She vaguely pointed towards the opposite wall, where at least ten pictures were hanging.

« Which, dear? »

« Come with me », she said with a sigh, and resolutely proceeded across the room.

« But you aren't feeling well; better sit down for a minute ».

« No, it's nothing ».

She stopped in front of a picture four and a half feet high and three feet wide, representing a window or rather what can be seen from an open window: the back-yards of a lower middle-class section of London: in the foreground a narrow and very long terrace, or rather, not a terrace, but the roof of a low building, which went on to an infinite depth, dotted at irregular intervals with chimneys that kept on growing smaller in perspective and finally faded away in the distance, amidst the trees of gardens and pergolas; on either side, the gloomy backs of the houses, with the window shut and the iron fire-escapes; in the back-fround, beyond the trees, distant steeples, factory-chimneys, more houses, a tangle, a jungle of gardens which it became impossible to distinguish from one another, and the high, grey sky, the sky of London. The whole picture was grey, a delicate, silvery grey, barely enlivened by the green of the trees and the tints, here and there darker, the reds and blacks of the houses.

« Don't you remember that window? » Twinkle said, with the ghost of a voice, as soon as she reached this picture. And before helping me to remember, she drew closer to the canvas, bent down and examined the corners carefully.

« It isn't signed », she concluded. « But it can only be by *him*. Look there! »

She opened her purse and pulled out an old leather photograph-case, in the inside of which, protected by a transparent film, was a pencil-sketch jotted down on a page torn from a note-book, and representing, on a smaller scale and in a sketchy fashion, the same subject as the picture.

« It's the window of my old flat in Fulham Road, don't you remember? »

I looked at the picture with increased interest. Yes, now I remember. Twenty years ago, Twinkle lived in a small studio on the mezzanine, in a street off Fulham Road, a squalid out-of-the-way neighbourhood which, with one of her impetuous and exaggerated decisions, she had chosen in a moment of impatience with the gossipy life of the West End.

« Only he can have painted this picture », Twinkle repeated, upset, looking at the painting and comparing it with the sketch.

« Whom do you mean by 'he'? »

« Why, him, don't you remember? Gino Petrucci, the one that disappeared! And this is the first sign of him, in twenty years! So he is alive, do you realise? He's alive! He's here in London! »

« Gino Petrucci? »

Yes, I did remember a Petrucci, a Gino Petrucci, a sort of Bohemian fellow, a rough-and-ready painter, a Tuscan, I think, whom Twinkle had warmly recommended to me, during her last visit to Italy, some twenty years back. I was at that time organising a series of performances in Venice at the Fenice Theatre; and Twinkle, who was about to go back to England, had brought this Petrucci to me, after getting me to promise that, somehow or other, I would obtain work for him as a scene-painter or costume-designer. After Twinkle had gone, I had kept my promise, and I had made use of Petrucci as assistant in setting up and retouching the back-drops. But he would come to work spasmodically, and really never did anything at all. I would see him only on Saturdays, when he came to get his pay which, but for Twinkle's warm recommendation, I would have withheld altogether. Until one Monday morning, after the third or fourth week, I received a note from him: he apologised for having to interrupt his work, but he was going abroad. A few months later, on my way back to New York, passing through London (and that was precisely the last time I had been in London and that I had seen Twinkle), she explained to me that Petrucci was there, out of work of course, and she apologised to me on his behalf, and begged me, in spite of everything, to do something for him again. The young man was repentant, she assured me; he had made up his mind to turn over a new leaf, to work seriously: why didn't I take him to America with me? I remember how this time I had been certain I had taken his number and doubted, as usual, of any possibility of conversion, and how I had tried to ward off Twinkle's insistence. But soon I had given way, and on the very eve of sailing from Southampton, I had consented to come and have tea at her flat in Fulham Road, where, Twinkle told me, I should find Petrucci profoundly mortified and humbled.

I remember going there about half-past four in the afternoon, and that Petrucci wasn't there. Twinkle, from the very beginning, struck me as nervous, agitated, irritated. Six o' clock came, and seven: Petrucci did not show up, although Twinkle, less and less able to conceal her vexation, went on assuring me that at any moment he might put in an appearance.

I remember how, on that very afternoon, I had decided to try once more (but without overmuch confidence) to appeal to my friend's heart; I wanted to ask her to meet me in New York at Christmas. In New York, in winter, life is so entertaining! But as the hours slipped by, her excitement reached such a pitch that I couldn't find the courage to say a word, and did not even make my customary protestations of resigned and unhappy devotion. At half-past seven, without thinking of Petrucci any more, I got up to go. With a vehemence which struck me almost as a sign of anger, Twinkle jumped to her feet and told me that she wanted to come and have dinner with me, if I had nothing better in view, and, on the following day, she would come as far as Southampton with me.

We dined in an Italian restaurant, in Soho; we stayed together until late in the night; the next day she came to Southampton with me; she was tender and full of emotion. At the last minute, as I embraced her at the gangway, I could see that her eyes were full of tears. But the tears were not for my departure; on the previous evening, and during the whole day, her odd behaviour, the behaviour of a woman who felt offended and embarrassed, had made me understand quite clearly that in her distress I had no part whatsoever, and that she was suffering because she could not find the courage to tell me about her suffering.

From New York I wrote to her and, as so often happens, I was bolder than I had been orally. I hinted in passing at the unrest which I had noted in her before my departure, and invited her, very warmly, to get her mind off it by paying me a visit. She answered with a very short but affectionate letter, refusing. And very soon after, in another letter, she told me the news, at first quite *en passant*, that Gino Petrucci had disappeared; ever since that afternoon when she was to re-introduce him to me in her flat in Fulham Road, he had not shown any signs of life. He had not gone back to Italy. Scotland Yard itself had been informed, and all possible steps were taken for tracing him, but in vain. Twinkle had an idea: she thought that one fine day he would turn up in my office at the 'Met'.; she begged me, in that case, to help him and to inform her at once by cable.

Then I understood, to my humiliation and surprise, that that little pseudo-artist was a very important factor indeed in the life of my poor dear Twinkle, and I guessed, but a little late, the reason of her strange behaviour on the eve and the day of my departure. This scant perspicacity of mine will not amaze anyone familiar with the ways of those whom Cupid's darts have pierced.

Gino Petrucci (I had given the name to my reception-clerk, and to the secretary, telling them to let him in) never put in an appearance in my New York office. Twinkle did not venture to write to me about him again. And I gradually forgot him altogether.

And now here he is alive again, with this picture of his; and here is Twinkle, an old woman by this time, clinging desperately to my arm:

« I *must* find him again, no matter what it costs. You will help me, dear? »

« Nothing could be easier », I replied, although, inside myself, I was wondering how, in the interests of Twinkle, I could prevent or at least delay such a meeting, after twenty years. « It will be enough, darling, to go to the secretary of the Exhibition and ask for the painter's name and address: the pictures are on sale here, aren't they? »

« What a fool I am, you're right, of course they are. It hadn't occurred to me! » exclaimed Twinkle with a joyous

laugh, bubbling over with excitement. « Come, let's go! »
We immediately went to the secretary's office. Some
pictures had been entrusted to the Exhibition for sale, and
for some others one had to apply directly to the owner or
the painter. Fortunately our picture belonged to the latter
class. But the name of the painter was not Gino Petrucci.
The name was N. N. And the owner (or in any case the
person who had sent in the picture) was J. M. D. Warwick,
3 Scarsdale Villas, in South Kensington.

During the drive to Kensington in a taxi, Twinkle gave
me further details. The window depicted in the painting
had been the path chosen by Gino Petrucci for disappearing
into the great unknown. Yes, that afternoon Gino had come
to the flat in Fulham Road. In fact he had lunched there,
tête à tête with Twinkle. He had thereupon at some
length admired and extolled the strange fanciful view of gardens, trees and chimneys to be enjoyed from the windows;
and while he waited for me he had drawn that little sketch
that Twinkle still kept in her purse, the last keepsake from
the vanished man. Then, as the hour of my arrival drew
nearer, he may have regretted his behaviour in Venice, or
perhaps he was reluctant to go to America, or, in any case,
to be obliged to work. The fact is that just as Twinkle was
preparing sandwiches for tea, he had jumped onto the window-sill, from which he descended, a yard lower down, onto
the long roof of the warehouses, and from there he had gone
on, walking up and down between the chimney-pots and
every now and then coming back to the window, exchanging
a few words with Twinkle and asking her for the time; and
in the end he took a still longer walk. Twinkle could still
see him, down there, a tiny figure amidst the last chimney-
pots. A minute after she had looked out again: he was no
longer to be seen. At first, you understand, she did not worry
particularly. A bizarre fellow, a talented boy who enjoyed
playing pranks. But meanwhile a quarter of an hour had

gone by, and when I rang the door-bell, Gino Petrucci had not come back. She was ashamed, you will readily understand, to tell me about the affair; and while we were having our tea, Twinkle, without my noticing it, had kept on looking out of the window. Besides, how could I have suspected anything so odd! I must certainly have been aware that she often looked towards the window; but no doubt I attributed her behaviour to her agitation, which I had not failed to note, and which I associated, none the less, with Petrucci's non-appearance.

The window! He had gone out by the window. He had, so to speak, gone into his picture, and he had not come back any more. Convulsively, excitedly, now, as we got nearer to South Kensington and to the explanation of the mystery, perhaps to some dramatic solution, Twinkle told me all about it, about her irritation during that afternoon and how, on the following evening, when she got back from Southampton, she had been convinced that she would find a note from Gino (she had started to call him simply by his first name) waiting for her in her flat, but had found nothing; and of her rage and suffering for the two ensuing days, and how she had thought that Gino, by disappearing, had simply not wanted to see her any more; until, on the third day, she had gone to his hotel, and had learned that Mr. Petrucci had not left, but that neither had he come home, since that very day of our appointment, which had been a Saturday: he had left his suit-cases and belongings in his room, and had not returned.

Then worry, and dismay, and terror lest some accident had happened to him. A telegram was sent to Arezzo, to Gino's mother. A telegram was sent to Rome, one to Venice, one to Milan, one to Paris, wherever Twinkle knew that Gino had friends. And all the answers were negative. At last Scotland Yard was informed, and the police undertook a search in the houses adjoining the house in Fulham Road, in the neigh-bourhood of the hotel, and everywhere, in London, where it might be conjectured that Gino had any acquaintances. No clues, nothing at all. And gradually, as the weeks and the months and the years went by, the mystery became familiar, her sorrow became habitual, her uncertainty: what could have become of him?

At first, in spite of the opinion of the police, Twinkle had insisted on supposing an accident. Then she had ended up by doubting too, at least by doubting. It is impossible, unless that is what you are aiming at, to disappear from the world without leaving any traces behind you. But it was only a doubt.

II

Scarsdale Villas: a squalid, solitary street, two-story villas, cuddling close to one another, with heavy cement stoops, all absolutely alike, leading up to the main story from the sidewalk, striding over, and half concealing, the gloomy basements.

The taxi stopped at number three. A yellowish light leaked out from a window on the main floor. I paid the taxi, which drove off and disappeared in the dark twilight air. Not a soul was to be seen anywhere. The noises of the city, of the Earls Court Station, of the busses in Kensington High Street, penetrated as through an immense distance. In the sky, beyond a veil of light mist, a star shone. Our hearts sank. Even Twinkle, who until now had struck me as impatient merely to get there, looked at the yellowish light that trickled through the dirty curtains of those windows, without daring to move. She clung to my arm without daring to take a single step towards the stairs.

« It was a mistake to send the taxi away », she said *sotto voce*. « Perhaps I ought to have waited, and taken a whiskey first ».

« Shall we go back? There must be a pub in the neighbourhood ».

A dog barked briefly from the house we intended to enter.

« No », said Twinkle. « Let's go up, come on. Do you know that during the bombings I never left London? And I never went down to the shelters, not once? How could I be afraid of this meeting? And besides... » she said, smiling sweetly, « and besides, you are here. And you are my dearest and oldest friend ».

« Yes, Twinkle », I said.

« Well, then, let's go ».

We climbed the few steps slowly, without hesitating. We stopped before the glass door. I rang the bell. Once more the dog barked. It was there, behind the door. Distant foot-steps approached, a tiny voice bade the dog be quiet. At last the door opened, but just barely, and through the chink we could see the small face of a woman, scared and wrinkled, two little black eyes blinking at us, like those of some nightbird captured and brought into the light, and a shock of smooth coalblack hair, undoubtedly dyed, half-covering her forehead with a fringe of bangs, with two funny little curls plastered down on her temples. A cigarette-stub hung from her thin lips which were tinted with lipstick.

« Does Mr. Warwick live here? » I asked, hesitating.

« Oh no! *Miss* Warwick! » the woman answered, making haste to shut the door a little more; and in the tone of her exclamation I could note amazement and fear at my ignorance.

« Excuse me, I didn't know. Does Miss Warwick live here? »

« Yes, certainly. What do you want? »

« I will explain to you immediately. Can't we come in for a minute? »

« I am afraid not. I am only a guest here », the woman answered, shutting the door almost completely. « Miss War-

21

wick is not in. If you will tell me what you want, I will give her the message ».

« We were given this address at Burlington House », Twinkle interrupted, impatiently, before I could prevent her. « A picture was sent to the Exhibition by J.M.D. Warwick, 3 Scarsdale Villas. Perhaps there has been some mistake? »

The door opened, as though by magic, further than it had been opened the first time; we could catch a glimpse of a squalid hall faintly illuminated, a little wooden staircase in the background, and a huge dog whom the woman held by the collar.

« Why, no, I don't believe there's been any mistake, if they really gave you that name and address ».

« So the picture », Twinkle went on, « was really sent to the Exhibition by Miss Warwick herself? »

« I didn't say that! I didn't say anything! » the woman stammered, as though terrified, and once more shut the door to a crack. « I know nothing about any picture. I am merely a guest here. What shall I tell Miss Warwick? »

« At what time will Miss Warwick come home? » I asked.

« I don't know, I don't know ».

« Because », I explained quietly, « we might be interested in purchasing the picture, and... »

« Do you know the man who painted the picture? The Italian artist Gino Petrucci? » inquired Twinkle outright.

This time, whether because we had mentioned a purchase, or because of the name Petrucci, the woman opened the door wide, looked at us for a moment with a last glimmer of suspicion, and at last, « Come in if you want to », she said. « Miss Warwick will be coming home any minute now. You can explain to her whatever it is you want ».

She led us along the hall into a room looking onto the back of the house, a small rectangular room almost entirely filled by a wide pallet and a lounge, standing opposite one another, along the two longest walls. In one corner of the room, on the floor, an electric heater was turned on. There was a small, low table with an empty bottle of beer and a couple of glasses, an ash-tray filled with stubs, the light was dim and the air hot and suffocating, saturated with the smell of *patchouli*.

« Sit down, won't you? » said the woman. Twinkle sat down on the lounge, I on the pallet; the woman remained standing by the heater; the dog, yawning and relaxing heavily, lay down in the centre of the room; he was so long and big that we should have been unable to leave the room without stepping over him.

« So you don't know Gino Petrucci? » Twinkle pursued.

« I don't understand », said the woman. « I don't know anybody ».

« Ge-no Pe-trouch-y », Twinkle spelled out. « An Italian painter. The man who painted the picture Miss Warwick sent to the Exhibition ».

« I'm sorry, but I fear I don't. I know nothing of what Miss Warwick does, I am merely a guest here ».

« But since when have you been living here? » Twinkle insisted, impatient to hit upon some trace of Gino.

The woman hesitated before answering.

« Since when? To tell you the truth, I... I don't live here. I'm only here to-day, by chance. I know nothing about the picture, I know nothing about anything. But I let you come in because I thought Miss Warwick might be interested in seeing you. I'm sorry you should be obliged to wait ».

There ensued an extremely lengthy silence. The woman pulled a cigarette out of a pocket in her black jacket, lit it, inhaled deeply. Blinking her little black eyes like a nightbird she looked first at Twinkle and then at me, and her expression was still suspicious and frightened. At last she attempted a smile and said:

« Won't you have a cup of tea? »

We thanked her. She came forwards, stepped over the dog, picked up the bottle of beer, the two glasses, the ashtray, and went out saying she was going into the kitchen to prepare tea.

As soon as I was left alone with Twinkle I reprimanded

her for having blurted out Petrucci's name so inconsiderately, thus giving away, right from the outset, the purpose of our visit. Twinkle protested ingenuously, why not go right after what one wanted? What harm could there be in that?

I endeavoured to explain. A woman of that kind, the atmosphere of the house, the furniture of the room, the very perfume, hadn't they told her anything? Twinkle answered, abruptly, that she hadn't noticed. What did she care about the place, the behaviour, the persons? What mattered to her was finding Gino again. She didn't even look about her. All this was simply a means of reaching her end.

She was most excited. I tried to explain to her that she must, on the contrary, remain perfectly calm, and keep both eyes well open. Difficulties might arise. For instance — in my opinion — the woman was not sincere.

« Do you mean she's lying? that she does know Gino? »

« May be », I answered.

« But why should she lie? »

« Why, I don't know. But for that very reason I entreat you, don't forget, when you talk to her, the kind of woman you are talking to ».

« As far as I can see she is an excellent person. I'm sorry for her, so there, and that is all. She must be a woman who has suffered no end. She is scared, she looks as though she were alone in the world, and poverty-stricken ».

« Yes, but do look about you, Twinkle! »

« The house is none too clean. And so what? I'm sorry for this woman. I confess to you that when she mentioned tea, the mere idea of the way the cups would probably be be washed... in short, I accepted without great enthusiasm. But I accepted none the less, because I was reluctant to humiliate her by refusing ».

« It's not that, Twinkle! » and I leaned towards her; I murmured in her ear: « have you understood, yes or no, that we're in a house for clandestine appointments? »

As I leaned towards her I jolted the dog with my foot,

and without moving his huge bulk he slowly raised his head towards me, and looked at me with one eye as though to let me know that he understood what I was saying.

On the other hand Twinkle, big-hearted Twinkle, did not, or would not, understand.

« Do you really think so? » she exclaimed.

« I haven't the slightest doubt, my dear ».

By way of answer, Twinkle rose to her feet and began to walk about very slowly, stepping around the outstretched dog, going over the half-darkened room, examining the walls on which, here and there, some little pictures and photographs were hanging.

Suddenly she cried out: « Gino! Look, here is Gino! A photo of Gino! »

I got up, stumbling over the dog, who got up too.

In a dusty old frame, under a dirty cracked pane of glass, there really was a photograph of Gino Petrucci, in hunting attire, with boots, a double-barreled shot-gun, and a Glengarry cap; moustache and goatee *à la mousquetaire*, melancholy eyes, and a sensual mouth; in two words, the perfect *Italian*, artist and dilettante, such as old maids in England dream of. Even the background was *de rigueur*: a landscape in the Maremma, a deserted farm-house, an Italy infested by brigands and mosquitoes.

« I remember this picture perfectly! » said Twinkle, gazing at it, and her eyes filled with tears. « There can't be the slightest doubt now, the painting is by him, and Miss Warwick knows Gino! » and as the woman came back at that moment with the tea, Twinkle pounced on her, pointing at the photograph: « This is Gino Petrucci, you see? This is the Italian painter I was telling you about! Don't you recognise him? He must be a friend of Miss Warwick's. Have you never seen him here? »

« I'm afraid not. I really couldn't say. Have you been to Italy? » the woman replied, pouring the tea and evidently attempting to change the subject.

« Yes, I lived in Italy for some time », Twinkle answered,

« but a long time ago. This gentleman.... » (and she pointed towards me) is Italian ».

« You don't say so », replied the woman and turned towards me with an enthusiasm I should not have thought her capable of. Her face suddenly lit up; she laughed with all the tiny wrinkles in her meagre face, and even her eyes, until then as it were dazed and dull, now laughed and became small, black, vivacious. You realised that she must once have been young, and that in her youth she must have been pretty, and you even guessed in what way: dark, slender, piquant, petite, but well-proportioned. « Italian? I should have taken you rather for a Frenchman or a Belgian. I'm so pleased. I lived in Italy, too. Not for very long, unfortunately. But those were the happiest months of my life. I have been to Sorrento, and Amalfi, and Portofino, in Florence, in Venice. Oh, it was lovely, lovely! The sunshine, all that sunshine! I am really delighted to meet you. My name is Madeleine Clarens ».

While the woman went on talking with this amazing enthusiasm, Twinkle looked at me, indicating the woman, and smiling eagerly. There was no doubt that, at least in part, I had been wrong: Madeleine was no vulgar soul.

Twinkle inquired once more about Petrucci, and once more the woman protested that she had never even heard of him; that she had never noticed the photo. Then, suddenly, the dog got up; we heard a slight noise in the hall, and before we could prepare ourselves for the extraordinary vision, a woman appeared in the doorway, tall, enormous, with a great shock of red hair. Her face was large, round, red as a peony, covered with freckles; two hungry, restless eyes probed us at once as though the woman wanted to swallow us; a potent breast, in spite of her age, which could not have been less than Madeleine's; hips like a female wrestler; and, to crown it all, she wore a shining transparent raincoat, of a bright scarlet hue.

« Who are these people? » she asked Madeleine after a

moment, in a hoarse voice, and without removing the cigarette from the corner of her mouth.

Madeleine by contrast seemed humbler, smaller, blacker; she answered that we had come because of a picture, and had inquired about an Italian painter, and that I was an Italian.

I introduced myself, and then introduced Twinkle. The colossus came forward without shaking hands, and pronounced her own name awkwardly: Dawn.

Twinkle, growing cautious and ill-humoured at this reception, started to ask her if it was she who had sent the picture of the window to the Exhibition. Dawn did not deny it, it had been she. But how had that picture come into her possession, Twinkle asked. « I am under no obligation to tell you », the colossus answered. « Anything else? » and she made a gesture as though to dismiss us.

Then Twinkle pointed at the photograph of Gino and asked her if she knew Gino Petrucci, and could she tell us his present whereabouts. Dawn did not answer at once: she looked at Twinkle askance, as though suspecting a trap. Then she said no, she knew no Gino Petrucci. What about the photograph?

« The photo was in this house, with the furniture and all the rest, when I bought it a few years ago ».

« Then, of course, the painting was in this house too ».

« I am under no obligation to answer. Do you people belong to the police? »

« No », said Twinkle, trembling in her effort to control herself; « we are simply two old friends of Mr. Petrucci's, who have lost sight of him and would like to find him again... with the aid and the kindness of whoever could put us on his tracks ».

« You've come to the wrong place, then. I have nothing to tell you. Good evening. This is the way out »... and she made a gesture as though to escort us towards the hall.

« Tell me at least », Twinkle said without moving, « to whom did this house belong before you bought it ».

27

« If there is a law that obliges me to answer you, I will answer. I will answer in court. Otherwise not ».

« No law », I said smiling and taking Twinkle by the arm to lead her away; « only an elementary sense of decency. Every time that I do not find this sense in a fellow-creature, as far as I am concerned, I feel extremely sad. Good evening ».

And we went away; Madeleine, who had followed this scene in consternation, blinking desperately, remained motionless in the room, without saying a word. The colossus followed us down the hall and, as soon as we had gone out, shut the glass door behind us, slamming it.

« Let's go and have a drink », I said to Twinkle, walking off with her rapidly in the direction of Cromwell Road. « We shall think over very quietly what we ought to do next. Perhaps it would be best if you asked your lawyer for advice. That woman was half drunk this evening. The lawyer will find a way to talk to her. Perhaps a little money might do no harm. They don't look as though they were living in the lap of luxury ».

« I couldn't say, I couldn't say », Twinkle murmured, almost crying with humiliation and rage. « But something tells me that woman is very close to Gino. She certainly knows him, of that there can be no doubt! The photo is proof enough. It was a snap-shot that Gino always carried on his person. And if that woman behaves in such a fashion, it is because she sees an enemy in me ».

I said nothing. I had no facts before me, only evidence. And I did not want to upset Twinkle with simple conjectures. Seeing that I remained silent, she resumed:

« Or do you by any chance really think that woman bought the house with the picture and the photo, and knows nothing about Gino's existence? »

« That may be too », I answered, mainly in order to calm her. We had reached the corner when we heard hasty steps behind us. We stopped and turned.

It was Madeleine who was rushing towards us and, as

she ran, beckoned to us to walk on. We turned the corner.
The poor thing, gasping and out of breath, caught up with
us after a few seconds.

She was disheveled, terrified, clutching her breast with
her emanciated fingers, yellowed with nicotine, and she gasped
for breath before starting to talk. At last she said, *sotto voce,*
and looking around the corner every few minutes as though
she were afraid of having been followed:

« Do you want to see Gino Petrucci? »

« Yes! » Twinkle almost shouted.

« Well then... well then, come tomorrow, at half-past three
in the afternoon, to a milk-bar at the corner of the Strand
and Little Newport Street, a stone's throw from Charing
Cross. I can't tell you anything else, for mercy's sake let
me go home. If she finds me out she'll kill me! Until tomorrow! See you to-morrow, you Italian! »

In spite of her terror and agitation, she succeeded in
smiling at me for an instant, squeezed my hand and ran off.

I spent the evening with Twinkle. My friend was stupefied and happy. She was living in her romance. To-morrow
she would see Gino once more, who could say in what shape?
— but after all she would see him again.

As for me, on the contrary, I deemed the situation to
be obscure, complicated, dangerous, and, in addition, ridiculous. But could I have sworn that, in my ironical distrust,
there was not some element of jealousy? After all these years
I had grown old, and Twinkle was old, and I had come back
to London to spend a few restful months, with the certainty
of her dear friendship, and in tender regret for something
that might have been and had not been. Why did Gino
Petrucci have to spoil all that for her?

The Italian Italian, the bungling, idling, brilliant, unreliable Italian, the Italian whom foreign men despise and
fear, and whom foreign women despise and adore, had always
been, during the long long years I had worked abroad, my
torment, my cross, my nightmare. What vexations and worries
had not come to me because of him! And now once more,

now that I had reached the Sunday of my life, I was to find him obstructing my path once more!

I listened patiently, the whole evening, to Twinkle's complaints, I associated myself with them, I raised my glass to her newly-kindled hopes, and when I left her, at the door of her lodgings in Brook Street, I answered her smiling and confident « See you to-morrow! » with an equally confident and smiling « See you to-morrow! » But in my heart of hearts I had sworn a righteous war against Gino Petrucci. On the following day, I would keep my eyes open. I would keep them open and watch over and fight for Twinkle's welfare, and for my own peace of mind.

III

Charing Cross, on Sundays after dinner, is the haven and the avenue of all sorts and conditions of men. Foreigners, out-of-works, provincials come up to town for the week-end, working-people come to the centre from the suburbs in search of entertainment, idle about preparing to shut themselves up in one of the neighbouring picture palaces or gather in dense groups about a painter who with coloured chalk draws a fugitive marine fresco on the stone pavement, or about a mountebank, a clown, a street musician. Right at the corner of Little Newport Street where Twinkle and I had anxiously, even earlier than the appointed hour, occupied a table in the milk-bar, there was a silent, extremely serious crowd, drawn up in a circle and all intent on the spectacle provided by a poor devil who had sewn up his accomplice in a bag, binding him (or her) very closely with a lengthy chain. In an extraordinary voice, and a Cockney accent, which made all that he said almost incomprehensible for me, the man was haranguing the crowd. As Twinkle explained, he was an-

nouncing that without any trick or fraud he was confining
with forty-eight turns of an unbreakable chain (a chain which
previously he had asked those present to examine attentively,
and with twelve absolutely insoluble knots, the creature enclosed in the bag, and that the latter, when once the operation
had been concluded, would succeed in rapidly, under the eyes
of the crowd, getting free from his bonds and escaping from
the bag.   The man shouted; the crowd, mute and grave,
looked on with an almost scientific interest.   Every now and
then the man would stop binding and shouting.   He would
bend down over the head of the person shut up in the bag,
and who was smaller than he, and embrace him as though
he wanted to kiss him through the sacking, and murmur a
few words that no one heard; then he placed his ear where
the person's mouth was and listened to his answer.

I looked at my watch.   Half-past three had passed several
minutes before, and there was no sign of Madeleine.   I pointed that out to Twinkle, and also informed her of my suspicion
that most probably we should wait in vain.   But Twinkle
did not hear me.   She stared as though fascinated at the
human form in the bag, and was eagerly intent on seeing
him come out.   I easily guessed what was going on in that
romantic mind of hers: she actually suspected that Gino Petrucci was in the bag, and that that was why Madeleine had
made the appointment at this spot.   After all, why not?
But I did not tell her that I had read in her mind, so as not
to humiliate her needlessly if it did not prove to be true.

Madeleine arrived, all out of breath, ten minutes late.
She sat down at our table, immediately proceeded to light
a cigarette and, resuming her mysterious and furtive tone of
the previous evening, when she had come running after us,
apologised and explained that she had escaped from the house
while Dawn was asleep and that she was afraid of her re-
proaches when she would be going home.

« When she wakes and doesn't find me, she'll be a fury! »
she added. « Heaven knows how she'll carry on at my return! »

« But what about Gino? » Twinkle asked anxiously, though without moving her eyes from the bag.

« What do you mean, Gino? » asked Madeleine.

« Yes, where is Gino Petrucci? »

« Where is Gino Petrucci? » repeated Madeleine, as though she had forgotten the purpose of our appointment.

« I thought he was going to come with you? » said Twinkle.

« With me? Oh no, that's out of the question. A pretty kettle of fish, that would be, for me and him, poor dear, if he were to be seen going about with me! You don't know what that woman's capable of! »

« And yet you promised me you would bring him here to-day at half-past three! »

« I'm awfully sorry if I didn't make myself quite clear », Madeleine answered, in great confusion. « But I didn't say that exactly. I said that perhaps you'd be able to see him. That was all ».

« And shall we see him? Will he come? » insisted Twinkle.

« Let's hope so, let's hope he can come, poor dear ».

« But did you tell him to come? »

« Of course I told him! »

« And what did he say? »

« He... he... to tell the truth, he didn't say anything, poor dear ».

« But how can he possibly not have said anything? » Twinkle remarked, in amazement.

« Excuse me », I intervened. « When did you see him? This morning? »

« But I didn't see him at all », Madeleine retorted. « I... yes, I succeeded in getting a note to him, a note fixing the appointment ».

« And what did you write in the note? » I asked.

« Not a great deal-oh, not a great deal at all... I don't have time, I had to write on the sly ».

« You didn't even write our names? You didn't tell him that two old friends of his wanted to see him? »

« Yes, I hinted at that, vaguely, as well as I could manage... Oh, if you only knew, it was terrible, for me, to manage to write that note at all ».

Twinkle got up. A slight disturbance had occurred, in the circle formed by the crowd. A policeman had appeared on the scene, had approached the man, and had forbidden him to go on with his act. Now he was waiting, with legs astraddle and arms crossed; and the fellow, murmuring, had started to untie his bag. The crowd of onlookers, too, showed its disappointment by grumbling. And gradually they had all begun to fling down small coins, threepenny bits and even sixpences, on the ground around the bag. The man untied the bag and gathered up the coins that were being showered down in rapid succession, and went on untying and gathering. I admired the kind heart of those people, who, cheated out of their anticipated enjoyment, in order to protest somehow or other against the instrusion of the policeman, made an offering certainly more generous than what they would have given if they had actually seen the performance of the escape from the bag. At one time there was a real shower of coins on the pavement. Little boys made haste to run after the ones that rolled off and brought them back to the man who pocketed them without ceasing to complain and to untie the chains. The policeman watched the scene impassively.

The last coil of the chain fell noisily. The man untied a little bit of string that fastened the bag at the top, and there appeared a woman, a brawny, extremely plain girl, in a sweater and slacks, with closely-cropped hair. Her face looked as though she were choking. The man put the chains and the bag away in a small satchel and walked off with the girl across the square, followed by four or five street-arabs. The policeman with a gesture invited the crowd to move on. Twinkle sat down again on her chair; I couldn't quite make out whether she was disappointed or relieved.

« There is no call to feel sorry for them », remarked Madeleine, lighting another cigarette. « They have taken in enough money as it is ».

« It is past four », I said, returning to the subject; « and Mr. Petrucci has not shown up. Frankly, do you believe he may still come? »

« I'm afraid not », Madeleine murmured humbly. « You will readily understand that since I sent him the note I couldn't find out if he would come to-day or not ».

« But it's Sunday! » said Twinkle, exasperatedly. « What does he do on Sundays? Surely he doesn't work? And where does he work? Where does he live? Why don't you give us his address? Let *us* worry about finding him ».

« How easy you make everything sound », Madeleine answered with a sigh. « His address? If there was nothing but that to it! But I don't *know* his address. Where does he work? I don't even know what sort of work he does. Perhaps he isn't working at all, at present ».

« When did you see him the last time? » I asked, trying to come down to brass tacks, if that was at all possible.

« The last time, you say? Well, I hardly know, a few days ago ».

« Do you see him often? » Twinkle asked, concentrating all her inquietude on Madeleine now.

« Often? Oh, very often. Almost every week, almost every day, in fact! But I only see him for an instant, when he passes down the hall to go upstairs, to Dawn's room, or to go downstairs, to the kitchen ».

« Ah! I understand », I said, taking it upon myself to put those questions which Twinkle would not have been able to ask. « Because Mr. Petrucci comes to Scarsdale Villas to see Miss Warwick? He's a *great friend* of Miss Warwick's, in short? »

« He's my friend, too, for that matter », Madeleine protested, with an odd sharpness.

« Forgive me, I understood you to say that you barely knew him by sight ».

« I? By sight? How could I have promised you what I did, if I didn't know him well, extremely well, perhaps better than Miss Warwick knows him herself? Gino is an awfully nice boy! But he's so good, so weak, that any bully can easily victimise him. That's how Gino is! Oh!... there was a time, in the past, when we saw each other without any danger every day, you might almost say every hour. A time of real happiness, for both of us. But I'm talking of a remote time, unfortunately. Now Gino is changed too. It's all that woman's fault. She's a wild beast, that woman is! »

« Are you talking of Miss Warwick? I thought you two were friends ».

« Who? I and she? Friends? Oh, I'm her friend, yes, possibly, but as for her, she hates me! She is jealous, bullying, suspicious, she always thinks I want to take Gino away from her. But that isn't only love, you know. At bottom there's financial interest. Because Gino has to bring home the money he earns, every bit of it, down to the last farthing. Otherwise, do you know what she does? She beats him up. And do you know what Dawn does with the money? It all goes into drink. If you only knew how she drinks! To-day she fell asleep again after lunch because she opened a bottle of gin about ten this morning, and by two o'clock she had emptied it ».

« Forgive me », said Twinkle, who had grown pale; « it seems to me there is some contradiction in what you say ».

« Contradiction? Maybe. If you knew what kind of a life I lead ».

« Yes », Twinkle went on; « you said: 'Gino has to bring home all the money he earns'. But then he lives at your place. And first you said you didn't know where he lived ».

« You're right. But... but at first I didn't want to tell you. I didn't want to tell the whole truth ».

« So this morning », I concluded, « you did see him, at your place ».

« Yes », the woman answered, stammering. « But for mercy's sake don't tell Dawn! »

« And did you talk to him? »

« No, I wasn't able to... But I shut myself in the bathroom, and wrote the note. I kept it ready, waiting for the right moment. When Gino went out, I shook hands with him and slipped him the note without Dawn's noticing ».

« Did he go out before or after lunch? »

« After. If I had a little money I could easily find a way of talking to him by myself and telling him all about the two of you ».

« What way? »

« I would give the money to Gino for him to give to Dawn as though he had earned it himself. When Dawn sees the money, especially if there is a little more than usual, she quiets down immediately, she sends me out to buy a bottle of gin, and so the day goes by. Then it wouldn't be hard for Gino, especially if he had some money left for a taxi, to come to an appointment ».

« How much do you think will be enough for you to go on with? » asked Twinkle, opening her handbag and searching in her purse, without taking the trouble, at that moment, to throw a glance at Madeleine, which, after all those contradictions and absurdities, would at least have revealed something positive to her. Madeleine, in fact, at the sight of the handbag and the money ready to pop from it with such unforeseen speed, had looked on breathlessly: incapable of controlling herself, through the smoke of the stub that was hanging from her lips, she eagerly stared at the purse and blinked as though the banknotes dazzled her.

« I am sorry », said Twinkle, handing the money to Madeleine. « I have only nine pounds with me. Do you think that'll be enough? »

Madeleine was unable to answer immediately. She grabbed the money greedily and it disappeared in a flash.

« I'll try », she said at last, recovering her poise with difficulty. « I'll try: I'm *sure* that now I shall succeed in getting him to come. I shall have to use all my wits, so that she doesn't notice anything. She's a terrible woman, believe me. For instance, the picture was in the attic for a long time. I had entirely forgotten that the picture was in the house at all. Well, without saying a word to me, she sent it to the Exhibition. Naturally, if she had sold it, she would have kept the money all for herself ».

« What? » said Twinkle; « not even Gino noticed the picture was gone? »

« Oh! he.. he would have noticed even less than I! »

« And so she wouldn't have given him even a part of that money, which by every law of God or man was the rightful fruit of his labours? »

« Who? Dawn? To him? Don't make me laugh! »

« But then that woman is a criminal! « exclaimed Twinkle, turning to me indignantly.

« As to her being a criminal, I can't say, dear », I replied; « I should simply say that she is utterly unreliable ».

« And Gino? » Twinkle went on, gazing at Madeleine anxiously. « How does Gino stand all that? how *can* he stand it? »

« Oh, you know Gino... you ought to know him well, if you take such interest in him ».

« We were quite good friends. But a great many years ago », Twinkle answered.

« Well, you can be sure he hasn't changed », Madeleine explained quickly. « He's always the same nice fellow. Always singing. You might say that no matter what happens, he's incapable of being glum or worried. Always, always singing ».

« That's true! » said Twinkle with a sigh. « I'm delighted to hear he hasn't changed. Tell me, tell me, what does he sing? »

« Oh, Italian songs, I couldn't tell you all of them. *Santa Lucia! O sole mio! Surriento! Gelida manina,* and the one that goes, I think it's a famous opera:

Scante col sangue mie...

37

I don't remember very well. All I can tell you is that he's forever singing. As soon as he gets up in the morning, I bring him his breakfast in bed, black coffee, he likes only black coffee, and oh! so strong, terribly strong; and until he's had his coffee he stays in bed as though he were dead; then he gets up and bathes, and in his bath he begins to sing, and he sings, oh! ever so loud, very, very loud! the window-panes tremble, and we have often had complaints from the neighbours, oh yes!... we have also had to pay a fine once, they denounced us to the police for that very reason! »

« I see he hasn't changed! » said Twinkle, who had listened to Madeleine's words in a sort of ecstasy.

But I, who had no reason for letting myself be carried away, reflected that by this time Madeleine's words had made it perfectly clear that Petrucci was living permanently with the two women, and that, in all probability, he was in intimate relations with both of them. Madeleine knew about Dawn. Perhaps Dawn didn't know about Madeleine. But both of them were equally affectionate, and you readily understood that they did not want us to meet him. Dawn, violent and outspoken as she was, had denied all knowledge of him and had even put us out. Madeleine, timid, hypocritical and calculating, had had the idea of exploiting Twinkle's anxiety and getting money out of her. It wasn't even improbable that Dawn's terrible tyranny had been purposely invented, and in full agreement with Dawn herself.

All these deductions, I broke, but with the requisite gentleness, to Twinkle as soon as Madeleine had left us, fixing an appointment for the following day at the same place and time. Twinkle showed no emotion. She admitted (what could hardly be denied) that Gino and the two women had been intimate over a long period of time. But she obstinately insisted on believing in Madeleine's truthfulness, in Dawn's intransigence, in Gino's extreme need of help from us, and she complained especially of one thing: her inability, in the circumstances, to risk another visit to Scarsdale Villas — where she would almost certainly have found Gino — without risking a scene with Dawn, from which, because of her gentle upbringing, she vehemently shrank.

And so I passed another evening with Twinkle, in an atmosphere of romantic emotion. Gino Petrucci, though he remained invisible, went to the theatre with us, dined with us at the *Ivy*, and accompanied us as far as Brook Street.

Twinkle spoke only of him, all the evening. Agonised at knowing he was in such company, she yet exulted at the thought that — now there could no longer be any doubt of it — she had found him once more. Gino was alive, he was in London, he was there, under the same sky, he breathed the same air with her. Every morning, in his fine barytone voice, he sang *Trovatore* and *La Bohême*: he was the same as ever, in spite of his age! Now it was up to her, Twinkle, to raise him from the depths of his abjection, to bring him back to his true life, to redeem him. Who knows, it may be that the idea of her redeeming mission had always been, for Twinkle, all one with her love. For that very reason, perhaps, she had never accepted me. I had never, unfortunately, needed anybody to save me. And now the idea of her mission resuscitated a passion which age and absence had assuaged, carried all doubts away on a wave of enthusiasm, overcame all difficulties in a new plan of battle. The undertaking was desperate, that was certain. But for that very reason, her mission was all the more touching, noble, inescapable.

I tried to insinuate the misgiving that, according to all probability, seeing how, in spite of the war and all that, in twenty years Gino Petrucci had never shown any signs of life, it might be reasonable to surmise that he was perfectly happy as he was, where he was, with whom he was. He sang *Trovatore* and *Bohême* in the mornings: who could tell, perhaps he *wouldn't care* to be redeemed!

« But you don't know, you can't tell! He was so fond of me! He can't possibly not be happy to see me again! » Twinkle rebutted.

And I went on repeating, with all the delicacy of which I was capable: that it had not been he who had lost her, but she who had lost him. Twenty years is a long time, At any moment, Gino Petrucci, if he had only wished it, could have shown up again. But in twenty years that moment had never come.

« You don't know, you can't understand », murmured Twinkle, and that was her only answer. « You don't know him; I do; and I know that Gino is unhappy, so unhappy... ».

So unhappy that he thinks he is happy, I pondered; but Twinkle ended up: « ... so unhappy that he no longer has any will, any hope of his own. It is imperative for me to see him and talk to him. Promise me that you won't forsake me during these days, that you will help me until I succeed! »

I promised; and with this fine promise I bade her good night again, for the second time that evening, at the threshold of her door.

And yet I was fed up. Yes, with all the affection I felt for her, I was fed up. In Berkeley Square I stopped the taxi, got out, and started to walk towards my hotel. It was drizzling. At my age, that was the last thing I ought to have done. But I felt the need to be alone, without the company of Gino Petrucci, in the fresh air, in the wet streets.

I crossed Berkeley Square, went down Berkeley Street, turned down Piccadilly. The prostitutes were taking shelter from the rain in the shop-doors, between the dark, shining windows. A few of them were alone in their niches, others had formed groups of two or three. I walked slowly, evenly, and, under my umbrella, as I passed, I stole glances at them, and it seemed to me as though the shop-windows were passing before me, with the motionless tarts standing in them, squeezed in their glaring raincoats, their ornamental little hats, their rubber boots. I recalled my distant youth, and, to my delight, the thought evoked no regret, but only a feeling of peaceful gratitude that I had never, when there was time, offended life by rejecting it. Now life rewarded me;

it opened out like a spectacle before me, it unfolded slowly, like a stage-setting.

At the corner of Albemarle Street the setting suddenly stopped. Under the rain which was now falling more heavily, in a group of four or five women who were standing close to the wall, I had recognised (although she was indeed almost unrecognisable) Madeleine. She was wearing a full geranium three-quarter coat, her head was covered with a *cloche* hat, she had gloves and a handbag, and her face was made-up to such an extent that, at a distance, she looked like a girl. At first I was struck by her voice, when I heard her laugh. Then I went closer, taking care to hide behind my umbrella, and, with the pretext of lighting a cigar, I stopped as long as was needed to convince myself that it was more than a mere resemblance.

So Madeleine, about whose past I had never entertained any doubts, still walked the pavements. Her face was horrible. It made you wretched to look at it. Under the dense pink layer of make-up, you could easily discern the wrinkles. Her lips were greasy with lip-stick. A heavy necklace was meant to hide the creases of fat. She wore spectacles rimmed with yellow celluloid, perhaps in order to mask the general effect, perhaps in order to make the passer-by fancy that, when she took them off, the final impression might after all be less disgusting. She smoked, laughed, talked to the others. I conjectured that possibly she was out not so much on her own account as in the interests of a friend; or else she might be trafficking in some prohibited drug; or else, again, it was no longer for venal purposes that she visited the scene, at that hour of the night, but from a habit as inveterate as life itself, not driven by gain, but by vice.

I was unable to determine whether these fancies of mine were more or less remote from reality. And all I wanted, in any case, was a new argument with which, on the morrow, to cool Twinkle's enthusiasm. As soon as I had lit my cigar, I went on my way without attracting their attention. Five minutes later I entered my hotel, and ten minutes later I went to bed.

But, in contrast with my usual custom, I was unable to fall asleep immediately. I experienced an indefinable dissatisfaction, a vague bitterness, as though someone or something had disappointed me. It was a state of mind unfamiliar to me since a good many years, ever since no one and nothing had disappointed me any more. What could have happened?

I reflected and gradually discovered, to my amazement, that, possibly through Twinkle's influence, I had replaced my first impression of Madeleine, as she had at first struck me at Scarsdale Villas, with an indulgent, fanciful, romantic judgment. So that meeting her in Piccadilly in that guise had unconsciously distressed me. The stage-setting had brusquely stopped. And (I now realised) I had reacted youthfully once more. Reality had once more surprised and wounded me. At seventy I had again experienced the same pain as the child whose toy someone has broken, as the young man who beholds the woman of his dreams in his grasp. There was only one difference: I did not, now, yield to the opposite extreme; I did not, now, abandon myself to total pessimism. I knew, now, that, like the toys of my childhood, like the dreams of my adolescence, not even Madeleine was entirely a fraud.

IV

Twinkle was not astonished by my story. She went on, even after hearing it, seeing a beautiful soul in Madeleine, and a sincere friend of Gino's. But that day I had a plan of my own and, luckily, Twinkle still had enough common sense to approve it.

It was unquestionable that Twinkle ought not to expose herself to a nasty scene with Miss Warwick; on the other hand it was probable that Gino spent a great part of his days at Scarsdale Villas, so, while Twinkle went to Charing Cross to keep the appointment with Madeleine, why should I not pay a surprise visit to Scarsdale Villas? Even if I did not find Petrucci there, I could at least have a talk with Miss Warwick; and then in the evening, by comparing notes, Twinkle and I, by putting together what Miss Warwick would have told me with what Madeleine would have told her, we might succeed in getting closer to what looked like the impalpable existence of our lost friend.

In the afternoon, when the time had come, I accompanied Twinkle in a taxi to Charing Cross; when I left her I begged her not to give Madeleine any more money, and went on to Kensington.

Gino Petrucci — unless he was hiding — was not at home. Dawn came to open the door for me, and was astonished to see me. As soon as she opened it, even before she had asked me to come in, she committed, in her surprise, the imprudence of asking me whether I had not by any chance seen Madeleine. That was enough to confirm my suspicion that the two women were acting in concert. But this time, perhaps because Twinkle had not come along with me, Dawn struck me as being much more pliable. She asked me into another room, the living-room, which opened right onto the hall, on the left; she bade me sit down on a lounge cluttered with cushions, she sat down beside me, she offered me a drink and a cigarette.

This room was bigger than the other, but filled with ill-assorted furniture and wretched ornaments, and everything was in utter disorder and absolutely filthy. The curtains at the two windows, which both looked onto the street, were lowered, and enhanced the impression of a junk-shop. The air was, as usual, suffocating, saturated with the smell of *patchouli*. In a corner, covered with a dusty cloth and half hidden by an empty book-case, I noticed an easel.

Naturally, I at once spoke of Petrucci. And Dawn, with equal promptness, repeated her denial of knowing him. If

I was interested in purchasing the picture of the window, she said, she was ready to negotiate. She apologised for having been so rude the other day.

I had forgotten the picture altogether. On hearing her mention it, I had an idea. It struck me as a good one, as being extremely simple, and I was surprised that neither Twinkle nor I had thought of it before.

« If you intend », I told Dawn, « to sell the picture, just tell me the price; it's not at all unlikely that I may buy it ».

Dawn lit a cigarette and thought it over for a moment, her eyes shut. She was wearing a dress of green silk with a pattern of black flowers, very low in the neck. The skin of her huge breast was almost violet in colour and all coarse-grained, as though from frequent rubbing. But from her face and her carriage you could see that until a few years ago she must have been a handsome specimen of a woman.

« I know very little about pictures », she said at last, raising her green and slightly prominent eyes and looking at me; « I prefer you to make an offer ».

« I like the picture », I then said without hesitation. « I offer a hundred guineas ».

She lowered her eyes and remained motionless, silent, so as not to betray her satisfaction.

« A hundred guineas », I went on, « which, naturally, I am ready to hand over to Mr. Gino Petrucci, personally ».

« You make me laugh! Why, Mr. Gino Petrucci doesn't even exist », she snorted, staring at me furiously, viciously.

« In that case I must reluctantly decline to purchase it. I like the picture, as I have told you once before, but, between you and me, I am making this offer only in order to assist Mr. Petrucci who, I have some reason for believing, is financially embarrassed ».

« And if Mr. Gino Petrucci does not exist, are you not disposed to buy the picture at a somewhat lower figure? »

« No ».

« Not even at a *much lower figure*? »

« Not even at a much lower figure ».

With a weary sigh, she rose to her feet. Her tremendous bulk impressed me, as I remained seated in my chair, as though it towered to the ceiling. She began to walk to and fro nervously, following the tortuous space open to her, through the room densely encumbered with furniture. Her heavy body passed backwards and forwards in front of me, sending me whiffs of the same perfume that I had already noticed in the house. Through her silk dress you could discern the outline of the stays that squeezed her body; and you could follow the curves of her enormous buttocks, the edge and the clasp of her garters.

All at once she stopped short, turned about in a rage, and said to me:

« Why are we going on with this farce? I've had enough of it. Let's talk frankly. You've seen my friend Madeleine, haven't you? »

I hesitated, not knowing just what to answer. At last I said that I had met her quite accidentally, the previous evening, in Piccadilly.

Dawn seemed astonished and offended.

« In Piccadilly? Yesterday evening? So she's been making a fool of me once more. Fancy, she told me she was only going to see her brother at Shepherd's Bush. And what did she tell you, that hypocrite, that pickthank, that viper? »

I replied that Madeleine had simply confirmed what I had already, thanks to the picture and the photograph, supposed, namely that Gino Petrucci was a friend of theirs.

« But why should I try to hide that from you? What for? Did she tell you that, the viper? »

I deemed it prudent to remain silent.

« Well then, I'll tell you why I denied knowing Gino, I'll tell you myself! In order to respect his wishes. That's why ».

« I don't understand. What wishes? »

« His wishes. Gino is a sick man, a very sick man, and

doesn't want to see anybody, he *can't* see anybody. He can't work any more, that's why he tries to sell his old pictures. And if he's a sick man, you can believe me, the whole fault is that vampire's, Madeleine's, who has sucked the life out of him. But who knows what wild tale she may have told you, eh? She'll probably have told you that it was I who illtreated him, eh? Tell the truth! But I only did good to him, I gave him shelter here, I protected him like a mother. And I was a poor silly fool. I discovered too late that my friend, whom I had sheltered under the same roof, with the same kindness, was a venomous serpent whom I had warmed in my bosom. They carried on right under my eyes, you get me? Oh! he was to blame too. He was a coward, a traitor! with that smile of his, he kept on fooling me all the time. Now it's too late to make amends. Gino is a sick man, his sickness is beyond all remedy. But if you, and the lady with whom you came here, are sincere friends of Gino's, then do what I tell you: buy the picture and don't ask any more useless questions ».

« Where is he? In a hospital? Even if I can't see him, could I make myself useful to him? »

« Don't bother about anything. I alone, I *alone*, do you understand? can do anything for him. But unfortunately I am without the requisite means. If you have any sort of a heart, you must believe me. I'm not an Englishwoman, like Madeleine, I'm not a hypocrite, I can't pretend. I'm Irish I am. What I feel in my heart, I've got to say it with my tongue. Follow your own instinct. You're a man of feeling too, you're an Italian. Obey your natural impulse, and buy the picture. Poor Gino will bless you! »

With these words, she sat back in her chair, pulled out a Nile-green handkerchief from her purple breast and started to weep. While she was drying her tears I noticed, to my surprise, the hands with which she clutched the handkerchief. They were small, sinewy, extremely beautiful, thin, tapering hands (the nails were painted with cracked red enamel). The sight of her hands made me look at her feet. They were

small and well-shaped. This confirmed my belief in Baude-
laire's eulogy. A great body with small hands and feet: that
means a woman much given to amorous pastimes, and gifted,
in the exercise of them, with an exceptional intelligence.

« I'm terribly sorry », I said, as soon as she was able to
listen to me, « if I have, even involuntarily, upset you. Please
believe that I am doing all I can to understand you. And
I wish I could do what you suggest ».

« Oh yes, do it, do it for Gino's sake! Don't you see?
We are two old women, we can't work any more either, and
we can no longer help him as we used to do until a short
time ago! »

« I should ask for nothing better; but your obstinacy,
first in denying the existence of our common friend, and now
in not letting us meet him, is so strange, so absurd, that I
cannot consent. I haven't the faintest intention of offending
you, but you must surely admit that I don't know you, I
haven't the remotest idea who you are: why should I hand
over a hundred guineas to a perfect stranger? »

« You wouldn't be giving them to me for nothing, surely.
You would be getting the picture ».

« I've already told you that the picture would interest
me only to a certain extent. Who can guarantee to me that
the hundred guineas would really reach Gino Petrucci? I
hope you will forgive me for speaking so frankly ».

« I see, that's how it is, you don't trust me! I beg you
to believe what I told you about Madeleine. At least let
me hear what she told you, so that I can protect myself. She
must have been drunk, I'm certain of it. And if you give
her the money for Gino, she will rush straight around the
corner, walk into the first pub she comes to and drink it up
to the last ha'penny! »

« It is precisely because I don't want that to happen, that
I should prefer to hand the money over to Gino Petrucci
directly. If you insist on not letting me see him, or even
on not letting my friend see him, I will give you my word

47

I will respect your wishes. But tell me where he is lodged. I will give the money to the management of the hospital ».

« He isn't in any hospital! Why do you insist on thinking he's in a hospital? Did I by any chance tell you he's in a hospital? »

« Well then, where *is* he? »

« Come here, if you like; come here every day. Search, search the house, if you refuse to believe me! »

She rose to her feet, went to the corner where the easel was standing, pushed the book-case aside, removing the cloth (and at the same time raising a cloud of dust) and uncovered the first sketch of a painting.

It was still another version of the picture of the window. Half painting and half drawing. That subject seems to have been an obsession with him. But this painting was old, dried up, cracked. Even the tubes of paint lying on the ledge of the easel were old, dry, covered with dust. Dawn turned the canvas in another direction: it was a study, another unfinished study, of two hands, a woman's hands, resting on the edge of a table, beside a bottle of whiskey, a glass, an ashtray, and a few cards laid out for a solitaire. One of the two hands was holding a cigarette between the second and third fingers.

« Your hands, obviously? » I remarked to Dawn, recognising them.

« To be sure; but how did you manage to guess that? »

« Well, just as I understood that all this is old work ».

« Didn't I tell you he is sick and doesn't work any more? And yet he comes to see me every day. He can't get on without that. He adores me. When he was well, oh! he adored me then too, but he wasn't faithful to me. He pretended to be! If you only knew how cleverly he pretended. Now he's sick, he sees only me. Madeleine no longer exists for him. No other woman exists for him. I'm the queen of his heart. Look, here's his hat, he forgot it here the other day ».

She pulled a faded old felt hat out from a bunch of rags. I looked at it attentively: it was an old *Borsalino* (1).

« It's an Italian hat, isn't it? » Dawn cried triumphantly. « What did I tell you? And look there, that's his working-jacket! »

And she pointed at a velvet coat hanging over a chair; it would have done beautifully for the role of Marcello.

« Do you believe me now? Do you believe me? »

« It's not a question of me alone », I sighed; « there is my friend too, who is interested in getting news of Gino Petrucci. What am I to tell her? »

« Who? Your friend? Oh! I know all about your friend. Gino was forever talking about her... he spoke about her at first, that is. Now, for several years, he hasn't been talking about her any more. She's a tiresome bluestocking, who has always been pestering the life out of him. What does she want now? To see him? As for you, I don't know, Gino never mentioned you. But as for her, of all people, Gino hasn't the faintest intention of seeing her. And you can repeat that too, if you want, to the old witch. At best, Gino might make an exception for you, especially if you buy the picture. He needs money so badly.

The doctor's bills, the medicine, the shots cost heaps of money. As a foreigner, he can't claim free treatment, you know. I should be so grateful, for him, if you could let us have something in advance, just a small advance. If you 'phone to-morrow, in the early afternoon, I will tell you what Gino says. And you'll see that I shall succeed in arranging a meeting, but with you, not with her ».

My interest, my insistence — largely due to my desire to make myself agreeable to Twinkle, in part to my unfailing curiosity —, had fooled Dawn. She thought I must be an intimate friend of Gino Petrucci's.

I handed her a five-pound note.

---

(1) One of the best-known marks of Italian hats; especially a wide-brimmed black felt, once much-worn by artists. (*Translator's note*).

« Is that really the best you can do? » she asked, taking the banknote and pushing it away under her corsage. « I have an idea. Give me another five pounds, and meanwhile you can take this sketch », she said, pointing at the canvas standing on the easel. « When you buy the picture, it will be all right if you give me only another ninety-five ».

« I should say so », I replied. I thereupon gave her another five pounds, and took the sketch. I would telephone the next day; she was to persuade Petrucci to see me. And I went off, determined not to buy the picture without having established direct relations with Petrucci or at least through some thoroughly reliable person. I had by this time come to a very definite opinion. I was convinced that Petrucci was in a hospital, and that the two women, acting more or less in agreement, were trying, without saying a word to him, to get as much money out of us as they could. But then why had I given her those ten pounds? For Twinkle's sake, undoubtedly. And also because the canvas, especially the painting of the hands, was, in my opinion, worth something.

This Petrucci was not altogether without talent. He had, evidently, not studied his craft regularly. But he must have at least looked at the French impressionists. And just as the view from the window, in its silvery light, reminded you, in spite of its wavering and approximative brushwork, of Pissarro, those pale hands, against the dark-red cloth and the sombre, bituminous background, suggested Monticelli and Courbet. Especially (I examined the sketch in the taxi holding it on my knees) they somehow expressed a genuine feeling, they did not suggest an exercise. Or perhaps it was I who, being familiar with the model, read that feeling into the painting. I imagined long winter afternoons, interminable London weekends, in the gloomy living-room at Scarsdale Villas. Dawn, already mature but still desirable, drinking and smoking and playing solitaire. And Petrucci painting, in adoration, those exquisite hands.

V

Twinkle's hands were just the opposite. Not that they did not possess a beauty of their own. But they were broad, frank, almost rough hands. And they contrasted with her slim figure, her distinguished features, exactly as Dawn's hands, so subtle and refined, contrasted with her Gargantuan shape.

I went to Twinkle's immediately, according to our agreement. I found her in a state of excitement that dismayed me. Madeleine had brought her a note from Gino. I imagined that Madeleine had been to the hospital; and in spite of Twinkle's intense agitation, I was glad, because I deduced that at last we were nearing our goal.

« 11 c'clock. I'm going out. I don't want to wake you. The milk is in the kitchen. The dog has had his soup. Sleep well, both of you. *Ciao*. G. »

It was not, as I had hoped, a note addressed to Twinkle. But only a note that Petrucci, leaving Scarsdale Villas that morning, had left for Madeleine and Dawn, while they were still asleep.

It was scribbled in pencil, in a pale script, on a scrap of paper torn from a note-book. But Twinkle had no doubt, it was his hand-writing. This ended my convinction that Petrucci was in a hospital. I didn't know what to think. Madeleine had told Twinkle she hadn't seen Gino. He had come to Scarsdale Villas at night, perhaps just before daybreak, had rested and gone away, as the note said, at 11 a. m.

I told Twinkle about my visit to Dawn, omitting anything that might hurt her feelings more directly and making no allusion to the picture of the hands (which I had prudently left at the hotel before coming to see her), yet trying to make her understand that Gino had by this time grown fond of those two women, with whom he had been living for so many years, and especially of Miss Warwick, who struck me as having an irresistible power over him. In my opinion, it would be unwise to count on Madeleine in any way. The poor wretch was quite pathetic, I readily admitted, and might even strike one as agreeable. But, in her extreme need of money, she was capable only of lies and deceit. Twinkle confessed that she had, in spite of my advice to the contrary, given her some more money. And she answered my pessimism with one single objection: in spite of all they had told us, true or false, neither Madeleine nor Dawn had said that they had informed Gino of our presence. This, according to Twinkle, was the main point! Gino did not yet know that we were looking for him. Until we were sure that he knew, we couldn't give up our undertaking, no matter how desperate it might appear.

The argument was a strong one. What could be said to rebut it? I said nothing, and between the two of us, perhaps for the first time in the long history of our friendship, there ensued a lengthy and oppressive silence. In the charming little studio, between those walls wainscoted with delicately tinted woodwork, in the midst of her books, her rare trinkets, the flowers, the deep leather arm-chairs, into one of which I had let myself sink wearily, twilight had fallen. Only a pale diffused light trickled through the full hangings of white muslin, framed between draperies of cretonne, at the two windows looking out onto Brook Street. The noises of London had, as usually happens here, quieted down. I could see the streets of that aristocratic neighbourhood, as they always are at this time of day, quiet, deserted, in a bluish dusk. Twinkle was seated opposite me and watched me with her sparkling eyes, thinking, beyond a doubt, of Gino Petrucci. I was watching her, and thinking of her. I was thinking how charming that hour could be, letting the night gradually invade the cosy room, letting death gradually invade our long and faithful friendship; had it not been for Gino Petrucci.

She divined my melancholy and, as she had so often done in distant and for me equally unfortunate times, came over to sit down at my feet, adjusting her skirts around her ankles with the same graceful gesture of a girl wearing a crinoline, and laid her hand, as she used to do, softly on my knees. Thus she remained, and for some time did not utter a word. I have had a great deal, I have perhaps had too much from life. But if a complaint should ever cross my lips, it would be to ask: why, dear God, did you refuse me this companion for my old age?

« Poor dear », murmured Twinkle at last; « how I must have bored you with this whole business! Can you ever forgive me? »

I kissed her hair. She knew that I still loved her.

« After all », she said, « I never told you about anything. And you never asked me to. You were always so kind. Now, don't you see, I feel I must tell you. I must tell you what I never told you before ».

« Even now I don't ask you to tell me anything, Twinkle. The only thing I would even now really like you to tell me, the same as always, you can't tell me. So... ».

« I know. But it's me that needs to talk. I am always, I have always been, an egoist. The years haven't changed me. After my husband's death, and you know how I loved him, there has been only one other man in my life. Gino ».

And at that point, with the cruelty that is common to every love when it declares itself, she was silent for a long time, as though to enjoy the full flavour of this desperate declaration, as though the better to impose the full flavour on me.

And I, who already knew, to the full, what Petrucci had been to her, on hearing it so explicitly from her lips, I yet felt it pierce through my heart like a revelation. So this love, that felt the need of speaking so officially, as it were, must be even greater, even stronger and above all even fuller than I had supposed. For the second time in the course of a few hours, I understood that I had fooled myself like a school-boy; the wisdom I thought I had attained with years, was still, oh so far away!

There was, in fact, no excuse for me. A man of my

experience ought immediately to have grasped how things stood between Twinkle and Gino. I ought to have been satisfied with that sketch, jealously preserved and continuously carried on her person, after twenty years! And yet, so blind are we to what we dislike, that I had not, even for an instant, thought that, despite her love for Petrucci, Twinkle might have had a real love affair with him. I had given myself foolishly over to the idea that Twinkle had never, in her whole life, had decisive relations with any man except her husband. Her athletic, virile, virginal aspect had deceived me. I had always deemed her to be frigid.

Now she had not as yet said a word about all this. Her expression (« there has been only one other man in my life »), taken literally, was still open to a favourable interpretation. She might have loved him and no more. But the tone of her voice, so tremulous, so desperate, and, what counted even more, another, interior voice, from myself to myself, had revealed the bitter truth, without leaving me the consolation of any doubt whatsoever.

And it was Twinkle herself who had understood that I had not understood and who needed, now, in her loneliness, the ultimate comfort of confiding in me. This love, which she had lost, which almost, because of the extreme evasiveness, to-day, of its object, no longer seemed to be real, she herself wanted me to know how real, how corporeal it had been. And if that made me suffer, all the better. My pain would, at least, be a late confirmation of that remote reality, so remote as to verge on the unreal.

« So often, do you know, did I ask myself », Twinkle pursued after a long pause, «did I ask myself, at the time, why I had not chosen to be more outspoken with you. When Gino disappeared, he had been my friend for over two years ».

« Two years? Why then you really did hide the affair from me! You... » I took her hand, caressed it, carried it to my lips, and after all that I smiled... « betrayed me! »

« Yes, dear », Twinkle answered, understanding my meaning perfectly, for no engagement, no promise to be true existed between us two: « yes, dear, I betrayed you. But why, I so often asked myself, why? For many reasons simultaneously. First of all, I did not want to sadden you ».

« So you postponed it until to-day », I observed.

« To-day it's another matter ».

« Another? To-day, after all this time, you really might have gone on being silent ».

« Oh no, dear, don't be unkind ». She rose to her feet in tears, and embraced me.

« A man is unkind when things are unkind to him », I replied. « To revenge himself ».

« But the unkindness lies precisely in the revenge. And you don't want to revenge yourself, you didn't really want to say what you just said! »

« No, Twinkle », I replied, and the sweetness of her embrace seemed to melt any grudge I may have borne her. « I was joking. You were quite right, before, not to mention it at all. After all, I have gone on living, for so many years, in the consoling illusion that if you weren't mine you didn't belong to anyone else either. You were quite right, and I thank you ».

« But it wasn't only because of that, that I didn't tell you. I want to be sincere all the way. Don't think that I didn't realise what kind of a person Gino was. I knew you wouldn't like him, that you would have been violently opposed to our marriage... ».

« Ah, but why? even that? « I sighed, facing the new blow almost with sarcasm. Apparently the series of revelations was not yet ended. « So you meant to get married? »

« Well, I wanted to. As for him, he said yes, he said no, he said yes again, but at heart he wasn't willing, and when he would have had to make up his mind definitely, that was when he disappeared. I knew even then that you would have been opposed to our marriage, and that it might even have spoiled our friendship. I didn't want to lose you, you see ».

« That's all right; but when you married I should have had to find out some time ».

« As long as it was possible, I didn't want to lose you.
And besides, one of his chief arguments for not marrying was
this: he was out of work, he wasn't making his living. I was
rich. He didn't want to be supported by me ».

« He needed only to have gone to work ».

« But he didn't even *want* to work. He lived from one
day to the next, from hand to mouth, by means of little loans,
odd jobs, all sorts of subterfuges. You knew him. Then, by
sheer force of insisting, I succeeded in convincing him that
he ought to work, if only for his own sake. He promised me
that when he got a regular job we would get married. When
he got a regular job, he would be different: you would have
a better opinion of him, undoubtedly. And then you would
no longer be opposed to our marriage. That's another reason
why I said nothing to you. Last of all, (and this is the hardest
reason to confess, because it puts me in a shabby light), last
of all... ».

« If you don't care to tell me, Twinkle... ».

« No, no, I want you to hear the whole story. Last of
all, as you know perfectly well, I wanted you to be the one
to help him, to give him a job. To whom else could I look
but to you? So you see I was afraid, if I confessed to you
what Gino meant to me, that you mightn't be willing to do
anything for him ».

I got up, beside myself. At any other moment I should
have lost my temper. Now my irritation lasted for only a
fraction of a second. I sat down again, and took her in my
arms, telling her with simplicity that she couldn't really know
me very well. Under no circumstances could her frankness
have had anything but the contrary effect. I might possibly,
for the very reason that he was my lucky rival, have given
Petrucci the best job at my disposal.

« And not from generosity », I concluded. « Rather from
pride, from spite, for revenge ».

« Forgive me », Twinkle replied.

« There is no need for you to apologise. You thought I

was better, simpler than I really am. You thought I would
react with the vulgarity of an operatic tyrant. On the contrary, I am the confidant. A confidant who, on the side, has
a little unfortunate love affair of his own with the prima
donna, and tells all about it in a long tiresome air at the
beginning of the second act. As a rule, the air is *cut* ».

« How malicious you are », said Twinkle, smiling. In the
darkness, which had by now grown almost complete, her eyes
were still sparkling. « Your part as confidant has not been
cut at all. I acted it for you too, thinking of you too. Because Gino and I never got along perfectly. We had hours,
days even, of absolute happiness, out of the world, out of
life; but then we always quarreled. If that can console you...»

« It's you who are malicious now ».

« We quarreled for the reasons of which I told you. He
was too proud to live on my money, and too lazy to go to
work in earnest. But there were other reasons too. Our
meetings were always furtive, brief and violent. We loved
one another in secret, with beating hearts ».

« Why? Were you afraid I might find out? »

« Oh no, dear! I hate to have to hurt you again; but
it was not because of me or you. There is nothing I loathe
like having to hide. And besides, you were almost always
far away, and buried in work. To keep a secret from you
was the easiest thing in the world; it came quite naturally.
It was for his sake we had to hide. He used to have not
one, but two, three, loads of women. You might say that
in every city, in every country we went to, he had one, or
that one of them followed us there. All those women, naturally, he had met them before he knew me, and none of
them were to be taken lightly: they were no passing love
affairs. Each one of them was a pathetic case in herself,
complicated, immensely serious. The subject may have been
vulgar, the woman in herself; not her love for Gino. Gino
cannot approach a woman without upsetting her whole life,
without feeling responsible, himself, for her life ».

« You mean irresponsible ».

« No, I don't. You must try to understand him as he is. He used to tell me everything. I was different from the rest, for him. To me he used to talk *too*. That is why I might have been the only one. When he noticed that a woman was happy with him, he at once, and quite rightly, thought how unhappy she would be, afterwards, without him. And true to his generous instincts, he would promise to be true to her, forgetting, in perfectly good faith, that he had already made the same promise to other women ».

« How fond you were of him! »

« How fond I *am* of him, you mean. At that time I used to hate him, and for that reason. I was unable to understand him. My jealousy blinded me. It struck me as impossible that such a being could exist on this earth. With that melancholy, angelic smile of his, with those loving eyes that pierced you through and through, and seemed to leave his soul in your arms, Gino at times struck me as a monster, a criminal ».

« At times ».

« And only after years and years of solitude, and when I had finally come to the conviction that he must be dead, thinking about his character with the peace of mind that comes to you only when you think about someone who is dead, I got to accusing myself, do you follow me? »

« Accusing yourself? » I confessed that I did not understand her at all. Twinkle rose to her feet and began to walk up and down the room, in a fit of anguish.

« Yes, if Gino did go away, if Gino left me for good, if he cut himself off from the civilised world, if for twenty years he has been leading a wretched life, letting those two tarts support him, if to-day Gino is a sick man, a beachcomber, an outcast from society, the fault is mine, exclusively mine. That is why I shall get no rest until I have found him again, until I have told him, and done everything that lies in me to give him refuge in my house again. After all, in those days he never had a real refuge there. There was always a reservation. Stupid little egoist that I was, I always set up conditions. Almost as though I had anticipated sheer happiness from his visit, and then had insisted that he carefully remove his shoes at the door so as not to soil the parquet. How can I possibly — I ask you — have been so foolish? I was jealous. It was jealousy made me foolish. I no longer understood him at all. I claimed the crumbs of fidelity, and risked losing the whole feast. I irritated him continually with my cross-questioning, with my sermons, with my menaces: I thought I spoke in the name of a higher British morality, in the name of a higher Protestant religion, a morality and a religion in which promises were made to be kept, and in which one was not supposed to tell lies; and I did not even notice that, on the contrary, it was I who was the hypocrite. I spoke only in the name of my petty self-ishness, of an austerity which was convenient for me. How many nights did I not lie awake, listening for the steps that seemed to stop down there, in front of the house! How often did I not dream, with my eyes wide open, in a voluntary and obstinate state of passion, of his return! And even now, would you believe it? even now everything is ready here to receive him. I have a room here next to my own, the guest-room I call it, in reality it has always been his room, and in the chest of drawers there are still his pyjamas, his handkerchiefs. I was convinced that he was dead. But I was unable, after all this time, to separate myself from all these things, which during all those years had helped me to dream and to hope. Every year on March 23, his birthday, I went on buying a present for him. A scarf, a pair of gloves, a necktie... They are in the bottom drawer; I meant to give them to him, all together, on his return. There was a time, during the war, I no longer remember as a result of what events or symptoms, when I had become persuaded myself that he must turn up again at any moment. It was then that I couldn't sleep, because of the absurd fear that he might whistle from the street (he used to whistle in order to call me in Florence, when

I lived on a top floor in the Lungarno) and I might not hear him; it was then that I hardly ever left the house because of the absurd fear that he might come and not find me in. But before, when he was still here, when I could clasp him in my arms, whenever I wanted to, for an infinite number of hours, if I wished, had not my jealousy been much more absurd, which tore him away from me, with which I tore him away from me by sheer force, almost against the nature of things, and cast him far off, as though he had been something I could easily do without, and so lost him forever? And you are astonished that I accuse myself! Nobody bears the guilt of my unhappiness, besides myself ».

VI

« We were made for one another », Twinkle continued, « from the very first moment. It was in Pisa, on the lawn surrounding the Cathedral. I was alone, with my Baedeker. He was with a girl, and he was holding a bicycle. I came out of the darkness inside the Cathedral, through the door in the South transept, and saw him standing in the middle of the lawn, with the girl and the bicycle. The girl was looking at the Leaning Tower; he, with an ironical smile, was looking at the girl. I felt as it were a force of nature pushing me towards him. I crossed the lawn without hesitating, straight towards him, and, as though I knew him already, I greeted him in French. He answered me in French, laughing and staring at me, but without the faintest surprise. I might have thought up a thousand pretexts for addressing him, ask him where was the entrance to the Baptistry, the Bonanno door, the way back to town. I felt no need for any. He was wearing a handsome straw hat. Without any explanation, I took it and put it on myself, and laughing, convinced as I was that I was only joking, I said to him: « *Nous avons échangé l'âme* ». The girl laughed too, she was not in the least surprised. Perhaps she thought that we knew one another. I am English, I was carefully brought up, I had never in my whole life committed any such folly. That time it all seemed quite natural. We went back to the city together, the three of us. He accompanied me to my hotel. That evening, after dinner, he came to see me. I was waiting for him. He had not said a word to me; but I knew he would come.

« With him, I felt I was in a miraculous state of balance. That does not come to you twice in your life. We were friends, like you and me. I never felt bored in his company. There was nothing I couldn't talk to him about, nothing he failed to understand. At the same time I loved and desired him without even a shadow of weariness or remorse. I held my happiness in my hands. If only I had gone on like that, as we had gone on for two years; putting up with his breaches of fidelity, which now, as I recall them, strike me as things of no concern. Gradually he would have got used to me, his escapades would have grown less frequent, in time he would have been utterly happy solely in my company. With my own hands I destroyed that happiness.

« In Florence he had a girl, a girl of the people, who was also his model. Her name was Fausta, and she had been his friend for several years. I couldn't go to see him in his studio, because there was also danger that I might meet that girl. Naturally, instead of being satisfied with the immense happiness that was mine (he used to call for me every evening, we would go out together and dine in a *trattoria*, and then he would pass the night in my room) I was so blind, so foolish, that I desired only one thing: to go to his studio. One spring night I obliged him, with a scene of hysteria, to take me up there. And after barely half an hour we heard the bell ring from the street. It was Fausta. For some time he had always been sleeping with me; at last, that night, the girl had seen a light in the window, she insisted on coming up. So as not to meet her on the stairs, I had to hide in a cupboard in the anteroom. Filled with rage and shame I heard and saw through a crack how the little chit, who was younger and better-looking than I, in a short skirt, with thin skimpy legs, and her hair down her back, clutched him to her, kissed him, went into the alcove with him. To escape without making any noise I had to take off my shoes, and as I went down stairs I suffered horribly, and swore to myself that was the last time I would ever see Gino. I passed a night in Hell. But next morning at nine he came to my place with a big bunch of broom which he had gone on a bicycle to pick beyond the Cascine. We quarreled for a few days and then made it up. I had to go to Switzerland, to Interlaken. Gino went with me. Well, when later on I wanted to remember the loveliest, the happiest moments of my life with Gino, I would think, among others, also of those moments of torturing humiliation, which I never would have thought it possible I could have borne: the long moments when I was shut up in the cupboard, and saw Fausta come in, and then, while he was with her in there, when I went away in my stocking-feet. What would I not have given to live through that humiliation all over again! I was happier in the sufferings of those brief instants than during the twenty years of my restful dignified solitude. But I have been a very foolish woman. I understood what I had lost only when it was gone beyond recall.

« In Milan Gino had another woman. She was the wife of a petty employee, something like a sort of usher, I can't quite remember. She was a strikingly good-looking girl, from Trieste. Her husband was much older than she, and had married her when she was seventeen. They had two children. Gino had known her for several years, he met her when he lived in Milan and took a furnished room in her house. They were poor people. The husband earned a mere pittance, they could barely make both ends meet. Her name was Danitza, her beauty was amazing, she was intelligent, very vivacious, she deserved something much better. She wore herself out bringing up the children, running the house and dreaming of impossible things. Magazine-covers and movies — when she could save up enough money to go to them — made up her whole ideal: and Gino. Gino had become her lover when he lived in Milan at her house. In fact, the second child was his. But then Gino had gone back to Florence, and Danitza had remained behind alone, with her elderly husband, the little children, and poverty and hunger. Because of the second child, Gino felt he was partly to blame for her sufferings. I saw Danitza once; she was alone. We were passing through Milan on our way to Switzerland. Gino telegraphed to her; she came to the station. She did not know that I was in the train. I was able to examine her from the window. She too was younger and better-looking than I, short, slender, extremely blond, two great big light-blue eyes, a face as sweet as a Madonna's. In my opinion she could easily have tried to become a movie-star. Well, when Gino threw over the job you had given him at the Fenice to join me in London, I sent him a sum of money he needed for the journey and in order to pay for the various debts he had made in Venice and Florence ».

« I guessed », I interrupted her, « that the series of revelations was not yet ended. So then you knew that Petrucci would throw over the job for which you had recommended him to me, and you even gave him the money for the trip without writing a word to me about it. Oh, not that by any means his departure caused me any loss! He would show up on Saturdays only, to collect his pay ».

« My conduct towards you was unpardonable, I admit. But what could I do? I sent him the money he had asked me for. And he arrived in London two weeks later. He told me that he had gone to Florence to pay his debts, and to Arezzo to say good-bye to his mother. But the British consul in Milan, not knowing, or ignoring, my *liaison* with Gino, wrote me that he had seen him on Lake Como, at Villa d'Este, with a small, blond and extremely pretty woman. Danitza, of course. When Gino reached London, I made a terrible scene and even refused to receive him in my house. He ended by confessing everything. He had not gone to Florence, he had not gone to Arezzo, he had not even paid a single one of his creditors. He had gone to Milan and offered Danitza what the poor girl had dreamed of her whole life long: a fortnight in a big hotel. Danitza had left her children in the care of her mother-in-law, and gone off with the excuse of a cure she needed at Salsomaggiore, and from there, with the complicity of a friend, she arranged to have a few letters or telegrammes sent to her home. Nothing at that time could have struck me as being more abject and monstrous than what Gino had done. To spend the money I had lent him on another woman! But, as I look back on it now, nothing could strike me as more human, more generous. He did not think of his own dignity, he really loved both Fausta and Danitza, and the rest as well, and he suffered when they suffered, and tried as well as he could to alleviate their pain. I know perfectly well that such justifications, which I think up for Gino, might seem to anyone else, for instance to a woman-friend if I had one in whom to confide, the fruit of abject weakness. Only someone could have understood me who through intolerance had lost the only love of his life: until the day before yesterday, I believed I had lost mine. How everything concerning the beloved one appears to us then in a new light! How our resentment over offenses received is transformed into undying remorse over not having pardoned them immediately! His transgressions are no longer transgressions, but insignificant, innocent and sometimes even generous acts which, in our abominable selfishness we were unable to recognise as such. What would we not give to have him back with us again, ready to commit them again, once more offending us with them, but restoring us to life!

« I had been back in London for more than a month, and we had not yet been reconciled. He was living in a nasty little hotel near the Strand, on the charity, you might say, of an Italian friend, Marcello Prati, correspondent of the

Turinese newspaper, *La Stampa*. Prati had married an Englishwoman, and was living in a cottage at Hampstead. They
had no children, they were quite well off, and Gino used to
go there every day to lunch and dinner. Possibly he also
made love to Mrs. Prati, I don't know, it may well be. After
the first week he had not paid any of the hotel bills. He
couldn't go on like that. That was when you cabled me: you
were going back to the United States, you would be passing
through London. Your telegramme was a pretext for our
reconciliation, but oh! what a short time it lasted!

« The day before your arrival I went to the Pratis for
luncheon; I was a good friend of hers. I found Gino asleep
in an arm-chair. When it was time to go away, I asked Gino
to accompany me. But as soon as we had left the house,
instead of going down into the Tube, we climbed up onto the
Heath. We walked about on the Heath for half an hour,
perhaps, side by side, without talking. At last I explained
my plan. I told him once more that he knew how much I
loved him; and that I knew how much, in spite of everything,
he loved me. We were made for one another; but we could
not go on living like that. Gino had talent, he was still
young, he must work. I was certain you would give him a
job in the 'Met'. A few perfunctory words by way of excuse
would have been sufficient when you met again. If it turned
out that you were particularly offended because of the way
he let you down in Venice, I would take all the burden of
the blame on myself. Then he would join you in New York,
as soon as he could get a visa for the United States. America would mean a new life for him too. Soon after I would
join him there. There, very soon, we could marry. He did
not answer with a single word, he held my hand in his and,
as he gazed into my eyes, his own filled with tears. Then
he embraced me, clasped me close to himself, as though in
despair. Like so many Italians, he was incapable of calculating, incapable of making plans, incapable of coming to
any decision whatsoever unless in an unforeseen impulse. So
I am certain that at that moment he was not thinking of

escaping. But a secret instinct must have warned him that this was the last time we would be together. As for me, ever since then, I have never given myself either to him or to any other man.

« We went away late at night. The grass was damp beneath us. I gazed, supine, at the stars. And there is one memory of that evening on Hampstead Heath, that has not left me for twenty years. His thin, bony shoulder, against which I leaned my cheek. Every evening of my life, I could have leaned against that shoulder.

« You arrived the following morning. I went to meet you at the station. I persuaded you to help Gino. You were unwilling, but I talked you over ».

« It was so easy, Twinkle ».

« Oh no, it was not easy at all! He came to have lunch with me. You know the rest. I think the sudden impulse to run away came to him only because he was shy about meeting you. He knew he had not behaved any too well in Venice, he did not dare to face you. Undoubtedly, he was not at all anxious to go to America, and it may be that, unawares, knowing that you were leaving the following day, he simply wanted to avoid meeting you, to lie in hiding a few days, nothing more. Then... then something must have happened, I don't as yet know what. As soon as I see him, that will be the first thing I shall ask him ».

« Twinkle, dear Twinkle », I said, seizing one of her hands. « Are you really being quite honest with yourself, when you say, and think, that he loved you? »

« Yes, because when he was with me, he was happy. I haven't any doubt whatsoever ».

What objections did there remain for me to raise? What reality can overcome the reality of love?

Dusk had fallen by this time, and Twinkle was exhausted, did not feel like going out. She herself prepared a supper for us in her little kitchen, and I helped her. She was calmer, she even jested. The long narrative had as it were soothed her.

« In a few days », I told her, « he will be here, in my place, Gino; and he will cook for you ».

« For both of us ».

« I shall leave you as soon as you have found him again ».

« Oh no! » she said. But that was all she said; and I understood that, as soon as that moment came, I should have to leave.

However, the calm was only apparent. When, after dining and smoking a cigar, I was preparing to go back to my hotel, she grabbed me by the hand and with tears in her eyes entreated me not to leave her alone. She had had no rest for two nights. Ever since we had discovered the picture in the Exhibition, and the fact that Gino was alive. She could get no rest: the night was one long torment, filled with nightmares and fits of remorse. She could never cease recalling the past: all the things she had told me about, and all the rest, down to the minutest details; and she never ceased blaming herself. Every now and then she would be seized by a fit of terror: she thought Gino must be dead, his ghost was there beside her in the room, accusing her. He looked dreadful, he was undermined by misery, alcohol, vice. Like the faces of witches, the faces of two women, Dawn and Madeleine, alternated in this *danse macabre* with his. And for this too, and for his death, she, Twinkle, was to blame.

I said what I could to quiet her; I tried, dispassionately, to prove to her that remorse was sheer folly. In all probability, no matter how Twinkle had behaved, Petrucci would have met the same end. Everyone gets the destiny he deserves. And I ended up by letting her suspect that he was not so terribly unhappy after all: otherwise he would have tried to find her. This struck me as being, of all my arguments, the most stringent one. But Twinkle once more refused to bow to my logic: according to her, Gino had fallen so low that he could never have faced the shame of showing up again.

So I pretended to have forgotten all that she had told me in a moment of complete confidence, and to be unaware that the guest-room, to which, with a charming grace, she now led me, was, in reality, the secret room, reserved, in her amorous imagination throughout twenty years, for Gino Petrucci; and that the pyjamas which she was so neatly laying out for me on the bed, were his pyjamas.

The bed stood in the centre of a sort of alcove. Behind it, on the right, was a door leading to the bath-room; next to it, another door led to Twinkle's bed-room; facing it, an archway led to a semi-hexagonal parlour, a sort of bay-window, in which there was a writing-desk, a mirror, an arm-chair and even — here too — an easel, but this time one that had never been used. A silk hanging, painted Chinese fashion, shut off the great windows. All the furniture, including the bed, was lacquered a light green, with black and gold decorations.

When I entered that room and studied the sophisticated decorations, I experienced an obscure sense of shame, which I understood as soon as Twinkle, after bidding me good-night, had left me alone.

It was not so much from shame at finding myself, an indiscreet guest, an intruder in her dream; but rather for her, that this dream should be so equivocal, so effeminate, so stupid: the room, in short, that a Philistine old lord might have prepared for his kept mistress.

If I remembered Twinkle as I had left her twenty years before and as I still remembered her, simple, witty and of such pure and noble tastes that they might even seem to be plebeian, I could not, as I looked about me, believe my own eyes. And yet her long solitude, peopled with fantasies and remorse, explained even this corruption; and this too touched me.

She knocked at the door and stuck her head in. Might she leave the door ajar? Of course, I said. She thanked me. I could hear her going back to bed.

But every now and then, in the silence, she would call me *sotto voce*:

« Are you still awake? »

« Yes, Twinkle, do you want to tell me something? »

« No, thanks, dear. Only to know if you were still awake ».

I looked at that door standing ajar, and thought of a less solitary old age, in which Twinkle would have been my wife; and I put a question to myself, as a result of an immediate and quite natural association of ideas: if Gino Petrucci, after all, never turned up again; and if Twinkle could be got relatively to calm down, why should I not ask her, once more, to marry me?

At length, before falling asleep, I caressed the idea not only for myself, but for her sake too. She would go back to Milan with me. How she would love my apartment in the Piazza del Castello! And Italy — surely she had not forgotten her love of Italy? Far from London, far from this gloomy flat which, during too long a time, had sheltered her disappointment, she would once more become what she had been before, my dear merry Twinkle!

Why not?

Something had wakened me with a start. I turned on the light. Twinkle, standing beside my bed, completely dressed, with overcoat, umbrella, handbag and hat, was putting on her gloves and looking at me. Through her little veil, her eyes were gleaming as I had never seen them gleam before; they were no longer laughing or moved, but almost mad.

« What is it, Twinkle? » I asked her, terrified, lifting myself up on the cushions.

« Forgive me if I have waked you », she answered, with the *pianissimo* and the *rallentando* that are reserved for great occasions. « I came in to leave this note on the chest of drawers and the thermos with some hot coffee. When you woke up later, you wouldn't have found me. I'm going out ».

« Where are you going? Are you mad? At this hour? What time is it? »

« It must be about six ».

« Will you kindly tell me where you are going? » I asked again, although I had already guessed.

« I'm going over there. I'm certain that if I go there at this hour I shall find him. I haven't been able to get a wink of sleep ».

« So not even my proximity has been of any avail ».

« No, on the contrary. I thank you for staying here. I didn't sleep at all; but it hasn't been like other nights. I wasn't restless. Knowing that you were here gave me a strange strength, the capacity of reasoning. And I did reason, the whole time ».

« From the consequences, one wouldn't say so ».

« Oh yes, I realised that this was the only logical thing to do ».

« To get up at dawn? »

« To go there at a time when they don't expect me to come, so as to take Gino by surprise. My heart tells me that at this moment Gino is there. The simplest thing is to go there ».

I loathe being waked early, I abominate having to get up as soon as I am waked. But her slim figure, her smart dress, her nervous movements, her hallucinated eyes, her little veil, all that made me, for a few moments, see there, at the foot of my bed, in the half-shadow of that love-nest, a young woman of thirty. And even the sight of her distress, which until then had only saddened and touched me, for a few moments succeeded in seducing me.

I got up, resolutely. Of course I would accompany her. Twinkle tried to resist; but that was just what I wanted.

We crossed a deserted London — the sky, the houses, the asphalt pavements all enfolded in the same livid light, pierced, here and there, by the rubies and emeralds of the traffic signals — and very quickly reached Scarsdale Villas.

We prudently stopped the taxi a hundred yards before reaching Miss Warwick's house, and pursued our way on foot.

A little further on, three charwomen, armed with their dustbins, their brooms and their mops, were chattering; their discordant voices, piercing and hoarse, echoed lugubriously through the deserted street, like the cawing of crows in a mountain valley.

Seeing that we had stopped and stood uncertain in front of the house, they too gradually ceased their talk and all three of them turned about to look at us suspiciously.

« Are you 'unting for anybody? » one of them said, in an aggrieved tone, or perhaps it was her Cockney accent that impressed me, as a foreigner.

« Yes », said Twinkle.

« 'Oo are you looking for? »

« We are not certain whether the person we are looking for really lives in this house », replied Twinkle, with her customary frankness.

« We should not like », I added, in order to explain our hesitation, « we should not like, seeing how early it is, to disturb anyone uselessly ».

« Well, 'oo are you looking for? »

« Excuse me », I went on, drawing closer to them. « In this house, number three, lives a Miss Warwick, I believe? »

« Yes ».

« And no one else? »

« Yes, a friend of 'ers ».

« A Miss Madeleine Clarens? »

« I don't know wot 'er nime is, but a friend of 'ers lives there tew, a lidy », one of the women put in.

« Yes, indeed, that's the one you sy », another added hastily, the one with the red nose.

« And isn't there a gentleman too? »

« A gentleman? »

« Yes, a man ».

« A man? Not that I know of ».

« Perhaps he doesn't live there, but he often comes to see them. Don't you know him? »

« Wot can I sy, my dear Madam, 'eaps of men comes 'ere at all hours, it's a bit 'ard to know all of 'em ».

« But the one we are looking for », I specified, « is different from the rest. You ought to recognise him, if he lives here, or if he comes here often, as we have reason to believe he does. He's an Italian ».

The three women were silent and looked at one another.

« Did you sy an Eyetalian? » the fat one said at last.

« Yes, why? »

« A thin, dark man? »

« Yes », Twinkle answered, tremulously.

« With a moustache and a little goatee? »

« A pinter? » the other one added.

« Mr. Gino, in short »? the fat one concluded.

« Yes, yes, Mr. Gino Petrucci, so you do know him? Where is he? » Twinkle inquired, exasperated.

« Eh, my dear lydy, where 'e is... 'e isn't 'ere any more... 'e went awy... »

« Where to? »

« Are you relited to 'im? »

« Not I, but this gentleman here is a kinsman of his. This gentleman is Italian too. We have been looking for him for some time. Could you tell us where he has gone to? »

« 'E 's dead ».

« Dead ».

« 'E s' been dead for over two years », the three of them said in chorus.

I looked at Twinkle. I could see, as it were, a light go out in her. She stood motionless, silent.

« I'm sorry, dear madam », pursued one of the two chars; and pointing at me, she added to Twinkle: « you said 'ow 'e was relited to *'im* ».

« The lady », I explained, « was much attached to the Italian gentleman ».

« 'Er too? » the oldest of the three blurted out.

« But are you absolutely sure that the Italian gentleman is dead? » I made haste to inquire.

« Eh! I was there wen they took 'im awy », said the fat woman.

« I was there too ».

« Me too ».

« 'E died after the war », the first one went on. « 'E was very sick for two or three months. 'E orter have gone to the 'orspital, but 'e didn't want to. Per'aps in the 'orspital 'e might 'ave got better. Eh! Many's the time I did tell 'im so myself. 'E wouldn't go. I noo 'im very well indeed. It's me that does the cleaning at Miss Warwick's. A fine man, Mr. Gino, nice, cheerful, always singing, as long as 'e was in good 'elth. You could 'ear'm from the street. They sy that 'e was a pinter, but I believe that in 'is youth 'e must 'ave been a singer. You certainly noo 'im better than us ».

Twinkle thanked them. Then she turned to me, still with that extinguished look in her eyes, and taking me by the arm she said:

« Let's go home, now ».

Meanwhile the day had broken. On our way home, the taxi went through Hyde Park. We did not speak. The sun was rising, it shone brightly over the water of the Serpentine, tinting the grass on the huge lawn, whitening the mist which hid the edge of it, down there towards the Marble Arch.

VII

It is true that for twenty years Twinkle had never ceased to hope; but in the course of the years she had grown accustomed to the thought that after all Gino might be dead.

When, a week later, she had once more regained the

calm of this resignation, we decided to go back to Scarsdale Villas.

I telephoned first, to avoid further scenes and useless attempts at mystification: I said that now we had found out about Petrucci's death, and were coming in order to purchase the picture we had already mentioned.

Dawn and Madeleine received us in subdued melancholy, and for this occasion they had chosen to put on mourning.

Tea was ready in the big drawing-room, which had been put into some sort of order.

Even before we asked, they hastened to explain with a great flow of words why they had lied to us by concealing their friend's death.

They had done it from *force of habit*. For years on end, when Gino was alive, they were used to hiding him. And so, when Twinkle and I had appeared at Scarsdale Villas, and had mentioned his name, Madeleine's first instinctive reaction had been to deny all knowledge of him.

Then, they admitted, the extreme poverty to which they were reduced had prompted them to exploit the situation, to deceive us. But after all it was not, they explained smiling and humbly begging our pardon, such a very *low* deception; because, by pretending to us that Gino was still alive, they succeeded in fooling themselves a little as well, and found consolation for their bereavement.

« He was the only man that ever really loved me », sighed Dawn, holding back her tears.

« And me too », Madeleine added, in a low voice.

But Dawn turned on her violently:

« You keep quiet. You have no right to say that! »

« And why not, I pray? »

« Because he would not even have looked at you if you had been a loyal friend to me... if you had not seduced him ».

« That's not true! I never told you: but if you really want to know, I can tell you now, and I apologise to this lady and gentleman. It happened all at once, that time you went to Polperro for a week-end with Peter... ».

« You liar! Gino went away before me, he left in the morning, to go to Manchester to spend two days with his Italian friend, the ice-cream maker ».

« He pretended to leave. In the afternoon he came back, and with the money you had given him for the trip we went to Soho and had a wonderful Italian dinner. He had prepared everything ».

« If what you say is true, that's a proof you were in collusion. He came back here because he was sure he would find you ».

« Well, it's not my fault if I wasn't as good-looking as you, if I didn't have loads of acquaintances like you, to invite me down to Cornwall for a week-end... ».

Twinkle rose to her feet, exasperated. I cut the discussion short by telling Dawn that we were in a hurry and wanted to settle the deal for the pictures without any further delay. If they owned any other paintings, drawings or sketches, we should be very glad to purchase those too.

There wasn't a good deal. I offered a lump sum, and after rapid negotiations we reached an agreement. Nor did I forget to obtain a receipt so that, after the Exhibition had closed, Twinkle would be able to call for her picture.

At the moment of going away, from the midst of a few dusty albums and scattered sheets of drawings, which the two women were putting together on the table so as to make a package of them, there fell out a copy-book, apparently a drawing-album like the others, but a little smaller, which Dawn quickly snatched from Madeleine's hands.

« Not this; these aren't drawings, it's writing, all written in Italian, it can't possibly interest you ».

We protested that, on the contrary, it interested us considerably. Twinkle made a gesture as though to seize it.

« Let me see it ».

« Please », said Dawn, clutching the copy-book to her immense breast. « Everything that belonged to Gino is mine now, and I can do what I like with it. Our agreement con-

cerned solely paintings and drawings. Here there is nothing
but written words ».

« At least let me have a look at it », Twinkle entreated.

« It's a diary, or some notes, that Gino, three years before
his death, wrote in Italian for somebody he knew, perhaps
a friend of his. It's my duty to keep it and deliver it, naturally, only to the person in question ».

« And who is this person? »

« The name is written on the cover: Twinkle. *For
Twinkle,* is written on it ».

« But that's me, 'Twinkle'! » Twinkle cried.

« You can give it to her without hesitation, she is the
very person », I added.

« I am extremely regretful », replied Dawn, still clutching
the copy-book to her breast. « But are not you Miss Ruth
Cummings? »

Such was, in fact, Twinkle's real name, under which, of
course, she had introduced herself at Scarsdale Villas.

« Ruth Cummings is my name », said Twinkle, « But all
my friends call me 'Twinkle' ».

« That may indeed be so », said Dawn, compressing her
lips in a faint smile of triumph and holding the copy-book
close to her breast, in her well-shaped little hands. « That
may well be so: but what proof have I of it? »

« Come, come, don't be so stubborn », Twinkle replied,
nervously. « You too must see that Twinkle is not a name.
How could anybody be called 'Twinkle'? Impossible. It's a
nick-name, come ».

« But I don't say it isn't a nick-name. I do not say
anything at all, my dear Miss Cummings ».

« Well then, look at my eyes », Twinkle beseeched her,
coming quite close to her. « Don't you see how they *twinkle?*
That is why my friends have always called me 'Twinkle'! »

Twinkle's eyes, poor thing, had never twinkled less than
at this moment; they were small, half-closed with rage, and
filled with tears.

« I am ever so sorry », concluded Dawn, extremely calm, now that Twinkle was growing excited. « But I do not agree with you at all. My eyes, for instance, twinkle much more than yours. Look at them, look at them as closely as you like. Don't you see how they twinkle? »

And it was true. The *vieille putain's* eyes, wide-open and glaring at me, at Twinkle, were twinkling in a triumphant laugh, as though she were concentrating in them all the happiness Gino had given her.

« But Madeleine's twinkle too! » Dawn added, insatiate, beckoning to Twinkle to look at Madeleine, who had followed the scene, laughing, from a dark corner, and who now screwed up her face in extremely minute wrinkles behind the smoke of her cigarette, emitting two lively little twinkles from her little black eyes. « Madeleine's too, if you care for another instance, twinkle more than yours! »

There was a briefest pause. Twinkle made an effort to control herself. Then she exploded, bitterly:

« Thank you *very* much », she said icily to Dawn. « I hope I never meet you again », and, with the package of drawings under her arm, she left the room and the house with the rapidity of lightning.

I accompanied her as far as Brook Street. Naturally, the next day, without saying a word to Twinkle, I went back to the two women and with a few compliments and a few sovereigns I succeeded in wresting the curious little copybook from them. On the cover there was a little pen-and-ink sketch of the Lungarnos; on the left, beyond the roofs, the tower of the Palazzo Vecchio; in the background, the hills; in the foreground, the bridge of Santa Trinità. Under the arch of the bridge, as in a vignette, was written, in print hand: FOR TWINKLE, FROM HER GINO. LONDON, NOVEMBER 1939.

At the instant in which she handed me the little copybook and was taking the money, Dawn smiled at me and said:

« You must think me very venal? »

« No. Why do you say that? »

77

« And that I am convinced that at this moment I am committing a wrong against Gino's memory? »

« No, I assure you I think nothing of the kind ».

« Yet I would never have given you this little copy-book if I had not frequently heard you call your friend by her nick-name, which, between you and me, I must say I find quite unjustifiable ».

« But then why didn't you give it to her in person yesterday: you would have made her so happy! »

« Who can tell! » retorted Dawn, clutching her silk dressing-gown at the waist with the hand that held the money, and offering me the other, with unexpected coquetry, in a gesture of farewell. « It may well be that she will not deem reading what is written in that note-book quite so agreeable after all ».

I looked at her in surprise: from her resolute expression and the vigorous elegance of her last words, I thought I could at last understand her odd nature, made up of contrasts, a mixture of vulgarity and pride; I admire the rough aristocracy which is sometimes to be found in the most genuinely plebeian temperaments.

When I was alone in my hotel-room, immobile in an arm-chair by the window, I waited a long time until the sun sank, a mass of confused red and gold mist, behind the still unclothed trees of the Green Park.

And at last I turned on the light, opened the copy-book, and . . .

VIII

began to read:

« When you, my friend, my adored one, Twinkle mine forever, when you read these lines, I do not know where I shall be, how I shall be, or even if I shall still be alive at all.

78

« More than ten years have now gone by since the last time we met, and since that day I fear you have not had any more news of me.

« I say I fear? Yes, I fear. I have done nothing to see you again. Or rather I hid myself from you during all these years. But at the same time, I have never lived one sole instant without desiring that some fortunate and unforeseen incident might bring us together. I no longer know where you are living. Do you still have your flat in Fulham Road? I suppose not. However, during the first two or three years, thinking you might still be living there, I always very carefully avoided passing that way. Not my will, but destiny would have to make us meet. But so far destiny has not willed it. You always blamed me for being such a fatalist! You are so different! You think that will-power, decision, diligence, discipline can do so much, perhaps everything in life. Do you still believe that? You wanted me to want to work, to become a great painter. But I have always let myself drift. All that I have done, all the good and all the bad in my life, I always did it in that way: letting myself drift. How that attitude of mine used to irritate you! By way of compensation, you must admit that if I am void of will-power, I am also void of any pride whatsoever. I do not boast at all, really not at all, of the little good I may have done; it came, just like that. And I don't believe that I ever deserved the joys that life has given me and continues to give me: I thank Heaven, or God, or Whoever it is, because I have never moved a finger — not a leaf on a tree, in order to get a little shade or a little sunshine.

« It was inevitable, my disappearance from your life, or I should rather say, from my own life and from society. For the last seven years I have been living like a sort of Mattia Pascal. Do you recall that novel of Pirandello's? We saw the film together, if you remember? that June evening in Siena, when we had such a row because I wanted to go to the pictures and you on the contrary wanted to take a walk to Monte Oliveto. We did go to Monte Oliveto, a few nights later. It was a wonderful moonlight night, the crickets, the fire-flies filled the darkness, and the air, neither cold nor warm, the sweetness of the night filled our hearts and everything about us, and it seemed as though all that could never end, our happiness seened so natural, so simple, and on the contrary it was a miracle never to be repeated. I close my eyes and still see the fireflies, swarms of them, in the dark places under the shade of the cypress-tree. I can still feel your slender, vigorous waist and crush it in my arms. And our long silence punctuated by the crickets, hours and hours on end, perhaps, we two side by side, in the darkness, in the moonlight, in the sweet silence. But to-day, in memory, it is as though we had never ceased to speak, isn't it? We thought. my Twinkle, the same things, instant by instant, and it was as though we were continuously confessing them to one another, and we weren't bored for a single minute, all that June night: never have we been happier.

« I am the 'late Mattia Pascal'. I have no name any more, no civil status. I work on my own, at home, in this house, where I am the guest of two ladies.

« Don't be angry. If I could speak to you, if I could only tell you in all detail how it happened, you would not be angry... at least you would not be too angry, because *you would understand*. You are the only woman, indeed the only person, who has fundamentally understood everything about me. Don't you want to be that any more? So try, just this once more, to understand me.

« I didn't do it purposely. I told you that. You know it. I have never done anything purposely, in all my life. Not even the smallest things. Let alone something so huge, so enormous as that: to disappear!

« I jumped from the window of your flat onto that low roof only because I was impatient: it irritated me to watch you preparing all that buttered toast, with such great care and such scant ability, for the *Commendatore* who was to come for tea, the slave-driver who was to give me a good drubbing. You were never very much good in the kitchen, you know perfectly well. But woe was me if I ever ventured to tell you that. You *wanted* to be good at that too. It vexed me to watch you soiling your hands with butter and jam, your hands which were made for holding a pen or for dealing out caresses. Merely impatience. I jumped out. Then, suddenly, as soon as I was on the roof, I began to walk up and down, venturing out amidst all those chimney-pots, and coming back, each time, to the window, to see if you had finished. But you never finished. Each time I hoped to find you without toast in one hand and a little knife in the other. But you were terribly slow, awkward, accurate. If a piece of toast fell to the floor, you stamped your foot, 'damn!' you said, and you picked up the toast that had dropped with a paper napkin and laid it aside, not on the plate where the rest of the toast was being piled up, but on a little shelf, and you hid it with a book.

« Each time, going up and down over the roof, I would take a longer walk, each time just a bit longer. The spectacle that opened out before me, at each step I took, intrigued me like a virgin forest, or a magic labyrinth. Oh, you know the skimpy little gardens of London, and you remember your window, so even if you never thought about it, you will easily imagine what I saw. I even seem to remember how, before I jumped from the window, I made a little drawing of what one could see from the window, and left it on your desk. Did you by any chance find it? Did you even keep it, perhaps? I am sure it was a vision that struck me, and that attracted me from the very first moment. Otherwise I wouldn't have made that little drawing. I always recalled that view from your window so perfectly that I have often again drawn it from memory, and I even made a few oil paintings of it.

« But the motionless, silent magic that the view of those scrubby gardens filled me with as I looked out of your window, increased, opened and unfolded, as I gradually progressed along the roof in the midst of the chimney-pots, treading on what at first I had deemed unpracticable and as it were

81

a sort of back-drop. It was no longer the magic that had over-whelmed me at the first moment, that lively, pungent, inartic-ulate, inexplicable sensation, without thoughts or second-thoughts, which had obliged me to sit down at your desk and jot down the little drawing. It was something else. Each one of those grey, white, dark red, tar façades, was a house, a dwelling, and each one of those dwellings must inevitably contain within itself, although — as is only natural in England — no sign could be seen from outside, a life, a thousand lives. Behind each one of those windows, hermetically closed and enigmatically shrouded with embroidered curtains, men, women, husbands, wives, girles, widows, children were wea-ving and living or at least their thoughts were weaving. Outside nothing was to be seen. And it was this that lent to those constructions, which an Italian, snatched up and bo-dily carried here from Chiaia or Sottoripa, would swear were uninhabited, a mystery, a power, and as it were the certainty of tremendous vitality.

« But if I stopped moving (I had by this time gone so far from your window that when I turned around I could no longer see it: the labyrinth of roofs, with its turnings, corners, ladders, changes of level, had carried me who knows where), even if I stopped moving and stood quite still, I gradually began to notice something. A cat jumped from a window-sill into a yard. A curtain was held open by a hand and then immediately drawn close again. By pricking up my ears, I fancied I could hear, indeed I did hear, a baby crying behind that window.

« I never wear a watch, you know. When I once more thought, not of you, for of you, you know full well, I always think, because when I think of myself I think of you, but when I once more thought of the *Commendatore* who per-haps had already reached your flat and was waiting for me, amidst all that buttered toast and jam, I felt my heart shrink. I had noticed, at the mere recollection of the *Commendatore*, that with all my troubles, and my quarrels with you, and without a penny in the world, and without any desire to work, I was yet entirely happy.

« Go to America? Work? Follow a schedule? What for? What for?

« We should get married.

« Ah! and wouldn't that be the end of everything?

« No, you say; no; because we are fond of one another, and two beings that are fond of one nother, attempt, naturally, to stay together as long as possible, to live and die together. But I never tried to do anything, and I never tried to do that either, my Twinkle. I have always let myself drift. So I did not, then, not even then, try to run away from the *Commendatore*, not to go to America, not to marry you. I have never tried to do anything. I have never wanted anything. Simply, I detested the idea of going back, of seeing again the white face and the grey beard of your friend, his plump hands, his striped pants, his tender Neapolitan accent, his kindly smile, his intelligent eyes, his gold-rimmed lenses. For the time being, I said to myself, let's go on like this. Later on I'll go back to Twinkle, of course. This evening, later on, when he will have gone away at last.

« At that minute, or possibly many minutes later, I don't know, I can't remember, how long I walked and stopped amidst those chimney-pots, along those roofs, in that supernatural silence formed by the continuous, confused, remote, imperceptible noise of the busses and the city: at a certain moment, in short, a little window, half-hidden by an iron stairs, the little window of a basement at the bottom of an area which was right under me, opened with a tinkle. And I saw a woman with a great shock of red hair leaning out and staring at me, with a fixed, serious gaze, as though she had already noticed me through the curtains and now wanted to understand why I was walking over the roofs, a most unusual spectacle in the eyes of English people.

« When I saw that woman's serious face, I reflected that my oddness was unlawful and therefore suspicious. And I was astonished that no one else had hitherto noticed me.

But who could tell, perhaps I *had* been observed, and they had sent for the police. The British police have always filled me with great alarm. I thought of going back. But after a few steps a double fear stopped me: the *Commendatore* at your house, still waiting for me; and the length of the journey, in the course of which the police would have plenty of time to catch me. Thus, instinctively, I turned to the woman and asked her, courteously, the way out, out of that labyrinth and back to the freedom of the road.

« The woman showed me only the first part, how to get onto a neighbouring roof, down into the yard, into the house. The way out, she never showed me. From that moment I always stayed in the house... not literally in the house, for we have already moved four times; I mean, from the moment I stayed with that woman, I was no longer a free man, I was no longer myself.

« She was not, and she is not now, alone. She lived, and still lives, with a woman-friend, a woman entirely unlike her, a small, thin brunette. Their characters are exact opposites, they quarrel continually, they seem to hate one another, and instead they are very fond of one another. The real reason why I have never gone away may lie in this: that there are two of them. Their days of ill-humour alternate, the defects of the one make up for the defects of the other, and with the one or the other I can always get on, I always succeed in getting some peace.

« If, while I am helping one of them (the big one, the one with the red hair) to cook, and she happens to say something that hurts my feelings, a harsh word or a vulgar expression, then I think of the other one (the little brunette) who, like her, is my good friend too, and yet so different, gentle, delicate, devoted. And this thought alone consoles me, gives me strength to endure and to wait.

« If, while I am helping the second one to clean up, she in turn (for she too has her shortcomings) irritates me with much tedious talk, then I recall the first one; all afire and outspoken and brusque. And I try to be patient, for I know that very soon the music will change.

« Are you horrified by my way of living? You know me, Twinkle, you understand me, you who in your single self, woman unique in the world, contained for me, in the variety of your sentiments, in your manifold qualities, in your intelligence and your charm, in your gentleness and your strength, in your earnestness and your cheerfulness, not two or three or four but all the women of this world.

« Cooking, house-cleaning: what kind of a life do I lead? A domestic life. I read English novels. I have learnt your language accurately by this time. I think I must have read all Dickens's novels. How lovely English is, and how entertaining English literature! I rarely go out. Sometimes, but rarely, on an errand. And sometimes for the week-end I go to the country with my two good friends, in absolute harmony, the three of us together.

« I paint, alas! very little. I have also sold a few small pictures, but without signing them, to acquaintances of my mistress. (I call my red-haired friend that because she is always the head of the apartment, the landlady, you know what I mean). I'm very careful to avoid meeting these acquaintances of hers, because I don't want any trouble, I want to go on living and perhaps to die as I have lived during these years, incognito, almost a free man, and without any responsibilities. We hope there won't be a war. Things might change then. Unless you, my unique adorable Twinkle, miraculously appear in my life again. You, I feel, are the only event that might change it. There has not been a day, during these long seven years, when I did not think of you.

Of late I have been ill, quite seriously. An intestinal fever. Now I am beginning to feel a little better. For the last four days my fever has gone, and the doctor who examined me says I may consider myself cured. But I feel very tired, very weak; and this letter I am writing to you... (but is it a letter?) is a confession, an effort to unburden myself, a long-drawn-out confidence, a need to talk to you after such a long time and after the lonely nights of my illness, even if I know I won't send this letter off and that perhaps you will never read it. I don't even know any more where you live. If I were certain I am going to die, perhaps I might send someone to search for you. But where? How? They would have to go to Fulham Road, and hunt you from one address to the next. Perhaps you have gone back to Italy?

« During many nights, when I was ill, running a high fever, I was alone at home. And I would think of you, my sweet girl, who would not have left me alone. My friends can't help it, it would be unjust to blame them, poor dears. I think, in my fever, I must have called you. The only consolation for me was to call your name continuously, with the certainty that you still love me.

« As soon as I was able to, I wrapped the blankets around my legs, and sat up at the desk in order to write these things to you in this copy-book ».

Here the manuscript broke off. Halfway down the next page, Petrucci had begun again, in his thin, aimless, but legible handwriting.

« I resume this writing addressed to you, my own Twinkle, after more than a year. I haven't the strength to read again what I wrote to you then. I know more than a year has gone by, because I was ill, and that was in October. Now, this evening, it is November 25, 1939. The war has broken out. I keep on living hidden in London; I hope they won't find me out; and if there is a war with Italy too, but perhaps there won't be, that they don't send me to a concentration-camp. My friends, however, are determined to keep me well-concealed.

« Where afe you, Twinkle? What are you doing?

« The first year after my disappearance, when we were still living in the house I reached across the roofs, from the window of your flat, I had the constant sensation that I was

living in the same block as you, not far, that is, from Fulham
Road. And sometimes, looking out into the garden, I would
look in your direction, and think that in a few minutes, in
a few steps, almost by means of a simple gesture, I might
have reached you. That gave me a tender feeling, an infinite
consolation. It was just as though you were there, so that
I needed only to stretch out my hand to find you; and
perhaps I did not make the gesture merely because I had
the certainty of being able to make it.

« Then we went far away, to another part of the city.
I at once thought, however, that it would be very easy to
find you: I had only to take the Tube, or a bus. In half-an-
hour, in three quarters of an hour, I could be with you. Gradually, through the chain of the years and my various changes of domicile, and my absolute ignorance of yours, this certainty became more and more of an illusion. But — believe
me, Twinkle — I am not conscious that it is an illusion,
accustomed as I have been, for eight years by this time, to
your temporary absence.

« Or am I mistaken? »

« Could I not, if I really wanted to, if I ever wanted
anything in my life, find you again? »

« Have you forgotten me? »

« *M'as-tu oublié? Mon amour, mon amour, m'aimes-tu
encore?* »

IX

That is how the manuscript ended. I recollect that their
acquaintance had begun, too, in the cathedral-close at Pisa,
with a phrase in French.

I asked myself what I ought to do. I was in doubt
whether reading the manuscript would give Twinkle more
pleasure or pain. Petrucci's evasive character, a mixture

of cynicism and affectionateness, was here revealed unmistakably. Would it mean a blow for Twinkle? Or had she loved him such as he was, with these shortcomings, *for* these shortcomings, and would the manuscript, after all, teach her nothing new? Or, again — since all things are possible — would she, in love, and blind to the very end, not have understood even what Petrucci told her so clearly: that he had loved her with a love void of substance — a literary, imaginary love? whereas the two women, Dawn and Madeleine, alternating with one another, were his concrete reality, as concrete as Gino Petrucci's reality could be: since he had anchored, for the first and last time, precisely in this continuous and see-sawing evasion from the one woman to the other, in this alternate negation of himself?

I was prompted to give the manuscript to Twinkle by the reflection that a souvenir, even an offensive one, from someone we have loved and lost, is always dear to us.

I was held back by a delicate wisp of hope: that Twinkle, by reading the manuscript, might at last undestand who Gino Petrucci was and so might, even if only a little later, turn to me. I once more pondered my secret plan of ending my old age without being lonely. Twinkle would understand at last. She would consent to marry me. She would come to Milan with me. In this manuscript, I may have had the weapon with which to convince her. And I shrink from convincing her in that fashion.

In fine, since it was already late and the hour had come when I was to go to her flat to take her out to dinner as usual, I wrote her a note saying I was very tired, that I was not going to leave my hotel, and asking her to excuse me if I did not come to keep her company; but that I was certain I could make good my absence by means of a gift I was sending her.

Together with the note I sent the copy-book, wrapped up in tissue-paper, and a few roses. Whatever effect reading the manuscript might have on her, up to that moment she loved Gino; so I avoided being present at the moment when she held his last message in her hands, and would certainly prefer to be alone.

It was almost midnight, and I was just falling asleep, when the telephone rang. It was Twinkle. She had received Gino's message. She had read it. She had read and reread it, again and again and again, and an infinite number of times. Even now, as she spoke to me over the telephone, she was still crying and laughing at once, disconnected phrases, in which emotion, consolation and delirium were mingled.

« Thanks, thanks, thanks, dear. You cannot understand the joy you have given me... you are really my great friend... Now I can die happy... I know that Gino loved me... that he never ceased loving me, and thinking of me... I told you so. I knew it... I felt it... But now I really know it, I know it better... From now on, as long as I live, every day of my life I will read all his words at least once... And it is you who have given me this joy... I thank you.... God bless you, darling! »

Of course I made no answer whatsoever. I let her talk. And I asked myself if she had understood and loved him like that, or if on the contrary she hadn't understood at all. I have thought it over again, since then, several times, but I have always remained in doubt. What is this thing called love?

Twinkle, at the telephone, talked, if I am not mistaken, for an hour. She read out loud to me whole passages from the manuscript — which I, naturally, told her I had not even looked at. She told me about Siena, and Monte Oliveto, and a thousand other things. She would never again be afraid at night, now. Gino's words were his living presence. Before ringing off, she asked me to come to see her the next morning, she wanted to read me the whole thing in its proper sequence... almost the whole thing, she promptly corrected herself, for there were, naturally, some intimate things that belonged to her alone.

I knew what those things were. But how difficult it is

for English people really to know Italians! We are always less honest than they think! Twinkle never suspected for an instant that I had dared to read that manuscript addressed to her. And yet I had read it, not from curiosity, but in order to spare her pain, if there had been any danger of that. Always less honest, but always more human than they think!

« I'll see you to-morrow, dear », said Twinkle, sending me a kiss.

« To-morrow ».

I hung up the receiver.

This story too ends as it had to end.

A few days later, a little sooner than the date I had fixed, I left for Italy, and, of course, Twinkle was not with me.

(translated by Henry Furst)

POEMS

BY

GIORGIO BASSANI

I

How the wind resounds, Aniene,
as it twists, gloomy and slow,
between your chasm and the mountain:
it seems the voice of a brother
or now a serpent's whisper
as through the bitter, dark grass
he slides, in search of a vein.
The desolate intonation
sounds always at evening,
until, mirroring the pure air
in the depth of the plain,
you rise, o foreign city,
like a huge rose-colored ghost,
this weeping that will not remain
beyond the day, this lament
that returns with the sail
of the night, wind, time
that swallows all forms and cries,
that goes, and never rests.

II

From the towers of Ferrara
flies now the gentle light,
but at the black grating, miser,
what bears you, leads you,
o caress of the evening?
Who answers a prayer,
an abandoned weeping,
with this fragile fanfare?
Keep night from falling, no
night ever if it does not bring
you through space, through the fog,
sounds weak and distorted,
rare, timid signals
when the hours are more similar,
when the day is more distant
and every name is upon the sea.

III

How far (who calls?) travels tonight a lament!
It fords slowly the river through its grassy bank,
rises twisting (who seeks?), and is here, near the light,
from there, with its broken sounds, with its fright.

« Vide cor meum »: You, call? Oh the heart, nothing
else of me (You, seek?) reflects you from the depths.
Touch my heart then, not the eyes, the mind,
the insolent tongue, the mouth wherein I hide.

IV

House where I am led by a toilsome path,
house lost in the green, face thin and holy,
only you remain from every heroic tear,
nothing remains but you, and the light that is sleepy.

V

Let nothing of me remain but a cry, slow,
without words. Never a word: my reward
you were, o heavenly intimate, debris, alone.
In the still sky, this wave, this word...

VI

to M. C.

Dawn at the panes; the music of a drum and fife
flew to me with a lightsome, raving merriment.
And it was you passing by, life, you, my life,
who came unexpectedly, you, future to be innocent.

« Pitiless age to come, who press now at the doors, »
I said, with tears less bitter than were sweet,
« forget my name!... » I said.   And death, yours,
drunken, still, that martial music brought me sleep.

GIORGIO BASSANI

IN MEMORIAM

I

In a dream I saw my father: « You here? »
he said, with his stifled laugh, « not coming? »
Island! Childhood! O sea, serenely breaking!
Everything returned in the night that was near.

Ah how vain in the whirlwind it was
that suddenly rose over those who fled,
to struggle, and on the sand, that head
all silver, and in oblivion, never a sigh.

II

If here, against my own chest's living heart,
if I dared bury you within myself, offended
here in me you tremble — then let offence
lack never in the life that is left me,

tears at this entombed fountain
where, suspended, bending, you stand.

(translated by William Fense Weaver)

CANCROREGINA

BY

TOMMASO LANDOLFI

I

23 March 19—

...These instruments, twisted, round or smooth, these push-buttons, these keys, these levers, these complicated systems; bunches, bundles, knots of steel, of glass, of everything imaginable; these dials, these switches, these gears, these valves, these indicators, these instrument panels; these joints, these sockets and couplings, in short all this infernal machinery sparkling cruelly in front of me, its most minute particles distinct in the white, ghostly light that gives birth to small and indefinite patches of blue-grey shadows like those at noon on a summer's day which with similar deceit speak of hope and peace in that other world so much vaster but equally restricting. As always, I hear an uninterrupted, clear buzzing and hissing. It rises note by note up the scale to a piercing shriek, and finally, passing the range of perception of my ear, it loses itself in an inaudible, muted vibration.

The earth is below me, always in the same position with the same contorted features, its face recognizable to me by the outline of Europe, the continent of my birth; interrupted now and then by the passing clouds, covered and then uncovered, sometimes slightly different, now smaller, now larger, but usually unchanging — how blank is the human face with only the emotions to give it expression! Oh, could I not have been sentenced to meditate upon a part of the earth unknown to me and therefore less hated?

Above me is the moon, that romantic moon whose black and white mottled face and open eruptions of calcined stone have never inspired much hatred in man.

The corpse follows relentlessly and gives me no peace. But now that all that could have happened has already happened, I want to tell a story, to tell it from the beginning. To whom and why? To justify myself perhaps? And to whom, I ask, should I send this message? Even if it actually reaches someone, what good could they possibly derive from it?

I don't know and I don't care. Perhaps because I shall pretend to be only a reader of the story and therefore I shall be less alone. That is enough. Perhaps I will be more alone and that is better; it will hasten the inevitable end or it will give me courage to...

I was lonely and disconsolate. My immense gambling losses and serious disappointments in love, not to speak of other things, had forced me to live in the village in the ancient home of my fathers. I felt quite hopeless. A deep and innate ineffectiveness hampered me in any kind of work. I would evolve some crazy scheme and then lose myself in contemplation of its possible, probable, daily more unavoidable realization. The world seemed to lack all meaning, and for me at any rate, to be without any future. I was ready or at least I wanted to get ready to leave it...

One night (but how long ago and in what distant past did it occur) when I was as Corvo has put it, « weak and weary, » absorbed in reading an old book, or if the truth must be told, was holding it mechanically before my eyes without reading, someone knocked on my door. I lived alone and was not in the habit of opening to anyone. But the hour was unusual and on this occasion some instinct led me to depart from my custom. A man whom I did not know stood before me. He did not speak, but with a brief gesture of greeting preceded me up the stairs. He paid scant attention to my feeble protests, and as I am timid by nature, I did not dare to lay a hand on him.

« Close the door quickly, I beg of you, » he said stopping abruptly half way up the stairs. « Show me the way. » As though under compulsion I obeyed.

In the light he appeared to be a man of powerful build and very marked features with a black mustache concealing his upper lip and a voice that resounded through the room. He could not have been more than forty years of age. Sinking into a chair beside the table, he seemed to have forgotten the motive that had brought him to me, nor did he attempt to supply me with any kind of explanation. My own chief feeling was one of fear, indeed he inspired me with a terror quite unjustified by anything in his behavior. However my customary habit of observing people closely soon led me to perceive beneath his external self-sufficiency a kind of deep gentleness, or even weakness, which in spite of his appearance restored my courage. Had I known the real reason for the discrepancy, I would have lost such courage as remained to me. His eyes shone with an extraordinary brilliance.

With a restless hand he turned over the pages of the book which had remained open on the table and made a few intelligent comments on its contents. His manner was that of one who was resuming a conversation with an old friend, talking vaguely as in a moment of leisure and idleness, slowly picking up the train of thought just at the point where he had dropped it long before.

« But my good man, » I began, taking advantage of a long pause. He interrupted me immediately with the further development of his line of reasoning which he did not, however, pursue for very long. Breaking off in the very middle of a sentence, without looking at me, he remarked gently:

« I am insane. That is to say, others consider me to be so, » he hastened to add in response to my involuntary gesture. « I can only hope that I do not seem so to you. »

He looked at me for a moment with a timid smile dawning on his lips.

« I... I have heard them speak of you. I have read one of your books. And to whom else could I apply in this neighborhood? You, I am convinced, will listen to me. Either I am really insane or I am not. It depends on what is meant by the word, but you will not be afraid of words, you will not give more importance to them than they deserve, nor to the ideas which they may express. I can see that you are not afraid of anything. You are a scholar. » Was I mistaken or was there possibly a shade of irony in the unnatural brilliance of his eyes?

« Listen carefully, » he began again. « I have escaped tonight from the asylum of —. » He mentioned one of the best known in the neighborhood. « For two years I have waited for such an opportunity and you will easily understand my extreme haste in order to profit from my regained liberty. During the long time of my detention they were never willing to believe or even to listen to the explanations and revelations which I attempted to give them even though I spoke with the greatest composure (since I am not insane, as I have already told you). They did not want to believe in the existence of the child of my brain. I pointed out the exact place where it was hidden; they laughed and shrugged their shoulders when the lowest and crudest of them did not resort to certain of their methods of imposing silence on the inmates. I implored them to look for it, to give it publicity for the benefit of humanity if not for my own. I would have been content to remain all my life in that horrible prison among those unfortunates who are deprived of the light of reason, if only this child of my brain might be enabled to open new roads to all men of good will, to their bodies, you understand, and to their souls. If only the principles that had begotten and inspired it and that must inevitably find a wider application in the near future might have been shown to the whole world, and especially to that smaller world, the thoughtful seekers after truth. Alas, with such people it was.

all useless. I don't know nor can I ever know which action of mine (since in this world of ours only action is punished or need be feared) led me to be confined in that place in which I awoke after a long period of unconsciousness. Such action must have been violent and inadvised, or at the very least, contrary to the rules of our present cultured social system, since it was obviously regarded as unjustifiable. It must have been one of extreme violence (since I am, as I have already told you, insane) and of a nature that they cannot forgive, for by doing so, they would jeopardize the whole structure of the precious human race which certainly feels itself assailed and terrified to the degree of applying the same judgment to any of my subsequent arguments or actions. As you know, a lunatic has no claim to the right of revealing truth and even less of demonstrating it, lest their entire edifice should crumble and fall; and so like Galileo, I spent two years in offering them a telescope of which they consistently refused to avail themselves. »

I felt myself swept away by his flood of words, nevertheless a strange feeling began to stir within me. I had neither the strength nor the courage to check the speaker... nor for that matter, the desire.

« Now, the idea I sought to expound to them is extremely simple and easily definable. If time, as was already made clear by the poets long before the scientists intervened, notably by one who was more than poet, more than man; if time is a method, a conception which does not correspond to any physical reality, an interpretation; if time and space, relating back to my preceding idea, are one and the same thing, then why should not space itself be merely a method, a conception, or an interpretation? Naturally the question is purely rhetorical, but then I do not want to weary you with unnecessary details and considerations most of them of a strictly physical or mathematical nature. You are not a specialist and would not be able to follow me. It is sufficient for you to know that in the light of this principle, or rather in the light of its physical configuration, all beliefs which up to the present have been generally accepted relative to the density of planetary atmosphere, to the nature of cosmic ether and many other things, have been completely superceded; that is to say, they lose all their significance, and the practical and tangible proof of this, even though it is barely a beginning, resides in my invention. The secret lies in a machine, a vehicle, or whatever you choose to call it, which in theory is capable of crossing any interplanetary space, and, why not — interstellar? In point of fact it can span the distance that divides us from our satellite. »

Here he paused, not in order to judge the effect of his statement, since his eyes roamed elsewhere and seemed to be staring into the distance, but as one will pause who has reached the most important or difficult point of his narrative. He sat without speaking, and I longed for him to continue. By now that feeling which I mentioned before had invaded and mastered me entirely since I already knew where this long preamble would lead. Nervertheless I was unable to keep from stammering:

« I am happy for your sake in this great discovery and, since you wish it, for the sake of humanity. But where do I come into the picture? »

« Do you mean to ask me what I expect of you? » he replied looking at me fixedly this time. « That also is quickly explained. I wish to visit the moon and for numerous reasons I cannot go alone. Would you be prepared to accompany me? »

It was now sufficiently obvious that I was dealing with a lunatic and with one of the most dangerous species: one of those logical madmen. I had no belief in his discoveries whether physical or metaphysical and I believed even less in the existence of his brainchild, as he called it. Except for the fear of what might happen, what had I to lose? Was I not preparing myself or at least studying all the possible means by which to leave this world? Here was a man who seemed to have divined my intention and wanted to help me, even though it might be in a highly unexpected manner. And then again, was not anything better than my life and perhaps even than the death for which I was longing? Certainly nothing could be worse than my present condition whatever the truth might be regarding his invention. I was desperate and he spoke to me of hope or at least of something new. Existence was abhorrent to me, and he offered me some means of reconciliation with it through adventure, even though it was only by offering me a belief in something that would help me overcome the narrow limits in which I struggled as in a dark prison, and not in the material manner he suggested. Was it so certain that he was mad? So far he could scarcely be said to have offered irrefutable evidence of the fact. Had not all men of genius, all courageous inventors, begun by appearing to be as mad if not madder than he? It was very certain that I could not hope for help from the learned, or so-called learned; then why not seek help from the mad?

Moreover he had a strange persuasive force, more in his whole being than in his words. Neither did I exclude the fact that his influence on me could probably be explained by some secret affinity between us, or in simpler terms, by my own latent madness. I might add to this that to go to the moon had been a great ambition of my adolescence, as I believe it is with all young men who are just awaking to the existence of their own intelligence and senses. All in all, perhaps the unknown man had come to the right person. How could it otherwise be explained that I felt no astonishment at this unusual proposal? Instead it gave me a certain security. I did not reply, however, and he still sat staring at me silently.

« Won't you at least tell me, » he asked finally, a little abruptly, « if the idea of going to the moon perplexes you, or if you too doubt my ability and disbelieve everything that I have told you? »

He was obviously insane and so I was obliged to show him some consideration, but at the same time, since he was an intelligent madman, I had to keep my observations to myself and treat him almost as any reasonable man.

« I am in doubt about nothing, » I answered. « But you understand that your proposal is not one of the most common, and the decision which you have ask me to make is one of those... well... one of those that is important in a man's life... so that. »

« Yes, I understand, » he said calmly. « In other words you want ample guarantee before making a decision of such great importance. It is only natural. Well then tell me, would you be willing to go to the moon if it were proved to you that you were able to do it and were assured not only a good voyage and a pleasant sojourn but a quick return trip if you wanted it? The rest is up to me. You see, in order to convince you, I know so much about these two possibilities that I can speak with certainty. »

Put in this way, what could one say?

« I am not adverse to going to the moon and I might even confess to you that I have a great desire to go. But.... to begin with, where is this brainchild or machine? » I asked.

« If it were that only...., » he replied. « She is well protected in a place near here to which I begged them for two years to let me return, but they would never give in; a place which at least no one else can ever reach — only I, only we, if I dare to say that already. What time is it? » he exclaimed, jumping to his feet with unexpected fury. « Not yet midnight. Let's go! We will be at the place before dawn. You are aware of course that it is to our own interests not to call attention to our actions in any way. If anyone found out about our project we would not be able to leave. You will have to prepare some things, get together some supplies and check the different apparatus in order to leave for this grand, this extraordinary expedition.... Well my man, don't you hear your heart beating impetuously, your whole chest expanding at the whiff of another world? »

He seemed taken with a high fever and moved restlessly

around the room. Stopping abruptly he looked at me with almost a threatening air.

« But you haven't answered yet.... In short, are you staying here or not? »

With my usual cowardice I wanted to stall for more time.

« How far would it be... is this place? »

« Four hours by foot, less perhaps if we take the short cut.»

« And in what direction? »

« Towards the mountains. What the hell! Day after day, before my unfortunate experience, living and hiding in that place or going there every night for many years, piece by piece, I have put together, produced my creation... Don't you think I know where it is.... Well then? »

I have already said that I didn't believe in the existence of this thing, but it seemed to me that it would not involve me hopelessly in any difficult situation if I accompanied him there even though excursions into the night did not exactly agree with my nature or my laziness. For me it would pass the time. (But in relation to what?)

« All right, let's go!! »

With a scream of joy he rushed to the door. And so we left for that strange trip.

We crossed many valleys and hillsides with only the light of the stars lighting our path, sometimes brightly and sometimes more dimly. No one said a word. About two hours from the village the mountains became steeper and the dense forest and thick underbrush were almost impassable. He seemed to know the easiest trail between the tangled undergrowth and the cliffs, and so we advanced rather rapidly. At a certain point part way up the hillside we could see the waning moon, only just risen. Ragged and misty, it seemed to be rocking about at the bottom of a remote valley. This sight, anything but comforting, instead stimulated my companion like a radiant vision, and he began to speak:

« Look, our goal! It will not be long before we reach it. The moon is ours. And do you realize we will be the first to set foot upon those remote shores. The only ones, no. Because I desire that all mankind, although it does not deserve it, should receive the benefit from my wonderful invention as from all my discoveries. But after all, as the sole human inhabitants of that silver planet (which, as it happened, was at that moment a most unpleasant, soiled copper color) we could remain there as long as we liked, waiting for the world to pay us its debt of honor, and in the meantime we would be lords of vast dominions. We could send the world a message from our home, and..... Incidently, where would you like to set up your first house, by the Pool of Dreams or by the Sea of Nectar. I'm joking, you understand. Even so, these lunar pools and seas are not at all as everyone believes, dried up basins, but actual and real expanses of water. Excuse me if I abandon myself to emotion and enthusiasm, but these sentiments, after all, in one like myself who... »

And he rambled on in the same vein. However he calmed down before long, and after expressing several odd ideas about lunar toponymy, his discussion took on a calm and almost scientific air. He was like a teacher who has to work with a dull and grossly ignorant student, which indeed I was. Among other things he commented on the physical make-up of the moon and chuckled to himself at the universal opinion of the astronomers who thought that such celestial bodies were devoid of atmosphere. There was not the least doubt in his mind as to the existence of atmosphere, nor did he ever admit that even though it might exist on the moon it would be found in a very rarified form. He added that he had taken every precaution just in case some of his plans and calculations proved to be wrong, and in due time he expected to give me reasons for these precautions point by point. He even hinted at the hope, supported, he said, by concrete data, of finding up there not a desert but a flowering civilization.

In all this discussion the most disturbing point to me was the fact that he considered me by now completely involved in his project and his most devoted companion. But time and circumstances would decide and perhaps help me.

We were standing together at the foot of some of the loftiest mountains in the whole mountain range. They rose high into the air, a tumultuous confusion of peaks, jagged rocks, and ridges which spiraled upward and seemed to wind themselves into a circle or crater, or form gigantic nests of stone in many of which there were old look-out stations. The tallest peak, called the Devil's Horn, rose above all the others in a beautiful, lofty design which seemed like a broken-down tower, or more exactly, like a large decaying tooth. Until a short time ago it was thought impassable because of certain risky passes, impassable at least to the ordinary man. This was about all I knew of the mountain region around the village. I had never ventured up there. Judging from what I could see of those rugged mountain peaks, they were more suitable for eagles than for men.

My companion pointed out the Devil's Horn which was weakly reddened by that moon-bauble, saying:

« In no more than an hour we will be up there. Keep very close and follow me step for step. The trail is difficult and so far it is not dangerous. »

(I was already exhausted, and now it was only a matter of following in his steps).

He started up the rocky path with me close at his heels, and after a short time he began to climb up one of the peaks obliquely in order to make the ascent less tiring, choosing his way carefully. Soon he, or rather we, went down into a steep basin in the rocks where we had to begin using our hands, but we came out again, errors excepted, on top of what the Alpine climbers call an ice ledge. Using our hands and feet, sometimes making a traverse, sometimes climbing straight upwards, we made an almost complete circle of the peak. At the first juncture of a saddle on the ridge of the mountain another peak awaited us; then another and another, always more impenetrable and difficult. I was aided on this lofty path and over these dizzy heights by the scarcity of light which veiled the immense danger and the depth of the precipice around the brink of which we were climbing. Nevertheless it also made the visible details of that already sinister trail much more horrible. Not infrequently I found myself as though suspended above a bottomless abyss with the pale red rays of the moon lighting the walls down to a certain depth but leaving the bottom of the pit deep in dark shadows. Before my eyes, always greedy for horror of any kind, were able to penetrate the deepest shadows, I had passed by that point. I went on in a sort of unconscious daze, panting like a dog, and occasionally asking my companion, who showed no signs of fatigue, to slow down his pace.

By this time almost every step brought new and perplexing views. The large Devil's Horn which seemed within reach, although isolated from us by a deep ravine, now appeared to have lost some of its arrogance and great height. We reached the edge of the large fissure or crevice which stretched into the distance and cut directly across our path. From the depths I heard a distant roar and straining my eyes into the deep shadow, I seemed to see a glitter of rushing water. The mountain was split to its base at that point, perhaps by some formidable telluric action, and the proud Devil's Horn was completely cut off from the rest of the mountain range. So this was to be our crossing point! I estimated the large rift to be no less than fifteen feet wide.

« One last spurt, » said that man of iron candidly. « One last spurt and we will be there. On the other side the climb will be child's play. »

I was suddenly seized with unrestrained terror and with it a feeling of physical weakness. It was too late to ask myself what I was doing on the top of these savage mountains alone at night with a lunatic in search of an imaginary flying machine. In vain I cursed the thoughtlessness and desperation which brought me here. Meanwhile I drew back stubbornly from the abyss, more frightened than anxious, and almost

decided to turn back from where I came rather than attempt
this last step which seemed to me an impossibility. My companion tried to comfort me, pretending that there was a way
of crossing that large gap, but I dug my heels in stubbornly
and would not listen to reason. Finally, seeing all his attempts
of persuasion to be useless, he looked at me with glittering
eyes and said brusquely:

« We do not have much time to lose. In the meantime
dawn is coming and we will be visible here to all the region
below us. Now, do you prefer to follow me without any
danger to yourself or would you like to end up at the bottom
of that ravine? »

« You... you could end up down there yourself, » I retorted, horrified by his statement and my teeth chattering
violently.

« Yes, perhaps, » he said, approaching me from behind
resolutely as though to begin a struggle.

« Hey, calm down! What the hell! Be reasonable, won't
you? By what damned way do you intend to get over there? »

« I've told you again and again but you have never taken
the trouble to listen to me. We will use the same method
that I have used every time I have come up here. »

Having spoken, he stared at me for a moment and even if
I was not in complete agreement, at least I was quelled. He
moved several feet away and began to rummage around in a
pile of small stones behind a large rock from where he pulled
out a coiled rope.

« Look, here's a rope. Now give me a hand. »

From a deep crevice which had been covered with larger
stones we pulled out two long pine poles. They were two
pine trees that had been peeled and the branches chopped
off. Handling them like twigs he pushed one across until it
reached the opposite edge of the breach, and then placing
the top of the pole in a small hollow on our side, he wedged
it in with stone splinters to prevent it from rolling. The other
he thrust onto a ledge on the other side and let it fall against
the wall on which he was standing so that it fell a little

below the actual edge of the cliff, obliquely but solidly wedged between the two walls. Winding the rope around the first pole and knotting the end into a large loop, he turned to me with the rest of the rope coiled in his hand and said:

« I will go first. Watch carefully how I tie myself into it. In a moment you will have to do the same thing by yourself. Above all, » he added threateningly, « don't try to escape, it would be useless. I could reach you in a flash and then..... »

He tied the rope under his arms and then put it between his legs to form a sort of girdle. Stepping down to the lower pole and pushing the loop along the upper one, he moved swiftly and reached the other side with the ease and agility of an ape. He then untied the rope from his body, rolled it up into a coil and threw it back to me over the abyss with an invitation to do likewise immediately.

The most favorable moment to escape had come, and for an instant I thought of turning and running down the mountain. But that demon was capable of crossing back even without the rope. Actually the method he had used was very convincing and, as he had said, it presented no dangers. The worst that could happen to me was that I could be suspended by the rope in mid-air like a spider, but in that case, I could depend on his able assistance. I was gaining great faith in him. I tied the end of the rope to the tree trunk, wrapped myself in it as I had seen him do and stepped down to take my turn on the improvised bridge.

My eyes were tightly closed. The crossing went well until the moment came to climb the opposite ledge. I suddenly lost my footing. My hand slipped, and I would have fallen like the spider, had he not grabbed me by the collar, and holding all my weight with one arm, pulled me up to safety. The logs were taken up behind us, and he turned to me now with a completely changed and happy expression.

« Excuse me if I frightened you, » he began, « but I have heard it said that it is the best method to use with one who is going into battle for the first time. »

We found the path again and started upwards to the now tamed Devil's Horn. As he had said, the way was not particularly difficult. We were about to reach the top which he pretended was the hiding place of his invention. Having arrived at this point did I believe in the existence of this creation (if I must call it this) or at least in the existence of some object on top of this peak? I was unable to answer the question but that in itself was already half an answer. And all this time I was not even able to decide definitely upon the sanity of my companion or rather from what kind of madness he suffered. Would he have brought me all this way merely to indulge his own fancy? On the other hand... At the moment there was no definite reason to doubt him beyond an inherent unwillingness to believe in miraculous things, and as far as he was concerned, I was, except for my curiosity, in the position of an impartial but critical observer. I was only awaiting the final test in order to decide if he were one of those madmen who benefit humanity and whom everyone calls insane, or a simple and therefore dangerous visionary. If he were the former, everything was going satisfactorily and no real harm had been done. If the latter... but there was no longer any time to think of what I would do or what would happen in that case. Even if there had been time, of what use was such a thought. It was quite impossible to foresee or to define what could have been his motives in bringing me so far, or what his future behavior would be.

Because I had been slow we arrived later than expected. A violet light, precursor of the dawn, was already beginning to color the sky and the stars shone with a dimmer light. We circled the final peak of the Horn horizontally until we reached a large ice-covered passageway in the rock walls of its cone-shaped crest. The sky slowly became lighter, and it was day. Milky, cumulous clouds prevented any distant view and actually separated us from the world below. Here there were no happy voices to greet the coming day; only imperturbable and heavy silence among the lime rock peaks. Hesitating for a moment on the threshold of this huge gateway and stretching out his arms towards the east, my companion broke into an exclamation of exhaltation.

« Far away, » he said, « far away below our feet lies the world. Within a short time it will be even further away. Where are they, those blind fools who undoubtedly are searching for me frantically at this very moment? Where are your creditors? » (But how in the devil did he know that I had creditors — and many of them!) « How remote all their anxieties and agitations seem to us! Doesn't your pulse quicken with joy? Brace yourself, my friend, with this pure, fresh air while waiting to breathe another still purer. Nor is this all! Infinite space is open to us. In the meantime and from up there, » he pointed to the smoky disk of a moon that hung forgotten in a corner of the sky, « we will impose our will upon the world below, and it is our will that all shall be prosperous and happy. »

At that moment and with a certain sense of relief, I heard the very distant screech of an eagle.

« Listen, » he exclaimed, « to the happy omen. »

Without further delay I was led into a kind of amphitheater or sunken well, the lofty walls of which were stained with the most brilliant hues, and in places glistened with moisture. Feeling our way carefully we crossed the small, sloping glacier which was fortunately scattered with fragments fallen from above and almost completely covered by a brown mold. It is unnecessary to say that I had been suffering acutely from the cold, however I was still alive, and as for him, he did not seem to notice the temperature.

We reached a tiny, low passageway at the foot of the rocky wall, hardly more than a crevice, so narrow that it barely permitted one to pass without scraping the sides. Here he halted looking at me with an air of triumph. Where then had he hidden this miraculous machine?

« Wait for me here », he said, and slithered through the crack only to leap out again instantly. With a bound he came over to me, and gripping me by the shoulders he gazed into my eyes. His own had a look of deep emotion and seemed to me to be veiled in tears.

« I am about to show you my invention, the fruit of long years of study and labor, the thing, I might even say the being, which is nearer to my heart than anything else in the world; my own child. I am about to reveal to you its hiding place and to place it in your care. Are you worthy of my trust? Will you betray me? The moment has come in which you must decide, since, as I have understood perfectly, you are waiting for this test in order to judge whether I am mad or sane. Tell me; if it exists will you go with me to the moon? Will you solemnly promise to do so when you have satisfied yourself of its existence. Or is there something else holding you back? »

He stared at me with an intensity beyond belief. I stammered incoherently that I was perfectly free to go and that I had the greatest faith in him. I ended by giving him my formal promise with an inner conviction that I was right in doing so, but not without certain mental reservations. He released me from his grip, flung himself into the crevice again and began to throw out a number of stones from inside the hole. Finally he stuck out a tousled head and invited me to follow him.

The opening was just as narrow as I have said. I struggled somehow through the crevice which grew wider and higher as I advanced, affording a relative freedom of movement, although it was still necessary to crawl on one's belly. I followed his feet in the darkness along a kind of subterranean passage like a sewer. We crawled for a short time like two earthworms squirming through sticky mud. I thought of nothing, I saw no ray of light and was half stifled when suddenly I felt the shoe ahead of me, to which I was clinging with all my might, slip from my hand. I seemed to breath more freely now and a moment later, slightly beneath me and to one side, I heard his voice strangely amplified as though echoing from a large, vaulted chamber.

« Don't move. Wait until I give you a light, » he admonished me.

I heard him moving quietly some distance away from me, and suddenly a brilliant light pierced the darkness. Then I realized that I lay at a sharp turn in the tunnel. The light which struck my eyes and which intermittently burst out with more and more violent brilliance, as though powerful bulbs were being turned on one after another, gave forth an indirect glow, reflecting from the curve of the tunnel. However, the source of the light remained hidden from me. In short my situation, physically speaking, was the craziest, most ridiculous and outrageous that one could imagine.

« Don't come any further yet! » I heard his voice say, both imploring and authoritative at the same time.

My God, the fellow certainly knew how to maintain effects! I was however just beginning to move on as the light became dazzling and he himself invited me to come along.

The underground passage, rising slightly, opened out into a huge grotto which in that clear light presented a picture of fabulous magnificence with all its heavy vaulting, its columns, and stalactite. Primitive sconces had been placed around the walls, but in place of torches they held cylinders with long spouts from which impetuous flames arose with a subdued hiss and sigh. They seemed to be as brilliant as the flames of acetylene except that they gave out a slightly blue light. Altogether they illuminated the entire place more than the most brilliant light of the sun. At the far end there was a large workshop and beside it a laboratory well furnished with all the requisite equipment.

I saw in the middle of the grotto when I first entered a large object of a strange form that glittered in the light. I now contemplated it more with horror than with amazement. If I may refer to my first impression without comment; it was lying there depressed and quietly staring at me with a thousand eyes.

My companion approached me thriumphantly, and watching the expression on my face, pointed at the object with both hands in a very melodramatic gesture:

« There she is. Her name is CANCROREGINA. »

From that moment I was devoted to him and to his machine (which I will call by the name that he had given her), or rather one could say that I was in their power. To tell the truth I had already made up my mind; he was not not insane, or if you could call him insane, it was only by applying the vulgar usage to the word. I would not even consider it. In the light of reason one could really fear that he might be an inventor, a misguided genius, or even a deluded misfit in society, but such a suspicion never entered my head. As to the act or acts which had sent him to the asylum and of which naturally I must have been a little afraid of his repeating, I attributed them with touching good will to a temporary unconsciousness and to some grave provocation, perhaps one of those mental irritations of which the person himself is not aware, but which beat intolerably against the brain. I, in conclusion, was confident, blindly faithful and didn't have the least doubts about him.

He had remained up there, and I, after being accompanied by him to that damned pass, had returned to the village to get some of the necessary equipment and, most important, some food for him and for the journey. I had to leave these things in a chosen place in the mountains every night. He worked in his laboratory compressing the supplies into a more compact form, or, if possible, developing synthetic products in order to assure us of food for many years. From time to time we met in the mountains to make further arrangements and to discuss plans.

Such preparations took much longer than expected and our impatience increased steadily. Among the necessary supplies many were so strange and unusual that I had to go into the city to purchase them. In fact many days passed before we could even think of setting a date for our departure, days that were feverishly exciting for me. These delays seemed to increase my enthusiasm rather than diminish it, and I was unmindful of the outside world except for our great project. If it had not been already far beyond the beginning stages, I might have wanted to hurry it along. In his heart he was

113

also impatient, but he said that he didn't like to be surprised and everything must be carefully planned beforehand, thus reducing the risks to an absolute minimum. With the cautious and methodic procedure of all men of science, he worked without rushing, guided by his many precision instruments.

In the meanwhile, the day after that first night on the mountain top, while I was still resting from our long, fatiguing climb, the director of the asylum came to see me. With great circumspection, as he did not want to frighten me, he told me that a certain dangerous lunatic had escaped from the surveillance of his guards the previous night and had been seen in the neighborhood of my house. He feared that the man would hide himself in one of the many unused annexes of my house or in the large park which bordered on a forest. The director, accompanied by two tall and efficient guards who waited at the door, asked for permission to search the premises as much for my own protection as for his own curiosity. They could talk as much as they liked, these men, they would not shake my faith, nor did I ever for one instant think of betraying, as they called him. Had I never known his name? For convenience I will call him Filano.

The director looked around the house several times and then left perplexed and proccupied. In any case the man was being actively hunted, but his hiding place would be a challenge to them for a very long time and would provide many interesting and even dangerous hunts. During the visit of the director (I add this here although I do not know for what purpose) I had the unpleasant feeling that he was speaking to me as if I were one of his inmates. He repeated his sentences over and over again in order to clarify the meaning to me or to impress the words upon my mind, and he scrutinized me intently with the eye of a competent judge. For one in his position these were probably necessary habits but they made me quite angry and in the end I became almost rude to him.

I returned a couple of times to the Devil's Horn and

began to gain more confidence in Cancroregina. She was a machine of bizarre humor or at least she seemed so to me judging from the sounds that she emitted, from her puffs and snorts and various other reactions while Filano worked around her; to me, I say, who knew so little of her multi-formed and complicated mechanisms. But on the whole she appeared to be a useful and propitious force even though her sparkle was completely metallic. I even became accustomed to her looking like a sleeping demon somewhat between the obtuse and the metaphysical, most of the time harsh and opaque, comparable to the look of a large grasshopper. However she was the liberator who on wings (metaphorically speaking) would take me away (not metaphorically) from this ungrateful world and..... and that was enough. Concerning the future of our project and its possible benefit to the world, I differed from my companion in that I did not give it much thought and only aspired to leave this world behind as soon as possible.

Cancroregina was fitted inside comfortably and even elegantly for two passengers with all the necessities that everyday life demanded, because, as I had already understood, she would not fly at a great speed, but would cover the great distance which separated us from our goal flying relatively slowly. Her storage spaces would hold enough food for at least two or three years and her tanks would hold oxygen, reduced by some magic process unknown to me into small white grains, for the same amount of time. According to Filano we would not use even a small part of these supplies, but it was better to have too much than to risk running short. How the many serious problems of aereonautics and all the other things attached to an interplanetary journey were solved, I not know. Filano himself gave me long explanations and demonstrations so that I would become familiar with all the parts and functions of the parts of his invention. He had hoped that in this way I would be not only his companion on the journey but also a help to him. All was in vain. The infernal impatience which devoured me, my

115

many distraction, my absent-mindedness, the blind faith
which I had in Filano and in the success of the undertaking
and finally (or rather in the first place) my constitutional
incapacity to understand anything of this game of life, prevented me from understanding anything. Unfortunately the
small amount that I had understood at one time, was now
forgotten. Oh, did I not know that with this mental confusion I risk... my life? But what good is life? If I had only
known I might have given all my attention and time to those
things of which I was capable!... Actually I know nothing-
and I can say nothing precisely or completely about Cancroregina. My memory of the fundamental principles of the
machine is very vague, but I shall try to put down the little
that I do remember even at the risk of saying something
foolish. It seems that in those regions of space where the
atmosphere or means by which she runs are found in a form
too rarified to propel her, the machine emits from the front
a gas of the type that we put in her tanks while on earth
and to which, as it were, moment after moment she catches
hold and moves along. I do not know from where she draws
her motor power or means of propulsion or even of what
damned type they are. I do know that she must be fed
through a large and greedy mouth with some of those gran-
ular bits; however these are brown in color. How to steer
her or how to stop her are both a mystery to me, and as for
such things as external apparatus or propellers, there are
none. How to get out of this grotto is a question which I
have wondered about from the beginning.

« Look, » said Filano, « as you see, from that side and
straight down to the far end, the walls of the grotto are concave like a sail filled with wind. By careful estimation I have
determined them to have a minimum thickness of twenty-one
feet, and with some good dynamite twenty-one feet is nothing
at all. You have already understood the rest! When the
time comes we will simply hop over the rocks which remain
from the blast, and it is as simple as that. A small hole is
plenty, a hole exactly wide enough to permit her to pass,

as I, » he exclaimed proudly, « can steer Cancroregina with millemetric precision. More correctly, she will fly out of the grotto with the greatest ease with me at the controls. »

Then to prove his statements he invited me for a short experimental run. Cancroregina rumbled a little, coughed and yawned lazily as if she did not like the idea of going on a little spin merely for exhibition purposes. Then, even more incredible, she rose from the ground. I heard a hissing noise and we started around the inside of the grotto. She rose a few inches at a time, circled beautifully around a column, slipped through a narrow passage between two other columns, made various maneuvers and finally floated lightly to earth. My enthusiasm was without bounds.

The great day came. The sun had just risen on top of the peak, for us but not for the rest of the world below who still slept, warm in their nocturnal vapors. The air at this altitude was icy and limpid. It was, after all, a morning in October, a morning of great hope as we set about blowing up the mines, already expertly placed in the holes in the rock wall.

The fuses were lit and we left the grotto hurriedly, crossed the glacier and took shelter under a ledge behind the crest of the hill. After a couple of minutes the mines exploded almost simultaneously with a loud, repercussive roar followed by a whistling noise and the sound of falling rocks and splinters against the stone. Returning to the grotto we could see immediately that the operation had been a success; a large gash had been blown in the wall only about half of which would be enough for dear Cancroregina to pass.

« Let's not lose time», said Filano. « The explosion will have been heard in the whole valley. »

Although the mines had been placed so that they would blow outward and Cancroregina had been pushed behind a massive pillar with metal screens put around her to furnish protection from the formidable displacement of air inside the grotto, we had been worried about her. Her delicate mechanisms could easily have suffered from the explosion or from the falling fragments of rock, but there she was intact, receiving us with a happy smile. Wasn't there the least little bit of mockery in that smile? Filano gave a last look to see that everything had been done, we took our places inside the cabin, he pushed some levers (I have no idea which ones) and Cancroregina groaned painfully. It seemed to cost her a certain effort to tear herself away from her slumber, and also, as I believe I have said before, it was the same effort for her to stop again after having once started. She seemed endowed, if such an expression has any meaning, with a great force of inertia.

She groaned again, trembled and pulled herself off the ground with a weak, creaking noise. Making a short turn around the grotto as though executing a caracole, breathing heavily all the time, she flew out through the hole, still vibrating slightly. Finally she lifted herself into the open sky and continued to rise higher and higher.

It seems that Cancroregina could not rise except at a very slight angle or by going around in ever increasing circles. Because of this, she would have to fly towards the moon taking a spiral course of short but variable steps, therefore the distance to be covered would be about ten times that of the direct route between the earth and its satellite. Taking into account that Cancroregina flew at a speed of about six hundred miles an hour, one could easily see that our trip would take some months. That is of course, if we could even penetrate the sphere of lunar gravity where the conditions of flight might be considerably different than those of the stratosphere. These were my own reflections. Filano had no doubts and seemed to know in detail how everything would turn out.

The first circle which took about twelve hours brought us over the Sunda Islands and, since our point of departure had been very high, we were flying at an altitude of about forty thousand feet. The next day we were over Hawaii at about the same height as the day before. This information could have been verified by looking at the different dials on the instrument panel. The following day we flew over the Malayan Archipelago again, and so on like this, going rather slowly but climbing steadily. While we were in the lower strata of the atmosphere our flight was observed by many people on the earth. The strange shape of Cancroregina must have caused a great deal of curiosity and even fear as the radio on board kept picking up messages from many places asking for information and explanations of our flight. We did not answer any of them.

The days passed and each day revealed to us a vaster horizon. However we were never able to see the earth's curve, in fact, it even appeared a little concave, nor did the size of the moon increase noticeably. The water masses below turned brown looking at them from this distance and the land seemed clear in contrast. Later the water appeared actually dark and dull while the land was extraordinarily light in color. We had the first perception of the spherical nature of the earth at about three hundred thousand feet. Naturally the oxygen apparatus had been functioning since the day of our departure. The thermometer outside the plane already registered very low temperatures.

Life on board went on peacefully without any incidents worthy of note, ruled in its essential phases by the iron hand of Filano, who above all wanted to preserve our strength for later work, although by this time he had resigned himself to my ineptitude and he alone supplied the necessary labor. In any case Cancroregina was more in need of a watchful eye than of any material attention and did not even require steering. Once the many instruments had been set she went ahead, rising and turning, completely on her own. We spent most of our time in intellectual discussions of science and philosophy, in plans and conjectures of what to expect on the moon and in those persistent but useless attempts by Filano to make me understand the principles of higher physics.

Among the daily tasks was the production of water, a duty which because of its extreme simplicity even I was able to undertake. Water in large quantities would have been an excessive weight and therefore we brought none with us for the simple reason that Filano could make it as we needed it. He put into a large retort, which was in some way connected with the internal organs of Cancroregina where undoubtedly the principal action took place, those whitish grains of oxygen and also some of the other grains, evidently of hydrogen. In a moment there was a great bubbling and boiling and the water dripped out, clear as from a fountain. By further manipulation my companion resolved our excreta, already reduced to a minimum by the synthetic diet, into useful substances and gases. The slightest amount of air entering from the outside would probably have been fatal, therefore nothing must remain to be thrown out. Our cell did have two apertures which gave us some connection with the outside. Both of these were constructed according to the principle of the valve and were hermetically sealed. The first was the escape valve for the carbon anhydride produced by our respiration, which, as Filano explained, accumulated in a certain duct against a heavy flap until it collected enough pressure to force the flap open allowing the gas to escape. An automatic closing mechanism closed and sealed the flap until it was necessary for the operation to be repeated. The second opening was the door by which we had entered. It also opened outwards and was held in position by strong inside bolts. It would have been quite impossible for anyone to enter our aerial home from the outside while in case of extreme necessity we would have been able to force open the door and escape.

At an altitude of about six million feet we reached the stratosphere or at any rate we ceased to feel the earth's attraction. We had known for some time that Cancroregina was only very slightly influenced by the magnetism of our planet and taking into consideration our own movement, we had noted certain variations in the relative position of the earth. Finally realized that we had reached a state of complete independence from the earth. In the meanwhile the sky was

becoming gradually darker and the sun shone with a glow of
red hot metal. The moon and the earth had assumed a bright
but chalky luminosity. We were reaching complete darkness
in the midst of which these three celestial bodies and the
stars shone steadily without affecting the darkness in the
slightest. Such is the sky as I see it still except that from
here the moon appears very much larger and the earth,
slightly flattened, occupies only an eighth part of the celestial
sphere. (The earth if I am not mistaken is a hundred times
the size of the moon). For anyone looking at Cancroregina
from the outside, she must appear like a tiny celestial body
radiating a diffused light and because of the atmosphere
which she emits, surrounded by a small halo. (This supposi-
tion was in fact confirmed later). After we had led a most
capricious existence for what seemed to me quite a long
time, the night faded from the interior of Cancroregina and
henceforth only an unexpected eclipse could have simulated
that darkness.

The days went by and from now on they were not
without variety. I have already said that life on board was
very quiet, but such a statement really applied only to the
first days, for as far as I was concerned, soon after our
departure I had begun to notice something abnormal in Filano's behavior. At first I did not attach much importance
to these symptoms which I judged to the result of exhaustion due to his extensive labor, to the great mental strain
under which he had recently suffered, to the excitement
caused by the successful beginning of our undertaking and
to numerous other more or less plausible causes. I confident-
ly awaited his return to normal. But these symptoms seemed
to be intensified by the passing of the days and weeks
compelling me to regard them more seriously. Finally they
became so gravely disturbing that I was thoroughly alarmed,

and I began to be aware of actions to which I had previously closed my eyes.

It is hard to say what it was that alarmed me. Sometimes it was merely an attitude, a word, or a glance. Other times it was something more serious. One thing was certain: the general picture with regard to his mental condition was not reassuring. He was obviously changed in comparison with the man whom I had first known, and even then he hardly could have been considered a model of normal behavior.

But how was it possible that I had arrived at such a conclusion; who had accepted him in blind faith and frankly with great admiration, I who had declared that so far from being insane he was the only sane man in this world, preferring to attribute the first qualification to all the rest of humanity, who had met the arguments of science, in the person of the director of the asylum, with an inward smile of disdain. Well, it would be difficult to explain how my admiration had been transformed from hour to hour into terror as my illusions fell from me.

Had he always been as he was now, or had he really changed? In the present circumstances this question was becoming hourly more important. It appeared to me that he was day by day revealing his true nature which he had momentarily crushed and suppressed by superhuman effort for such time as he required to reassure me and drag me into this adventure; an adventure which in itself, as my companion's peculiarities increased, began to strike me as foolhardy, desperate and even fantastic. At first I had thought it safe and assured of great reward. Now that it was too late, when there was no longer any remedy, I began to realize my lack of judgment and my imprudence.

It was not that my person was threatened as yet or that he flew openly into rages, but it seemed as though his irritability was cumulative and that an explosion might occur at any moment. How can I describe it? It began with sidelong and unexpected glances, with abrupt and inappropriate laughter, with sudden pauses or deviations in the very middle of a sentence, with excessive irascibility, emotional reactions and any number of trifling peculiarities; and these had gradually assumed serious pathological proportions such as misdirected gestures, temporary aphasia, stuttering, arbitrary deductions, verbal associations, automatisms, and so forth. Generally speaking his utterances now gave me the impression of those little shoe-polish tins in which the street urchins make a hole in order to spin them on a string. His arguments, if we adopt a modern equivalent, seemed to spin crazily. Having seized upon some fact, usually of little importance, he would cling to it indefatigably and remorselessly for hours, twisting and turning it without succeeding in connecting it with the other facts or topics of discussion or making any sense of it. He did not appear to be fully aware of his condition. He would talk about himself endlessly, often late into the night (or rather during the hours dedicated to repose since there was no night inside Cancroregina). If weariness had succeeded in overcoming my terror I would be awakened by outbursts of laughter which would give me goose-flesh. The laughter which he had recently developed appeared to be a violent, nervous automatism, and it was ghastly. Quite suddenly in the midst of an argument in which, it is unnecessary to say, there was no reason for laughter, he would throw back his head, press his two fists to his temples, while a hideous grimace distorted his face, revealing all his teeth, and would tremble all over, or to be more exact, would vibrate in paroxysms of uncontrollable convulsions without so much as a sound issuing from his lips. Sometimes such attacks would last for many minutes, after which he would resume his occupation or continue his ravings just as though nothing had happened to interrupt them.

But why insist? I was compelled to admit to myself that he was raving mad. Had I still any doubts, I now observed that the pupil of his right eye, and of this eye alone, had become immensely dilated. He began to complain of visual, auditory, and tactile hallucinations. Despite his condition he continued to attend to Cancroregina with a fierce and jealous zeal, a zeal that made him keep me at a distance from all the instruments and machinery. What had formerly been a tender devotion to his creation had now assumed diseased aspects or proportions. It was perfectly clear that his mind would give way at any disturbance in his daily routine or at any new situation which might face him. Indeed we were entirely in God's hands. In spite of the disorder of his faculties, he had for a long time shown me a certain benevolence although he would frequently swear at me, but I now felt that any such kindliness had been consumed by his inward fires or had been transformed into its opposite, a more or less open aversion. For instance, his sidelong glances were almost incessant. I felt that he was observing me even when my back was turned, that he was spying on me when I slept or when he thought me asleep. It is useless to attempt to describe the kind of life I was now leading, helplessly confined with this lunatic in our narrow prison, literally outside the world.

I scarcely slept. I lived under a nameless terror and oppression, day by day, hour by hour, awaiting an inevitable explosion. My nerves and my strength were beginning to fail me, and I was becoming fearful for my own mental stability. I was quite unable to imagine what might happen after the explosion should I survive it.

Such was our situation until the fatal day. Events that have a deep and lasting significance in a man's life, even events that have permanent good or bad consequences for all humanity on into the future and which have their premises in a past of indeterminable duration, all such events have a time unit, a short, earthly time perhaps, but even if they are predicted they are unexpected when they occur. It seems to us that such great happenings as these could not take place in any given period of time, on the other hand we do not realize that they may be concentrated into an instant. Therefore when any irreparable action is accomplished, particularly if it is a regrettable one, it does not seem possible to us an instant later with such a potentially important action, we are unable to go back to the conditions which existed before that act in order to begin again, to reflect further on it, and if you wish, to do the same thing over again! But it is true. All that has happened is like a dream and cannot be a part of reality, yet all is so real that it is already a part of the past. (My nonexistent reader will think this a pompous introduction to such an unimportant event. But since you do not exist, think as you choose and accustom yourself, if you can, to my tirades). What happened to me was quite as unexpected, although I had been waiting for it for many days.

Filano's condition became worse, especially after we had reached eighty thousand miles in altitude or, as it were, in elongation. It happened at about the half-way point between the earth and the moon. We had then been travelling for slightly more than two months.

One morning Filano was particularly nervous as he got up from his berth where he did almost everything except sleep. He let loose a stream of abuse and abandoned himself to actions that had not the slightest trace of coherence. He actively showed an open hatred of me and paced back and forth frantically like a wild beast in a cage.

Quite suddenly he pushed me in front of him, began to shake all over and seemed about to leap upon my back. His inhibitory sense appeared to be completely destroyed. The daily tasks which he was in the habit of performing had lost even an appearance of coordination. With what seemed to be a complete loss of memory he prowled around Cancroregina aimlessly fiddling with her instruments and internal mechanisms. He laughed, cried, shouted, shrieked, raged and shook in uncontrollable agitation. He appeared to want to kill me with a look. Once he stopped abruptly in front of me and with deep emotion praised his creation because as he said, it would soon be no more and he would be alone in the world.

My own safety was obviously in immediate danger. Even if I turned my head and plugged my ears I could not bear to wait for the final outburst. With his physical strength which was multiplied a hundred times by his present condition, I would have no hope of restraining him by force. If he ever attacked me, I would be lost. My only course would be to try in some way to kill him first; yes, to kill him!

Towards noon his fury reached its height, but it had not as yet risen to the point that I almost wished for in order to resolve my unbearable tension. He began to rave more and more violently around the cabin, and all of a sudden (I could not even imagine how to check him) he flung himself against the door, unscrewing the large bolts and flinging them in all directions. He shrieked convulsively that he needed air. The door remained tightly sealed by the mere force of its springs. But possibly a last glimmer of sanity warned him of the terrible danger to which he was exposed or else his mind had jumped to another subject. He stopped, fell back against the instrument panel, turned a switch and raised a lever. Cancroregina for the moment did not seem to notice the difference and proceeded on her usual stable course.

It was then, while his back was turned to me and he stood facing the instrument panel, (a position in which he remained frozen for some time) that I heard the voice which still pounds, against my eardrums: that voice, calm, icy, and horrible, which had nothing in common with his usual speech. The voice said:

« I have been thinking for a long time. We cannot go on like this. The trouble lies in your presence, in your weight. You must die ».

He said no more. Almost simultaneously he wheeled round, gnashing his teeth noiselessly, his whole body trembling with hatred and epilepsy. His face was a livid blue. He threw himself upon me and lunged for my throat.

I do not know how I avoided his grip but I drove him back against the wall. Recovering his strength he sprang at me again. In an instant I had made my decision. The door, as I have already said, remained closed only by the force of its springs, which must have been considerable. I remembered having thought so at the time of our departure, but I hoped that if I pushed him against it, his weight would open the door sufficiently to allow his body to slip through. I would risk my own life as only a breath of the external air (or whatever it might be) would easily be enough to kill me. I had no choice, and to risk one's life is always better than certain death. Sooner or later I would succumb to one of his assaults. He was on the point of a further attack. Summoning all my strength and with the energy of despair, I placed my shoulder against the wall, put my right foot in the middle of his chest and with the aid of elbows, head and neck, I thrust with all my might.

The door yielded, but not sufficiently. It wavered for a fraction of a second on the point of closing with all the weight of Filano's body against it. Then the crack widened and he fell headlong into the void, (an expression which I suppose has its literal meaning here).

The door closed again with a sudden crash and a blast of freezing wind, paralysing my internal membranes and viscera, swept through the cabin. I was suffocating, burning; it seemed as though my vitals were lascerated and shrivelled. I lost consciousness.

When I regained my senses, my heart was hammering furiously and I had a thick ꞇ   ꞇ front of my eyes, but I recovered rapidly. My skin had become like parchment and remained in that condition for weeks. And the first thing that I saw was... FILANO.

I do not know why or by what means, (it will be familiar to the physicists) Filano's body had not fallen at all. Perhaps it was because up here the earth's gravity had lost a great deal of its force, at least on such a small body as this, or that it could not compete with the force of attraction of the nearer Cancroregina, or more probably because he had remained caught in the atmosphere which she emitted and was now a part of it. He followed his creation in space faithfully, oh so faithfully! Filano was easily visible through the rear window in a dim ray of reflected light against a dark sky. His body, without doubt dried and emptied of its internal organs as if preserved in spirit or rather in liquid air, was probably fragile like Bologna glass, but he was externally intact. His eyes were open and he bore on that horrible face the fierce grimace which had been his last living expression. He followed (or follows) Cancroregina into space, follows me, his murderer, into infinite space and eternity.

As he had fallen with his head thrown back, the attitude of his whole body made (or makes) one think of those hanging wooden images on the merry-go-rounds in Piedmont, like Zany, the soldier, the beautiful dame and the drunkard, who have no limbs and like sirens their bodies are elongated for the convenience of the children riding them. With the turn of the merry-go-round they spring into the air, one by one, with a fascinating zig-zag motion.

The second thing that attracted my attention was a buzzing noise coming from the main instrument panel. The small lever that Filano had touched hardly a minute before had been lowered and Cancroregina began to shake, vibrate, roll and pitch dangerously while she made threatening rumbles similar to those made by the gas in a kitchen stove. I gathered all my strength together in order to rise and attempt to push back the lever to its former position. I did not succeed completely, but in trying to do so I had the feeling that Cancroregina was turning and performing what I would call a « wing slip », that is, if she had had wings. For many days I was not aware, nor could I have been aware, of what had happened at that moment. I finally succeeded in pushing the lever back into place, and our flight went on as before. Then I noticed what had happened: for some reason, I know not what and will never know, Cancroregina had swerved from her course and was circling the earth like a very small satellite.

At the same time her speed had almost doubled and hence was the same as that of our own planet. For this reason I always saw below me the same continent, my beloved...

II

30 March.

Well, I have told the story. Why, I repeat once more, and to whom? If one day we should fall to the ground, she and I, who would be able to find a trace of us and of this manuscript? Before falling to earth will we not vanish into infinitesimal particles, or even after decomposition will we not still go on? Have I perhaps finally cheated the agony, the terror, remorse, weariness, cold, the exterior and interior emptiness and even the very desperation of my soul? Not at all. I have spent almost a week in this eternity which is now my life — a week is not very long for an eternity. In brief, I have taken a liking to it and I want to go on. Who knows? Perhaps to go on eternally one might even pass the limits of eternity itself.

« I write you from the honeycomb — of an orb hurled through space.... » Yes, it is something like that. But I do not know what the poet means by the « honeycomb, » and certainly I would change it into something else instead of a honeycomb. By now I have spent months (a millenium) since the death — the murder of Filano. I am alone in here, alone and without hope, feeling the same as I did before starting out on this foolish flight, perhaps even worse than before after seeing what I have written and what I feel. I am alone with myself and in myself, in the belly of this machine which by now has become my hated and mocking enemy whose course I cannot hope to change.

How many plans have I made up to now to change her stubborn mind, to guide her back to earth gradually, or even to compel her to land on the moon because then this endless journey, this circling without escape would cease! It is all in vain. I have already said that I know nothing about her mechanisms. I have sat alone and studied her in order to grasp something, but it is useless. Methodically, systematically, with aching patience, over and over again, daily and for hours on end, I have tried moving and fondling every key, lever and button, testing every conceivable combination, and coordinating their movements in every different way possible. But still nothing happens. She has not moved one iota from her tiresome course. The only reactions that I could get out of her were fierce and menacing rumblings, rattles, howls, tremors and vibrations so that I finally had to stop. To have continued would have ripped her away from her set course, and undoubtedly this would have thrown her, or rather both of us, into an empty chasm. I only know how to continue giving her fuel for this senseless and unending flight. I remembered that Filano had done nothing more than move one lever and turn one key, so why shouldn't she continue on her course as before, once I had put them back where they were? But that was long ago. By now I have given up all those attempts. I have resigned myself to my fate, if such a term has any meaning here. As for the radio I won't even speak of it. In trying to understand its different dials and plugs, I broke it. Besides, what could I have hoped for — communication with a similar machine?

And to think that all I need to guide me to safety is right here inside and within easy reach. It might just as well be some place else. I don't know how to use it; I never did and I never will.

There would have been enough food for two or three years if there had been two of us. However I am alone and do not eat or even swallow those pills. There will be enough of them to last an eternity — for all my life.

Alone and without hope. But how can one live like this without anything, without even a future or a distant hope. Actually I am waiting for something, I am waiting for the courage to die.

But was I not the one whose greatest desire was to leave

the world, the one to whom anything was preferable to life on the earth? Yet, strange to say, having left it I no longer hate it at all, I even... But why have I written, « strange to sap? » What can be strange in recognizing one's good fortune after having lost it or in believing the worst of all evils to be the lesser after having sunk from an abject condition to one still more abject? This would seem natural. And indeed it is, but not in my case. Actually it is not that I regret the world or desire it as the lesser evil. On the contrary I do not regret it at all and I have lost all desire for it. Rather, I love life itself which heretofore has never been very tolerable to me. I love it, or perhaps I began to love it (to do so is either a natural law or a matter of personal inclination) when my own life became hopeless. The more hopeless it became the more I loved life. Now I love it above all things. If then I say that I want to die, I mean that I want the will to die. What is contradictory in this? For example, isn't it possible to love a woman madly and at the same time know that any relationship with her is impossible even though this be only a personal impulse of which she is unaware? And what do you do then? Do you hate her perhaps? Not at all, you desire not to love her, which is the most passionate kind of love. The relationship still remains impossible, literally impossible, perhaps because we prefer it that way or because we love her only for this situation. But after all, does one not love that which is refused or refuse that which one loves?

Why, I ask you once more, did I not speak earlier about courage? I want to confess everything. (It would be absurd to try to pose since my reader is entirely imaginary). I am afraid. It is a physical fear of death and of what comes after death. In fact, having passed from one bad situation to another still worse, isn't it highly probable that I shall eventually sink to one still lower? In this present situation it is to be noted that the direction is obvious; that is to say, I am not moving toward any ultimate good or even toward a slight mitigation of my suffering. I say this having considered my whole life from its very beginning. I am moving toward an ever increasing evil. To be more precise I have come from an already impossible life into this intermediate state between life and death, to one even more impossible. What does life hold for me now? But what does it matter! Even if I could love this third state, the most impossible, with a passionate love... it would not be a solution.

6 April

Die! How does one die? I woke up this morning from my brief sleep with these words on my lips, however the meaning escapes me. One is born and one dies from the same womb.

What can this mean? Perhaps it alludes to the blind suffering of dying or to a hidden identity between these two supreme events. I imagine it means that to die one must find the way or the aperture, so to speak, as one must do basically in order to accomplish anything. (Is death an action or an experience? It all depends on the individual case).

A good explanation at any rate!... Oh, how terribly confused I am! I understand less than nothing of myself, of the... I cannot say of the world... well, of myself and of everything else.

Yesterday I awoke with another sentence running through my brain: If we arise from sleep so refreshed, with what new strength may we not arise after death?

And what in the world does that mean? What relationship does it hold to my previous thoughts? How can I tell! In any case I have dwelt consistently upon these sentences and upon everything relating to them if only in order to master my mental confusion by means of calm concentration. (But this is not true. There is another reason. Yes, because these words might be words of hope).

If we arise from sleep... The concept and the similitude themselves do not lead far, but going beyond these one may be led to data of a scientific nature. When, in other words, it is established that sleep represents death, or vice versa as in all the religious doctrines, that death is only a sleep, such a concept has only a poetical value representative of, or applicable to the most exclusive sphere, the most conceivable and yet least definable activity of man. If it is transferred to the field of philosophy, understood according to the comprehensive idea that the philosopher and the poet were formed by this science; if, in short, death is considered not as a symbol in the figurative sense, but in the real sense as the nightly rest after the terrestrial day that brings on tiredness and necessitates the refreshment of our physical and spiritual energies, these are more or less the results that might be obtained:

If we calculate that the average duration of the human life is seventy years or twenty-five thousand days in round figures, we could give this an arbitrary name or value, for instance a value of one million seven hundred and fifty thousand years; could not this millennial life then be considered as but a day in an even vaster life? For example this vaster life might be valued at forty-three billion seven hundred and fifty million years, and so on, if not to the infinite at least to the indefinite. Reciprocally following a reverse procedure (for symmetry seems to be the first necessity and almost a point of honor in our hypothesis and actually in the arbitrary dimension of everything) one could compute an indefinite number of deaths within our twenty-four hour day each preceded in their turn by other lives reduced in time but nonetheless complete, or by cycles of lives, one within the other. By deaths I mean those longer or shorter cessations of consciousness in wich our spirit and our body regain their strength in order to live. It is wonderful to imagine that each of these small steps, I mean these days, decades or eras, all these personal time units of man, could complete a step forward on the road to higher perfection in another sphere, and that they might converge thus on a higher level, forming one perfect life, estimable and valuable only when it is ended...

And... Oh well, why continue? To hell with it all! At least this speculation is a good pastime, but in the end it makes my head spin. Perhaps this kind of speculation is consoling for others, for those down there, but certainly not for me. Fundamentally it leads to the conclusion that human life is only a small cog in a large wheel, that life is practically eternal, and when one dies one does everything else but die, and so on. But by God, it is no conclusion. That death in itself, I mean to say the actual decease, is not painful, is all that I am able to discover, and that is slight comfort. Why did I throw myself into these meditations with a definite end in view? Perhaps in order to make my fear of « after death » seem less than the fear of dying itself. And yet it would be good if all this eternal life could converge into a higher perfection and this perfection be the ultimate end. But perfection in what? That is the point. As far as I am concerned, I am unable to think that I would fail to reach perfection at the end of time, but it would be a perfection in grief, anxiety and boredom.

Down there on the continent of my birth it is night, night which I have not known for months, and with it the sunset in its delicate and rich variations, its thousands of colors melting one into the other. Here I see only white and black, the two colors of horror. Down there a warm breeze rustles the grass, making the flowers in the fields and the tips of the trees sway lightly. It ripples the surface of the water. The animals are on their way to warm dens or nests. There are... There is also one, a man like many (like myself) going home after a day's work, and at home his mate and his sons await him. Even the well known soup is steaming on the table... There is, and there are... How many! How many!... Oh yes, but didn't I swear repeatedly that I had no tears for the world, that I wept for nothing, and now while I weep for it, don't I weep for exactly those things of which I thought the least? Men can be friends among themselves. They group themselves in families and societies. Men fraternize, they marry and beget children. How it once annoyed me; and the more it annoyed me, the more I refused to accept it and become a part of it.

7 April

I reread the last words that I wrote yesterday. But no, my present life and that one are the same in reality, or at least my life has been always this way. I was detached from the world, but not completely. I had lifted myself with great difficulty but I remained halfway between the point of departure and my goal, and there I began to go around in circles, to whirl without rhyme or reason, still attracted to the world which I left, always up in my sky, near but inaccessible to that other world... And our deeds which follow us...

No. It is not like that! I was excluded from the world, from all its simple and natural pleasures. A short distance from me, my brothers (in Christ only) fought and died, but to me all was dimly denied. I didn't have that which all other men had, and therefore I had to assume this attitude. I had to detach myself from the rest of the world and to spurn it, either because it gave me nothing or because of my pride, like the fox and the grapes. I always wanted to die or I wanted the will to die. I wanted to die out of desperation, not by vocation or choice. Thus it is not that I was a misfit in society and other men were my brothers in name only, but...

Of course if I were still alive, and as a result had readers, critics and literary worries, I would never have written like this. I know from my own experience that it is a good idea to suggest certain ideas in the mind of the reader surreptitiously. One cannot put them down just as they are under the reader's nose as it is contrary to all the rules of literature. The critics, whose high function it is to form and mould authors, a function which they perform admirably and faithfully, do not understand how to express anything, and if by chance they do understand something, they scream immediately that such a passage is too clear, such a parallel too immediate and such an image too commonplace. It is easy to see from this that they do not want to understand even the little which somehow sinks into their brain and that they will judge any such similar attempts to attack their ill-will as offensive and indecent. Their true passion and the ultimate need of their soul is not to understand anything at all.

9 April

It is always the same sight, the same route. It is always the same gyration, even though large, the same few celestial patterns; and it goes on, I repeat, without end or without aim. There are wonders in the sky; such as that bottomless darkness itself where those glittering rays of light mingle together but are as separate from each other as the many islands of the Pacific, minute lands in comparison with such a great void. There are marvels on the earth, but one can do nothing more than speak of them. On earth life goes merrily on its way, and hardly one span away everything is death and shadows.

The large sun is set in the darkness, the yellow stars do not twinkle; the phases of the moon, those of the earth; the new moon, the new earth; the full moon, the full earth. And then? Oh my God! Here nothing ever happens. You, you down there! And you say that you know anxiety, lonliness and BOREDOM.

Not much happened after the death of Filano. Once I saw something which seemed like flaming vapors pass across the large face of the moon. It looked like a faint greenish sail. I thought it was a diaphanous cloud; yes, just that, a cloud, in defiance to what the great thinkers may believe about the moon. Was it illusion or reality? Was Filano really right? Another time, three times in fact, I saw a luminous speck rise up from the depths of the darkness. It approached, receded and then disappeared. A small celestial body, I cannot define it otherwise, came so near that I could see something of its physical make-up. It was a desolate rock of irregular form, dry and sepulchral, with many iron-grey veins. It also had been thrown out to wander aimlessly through the void. If only one of these rocks would hit me, but there was little chance of that. It would have been like accidently dropping a grain of wheat from an open balcony and trying to hit a spider web stretched firmly across a door below. But I forgot. I saw tiny flames light up near the earth like matches being struck. And that is all.

This eternal silence! Well once more, this life is basically the same as my other life. I am almost happy that I didn't go to Singapore in my youth. What could I have found there that would have been different?

Filano, dear Filano, looking at me. You whom I have killed, find a way of taking me with you. I also feel the need for air. We can go on side by side for eternity following this wonderful machine, our executioner.

But how did it happen that Cancroregina changed her direction and left her course? I keep thinking that it couldn't be just an ordinary incident or an accidental happening. No, it was premeditated as it was in everything she did. I realize with horror that she has gone mad with her putative father, but hers was another form of madness, obstinate and monotonous.

Moreover — but how terribly confused I am!

11 April

I said in my precious moments of sincerity that I love life itself more than any one of its greatest gifts, more than all of them together, more than honor, glory, power, creative genius, kindness, gold, freedom, light, wine and happiness! (But I did not remember love and women in this list. How did that happen? There is a reason). I am deprived of all this as I have been deprived of so many things which make life divinely beautiful. My eyes are without sight, my limbs are mutilated, I am barely allowed the privilege of breathing, I am compelled to listen constantly for the steps of a mortal enemy upon the threshold of my existence; but I am granted life and I accept it without protest with all that comes with it. Plague, leprosy, cholera and shame do not terrify me as long as I may live. Even if I were to be compelled to beg for life in the most humble manner before the vilest and most abject enemy, I would kneel at his feet in the mud with a smile. I would bow my head before him were he the last man on earth.

Is this true? Yes and no. In my case I was speaking of real life, not this semi-existence. It most certainly is not life. But let us see what is lacking. I would like to point out that even if a man were to spend his whole life in solitary confinement like the man in the iron mask, I do not think that he could be as unhappy as I. No, he would not be as unhappy because at any rate he would be living upon the earth among his fellow-men even if segregated from them. In such a situation he still might find peace of mind; yes, even in such a desperate situation. Here we come to the point: peace of mind. By what cursed and diabolical reason am I unable to find it? Perhaps it is just for that reason. For example, I could resign myself to my condition whatever it might be, I could work and await a natural death serenely. I have always dreamed of work of a literary nature. It would be work of calm and coherent proportions, performed in absolute tranquillity. I have memories in abundance and in my confinement here I would be at liberty to employ Flaubertian time in the polishing of my works. What would it matter, then, if these works be consigned to destruction or if they find no readers? A great man has already made it clear that a work of art does not need to have a history and I myself was in the habit of saying, more or less contentedly, that literature begins where literature ends. I repeat, where could I possibly find a better opportunity. Let us not even mention the literature which lies imprisoned within this cell. To work, to work at any price! But how is it possible to work when one has been torn up by the roots. God in heaven, could it be true that peace of mind can only be found in the world among ones own kind? Is it my fault that I behaved as I did? It is all very well staying with one's own kind, but what if one is essentially different? It is said that everyone has his counterpart... However, it is obviously useless for me to dwell upon such problems for so long... or have I been wrong from the very beginning? Evidently one cannot live either here or there in the way that I lived and am now living. Should I not give my life another twist, another direction? Is there not something that might illuminate that life, this life, death, and all the rest for me? I feel vaguely that it should be so. One would only have to give it a name or to find a word with which to describe it, but I cannot, or rather, I do not wish to speak the word. Something prevents me from uttering it, something akin to pride, to an inborn, blind and possibly unconscious pride. Isn't it that I will not admit that I am beaten? Hell no! Beaten by what and by whom?... But haven't I almost said it, said that word?

I had better stop babbling like this even if it is only to myself. Above all I had better stop looking for explanations. The confusion in my head increases and I no longer understand anything. I spoke of having memories. I had them once, but I no longer remember them. I no longer remember anything.

It increases. There, I was unwilling to say it even to myself. I have waited until now to say it, but now, say it I must. I..... Isn't everything that I have written today rather queer? It must certainly be queer. Looking at my reflection in the polished steel wall before me, I see that I am laughing. I am laughing silently and convulsively. I am throwing back my head and with my fists clamped to my temples.... I am laughing just as Filano laughed so many times. Help me, my God! (There I have said everything).

15 *April*

I feel as though I want to follow Filano's fate. I speak to myself. I laugh like Filano. I rush around the cabin furiously and do all kinds of odd things. I will end up as he did. But I do not want to die, damned! And where, here? I do not want to lie without a tombstone. I want a pitying hand to arrange my remains in the coffin, I want my grave heaped with flowers, culled from memories and from tears.... And once more I desire that which I most despised.

Coffin, grave, flowers, tears: things of another world, of THE world. You must not let your fantasy run so wildly. Either that or this is your tomb. He is your companion forevermore. («He has also given me an inkling of my fate — to go on alone and without — heirs and when the time has come — to die without a hand to help me»).

Thinking it over well, do these things which I see around me really exist? Isn't Filano and all this story and even Cancroregina herself merely a part of my imagination, diseased as it is? Shall I not awake between friendly arms or even in bed with my wife?

Oh, how my poor head aches! This Cancroregina who will not release her prey. She is poisoning me, she is suffocating me with the gases of her intestines, or to be somewhat more classical, with the vapors of her hypochondrium.

17 *April*

I cannot understand how that miserable little clerk whom I see down there between the fortieth and forty-second parallels continues to exist; a little clerk with spectacles and a derby. (Isn't that in itself odd these days?) He is hurrying towards the office after having lunched with his beloved family; he will return home at the end of the day too tired to do anything or even to think; he will eat his supper and go to bed with his wife to whom, however, he makes love only once a week and in the morning he will begin doing the same things over again. His salary is not even sufficient to buy any new clothes; his elbows and his seat are shiny; his breath is offensive and his teeth always harbor some fragment of putrid meat. And then? What else is there in his life? Nothing. How is it possible to live thus? That is what I used to think. Now I envy him.

It is not a matter, as I now clearly understand, of her having gone mad together with her creator, nor was it her creator who drove her to insanity. It is she who has caused him to go mad and is driving us all mad. Just as a woman may suckle a siren who stares at her with venomous eyes, or for that matter she may suckle a viper, and yet she is capable of conceiving an offspring who devours her vitals. Perhaps this situation has never happened to a woman, but it has been known to happen with other animals, and that amounts to the same thing.

27 April

Thank God! The absolute silence has been broken. I have heard — I have heard a voice and I was unable to understand what it was saying or from whence it came. Finally I realized that it was Filano speaking. The poor devil out there was gesticulating wildly and seemed to be shouting in his attempts to be heard, but you know, with this window more than half a yard thick.... By putting my ear close to the glass I managed in the end to hear his words. They were few. He was only saying, « I am happy and I forgive you. » Then he fell back into his customary position. Oh well, so much the better.

But there was one strange thing; it was not the only

voice speaking. And what can be the meaning of that?
There must have been someone else. Possibly Cancroregina
herself who may be a ventriloquist.

1 May

Today is Worker's Day in almost every country of the
continent of my birth. There they are in the streets of
Milan, a large number marching in parade, with signs, stand-
ards, flags, banners, floats and all the usual panoply, with
songs too. Well, what difference do the workers make to
me? But wait, it means something to me, or at least it once
meant a great deal to me. I don't even say that they are not
doing right by agitating or that they don't have a reason;
but there is nothing that revolts and depresses me more than
parades, songs, posters and flags; parades of organized people.
I know of nothing more sordid or tiresome. And there are
so many like me, so many who are possessed of intellect and
heart. Is it possible that they cannot get along without these
posters and flags? They might at least change the name
« workers » if they wanted to further their cause, but to what
group can the mass of workers attach themselves; the Union
of Workers, the Confederation of Laborers, or that other
name which has a sound like the rumblings of an empty
belly, the Proletariat? They might change the name of their
directors (another beautiful word, and for those who are
being directed a most honorable one). Have you ever known
of anything with such names as these to have any soul or
any destiny? When the last war began a certain Gamelin was
placed in charge of the French forces. I said to my friends
(what friends?) that France had already lost. An easy pro-
phecy, as one can see from the beginning whether a name,
I do not speak of the man himself, is destined for something great and noble. With all respect to his undoubtedly great ability, can you imagine a victorious Gamelin in his
country's Hall of Fame? Look at their names. Can't you

imagine some of the more dull and hollow ones? Is there even a slight hope that those who bore them were generous and liberal men of good soul and superior character? Without the soul it is impossible to solve even the problems of filling the stomach, a matter which seems to be a special passion of these people. How can the workers believe in such names? To return to the group feeling at the basis of « work, » why do they put up with all this wretchedness, abjection, and human shame? Is there not a single worker, I ask, who is not convinced in his heart that work degrades man? (It is curious that in this case they should pretend to attribute blue-blood to only a few natural functions. After all work is hardly a natural function in the best of hypotheses). Only one great man occupied himself with the question, and he was careful to call himself Lenin, which is to say « the Lazy One. » Now why do those disgusting initials still prevent the less common people from reading the newspapers? Who invented initials and abbreviations which are the graves of all words, and as a result of the..... Why do they generally insist on banishing poetry from those wretched lives? Poetry is actually the one thing that can help the workers. In it alone is salvation, not in organization or technique, which is only useful to the demagogue. But why all this bitter invective? Certainly man is not encouraged or aided to stay among his own kind and to be happy with them. Even more, everything is done to make him loathe his fellow-man. One must speak, I repeat, to their, to our divine imagination, and even such a man as one of those racketeers whom one sees in cartoons, with a high hat, a big diamond ring on his finger and a heavy gold chain across his paunch, has some imagination.

If I were still alive I might never have written these things, for who knows what would have happened if I had. Some people would have said, « What right has he to set himself up as a judge, etcetera? »... Others, admitting that I had the right, might say, « Mr. Everyman (down with this revered and insignificant name) affirms that..., » with the usual interpretation *ad usum Delfini*. They would have done everything to get me on their side. But wait friends! I speak of the workers because my sympathy is so much with them that I feel myself betrayed by them. I succeed in speaking of the others only with difficulty, for the simple reason that even though they are dangerous, they do not really exist.

Why and to whom do I make these explanations? Let us finally decide: am I alive or dead? Anyway, what is my relationshp to those people down there? Actually nothing at all. Oh how I wish that I were a worker; or worse, a director; even worse yet, a priest or a pope; if only to...

5 May

The death of Napoleon Bonaparte. Is this a real name or not? Well, how should I know? I didn't even want to speak of Napoleon Bonaparte. I wanted instead to say, God, I thank Thee again for now I have companionship.

They came out of my mouth, my nose, my ears, my umbilicus, and my anus. Others, but much smaller ones, came out of my eyes and my prick. They are black and shiny — too bad that they stink. Those which I have tried, taste of ants, iron and women's breasts. Anyway here they are and I can even talk to the larger ones. I have read over several passages of this manuscript to the most intelligent one, to the one who seemed to me to be so, and he approved. However, they all appear to be immortal, and that worries me a great deal. Yesterday, as I lost my temper for some reason or other, I hurled several of them against the wall and floor (however not the most intelligent one who is useful to me as a general listener); then, to prevent them from contaminating the air, I ate them, and do you know what they did? In a few minutes they came out again from the same holes, bright and shiny like new shoe-buttons.

I speak and speak; we talk and talk.

7 May

This is dust, real dust and cannot be anything else but dust from my home planet; a minute particle of earth which I carry with me. This other dust which I have in my brain, that comes from here. Dust and cobwebs on my brain. It is like waking up from a troubled sleep, but much more intense. And devouring flames, tortures, lacerations —.

Oh Lord, You Who died upon the Cross, save me! Save me from this evil, from this fear, from this solitude. There was no place for me on the earth, nor is there one for me here. I don't know how to pray. Even now my words become futile, trite and literary. But what does that matter to You? I speak as best I can, and You can see inside of me. Listen: « Nous sommes nombreux, nombreux, nombreux: — n'en demandons pas plus pour être heureux. — Une petite maison de campagne au bord de la mer, — ou en proximité d'un petit ruisseau clair... » They are the simple words of a folksong; with my friends, my lifelong companion, my children, in peace with You, with Your law which is the law of the heart... That is what I wanted to feel and to have, that is what I wanted to sing to You in thanks. That is what I wanted my prayer to be. You are my witness, and if I said that I was like no one else I did not mean that I was better than the rest. I am not even better than the lowest worm on earth. They at least can have children, and they even let the smaller ones eat their intestines... But not I. Children; for the third time, what must one do in order to have them? I bless You for all the things that you have not given me!

Lord, have pity on Your poor son. Let a tear fall, a tear of heavenly dew fall on his flaming head. Send peace upon his wretched soul, his tortured limbs! But didn't Gogol say the same thing? Are these not the best words to use in speaking to You?

Oh, call me to You. Take me at least to the bright shores

of the moon. Perhaps among those gentle creatures I shall find peace and happiness, should those two things not be the same.

12 May

I killed them all off by an ingenious method. They began to get on my nerves and they took up too much room because (lucky things) they multiplied unceasingly. My method, however, is too long to explain. To be frank, I don't even remember it, though I know it was ingenious. Basically the general principle was this: being immortal I had to surprise them in order to kill them, that is, not give them a chance not to die, and I succeed. Having killed them I didn't even eat them for fear that my internal fluids would revive them. Then (I am not so crazy as to open the door again) kneading the largest ones into a sort of dough and rolling them into long rolls like worms, I pushed them one by one into the outlet of the carbon anhydride tube, from which they were shot out as the pressure of the gas forced open the flap. What long and stupid faces they had in death!

The only trouble was that they also proceeded to follow us. They all floated along in a semicircle around Filano and on we went with them following. This black flock bothered me slightly, but at least I have stopped the invasion.

Now, however, I have these others around my feet. I don't know. I see nothing and every once in a while I feel that I am being touched by large forms with intolerable and impossible faces. I think that they are going to swallow me. They are like women's breasts or hips, but hairy even though pleasant and smooth to touch, and if I try to catch hold of them, they evade me. Who knows what they are or what they want of me? There is no doubt that I must invent some other system to free myself from these creatures.

A strange accident has happened to the Mont Blanc (I call it this jokingly). A vampire, not a bat but precisely a large vampire, I don't know from where he appeared, came in and began to flit around the room. Did he really enter this cabin and begin to flit around? No, only in my brain. First he remained caught in the strands of the web, and having broken them by striking them hard, he kept hitting obstinately against my forehead like large bluebottle flies against a window. He came in from somewhere and did not know how to get out. Sneezing more and more I pushed him away, I took him and rolled him in the palms of my hands and then with an iron roller. Afterwards I folded him in eight pieces, and stretching out each piece like dough, I put him in the same tube from where he floated out to join the others. Boy, the party is certainly getting large!

Cancroregina is becoming more and more despotic, surly and acid. Now she demands that I keep quiet. To hell with her — she can just wait! Her nasal voice, stinking and greasy, excites my antipathy more than I can say. War is declared between us! Who will win? I don't know. How should I....?

Devouring sesquipedalia and dragons is as useless as tilting at windmills.

13 May

The inhabitants of the moon, which I can see very clearly now, are just exactly as I have always maintained in all my works through superior powers of perception. Their third foot is like the ivory of the towers of Castelnuovo in Naples, like the mother of pearl of the women of Luco. What is most striking is the extraordinary clearness of their hair. I do not even speak of their oviducts, their foreheads or their good looks. Because I hope so much that...

17 May

In the last days unheard of quantities of various (and varicose) objects entered the cabin by different means. In what a chase, worthy of the Duke of Athens, in what a deopercolation of Prague I took part! I threw myself raging on each and every one of them, and within forty-eight hours I cleared up the whole damned mess. What a lot of trouble since several of those thing, which I had never seen before nor knew the use of, did not permit themselves to be liquidated. Behind us two now mortal enemies floats an exterminated and disorderly (if one regarded their different positions) crowd of dead objects and persons. It seemed to me that almost everything that exists in the world was there with infinite eyes, mouths, eye lashes and limbs of iron. I ate a lot (12) rubber balls, and now their constant bouncing hammers against my little brain.

In order to free myself from these round and hairy creatures I did as follows: I was ready with the iron bar and was about to beat one of them. I hit my own hand very hard, the hand with which I was holding him tightly, but at least I bruised and wounded him so that he was quiet until I finished beating him. And so little by little all of them became soft and mushy. At the end of all this work, and after having scooped out all the air carefully in order to catch every last one of them, I collected the empty skins. First I wanted to keep some for hides but then I thought better of it and got rid of them in the usual manner.

Now finally I am alone once more. I am really alone this time. I broke my hand doing it but there was no other way out.

22 May

Two months have past since I began these notes. Two months! An eternity? Or rather a moment. Perhaps both in one. Here time is no longer measurable. Now and always this life without end, this space and this time without reason. « But one will live, alas —. One will live anyway... » I suspect, having read over the last pages, that I suddenly had

148

a long seige of madness. « I suspect » of course is only an expression. How can I doubt it after once going over that stuff? Even now I don't know whether writing in that willy-nilly manner has past. I feel clearer and calmer than ever. My God, what a mess! Tomorrow I will make another attempt, the supreme attempt to bring CANCROREGINA back to earth or at the worst to induce her to land on the moon. I want, I must do it after letting myself go for so long.

23 May

The attempt failed!

I: Will you make up your mind to give up this useless race and land somewhere?

CANCROREGINA (*from the liver, with a muddy, muffled voice*): No.

I: But I shall force you to do it.

C: Brr, trr, hmm, grrr, frrr, muu, bof bof.

I: All right, all right! I am only joking. Let's speak calmly. Why the hell do you insist on doing this to me?

C: (*from the spleen in a jaundiced voice*): Because I do. (The old bitch answered the same thing to all my inquiries).

I: But look, isn't there some way of coming to an understanding? Have you no heart? Have you no pity, if not for yourself for me?

C: (*from the ovaries, hysterically*): My answer to all three of your questions is categorically no, no and no.

I: You cursed old slut, you squint-eyed whore. You'll see!

C: Fff, sss, zzz, bbrrr.

I: No, no! What are you doing? No! Let's discuss this quietly. I apologize. In the name of God have some compassion.

C: (*from the Fallopian tubes, tartly*): Suppose you tell me who you think I am fornicating with when you call me an old whore? You for instance have many mistresses

and no lovers, not even a wife. And you shouldn't talk
about things of which you know nothing.

I: Everyone knows that much. But why do I attempt to
argue with you! Then there is nothing to be done?

C: (*from the stomach*): No.

I: And this is to go on forever?

C: Yes, forever.

I: Even after death?

C: Even after death.

I: Lord help me!

C: (*from the entrails, vociferously*): Ha, ha, ha! Did you
expect me to admit defeat?

24 May

Lines written in hours of insomnia

THE PRAWL

A prawl! What kind of a beast is a prawl? I'm sorry
to say that I myself do not know, and I am equally ignorant
as regards the slut. The prawl seems to be something between the tapir and the hog and has practically no neck. He
comes out at night running like a hare with the sunshine
piercing his ears, and from the shade he spies upon me and
broods over my madness, crouching like a cat, or better, like
a cow-turd, with eyes of yellow flame.

For a long time my life has been obsessed with the research and cataloguing of words. The prawl is a prowling
shadow in the darkness. The prawl comes and goes. The
prawl is a mass which I am unable to swallow.

The prawl is not an animal it is a word.

What difference does it make to me? I may say that
my life is not at all obsessed with research and that here
there is neither night nor darkness. It is useless to mention
them to say the least. But hasn't someone had the idea of
attributing this poetical fart to my pen or of cheating me?

First,this writing cannot even be called a decent imitation; second, who would recognize my style? Oh no, here is the hand of a lousy, misbegotten, misterbegotten, missesbegotten, masterbegotten, son-of-a-bitch with a persecution mania, or of a shameless genius. What do you want from me, if you please, what do you think I am going to do? It is useless to hope for any help from me, and equally useless to try to suffocate me with these idiotic jokes. I shall not give in an inch.

In any case this is what happened. I was standing near a window peacefully observing the cataflections of the sky, constructed according to a very interesting musical system, when unexpectedly this sheet of paper which was perched on a kind of writing pad rose up of its own accord, and floating through the air placed itself exactly before my eyes as though to give me every opportunity of reading what was written upon it: namely, that which you have already read, and which was written as I have said, by an unknown hand (I myself added the date). That is not to say that any invisible person has been admitted to my prison lately, as I certainly am not a simpleton, and at that very moment I started to make passes in the air with my hands, waving them all around the paper which then floated back to its original place by the same means. What can such a thing mean, I repeat? It really seems inexplicable.

I shall die soon, I feel it.

I shall die, and then, among other things — she wants to say — we will see it with Cancroregina — Cancro, the queen, Cancro, the queen, Cancro, the king, the princess, the royal family; Cancro the etcetera, Cancro-Ancro. Has Cancroregina perhaps taken it into her head to rule the universe?

30 May

Have I not said that I felt it? I have been dead for two days. You were perfectly right, nothing has changed.

Oh, if I had only known that it was so easy and that nothing would change, I would have been dead sooner. Why do it if nothing would have been changed? Eh, I don't know, but it seems to me in every way better to be dead than alive.

Now that I am dead I feel that I must tell you the whole story, to tell it to you from the very beginning. I was lonely and disconsolate... Oh to hell with that story! Why do I bother? If I am dead, what mistaken reasoning makes me tell it? Better, with the serenity that comes to the old and wise, better by far to contemplate these slippers. The best way of escaping any villanous attack is to do nothing at all. Look at me — behold I am happy and contented! With the utmost inner composure I can sing: « Long live England and Engsea! »

And still whenever I think about them I feel the need to relate this story and to tell it from the very beginning. I was alone and disconsolate......

III

SCENE ONE

A corridor of the insane asylum

A LUNATIC, FIRST GUARD, SECOND GUARD

THE LUNATIC *(is visible through the bars on the door of his cell. He is holding a pair of hospital slippers in his hand which is raised slightly above his head. Staring at the slippers intently in perfect immobility, his feet together, he is in a position of perfect attention except for the raised arm. He remains in this position throughout the entire scene).*

1ST GUARD *(overtaking the other one)*: Heh, he's a new one, eh? At least he won't give you much to do, quieter than...

2ND GUARD: Now, yeah. But you should have seen him last night when they brought him in.

1ST: Really?

2ND: You bet. I've never seen anything like it. Four of us couldn't handle him and we're not exactly weaklings.

1ST: Poor devil.

2ND: You weren't here. Poor us, is more like it.

IST: Then what happened?

2ND: We put him in a straight jacket for a while and all of a sudden he calmed down.

1ST: Luckily.

2ND: He ask to be allowed to write.

IST: To write?

2ND: Yeah, and you know, he begged and pleaded so much that I... He seemed completely recovered... My God man! I have a heart too.

IST: And how! But you know it is strictly against the rules. What did you give him?

2ND: Oh, a couple of sheets of old paper, he asked for more later, and a pencil stub no longer than this. What could he do with that?

IST: He could swallow it and then...

2ND: Oh, well, everything went all right. He wrote all night long. And now there he sits.

IST: What did he write?

2ND: Here it is. Look!

IST: *(unfolding the manuscript):* There. What, what? He writes about a machine to go to the moon.

2ND: Yes, and a lot of other things. I've only read a couple of pages. I'll give it to the director. He's always looking for this sort of thing.

IST: Better take my advice and tear it up before you get yourself in a mess.

2ND: Maybe, but I'm sorry for him. Who knows how useful this might be to understand something about him.

IST: What an idea! Oh well, do as you like. Goodbye.

2ND: Goodbye.

SCENE TWO

Studio of the director

THE DIRECTOR OF THE ASYLUM, A LADY

DIRECTOR: Yes madam, how may I help you?

LADY: What is the matter with him? It happened all of a sudden. He came home at the usual hour, a little late perhaps as they have lots of overtime work, he ate, changed his shoes and began to read the paper just like any other day. Then suddenly he got up and went to the other side of the room, and I heard all sorts of things... I don't understand... *(she begins to cry)*.

DIRECTOR: Now, now.

LADY: I ran, but immediately I understood everything from his face, from the look on his face, as if nothing was there, as if he were not...

DIRECTOR: Yes, yes. We know all the rest.

LADY: I thought first of the danger to the children.

DIRECTOR: We know that too. How many children have you?

LADY: Five.

DIRECTOR: That's quite a few. But I want to know, have you ever seen anything abnormal, let's say strange or exceptional in your husband's actions lately?

LADY: Oh no. Absolutely nothing. Except for that flair he had for literature and poetry, he has always been a very peaceful man, you might say without any bad habits or anything like that, but you understand, with his wages and a large family...

DIRECTOR: And what about his anamnesis?

LADY: What?

DIRECTOR: I say, ahem... about his case history, about his family and that sort of thing. Has there been any insanity, for instance, uncles, aunts etc.?

LADY: Not that I know of.

DIRECTOR: Very well, thank you. There is nothing else for the moment. I hope you will be all right.

LADY: But sir, I would like you to tell me frankly... as you you know about these things...

DIRECTOR: I see. You want to know if it is serious or not?

LADY: Exactly.

DIRECTOR: Truthfully, I cannot tell you as yet. We must first put him under observation and study the case. Can you tell me just when the catalepsy occurred...?

LADY: Oh! *(she cries)*

DIRECTOR: No, no. Don't be distressed. It is only a state of immobility and indifference to external stimuli, which hinders us in our observations and diagnosis... ahem...

LADY: But...?

DIRECTOR: All that I can tell you is that it seems to me to be fairly serious, and, as I don't have the right to hide it from you, a grave form of... of a brain disease, that is... ahem... of manic-depressive psychosis with some complications.. mmm, schizophenia and dissociation aspects... In short a type of melancholic insanity.

LADY: Melancholic! Oh my poor husband *(she cries)*.

DIRECTOR: But we will let you know more as soon as possible.

LADY: Give me at least some hope, me and my poor husband. Will he get better?

DIRECTOR: Who can say? We will do everything within our power to help him. I do not despair, quite to the contrary! *(aside):* I wouldn't give that guy two months to live in his condition. *(To the lady):* It is certain that these unexpected forms are in general either very serious and with no hope of recover, or, in spite of the appearance, slight and easily curable. But again, we hope everything will be all right. Have faith. Goodbye.

LADY: *(exits crying).*

DIRECTOR: *(alone):* A very interesting case! However, from what has already happened I must hurry to study the case. I will be able to write a study for the *Pschiatric Annual* and perhaps finally get... I can quote from this

manuscript that the guard brought me, it will be an
excellent study, solid and... and perhaps finally I will...
That guard must be punished. If he had killed himself
with that pencil as in the case of? — But of all things!
This manuscript is really a juicy tidbit!

IV

We wanted to give in part just that little tidbit to our
twelve and a half readers — we don't know why.

(translated by Jack Murphy)

ATTILIO BERTOLUCCI

FROM « THE INDIAN HUT »

1

Behind the house in the mist of November
It raises its indecisive peak:
A simple rural edifice
At the end of the fields, a graceful
Apparition in the thinning fog;
One might think it an Indian hut.
Here where the working equipment
Lies overturned now that the sun
At the end of the season has closed
The cycle of sowing, with intentioned hand
These stakes were set there, one
Against the other thus to form
A pavillion quiet in the autumn.
On the hardened earth that leads
To the lonesome shelter skips
The little bird people call winter's
Who is unaware of the others present

157

On the path, intent perhaps on some
Last berry, glowing, to his acute
And peaceful eye, in the distance.

But we, what promise brings us
In the morning's cold air to such
Abandonment? What sweet food
For our youthful mouths
Beyond the familiar silence,
Beyond the last rotting straw, where
The path ends, where the path dies?
Now the day is serene over all
The plain till the point where the city
Appears, a dream closed to us, a secret,
Of red and grey houses silent
Through the naked trunks of the woods.
Oh, there will be a time so calm
Barely marked by the kindly invitation
Of the traveling peddlar in the noon's
Sunlight, by the sharp sound
Of a stone against the blue guttering.
Then in the silence we will hear the shout
Of our dear ones, closer and closer
And anxious, then weakened, lost
In the fog that rapidly thickens
In these days when the sun turns
Past noon, and it seems that the night
Descends now, without hope.

The grass that coldly touches our bodies
Extended and huddled within the darkness,
Our hidden faces, our aching knees,
Is already the hard, dead grass of winter.
Yet it is the sweetest time of the year
When the barren hedge that encloses

With its arm the deserted dominion
Becomes the hiding-place of the stray
Sparrow, who is already the earth's color.
Here we have come where we desired,
Walking through the foggy morning
Untired, and when a cart passes
With the noise of milk being splashed
In the zinc that shines in a fugitive
Sphere of sun, the man is sleeping,
Even the horse is asleep as he goes
Trotting, uncertain and patient.

The house could barely be seen, seized
In the sad sleep of a common dawn
In November, at a turning where near
Easter the bells, undone, are heard
Vibrating over the earth that is kissed.
It was that hour when behind the shades
The family stirs itself bitterly,
The last of the flies buzzes, near death,
In the close kitchen where the ember
Of the first fire of autumn lasts
Till the first woman, chilly,
Youthful witch, false moutaineer.
At her breath, her adept handling
Of sticks, already the room is bright
That now the open window fills
With mist in intermittent gusts.

But the time passes and other windows
Open without desire to the day,
Slowly touching the torn ivy
And the fragile plaster. We are
Seated on the plowed earth, quiet,
Looking about us, grinding a clod

Just barely damp with the breath
Of fog that is slowly rising
In the steps of two boys first
Alone, then closer and closer,
Until they are seen advancing together
And disappear chatting, the friends
Of so many long days in a time
That never comes to an end.

And how gently the day grows
On the plain by now sown,
Prepared for its winter rest and yet
Lost today behind the last sun
That ripens on the brush rare grains
That even the starlings have overlooked.
In its heat the wall of the house
Grows warm, a scrap of mortar falls
With a thud softened by the twigs
Of arid rosemary, a woman
Sings happily from an open room
Invisible from here, the solitary
Voice of good weather and forgetfulness.
No one remembers, so dear
Is the hour passing over the earth
That a distant, silent bird
Marks with his fleeting shadow;
No one remembers us any more.

(translated by William Fense Weaver)

ANGEL ISLAND

BY

GIUSEPPE DESSÍ

In February, 194..., I made my way home after long imprisonmente.

I had been away five years, leaving behind my mother, my sister Giovanna, her husband and two sons, Giovanni and Lino.

Also my fiancée Maria, who was virtually a member of the household.

When I returned, it was my good fortune to find none of them missing.

Our village escaped the destruction of war and there was relatively little suffering. Except once when a fleet of fishing boats was attacked at sea and four men perished.

Many of our youths, however, died in action while others vanished, leaving no traces of their whereabouts.

In my first year away, I was reported missing. Then one Mario L., a barber and my companion since grammar school, spread the story that he had seen me collapse on the field with a severe head injury, that he had nursed me until my last breath and then turned over my identification tag and money to Lt. Cristoforo R., who was killed in action shortly afterwards.

How this man, one of my closest friends, could have been so mistaken is beyond my comprehension. I cannot believe that he deliberately lied; and since he no longer lives in Sardinia I cannot demand an explanation from him.

After a year and a half of prison in Russia, I managed to escape. The Germans, however, recaptured me and sent me to a concentration camp in eastern Germany. There I agreed to become a collaborationist; but once across the Italian frontier, I deserted with three other Sardinians from my village and together we traveled on foot to Forte dei Marmi, where we stole a sailboat and set out for home, landing after four days and nights at sea.

I had known much sorrow; but what I endured during those war years was a separate experience, unrelated to the events that were to come.

All during my internment in Russia and Germany, I had tried to communicate with my fiancee and my mother, but not a single reply ever reached me. Between us was war, and not until the end of the cataclysm unloosed by mankind could we hope to be reunited.

My despair at first was followed by calm resignation, relieved by faint flickers of hope. Then a dull, heavy apathy settled over me which I could throw off only by escaping into day dreams; and I would lose myself, not in rational thoughts evolving from some logical starting point, but in bizarre fantasies that gave me refuge from the precariousness of my existence and encouragement in the face of the remote possibility that I would ever see my homeland again.

For the most part, I would dream of reunion with my family and fiancée. As if telling myself a story over and over again, I would improvise variations on the same theme, creating every possible hypothesis within its limits. For example, I would imagine finding everyone at home safe and sound — as eventually I did — Mamma, Maria, Giovanna, Rodolfo and the boys; or else all except Mamma, who was already old and ailing when I last saw her. Then I imagined the joy of my home-coming darkened by the sadness of her death and felt the consuming grief of returning after so long to the house where I had grown up under her eyes only to find her gone. I could see the others lavishing me with embraces and loving attention because I learned the news of our loss only at the moment of my return, whereas they were already resigned to it. Or else I would imagine that Maria had died. This, even more than the possibility of my mother's passing which, one might say, would have been only natural in view of her ill-health, struck me as the worst ordeal that could await me, were I to survive the war. I would feel something crumble within me, as if all life were beginning to disintegrate. And while I saw the other fantasies in a kaleidoscopic succession of images, this one of Maria's death remained steeped in darkness like a towering wall rising high into the night; and that unreasoning torment recurred with growing frequency, as if some dispassionate, inevitable destiny were bursting in on me from the outside world.

Slowly, cautiously, like a boatman hoisting a sail into the wind, I tried to create a picture of my life without Maria, just as I had imagined life without my mother or my sister.

The first thing that rose to my mind was a vision of the church of S. Ignazio, which stands in the lower part of town beyond the lighthouse and where we used to go for evening worship. I could see her again under the arch of the chapel of the Rosary, veiled in black as when she mourned her mother.

Thus I accustomed myself to the idea of her death, first by recalling her in mourning for her dear ones, then by imagining that she herself had passed away. My despair abated; I became almost resigned to it, as if she had died a long time before and my fancies were only remote memories.

Sometimes, through sheer force of will, I managed to throw off these morbid reveries, saying to myself: « What's all this nonsense! Of course she's alive! »

I would live through years of stormy passions in the course of a single day.

I would mould my thoughts to my moods in the same way an actor uses his face or a musician employs his instrument to play a piece that expresses his feelings.

This sort of thing, I am sure, can easily drive one to insanity.

There have been other women in my life, but none as necessary to me as Maria, even though in appearance, according to prevailing opinion, she was the least prepossessing. Some considered her wholly unattractive, if not downright ugly.

This appraisal of her often hurt my vanity, although I was well aware that Maria gained in loveliness as one looked long and attentively into her face. She was a creature of rare excellence, to me at least, because her delicate beauty, which unfolded and ripened before my eyes the more I gazed at her, lay hidden as if in a secret chamber; once discovered, she became indescribably tender and pure, and an intimate transport of love would illumine her whole being.

No single thought or emotion is ever lost. Whatever befalls us at any time in our lives remains forever within us, even when we forget. Don't we sometimes search in vain for some familiar object that lies before our very eyes?

So it is with past sickness and sorrows; when they afflicted us, they seemed like tangled labyrinths of pain and despair. But everything merges with the flow of time, everything becomes time and man, with his hands, his feet, his breathing lungs and graying hair, is a living, sentient embodiment of the past.

The spectre of Maria's death had become so vivid to me during my incarceration that, had it been possible for us to marry after my return and always remain together, its shadow would have become a part of her, just as some inevitable fate, already discernible in a man's imminent future, becomes clearly defined, like the reflection of a mountain in a lake. Even now, today, we would have sensed in a kiss, let us say, or a glance an alien sadness, held at bay, perhaps, but still unvanquished, still to be driven off, as fixed in my mind as the vision of the snow-covered plain surrounding my little hut, a memory I carried with me through so many bleak and lonely winters.

I remember the exasperating clarity with which I could almost see in my thoughts the house on little Angel Island where Maria used to spend the winter with her aging father, or her aunt's house on the beach beyond the town, where she lived in summer. I could see the vineyard, the vegetable patch, the hedge of prickly pears, the cove tucked away among the high cliffs where we used to meet. Everything became silence and space within me until in the empty stillness, I could even hear the baying of the vegetable farmer's dogs.

I tried to fight off the oppressive gloom spawned by a nightmare I myself had conjured up with such painstaking care, at the some time cultivating unwittingly an indefinable sense of remorse, almost as if I were somehow guilty towards her. Thus, I persuaded myself that my fantasies bore the same mystic import as do certain dreams of death which, paradoxically, signify good luck, since to dream of a beloved one's decease, according to peasant superstition, prolongs that person's life.

Out of the very despair, therefore, that plagued me so insistently, I formulated an article of faith; and when I set sail from the Italian coast for my native soil in the dead of that February night, I knew that, were I to land safely, I would find Maria alive and well.

We encountered Gerolamo, a fisherman from Maddalena, off Cala Daria after four days and nights at sea. He was the first to tell me that she was married.

This was the one speculation I had never made.

Faint from exhaustion, we gave the oars to Gerolamo. The boat moved slowly towards shore.

All at once my fatigue lifted, my mind became sharp and clear.

In a flash I recovered my proper place in time, which had passed over this land without me, and in life, from which my little world had excluded me.

What had happened had to happen.

The mountain contours and the profile of Angel Island rose up against the clear, pale morning sky. Immutable in the limited span of human history but fluid as clouds in the vast aeons of cosmic time, they gave me an acute sense of the brevity of my life, of the irretrievable years torn from me and lost in the swift current.

Gerolamo wanted to hear my story.

I told it briefly.

The sun shone full in his face. He kept his eyes closed, squinting at me occasionally, first with one eye, then the other, to verify my words by my expression.

He told me they thought I was dead. My mother and sister were still in mourning.

I asked him again about Maria.

He looked at me; then he explained that after a short betrothal, she had married Piero T., now her father's business partner.

He would also be my partner, I reflected, presuming that I still owned my share of the quarry.

We landed at Cala Doria so that Gerolamo would have time to notify my family and prepare my mother. Without convincing me, he kept insisting that good news no less than bad can be fatal when it unexpectedly disrupts the normal course of events.

There must be times, I mused, when it is hard to renounce one's inner resignations.

When he was about to go, I caught his arm. « Do you think I ought to go away without saying anything? » I asked him.

He scrutinized my face, examining my eyes, my mouth, my forehead and again my eyes. His own eyes were small, shifty, malicious.

« If it weren't for your mother », he said.

« Will you tell her? »

« Not me », he answered, « it's none of my business. That's up to your family ».

He looked as if he were setting out to convey bad news.

When he had gone 200 meters, I called after him.

He stopped and waited. I went to him.

« Let's hold off until tomorrow », I said. « It's almost dark now ».

We pooled our money and sent out for brandy and American cigarettes. Gerolamo prepared a fish soup. After the meal, we threw ourselves down on the floor and fell asleep.

When I awoke, it was night.

I struggled for a moment to find my bearings. Then, just as it happenend in the boat, suddenly I was wide awake, alert. I felt strangely intoxicated, like one drunk with despair. I wanted to run, to shout.

The others lay on floor mats, breathing heavily in their sleep. Gerolamo was crouched on the table, his knees drawn up against his chin in one of those postures typical of sailors, who seem perennially youthful even in old age, if one does not look into their faces.

I lit a cigarette and went outdoors.

Strolling aimlessly, I tried to repeat her name aloud, the name that had sprung from my lips so many times before, as if she could have heard me.

All at once, I was seized with an impulse to go home, to see the house as it was while they still thought I was dead.

I struck out; but soon I realized that I was not heading towards home. It seemed as if some invisible escort were directing my steps, forcing me to take a different route.

I had been in Piero T.'s house many times before.

All the windows were closed. A single ray of light fell between the shutters of a window on the ground floor. I heard a woman singing softly to an infant in her arms, tapping her rocking chair in rhythm against the wall. She must have been a young girl; one could tell from her voice.

I circled the house and climbed up the slope. Then I scaled the garden wall and, balancing myself by the branches of the orange trees, advanced towards the house. The wall was a meter and a half high on the garden side, dropping four meters on the outer side to the cobblestone pavement below. In my boyhood, I used to play cops and robbers with Piero in this same garden. I recognized its damp fragrance, remembered how the soft, leaf-scattered earth felt under my feet.

I went as far as the terrace. Once when I was a lad, I hid under the bed in the ground floor room where Piero's pushed it open.

I leaped down. The door of the room stood ajar. I pushed it open.

Moonlight fell across the dressing table and the mirror. A woman's dressing gown lay on a chair by the window. The bed was turned down for the night.

I picked up a big tortoise-shell comb from the dressing table, examined it against the moonlight, sniffed it and put it in my pocket.

In the hallway outside, the girl's drowsy lullaby sounded louder as she continued to rock the baby to sleep.

Apparently there was no one else in the house.

I retraced my steps to the slope.

Then I realized that all this time I had been clutching my pistol in my left hand.

My legs ached with fatigue, I felt unable to take another step. I jumped off the wall and stretched out on the grass. Releasing the pistol's safety catch, I pressed the gun barrel against my temple and held it there until the sensation of cold steel passed off.

The tall, thick grass hid me completely.

I woke up in broad daylight.

The windows of the house were still closed.

Maria, I recalled, was sleeping in the ground floor room, now the bedroom of Pietro T., a stranger. This thought had plagued me every moment of the night, all during my sleep. Yet it was only natural that she should be there, I reasoned, even more natural and understandable that it had seemed the day before. But the more I accepted as natural the unhappy consequences of my falsely reported death, the more I suffered, the more unendurable, became my distress. I should speak of my *sorrow*, although those who suffer it find this simple word inadequate to express the full measure of true sorrow, which floods the soul and becomes many different things. Mine was an emotion that alternately plunged me into the depths of despair and exalted me with intoxication: a dark, soundless intoxication, full of images in action, like race horses, motor cars, aeroplanes, machine guns firing at random.

I fancied Piero standing at the terrace door. I fancied myself raising my loaded pistol, taking aim, firing. I could see him fall backwards, his body disappearing from sight, only his legs still visibly, projecting from the room.

Had he really appeared at that moment, I know I would have killed him.

The sun was already high when I returned to Gerolamo's. The house on Angel Island where Maria's father lived gleamed in the light, even its chimney distinctly visible. The funicular cables looked like a spider web.

My companions were waiting. Gerolamo searched my face, first with one eye, then the other, in his odd way, then lifted his chin in a query. I shook my head.

« Then I'll go », he said.

Everything happened in the most natural way.

My sister, my brother-in-law and the boys came running towards me. There were kisses, embraces, tears. Even I wept.

We made our way home together, crossing the fields and vineyards to avoid neighbors.

I waited outside the house with Giovanni and Lino.

Then I saw my mother at the threshold. I darted forward to support her frail figure. She clutched at my arm and fainted.

Regaining consciousness she took my hand and pressed it against her cheek, murmuring that she always knew I would come back. Her voice was strange and mournful, her mind seemed to be wandering.

While she dozed that afternoon, I gave the others a disordered account of my experiences. I felt animated as never before; and my listeners followed with such rapt attention that my narration, in reality a recital of dull, monotonous facts, took on the thrill and excitement of a fascinating adventure story.

Giovanna stood behind my chair and leaned against me. I could feel her eyes glued on my face as I talked.

Lino spoke. « Now everything seems all right again », he said. « You know, Uncle, we always felt there must have been some mistake. It just couldn't be true that you were dead. We never believed it, did we, Mamma? »

Giovanna's fingers dug into my arm and tightened. From her downcast eyes, tears flowed silently and unchecked.

Nevertheless, no one can blame Maria for believing I was dead.

Allowing that Giovanna and the boys, especially Lino, knew instinctively that I was still alive — even though they probably never dared hope to see me sitting there at the family table again — one must ascribe their faith to the fact that I was not indispensable to them as I was to Maria. Whatever happened to me, their lives would go on unchanged; but not Maria's. My mother, they said, kept insisting that one day I would return. But it is entirely possible for a mother, who conceives a child out of nothing, who sees him grow and take form out of nothing, to convince herself that the earth can restore him to her, almost as if it were yielding him up in a second birth. Moreover, my mother was devoutly religious and therefore believed that she would see me again in the next world after her own death, for which she had begun preparing years before. Logical argument is powerless against a conviction of this nature when it is anchored firm as a rock in simple souls; yet upon such a foundation one can gradually build up in his mind a preternatural faith in resurrection.

No, no one can blame Maria for believing in my death; nor can it be said that she failed in her love because she clung to no illusions. It would have been sheer madness on her part to think for one moment that Mario, my companion since childhood, could have been mistaken.

On the other hand, I can well understand how Maria must have sought desperately to free herself from grief. Whatever recourse she might take, I know that her love for me would have remained undiminished in her soul. Certainly, there has been nothing else in her life to equal or overshadow it.

I met Maria twenty days after arriving home. By that time, everyone assumed that I had humbly accepted my lot, judging from my outward tranquillity, and that I would soon resume work on my mother's land and at the quarry.

I had neither attempted to see Maria nor avoided her. Several times, on foot or on my bicycle, I passed her house — or rather Piero's house — where I had spent that first night in circumstances so fraught with danger, so similar to the hazardous life I had been living, that the incident might well serve as a fitting last chapter to the story of my war experiences. By now, however, I had settled down to a normal existence with the satisfaction a man always feels coming home from war or even only from military service, and that strange night excursion seemed like a remote dream. I had resolved not to intrude on Maria's life, even if I could have done it without the smallest effort.

Thus, whenever I passed her house, I would look up calmly to observe the facade, the balconies and the windows which, facing the north wind, were always kept shut.

From my sister's house I could see Piero's garden, the round pergola and the little, rusty iron tables.

One day I saw Maria come out of the house to hang up some laundry. My heart began to pound like a hand that opens and closes as if it were trying to breathe. Then that strange exhilaration came over me and, although I only strode up and down the terrace, I seemed to be galloping on horseback. My agitation must have shown in my face because Giovanna asked what was the matter.

This brief paroxysm passed off, leaving me empty, apathetic, drained of strength. I had to sit down.

It was one of the last days of winter, cold and grey. The wind blew the clothes off the line into a disordered heap against the house; but Maria never appeared again all morning.

Our first meeting took place early in March.

The weather was still the same: grey skies, wind, the turgid morning sea subsiding towards noon.

I encountered her on the beach.

Carrying a pocket book and a bundle under her arm, she stopped and waited for me. The wind whipped against her and she turned aside to straighten her clothes and pin down her skirt. One could not tell from her expression what she was thinking. The muscles of her face were drawn; perhaps she was pale from the cold. She looked somewhat aged.

I held out my hand, thinking how much better it would have been for both of us if I were really dead. We stood looking at each other, not knowing what to say. In former times, we would have exchanged greetings in the tenderest terms, we would have embraced, we would have considered our two lives fused into a single existence, stronger and richer.

She grew even paler. I was afraid she might faint. Her lips trembled.

« You're very cheerful, I see », she said.

I was far from cheerful inside; but that uncanny exaltation that overpowered me whenever I saw her or thought of her apparently made me appear cheerful when, in fact, my whole being was inundated by a torrent of emotions, like a flooded river on a rampage. And what I felt was nothing else but sorrow.

Without another word, she turned and went away.

The beach was deserted except for small black dots of women a hundred paces away and a boy on his bicycle. Long bands of green streaked the sea.

I remained standing there long after Maria disappeared off at an angle. At last I stirred myself and went to launch my boat, moored nearby.

During that month, I saw her several times again.

She had really grown older and thinner.

We never met alone. Once she was with her husband, who congratulated me on my safe return in words that sounded sincere enough, however absurd their meaning.

Maria appeared irritated with me. She behaved exactly as when we were betrothed, flaring up jealously whenever I paid other girls little attentions purely out of courtesy, or losing her self-command when she failed to understand at once how and why I did something. She was still the same Maria. The intervening years had left their mark, to be sure; the physical demands of matrimoniy, pregnancy, breast-feeding, housework, all these things showed traces in her face, on her person. But her inmost self remained unaltered. I knew it from her voice, the deepest secret I remembered about her.

I went to the quarry on Angel Island every day, usually in my sailboat, occasionally traveling by the little freight railway. On the way, I could clearly see the red roof of her father's house rising out of the rocks, and my thoughts troubled me more than ever because I would recall the happy times when Maria lived there; and my torment grew until, between the breakwater and shore, it merged with the island shadows falling over the water.

One day, not wanting to go as far as the island, I decided to change course and put in at Cape Daino on the left.

I hoisted the sail and set the rudder.

The boat described a wide curve and sailed into an inlet hidden by a great volcanic rock where Maria and I used to meet. I would either sail or swim to the spot, while she came by way of her aunt's vineyard and a narrow path I had cut through the hedge of prickly pears. We had no real reason to conceal ourselves; but love, by its very nature, is enriched by apparently useless secrets.

I hauled the boat up on the dry beach, then stretched out on the sand.

The basalt rock walls formed the cove in the shape of a funnel, like the open crater of a volcano.

At the botton, a strip of sand about a meter and a half wide rimmed a mirror of still water.

I lay there perhaps an hour.

Nothing was visible from the sea except the green tip of my boat's mast.

I began visiting our old secret haven regularly.

Often I took a book along.

Sometimes I stripped and bathed in the water.

It was now mid-May, the season when the world yields itself to the blue heavens and bursts into color in the warm spring air.

One day I discovered footprints in the sand.

I stood transfixed.

They could have been a boy's footprints or, more likely from the evidence, the imprints of a woman's shoe. I pretendend to weigh these alternatives without drawing any logical conclusion; I recognized those footprints only too well.

She must have been there. Perhaps she was even watching me at that moment.

There was a small recession in the rock, as high as my shoulder, where wild doves used to nest. In this secret vault we would leave messages, fixing a rendevous for the next day, for example, or conveying some sentimental trifle, or reproaching each other on any pretext whatever so that we could forgive each other in affectionate reconciliations.

I got up to examine it.

Removing the stone that covered the opening, I found the hollow empty, but clean, as if someone had just brushed out the pebbles, and dust.

I tore a sheet from my notebook and wrote: « I will come back every Saturday at six ».

No sooner had I replaced the stone then I heard footsteps near by and a sound of rustling. I turned around. She was there.

She asked if I still loved her. I said I did. Then she declared that she had always loved me, that she had never ceased loving me even when she thonght I was dead.

At first we saw each other only once a week. Taking precaution, we changed the day of our tryst every time. What was once a simple, joyous game was now a deadly serious matter.

But we had to see each other and talk, talk, talk.

We even kissed.

Non one will believe that nothing else happened in our little retreat.

We exchanged tender kisses as we use to do; but nothing beyond kissing ever passed between us, either then or now. For me she remained as she was in girlhood, inviolate.

Nevertheless, a kiss is no less momentous than an embrace, whether an act of love uniting two lovers or a caress that leaves them still two separate beings.

Our trysts became more and more frequent. In addition to the notes she left in our little depository, Maria wrote letters and sent them though the mail. I answered, also by mail, even though I was not unaware of the risk we were running.

Gradually, almost without realizing it, we found ourselves caught in a web of lies and degrading subterfuges. But like all adulterers, we considered our situation both exceptional and temporary; moreover, we believed in the innocence of our love, since we had never possessed each other despite our driving desires and the convenience at hand to fulfil them.

One day my brother-in-law Rodolfo called me into his room. Handing me his binoculars, he motioned towards Angel Island.

I adjusted the lens and looked.

The island was still and blue as a cloud.

The hollows that scarred the rock coast were filled with shadows.

Sighting the thread of cables, I followed it to the tiny port where workers were loading the freight cars.

I removed the glasses and looked at Rodolfo.

He returned my look, silently for a moment. Then he explained that with those same binoculars, he had been observing me as I trained my sea glasses on Piero's house at the same hour every day.

It was true. I had been watching Maria through my glasses as she stood on the balcony on the terrace.

I had also been looking to see if she had left a strip of red cloth on a rock at the mouth of the inlet as a signal. When it was there, I would hurry down along the wide canal to my boat.

I asked Rodolfo if he thought anyone else knew.

He replied that there was much gossip going on about us and that certain persons were keeping a close watch on our actions, expecting sooner or later to amuse themselves.

Divertirsi: he uttered a word that even now arouses in me a feeling of disgust for people.

I lacked the courage to tell Maria at once. Instead, I tried to behave as circumspectly as my impulses would allow, although I knew that any further precautions were useless.

Seeing me preoccupied, one day Maria asked the reason why. I told her everything.

« It's true », she said. « Everyone is talking about us ».

Before we separated, I declared that the only recourse left us was to go away together.

Se gazed at me pensively. I knew she was thinking about her child. « Could you really do such a thing? » she asked.

« Why shouldn't I? » I replied.

« But I belong to someone else », she said.

« You belong to me », I answered, « because you've never loved anyone else ».

We clasped each other in a tight enbrace and, in a kiss, she offered herself completely.

Thus she became mine.

We agreed to go away within the month and arranged to meet the following day to discuss the necessary preparations.

She hoped her husband would give her the child for at least a year; during that time, something unforeseen might occur. Without putting it into words, we were both thinking of Piero's death.

I watched as she moved away and disappeared among the rocks, then pushed my boat into the water. At that very moment, something happened.

Although I had wanted to see Piero dead — I had even contemplated murdering him myself — nevertheless, I had never really hated him in the true sense of the word. Rather, I had accepted him as nothing more than a passive instrument used by destiny against me. Perhaps out of the unconscious self-defense that often prompts us to close our minds to painful, ugly things in our lives and conceal them from ourselves, until that moment I had never allowed myself to think about the conjugal intimacies between Maria and Piero. But now with the rapture of possessing Maria hardly spent and subsided into weary gratification, this new ecstasy struck me as something wholly physical, wholly apart from everything I had always cherished in her; and the resentment I had felt in my soul for the man who united himself to her before me turned into bitter jealousy and hatred.

I had loved Maria chastely before going to war, I had thought of her chastely in far distant places, I had continued to love her chastely during those past months.

But after she became mine in that little haven which had sheltered us for so long, suddenly that man stood between us, no longer as an abstract barrier to our happiness but as the man he really was, a man who discovered her loins and penetrated their secret depths before I did. And all at once, the physical embrace, which lovers remember as a single act, as a momentary thing like a kiss or a breath of inhaled air, broke into a hundred pieces, and I saw him in my place, performing those diverse actions, breathing in Maria's face, his body weighing on her breast.

I missed our rendezvous the next day.

And again for five consecutive days.

When I returned to our inlet, I saw her footsteps in the sand, and I was seized with an irresistible desire to have her again.

I waited in vain for many hours.

The secret vault was empty. Beyond doubt, she had come back to remove the letters I had not collected.

I left a note saying I would return the next day and explain my absence. I asked her pardon and declared my need for her.

I needed her desperately, in fact. I wanted her love, but I also wanted to make her suffer as I had suffered. Because I would never have believed that anyone could endure so much.

I went back morning and night for many days.

Maria had not touched the note. She had not even been back to the inlet.

Rancor against her and remorse alternately welled up within me. Once I fell on my knees on the very spot I had taken her and, crying aloud, begged her to forgive me.

From Angel Island I kept a watch on her house through my sea glasses without seeing her once. Only the serving girl appeared on the balcony, sitting there with the infant bundled in a red shawl.

After eight days I turned to Giovanna for help.

My sister could hardly believe that I had not been told: Maria had gone to Milan with her husband to take a cure.

Giovanna reached for my hand and squeezed it.

But what I needed was to move, to run.

Giovanna was surely far from suspecting what was happening at the very moment when a rapid exchange of words passed between us.

It was about ten o'clock on Thursday morning.

When the mail arrived on Sunday, Rodolfo came looking for me.

I could hear my sister's muffled sobbing in the next room.

Maria had died on Thursday.

The train was roaring through a tunnel somewhere between Rome and Florence when the door of her compartment was found open.

Piero was arrested, then released.

This is November.

Maria died in July.

Nothing has been erased in this brief space of time.

Inurement to grief affords little comfort when the loss of a loved one is no mere conjecture but grim reality.

That was what my death meant to her: reality. I am glad that I never accused her, not even in my thoughts, of infidelity.

(translated by William Packer)

THE FUNICULAR

BY

GIORGIO CAPRONI

Where does it carry us, friends,
the funicular in the night?   Electric
and dead, the bulb presses the walls
in the steam of breathing — and press quiet
rumblings, veiled with dust and with oil,
the fluent cable.   And how vibrant,
how profoundly vibrant in the black
panes of the tunnel, is that lazy
inflexible cord that carries away
de profundis the patrons at its mercy
in its felted starts!... White bench
is it? or tomb that high in the arcade
now faintly shines through, while the air
is already scented with dawn?   The open,
and it is there the cable goes — not now
the hour, in darkness, to ask for the stop.

It is sudden, the breeze that opens,
at the mouth of the tunnel, with the thorns
of its acid light, the swollen and
delicate veins lighter than lacework
of blood, or than hair with the eyes
suddenly wounded — and it is sudden,

181

the dawn with a stench that comes from
crockery and cold garbage, and on a face
through the damp windows opens a city
whose deserted pavements are already pressed
by the first sounds of carts. A crowd
of pressing street-cleaners whose ears
are red with the alarm-clock shouting the hour
in the depth of the blood, not even here
can the cable find peace — not now
the hour, in chaos, to ask for the stop.

And slowly, as if in a shudder, the ark
from debris to debris, within the light
nausea, enters — swaying, cuts off
the markets of fish and greens, the foot
presses a felted path beyond the white
rocks of the dawn. And where a color
of fever passes over the benches
that still are drowsy, at once in the sun
ah what orchestra freshly breaks the sea
with its plectrum's breath! The brass
of a first melodious tram in the salt
that vibrates in the air, amid the rigging
of a port still tender, heve is a dawn
made of mandolins in which already
another impetus is closed, buzzes — again
an hour impossible to ask for the stop.

And on, past the freshest of rocks and air,
in tremulous Genoa, the ancient
wood of the rope-drawn boat in the air,
black, passes the bridges — the network
scans in oblique deviations, to arrive
by terraces to know the transparence

of the open world. Where if the eye,
still damp, bites a more certain descent
of crystal and slate, then woe,
if the patron forces asail the magic
past the cable's closed pace! The pane
is veiled at a steamy shout, the breath
nebulously condenses its words as they
with vain names becloud the air —
that crystalline presence wherein the hour
has fled when to have asked for the stop.

This hour that is lighted by the white
curtains stirred in the first breeze, brings
girls to the sea, their swarm so fresh
descending the stairs — shines in light
sweaters, the wool and the sharp surfeit
of hair and laughter, hour that restores
the reddened heels, pungent in sandals
amid left-over shells and glass. The sides
vibrate in the muted harp that inclines
monotonous to other leaps, but now red
Righi, of another Genoa the summit
draws the cable inflexibly — from the cries
the ark and from the green shutters the hour
breaks off like a sigh, beyond which lies
all fresh with mirrors the only room
where it was lightsome to ask for the stop.

And the hand... Who moves, now? who lights
that hand of coral that is greeting
trasparent of bood, now that the boat
with a start experiences the gloomy
mace of midday on the wavy rigging
that rolls?... And at grey Oregina

with houses where the hard wagon
clambers up, alas already the peak
of the cable bears us, while a stoning
shatters completely that blood, while the shadow
of the cart darkens the frigid grass,
midst rubble and laundry, and for a war
that exploded in shouts, a roof drips
like a hailstorm. Perhaps it is here
a halt is feared? or perhaps it is time
among the bleached clothes, to ask for the stop?

Perhaps here is the knock... But no! to Zerbino
high over the prisons, in the grey
breath of the wind, now a child runs
made of feathers, bringing his face
a palm from the windows, and if he flees
at the blow that with shadow blackens
the air, in the air's ruins appears
the black reserve of the Genovese
gathering — the game of bowls that calms
the noise with slow, slow steps, and in rhyme
closes the thuds of balls within the ark
with the sharpness of guilt. Bends
the ark at that weight of darkness, still
its cord does not halt — it is made
to slip off in silence towards an hour,
where it is probable, an unsteady stop.

And the lights... Can evening have fallen?
what night is preluded? An unearthed
zone shines with crockery and the silent
moon that now covers a silence and airy
light of promised rain. The ark now
turns its prow at Staglieno; if the patron

brings his hand to his mouth, his forehead
is unexpectedly spattered by a distant
swarm of gelid drops that can forbid
the heart's abandon. He draws down
the windows, but now a colorless music
creates still other windows — rare, it streaks
with glimmerings the night, silently skimming
the unscented promise, the quiet
boat proceeds towards another hour
perhaps drawing near to ask for the stop.

And meanwhile what cool rain falls,
nocturnal, on the dark funicular
that now slowly slides and pervades
with silence the zone? While away,
on and on it climbs, vibrating, subtle
in the gentle shade, from a balcony
that a cloud rinses, high, subtle
water of silver is lighted, a rain
more fresh than the breath from the sea
that opens its heart to the patron, now
as he touches timidly the wire whence starts
in the far distance, a drum. The mouth
opens, awed, at that trill, but again
from the washed pavements the city
in the depth proffers voices — another hour
in which the nickel plate cannot read: stop.

And the gentle funicular — where
does it rise, wet and blue, in the basin
of another city damp with sea? where
with its cable, well-oiled, nocturnal,
does it gain other cliffs, and a parade
of girls in love? To the sailors

185

they proffer, departing, their spattered
shoulder on the stones where they sing, where
ever a minute rain falls, more fresh,
on the warmth of these breaths. And at sea
that, most tender still, refreshes
the night with its light, ah, if a moon
appears through the clouds, scenting
the stone like a fish!... The cable —
why not cease here? Is not the hour
this, even in sleep, to ask for the stop?

But the breeze has power, carries away
like the inflexible cord, even the sound
of those fresh sandals and the first voice
that rises above the others. In the white
thunder the sea creates on the bench
overcome by the ark, in a new glimmering
a fog grows thicker — it is the first
pearl dawn that has not the warmth
of figures and sounds, and towards it
the most silent ark dreams of a
probable goal. In the dark bars
along the sea, alas, the lamp of coal
that is lighted for the solitary
woman who scrubs the floor — who knows
now among the glasses of milk the hour
when the passenger can ask for the stop!

For it is fog: fog is fog, and the milk
in the glasses is also fog, and in the eyes
of the woman is fog, who in her slippers
washes the doorway of those meager bars
where Erebus is sure. And Proserpine
or a faded girl, while she rinses
the befogged glasses, it is she

who opens the morning that water
(only water of fog) has in the fog
softened by sun where evanescent
the ark disappears from sight: the white
fog of dawn covers her, and the funicular
already remote is now wan, discolored
in the milky fog where dissolves
the last desire to ask for the time
within that shroud to ask for the stop.

(translated by William Fense Weaver)

TWO SHORT STORIES

BY

JOYCE LUSSU

THE MATRIARCH

Raimonda Orrú was often called Donna Raimonda because she had the finest house in town, boasting a glass cabinet crammed with porcelain knick-knacks in the dining room and even an overstuffed sofa and six chairs to match. She was a pious soul and a true Christian, as the Bishop declared the time he dropped in for refreshments after dedicating the new convent. Once very beautiful, Donna Raimonda now maintained a proud, formidable air, the more awesome because she was totally paralyzed in both legs. She sat up all day in an armchair and every evening her daughters carried her bodily to bed, bringing her downstairs again in the morning after washing, combing and dressing her with loving solicitude, encasing her legs in warm woollen stockings and slipping stylish new shoes on her dead feet. Efisia, the eldest daughter, had white hair and looked even older than her mother. The next was Felicina, who was always silent and would sit for hours on end with a prayer book in her hands. Marietta, the youngest, was thirty-five but looked considerably older because she did almost all the work with only the assistance of an old serving woman who had been in the household employ so long that by now she was virtually one of the family. Of eleven children born to Donna Raimonda, only these three were left to her, except Giovambattista, but he was a good-for-nothing who spent his time wandering aimlessly about the plowed fields and pastures,

never venturing beyond his mother's estate, not even when
he married the daughter of Uncle Pietro, the grain thresher.
His bride had been a vivacious girl, as quick as an ant and
cheerful as a nightingale, and everyone believed she would
rouse her husband from his stupor and persuade him to go
and live in the city. Donna Raimonda, however, insisted that
she spend at least the first year with the family so that she
could absorb the household traditions and learn to cook in
the manner to which Giovambattista was accustomed; but
after a few months, the poor girl contracted pleurisy and her
lungs gave out and finally she passed on to a better world.
It was a grievous thing for Donna Raimonda because her
daughter-in-law had been a tractable girl who soon learned
to suppress her exhuberance, to move about the house in
silence and perform her tasks with diligence; moreover, it
would have been comforting to have a grandson carry on the
family name. But all that had happened long before, and the
ways of the Lord are infinite and at least there were still her
three daughters to stay with her and take care of her and
have everything done according to usage, indeed it is a sad
fate for old people when their children move away and leave
them in servant's hands or abandon them to strangers.

Efisia never considered matrimony because she limped,
having injured a leg in a fall when she was a little girl. Felicina once had a proposal of marriage, but that was twenty
years before; it came just at the time of the accident and
naturally when she saw her mother paralyzed for life, she
knew she must stay at home with her and therefore had to
decline. Marietta was likewise devoted to Donna Raimonda,
even more devoted than her sisters. She was always with her,
always smiling and trying to cheer or amuse her, never betraying the slightest impatience when Donna Raimonda flew
into fits of temper; on the contrary, she would stroke her
hair and call her « my spoiled little mamma » and often sit
on a stool at her feet and hold her hands, as she did when
she was a child. She would cook succulent roasts, comb her
mother's white hair as if she were a queen, supervise the ser-

vants, transact all business with the tenant farmers and collect the family's share of the profits, always treating others with such gentle sweetness that everyone wished her well. She was moreover very devout and always the first at Sunday mass, going with the old woman servant at five in the morning and returning later with Efisia and Felicina. Except for a few pious worshippers, the church was almost empty at the first mass and it would have been better for her had she always found it so empty, but one morning as she pushed open the door to leave, she heard a man's voice close behind. « Marietta », he called.

« O Corraine! » she exclaimed in surprise, and a red flame flared up in her cheeks. In the church, Corraine had been watching her from a distance. Filled with pity and tenderness, he had observed how bowed and gray and faded she was, so different from the Marietta he remembered, a young girl learning to weave or playing with the daughter of Uncle Pietro, the thresher; and seeing her blush, Corraine reflected that even now she was worthy of far more than a man's mere pity and tenderness.

« You've returned to town », said Marietta, « and not come to see us? »

« I have come », Corraine replied, « but they wouldn't let me in ». He glared at the servant woman, who stood her ground silent and unflinching, as tall and erect as a pillar. Then Marietta felt all her brief happiness recede into the depths of her heart and lie there like a heavy stone at the bottom of a well. Hastily she bade him goodbye and left the church, sensing the servant woman's gaze pierce her back and a dark cloud of guilt gather over her thoughts.

« The mistress told me not to admit him », the old woman said. Marietta was too rattled to ask the reason why, atthough she could well imagine, and she knew that her mother was right and she was wrong. For the next seven days, she lived through the long, empty hours as if in a fog and when Sunday morning came, she dressed as usual for mass, determined to go at all costs. The servant was sitting in the hall, pulling out wool to restuff the mattresses when she saw Marietta. « Wouldn't it be better », she asked, « to finish what we're doing and go to the eight o'clock mass? » But when Marietta started for the door without replying, she wrapped her black shawl over her head and followed.

In church, Marietta went directly to her pew, looking neither to right nor left. When mass was over, with lowered eyes she hurried to the door and slipped out, not even pausing at the holy-water fount. Corraine caught up with her at the foot of the steps outside. Reaching out to stop her, he placed four fingers lightly on her wrist and, although he hardly touched her through the wool sleeve, to his amazement he realized he was trembling. Marietta stopped abruptly and withdrew her arm. She, too, was trembling.

« Marietta », said Corraine, « when can I come and talk to your mother? »

« O Corraine! » Marietta murmured in a low voice. But then her courage failed and she allowed herself to be dragged away by the servant woman, who accompanied her home and took her straight up to her room, without stopping in as usual for a moment's chat with Donna Raimonda.

« I'll tell the mistress you don't feel well », the woman said, and added: « Remember, your mother is a saint ».

And I'm a sinner, Marietta said to herself, sitting on the bed and clasping her temples between her palms. But why, why mustn't I see him? I want to see him, see him, see him. Only for ten minutes, but ten minutes all for myself, for him and me alone, the two of us together without anyone watching or spying, to see him for ten minutes can't be sinful, I don't mean any evil, blessed Virgin, I've prayed to you so many times, let me see him for ten minutes, it wouldn't be a sin, even Mamma got married, O blessed Virgin Mary, please help me, please tell Mamma it's not sinful. And Marietta grasped her wrist where she had felt Corraine's fingers through the wool and pressed it against her cheek and then she dropped her hands in her lap, having no strength left to clasp them in prayer.

Suffering great torment, thus she passed another week. The servant woman watched her and said nothing, her sisters watched her and said nothing and her mother watched her and scolded her for not doing everything the way she always did. Until Saturday night when she could no longer endure the raging passion and, closeted alone with her mother for a few moments, she summoned up all her strength and said:

« Mamma, I've seen Corraine Sulis ».

Donna Raimonda lifted her head and sat very still, staring at her daughter without blinking an eye.

« I've seen Corraine Sulis, Mamma », Marietta repeated, and her words sounded like a sob.

« If you've seen Corraine Sulis », said Donna Raimonda in a clear voice but hardly moving her white lips, « then I don't wish you to see him ever again ».

Marietta fled to her room and writhed on the bed, beating her fists against her forehead. The servant, having heard everything, followed to spy outside her door. « Dear Virgin, dear blessed Virgin », the old woman heard her lament, « why why must it be a sin? » Then she cried for many hours until at last she was apparently quiet again; but suddenly in the middle of the night, she got up, all disheveled, with clutched fists and a wild look in her eye, and she began to rant: I hate her, that old woman, I hate her I hate her, why doesn't she die, what's she waiting for to die, she's the one who's damned, not I not I. O dear Virgin, if you love me, kill that old woman! The servant wondered whether Marietta was losing her wits and she ought, therefore, to go into the room, but she decided it would be better to continue keeping guard outside and so she remained squeezed in her dark corner, stiff and immobile, not even stirring when she saw Marietta leave her room a little before dawn wearing her best dress and a silk shawl, her neatly combed hair bound in a blue scarf, as if she had fixed herself up for a tryst with her lover. But the serving woman knew well enough that she was not going to her lover and she began to calculate how long it would take her to arrive at the river and how long it would be before the villagers brought the news. Meanwhile, she sat in the hall, pulling out wool for the mattresses and pondering what she could say to keep the truth from Donna Raimonda, because it would be wrong for such a pious woman to suffer, knowing that the flesh of her flesh had harbored a damned soul.

THE BAMBINA

They were happy when the new baby was born because it was a girl, while the other five were all boys, even the three that died. It is no simple matter to bring up six children and each time another one arrived, Antonia hoped it would be the last, instead every year she found herself pregnant again. Still, children are sent by Providence and one must accept them in humble resignation. After an extremely difficult delivery the year before, the doctor had recommended an operation with a warning that Antonia would almost certainly not survive another confinement; and when she mentioned it at confession, Don Gesumino rebuked her because it is a sin to reject children sent by Providence, and he quoted a verse which said something about the Lord feeding birdlings in their nests and not letting them die of hunger. Thus, when Antonia discovered that she was carrying another child, she bore it with the same equanimity as one accepts a hailstorm or the loss of an ox killed in a fall over the precipice. The last confinement was difficult too, with Antonia hovering between life and death for three days, but both mother and daughter were brought through safely, and Antonia at bottom was really very pleased that it was a girl because girls are always a consolation to their mammas and this one was especially adorable, with a tiny, wide pale face and big black eyes. Antonia doted on her with the same loving tenderness she had felt for her first-born so many years before, as if she had forgotten all the pain and drudgery of rearing five sons. She smiled like a bride again when she held the infant to her breast, calling it her morning star, her precious gold Napoleon, the most beautiful little girl in all the world. Even Egidio was pleased, and when he came home dead tired after hoeing the field, an hour and a half on foot beyond the stream, he saw that gentle smile on Antonia's face as she clasped the child in her arms and he recalled the first time he had ever spoken to her, once when she and her girl friends, armed with long sticks, were on their way to gather prickly pears. She had thick, black tresses then and she would toss back her head to shake them out, always looking straight before her, and she was exhuberant and ripe as a pomegranate about to burst, whereas now she was as withered as a winter apple, with sparse hair and even some of her teeth missing. But for the baby girl she found her youthful smile again, as if there were still some mysterious charm in life, something more than the squalor and the dirty kitchen and the boys forever shouting and hurting themselves and the rags to mend when thread was so dear that he had no idea how he could buy it, and the shabby bed without linen and only one greasy, threadbare blanket reeking with a stench of the ague, which was bothering Egidio at the time, and the five small brothers, some lean, some swollen, but all with sallow faces and big eyes round with fever.

The baby girl also caught the fever and her face became thin and sharp like parchment, her eyes wide, and she whimpered constantly. She was a very good child, she never cried noisily, indeed tears never even came into her eyes as she stared around her, appearing to understand everything. Then, when the fever abated and she seemed to be getting well again, she caught dysentery and could not digest her mother's milk; in fact, Antonia herself was so wasted away that she gave no milk, only a thin, watery fluid.

The doctor came to call and afterwards went directly to see Don Gesumino for a confidential talk, saying it was the priest's fault that Antonia was breaking her already ruined heart and asking what he was doing to these poor people. Their real sickness, he declared, was hunger; they were so badly underfed that it was an ironic joke for a doctor to give them prescriptions and put them on diets. Don Gesumino folded his hands and said we're all poor in this village, Signor Doctor, what misery, what misery, the Lord is punishing us for our sins; but then that evening he thought it over and instructed the servant to kill one of the chickens that had ceased laying eggs and take it to Antonia to make a broth for herself and the *bambina*. When Antonia saw the chicken, she began to weep; she caught the infant up in her arms and kissed it and declared that the Virgin Mary had not abandoned her after all at this wretched time when she had been without bread for so many days because the drought had destroyed the crop and it was no use even to re-sow the parched fields. But when the broth was ready and Antonia saw the five little boys standing around the pot and watching it with shining, feverish eyes, she lost her courage and could not swallow even a spoonful, and so she told them that the broth was all for their little sister because she was suffering from dysentery and had to get well.

But deep inside, she knew the *bambina* was not going to get well. The other three had also had that opaque film over their cheeks and that same grave look and those pitifully inert little hands, and they had died in the very same way, they, too, had died from dysentery. She fed the child spoonfuls of the broth, but without hope, then put her back in the big bed, tucking her under the rank-smelling blanket which she could not wash because it was the only one she possessed. From under her little baby's cap saturated with sweat, the infant fixed her dry eyes on her mother and Antonia's heart sank, she no longer had the fortitude to smile and call her my little morning star. « This one will die, too, I'm going to lose this one, too, » she murmured over and over again, lost and defeated and filled with a strange anguish not unlike remorse, as if it were all her fault.

Egidio could not stay home that night because the grapes were ripe and unless he kept close guard, thieves would surely strip his little vineyard of the fruit. He told Antonia that he would do this: he would carry the little one to the cemetery the next afternoon because he wanted to be present at the burial too, but he had to work in the morning and absolutely could not go before afternoon. He leaned over to kiss the child and she stared at him with wide, round eyes and drawn lips; her little cheeks were yellow and sunken and there was no doubt about it now that she was going. When she passed away at daybreak, Don Gesumino came and said many things to Antonia as she stood at the fire like an automaton, preparing a soup for the boys. We are all sinful, he said, and we must bear our sorrows with resignation; a little angel as white as snow has flown up to Paradise and other little angels as white as snow are descending to earth. And as she stood against the sunlight streaming through the open door, he observed that she was pregnant again and, tapping her on the shoulder and smiling, he cited several verses which said something about divine Providence never abandoning the honest and the good.

(translated by William Packer)

POEMS

BY

FRANCO FORTINI

FOR A COLLECTION OF VERSES

Without asking of these voices pride
Or power or delirium; in still syllables
To rest. The avenues beyond the curtains
Of the window; the city; the people;
The events; all now I know
Certain of names necessary and exact.
In this light, a moment, I rest.
And from here I say words to the listener
While the day lasts. I know the darkness
How it enchants the skies and the cities
How it floods in the heart. An hour at least
To name the things hoped for
By men who come, and return
From work and in these evenings watch
With even silences
The avenues that go into winter.

THE WORKSHOP

This vast workshop
Of things and of skulls
Where we work
Hardened at heart
Traitorous workshop
Of disorder and ashes
Of sickness and sores
Sometimes beyond the windows
A blade of grass stands out in the fields
Or a tiny leaf
On delicate branches

Hardened at heart
We observe it.
And thus we know
What is evil and good
The shade and the light and all
The living opposites
Of the sound of the white-hot
Hammers of the workshop
Amid dust and disorder
Our hearts in agony
And in profound joy.

FRIENDSHIP

A single word
A single word can do
A single word
From the friend with the live black eyes
And his familiar patience
To live and to watch
The dusty bay-wreaths
The habitual symbols

Of Florence and the indifferent heavens
Where one day miracles passed
And his knowing
His dying and of joy
A single word
And a single hope can do.

Weak infinitely weak
Delicate unsure improvident amused
Lost in the mists
Of vague loves, of obstinate pains
And resistent to the good
A single word
Does for a day. Thus from misery
Rises friendship and desire
Like the lovely rain
That breaks the dried leaves, washes everything
And shines and revives.

TO HIS WIFE

— Where are you, white heart
Only closed to you heart
Confidence of the veil
In the curve of the wind,
Feather of air, you, free
Cloud that varies in the wind?

Where from every ill
Can you retain your form?
Without print or sign.
My mind thinks of you,
Here where all is time
And labor of ashes.

— Why do you call afar
If nothing separates us
Why extend your hand
As if you were alone?
If you give me your hand
Everything will return.

Things bare and pure
That love those loving
And a place amid the air
For our two faces
For our smiles
A place without pain.

— *Where are you, white woman*
Closed within my shadow
Rose of all my future?
When over my mind
It is evening, amid the shadow
You rise, intact, rose.

— Don't ask afar
Sad man, rest.
If you sleep, I am then
Like that girl
I was, and there is nothing
That is not hopeful for me.

— *Where are you, my hope*
Moon of the morning
White dew of peace?

— Don't seek afar
Look, here is my hand
Listen, here is my voice.

(translated by William Fense Weaver)

THE GIRLS OF SANFREDIANO

BY

VASCO PRATOLINI

A TOUGH DISTRICT

The Sanfrediano quarter is on the wrong side of the Arno, a huge pile of houses that lies along the left bank of the river, between the church of the Carmine and the slopes of Bellosguardo. Seen from above, it seems to be surrounded by the Medicean bastions and Palazzo Pitti, as if they were buttresses; and there the Arno runs at its widest, finding gentle, broad, and wonderful the curve that washes the Cascine gardens. Whenever civilization has become nature itself, the smile of God, terrible, fascinating and immobile, what perfection remains then, surrounds Sanfrediano and exalts it. But all is not gold that glisters. By contrast, Sanfrediano is the unhealthiest section of the city; in the heart of its streets, as densely populated as anthills, are located the Central Refuse Dump, the public dormitory, the barracks. The greater part of its slums is the home of rag-pickers, and of those who cook the intestines of cattle to make their living from them and from the broth that is the product. The broth, by the way, is tasty, and the Sanfredianini, who despise it, are nourished on it and buy it by the gallon.

The houses are ancient because of their stones, and even more because of their squalor. One backed up against another, they form an immense block, broken here and there by the openings of the side streets, where the sudden, incredible breezes enter from the river, and by the squares, vast and airy, extended harmoniously, like parade grounds. The

201

happy, bickering clamor of the people brings these places to life: the sounds of the second-hand man and the ragpicker, the worker in the nearby repair shops, the office clerk, the artisan who works with gold, or in marble, or with furs. And even the women, most of them, have a job. Sanfrediano is a little republic of women who do work at home: they make the straw coverings that go around demijohns, they sew trousers, take in laundry, weave mats. With their work, substracted from the cares of the house, they earn what they call the « minimum extra », a family needs, when it is numerous — as they almost always are — and when the work of the man, if there is one, brings in only the bread and what goes with it.

These people of Sanfrediano, the toughest and liveliest of the Florentines, are the only ones who retain authentically the spirit of a people that has always been able to make something graceful even out of clumsiness, and whose ingenuity is a perpetual effrontery. The Sanfredianini are sentimental and pitiless at once: their idea of justice is symbolized by the enemy's remains hung to a lamp-post; and their idea of Paradise, summed up in a proverb, is poetic and vulgar: a Utopian place where there is an abundance of millet and a shortage of birds. They believe in God because, as they say, they believe « in the hands and the eyes that made us »; and logically enough, reality seems to them finally the best of all possible dreams. Their hope lies in what they can make from day to day — which is never enough. Precisely because the foundation of their spirit is paved with incredulity, they are obstinate and active; and their participation in historic events has been intelligent, constant, even prophetic at times, though perhaps disordered. They have only covered over with more modern ideals their myths and banners; their light-heartedness, their intransigence, and their predjudices have remained the same. And if the shades of the Great move between piazza della Signoria and the tombs of Santa Croce to light up the icy spirits of modernity with the sacred fire, then in the alleyways of Sanfrediano the people that was contemporaneous with those Fathers moves still in flesh and blood, next door. The few of them who won a humble, malignant glory continue to exist; Boccaccio's Buffalmacco and Burchiello are alive. Those same women and maidens of whom the ancient romances and chronicles are full: lovely, genteel, audacious, shameless; those faces, the speech, the gestures in which chastity itself acquires a mysterious and irresistible enticement, and licentiousness becomes explicit, unaware and disarmed by candor — take one step here, and you meet them all.

Among the girls, because of her youth, her beauty, and her toughness, one who works covering chairs with straw is the standard-bearer. It was she who wove and then sprang the trap that caught up Bob and his girl friends.

It is an adventure of our own time, and it deserves telling.

TOSCA, TOSCHINA

Her name is Tosca, she is eighteen, and she has had the straw strips in her hands since she was born; she played with them in the hamper that acted as her crib, set on the pavement on the fine days, near her mother, who rewove chairs and, to feed the child, arranged her schedule by the Cestello bell, which rings every hour like a clock. Now Tosca is quicker than her mother, she turns out more « pieces » in the course of the day; even if her mother still works nearby, her fifty years weigh on her arms; but more than the weight of her labor there is that of the mourning for her son dead in Africa ten years ago. This is a grief which Tosca has not suffered deeply; she was in the second grade when her brother left, and in these years so many things have happened to her: all the things that happen that happen in adolescence, at the first discovery of girlhood, in Sanfrediano.

Tosca grew up in the war years; she saw the side win which she had heard them whisper ought to win. No particular sacrifices were imposed on her, at least none different from those to which she was accustomed; her father hasn't stopped going to the shop, and chairs to reweave haven't ever been wanting. While her body was developing in health and beauty, her spirit suffered none of those troubles that leave a mark. And when the first adverse blows came to her, she knew instinctively how to defend herself. She is a being that life will have to be clever to humiliate, and perhaps will never succeed. Nobody will succeed, and Bob, whom she was there to punish, will remember her tiny face for a long time. Not exactly that face of peaches and cream, as it appeared to him in the summer of '44.

She was sixteen when the war arrived in Sanfrediano, when the shots rang out below her house. There were days of shelling and then others of insurrection. Tosca carried water to the partisans, here and there, through her streets that seemed to have changed their expression, like the people. It was an order she had been given; it was an amusement, too. Her body was bare beneath her slip, and the partisans let their eyes wander when she leaned over to set down the jugs and always a second later, she put her hand to the front of her dress.

« Is Tosca really your name? » they asked her.

« Of course. Why? Are you just discovering me today? »

As a matter of fact, they had been in the mountains, the young men who should have discovered her; she had been a baby, not even a year before, and in the meanwhile « you've exploded », they said to her. She had become a « different matter », a woman; they whistled trying to find an adjective for her; and even in the boldness and self-confidence that their situation had given them, she intimidated them somehow. They weren't able to forget her as they thought they had left her, and their compliments were infantile, like the picture they had kept of her.

« You've become international », they said to her.

And her ready reply always put them off.

« Like the war? »

« It was just to get things started », they said.

« And I'm stopping you », she answered, « here, wet your throat ».

One day, the second day that they were down from the mountains, and Sanfrediano was in rebellion, when the advance guard of the Allied troops had arrived, the bridges were blown, and this side of the Arno was in a state of seige. With the Fascists still shooting from the rooftops, the partisans lined up three « blacks » against the wall in the square of the Carmine. Tosca was opposite, watching, among the people backed up against the houses, who were quiet or else slipped off down the side streets. The windows were all shut, and a monk came and went from the group receiving justice and that of the corpses; there were six, the dead and the still living, whom the monk encouraged and blessed. There was an almost legendary silence, that of a Christ stopped to listen; the rough voices giving orders rang out sharply, with the echo of the shots, in the ruinous light of a suffocating August noon. The wall, marvellous as it was, with the green of the trees that overflowed it from the garden of the convent beyond, was a backdrop, and the sky was so blue as to give it perspective, to relieve it, to blind.

The squad with their red scarves lined up, fired, the three with their backs to the wall cried *viva* (Viva *what* nobody knew; they didn't have time to finish).

« They fell like puppets », Tosca said.

A woman, a wife, near her, made the sign of the cross; Tosca looked at her and smiled.

« Perhaps I spoke out of turn? » she asked, and made the sign of the cross also.

« It would have been better not to speak. Now that they've paid, they're wanting prayers ».

« I'll remember them tonight; now I have to give drink to the thirsty. I'm obeying a commandment. Or am I wrong? »

« You're not wrong », a man said to her. He was missing a leg, and was leaning on his crutch, looking into the sun so as not to see the other three « blacks » whose turn was about to come.

He was an elderly man, who rented out carts, a friend of her father's who had watched her grow up under his very eyes, as he reminded her:

« You're not exactly wrong. Do you think I could have any love for them over there?... My name wouldn't be Barcucci if I didn't say down with the lot of them. Better an innocent man should die, if there is anyone innocent among them, than run the risk of keeping alive one of those that should be done away with ».

« And so? » Tosca said.

« But it's for me to say these, Toschina, because I have white hair, and can say them ».

« O, Barcucci », she exclaimed, « it seems to me you're getting off the track ».

And as she went away, the cripple shouted after her:

« You're growing up all at once... that's what I wanted to say to you ».

« I'll put weights on my head, then », she answered, and she went about the square with her jugs of water, one in each hand.

Suddenly, a partisan popped out of a doorway and drew her in, making her spill half of the water.

« Idiot, don't you see that you're under fire », he said.

« They're firing at those men over there, not at me, after all ».

« Do you think the bullets are on springs then? »

« But if I'm halfway across the square... » she said.

Tosca watched him drink, noticing that as he drank from the jug his hands trembled and the water ran over and wetted his red scarf and his jacket.

« Do I know you? » she asked.

« Of course, you know me. You're Toschina. I used to

be a friend of your brother's. He was a little older than me ».

« And you're from via del Campuccio. You're Bob, of course. How stupid of me. Who doesn't know you, Casanova? You're Leda's boy friend ».

« I used to be », he said, « about a thousand years ago ».

They fired, and Bob shut his eyes, raised his shoulders as if to take cover; it was an instinctive movement, over in a flash. This time the three who fell didn't say *viva anything*, only one of the three cried *alala'*, then they heard a voice in the group of partisans, in the middle of the square, that began a song, and the chorus joined in.

« I've got to leave you, beautiful », Bob said, « Give me another gulp ».

« What were you doing behind the door? » she asked, a little suspicious.

He set the jug down. « I was on guard », he said.

« Guarding what? who? The walls? »

Now Bob was no longer upset, he winked his left eye, and laughed. He had white teeth and a smile that tore the hearts out of the girls of Sanfrediano.

« Keep me in mind », he said. « When the party's over I'll come and see you ».

And he went off, running towards his companions, lifting his Tommy-gun and balancing it on his shoulder with the heel of his hand; and she was left with the doubt that his reddishness was due, not to the heat, but to fear; and this impression, instead of leading her to despise him, gave her a strange sense of tenderness, of faith.

« Yes, come », she replied. « I have some cordial made with arsenic I can offer you ».

Then the rest of the city was liberated, and soon everything became a memory; her father was back in his shop, somebody had taken up the chair business again, and in her girl's life, the war having passed, love came to take its place.

Not yet *love*, but the waiting for it, the listening to every feeling and thought during the day, the attention to herself, her hair, choosing the right lipstick and the right clothes, the talking and discussing about love, and arguing about it with her girl friends; and then the excitement, the perplexity, the indifference, always disguised by a nonchalant haughtiness, with which she welcomed a glance, the casual compliments of the street, the familiarity of the boys who had known her as a baby, who had been wet behind the ears when she was too, and who now invited her to dance, offered her a treat, a cigarette; and at the dance, the strangers, even those from the other districts, the contact of their bodies, the insensitivity or the attraction they inspired in her. The revelation, in all of this, of her feminity, which became the knowledge that she was beautiful, and capable of loving, and her own fundamental nature, noisy and exclusive, which adapted itself to this sentiment, the devotion and the animosity together with which she wanted to know it, her love. Which was Bob's already, and had been Bob's at once, as soon as Bob kept his promise, and broke his engagement with Silvana.

Then Leda was lost in the long night of time, and even Silvana didn't count for Bob any more, neither Leda, nor Silvana, nor the others had ever meant anything to him; they had been « episodes, that's all », just fooling around.

« The others? What others? I know about Silvana; she told me herself, we were friends. If I didn't know know that I love you so much — this is the first time it's happened to me — I wouldn't have done this to her for all the money in the world. Who are these others? How many of them have there been? »

« Zero », he answered. « All of them zero. I feel the same way you do. You're the first for me, too ».

« Listen, Bob », she said to him, « You're seven years older than I am. You're twenty-five, and I'm eighteen. You're a man, and I'm a woman. But if you leave me like you've left the others — who they are and how many there are I don't even want to know — I'll take those two eyes of

yours and make a pair of buttons. And that moustache of
yours — I'll make you eat it ».

« Good for you », he said. « Shall we try? »

« Remember », Tosca repeated, « I'm serious about us ».

Her voice was uneven, almost angry, loving.

« I'm a Sanftrediano girl, and don't you forget it ».

THE TOOLS OF THE TRADE

The girls of Sanfrediano, whether they are beautiful or
ugly, with faces that are pimply or like a Madonna's, are
to be recognized by their hands. These are their mystery,
their most secret pride, and their dowry; they are white,
milk-white, with fingers that are long and tapering. These
hands come out miraculously pure from the trials of a hundred occupations to which they are applied. With them,
the girls of Sanfrediano weave chairs: it is a trick of magic
how the strips of colored straw are pulled out on the form; the
girls handle the skeletons of the chairs like a piece of equipment, they roll it around before they give that snip of the
scissors that evens up the straw at the place where it is sewn.
Harmony is in their gestures; they sing and talk of their
loves, as they sit one next the other in a line on the side-
walks, during the good season. And another trial of patience
is the work of the linen seamstresses: what they edge and
embroider comes alive beneath their fingers, becomes flesh
and flower, as they say.

« Silk or cambric, it all ought to be treated like something alive ».

« It's like embroidering on rose-petals ».

« You have to get used to it, then the needle does all
the work ».

« It's easy, if you have good eyes ».

Silvana, who has now put Tosca in the list of her enemies
and considers her, with good reason, the chief of the lot,
is an embroideress whose fingers are worth gold, and in one
of the workshops along the Arno, she is among the most

highly-prized of the workers. The younger Countess Ginori, when she learned to whom she owed the splendor of her wedding attire, sent to the girl's house a box of wedding-candy. But since Silvana, when she read *Married Today*, felt her own wound open again, the kind gift went flying out of the window, precisely at the moment that the garbage truck was passing by, lovely and open, with a halo of flies, and the box of candy came to rest there.

« Bob still sticks in your throat, doesn't he, Silvana? » said her sister, who still wears short stockings and works as a box-maker.

« What an idea! He's the one who keeps hanging around me and can't make up his mind between me and I don't know who... ».

And then she burst into tears on his sister's shoulder.

« You'll learn in a year or so », she said, « what it is to be jilted and be left... ».

And the child, still bitter because of the candy now lost forever, said, « Why, Silvana, I'm ashamed to call you sister. What I mean is: God gave you two good hands, didn't he? Why don't you change that boy's face a bit? »

They stand behind the counters of the stores, the pastry-shops, with those fresh hands and fingers, smelling of sugar; they go into the factories, the washrooms, into the carton-makers, the laundries, and, dirty with ink, into the printer's; they separate rags and shreds, and with sand and brushes they rinse the bottles collected from the scrap-men, covered with filth, yet their hands come out neat, clear as the eyes that they raise from the embroidery frame after nine hours of work, white, crystal hands, with nails whose enamel is a kind of blood that asks to be sucked. The hands are their souls, which they wear displayed, to show, unknowingly certain, that their spirits are loyal, industrious, lovable, passionate, and also when necessary, destructive and explosive

And after their hands comes that other mirror, their eyes, those lights opened wide on the hearts that belong to them. Even where the features of the face are vulgar, and the limbs perhaps graceless, the expression of the eyes can always lighten them, convince one of the absoluteness of their feelings. On such faces as theirs, even hypocrisy (and there is that also; Gina in full of it, in spite of herself, to the roots of her hair) declares itself and becomes a virtue.

Gina met Silvana and said to her: « You look a little rum down. Why is that? »

« I've got a cold, do you mind? »

« Who knows where you got it? »

« Well, not from you, anyway. I'll always be able to take care of you ».

« Good-bye, Miss Light Fingers, and if you should see Bob tonight, say hello to him from me ».

She went to see Tosca and sat down beside her on a bench, among the strips of colored straw.

« We've always been friends, and since I'm a year or so older than you are... ».

« Now listen here, Gina, for days now you've been coming here to give me these heart-to-heart talks, ever since I told you I was engaged, telling me that I should be careful, that he's a ladies' man, and so on and so forth. You wouldn't have any personal interest in Bob, by any chance? »

« Me? With me Bob never tried anything », Gina said hastily, eating her words, « he knows how I am... and besides, I'm getting married in a month. It's not me; it's someone else whose hands are burning ».

« I can present her with a cake of ice, this someone, if you feel like taking it to her ».

« There's nothing for me to say about it. You were born right here in Sanfrediano, you, Silvana, all of you ».

« And you were born in the Palace of the Signoria, if I remember rightly ».

They are always in love, the girls of Sanfrediano. Their nails were made for scratching, and naked, they are garlanded with bashfulness. If they have ten fiancés, it is always the first of them that they end up marrying. And he will find his wife a virgin certainly, and an expert in kissing. But if he is slow in making his peace, or in the interim is too ostentatiously jealous, or isn't jealous enough; if he becomes involved with another Sanfrediano girl instead of courting the « sluts » of the other quarters, she — his first — « just to spite him » will give herself to the first one she thinks of, perhaps the least likeable, among those who are courting her. And she'll let her man know about it. Then he waits for her where she works, or at the door of her house, and he slaps her and tells her to hurry up with her trousseau, because in a few months they have to get married, wasn't that the agreement, in spring? Naturally, other slaps — but with the fists doubled up — will have been given earlier to the man who enjoyed her, who will defend himself, but not pass to the offensive. This all happens, of course, when it happens; but that isn't seldom. Generally, the girls make it perfectly clear when it is the moment for their man to come back to them, and he (if it is really *he*), the first, doesn't wait for a tick of the clock.

Not Bob, however. He is the friend of all, and a Sanfredianino like them all, but still he goes into a category by himself. He has always been the first one for all of his girls, and every time he has let the wheel go on turning; he doesn't know how to give that kind of slap. He is an elegant and handsome boy, and he insists that life is a carousel that you have to know how to turn, and that girls are oranges to be squeezed. « You make a little hole in the top, like in an egg, and then you suck in the juice; and afterwards there's always someone who'll trade the shell for a fresh egg ». Bob is as bright and as vulgar as the brilliantine on his hair, and most probably, in the stories that he tells of his feats, truth is overcome by exaggeration. Anyway, we believe that he's met the person who can mess up the part in his hair. In the meanwhile, Tosca has begun to call him by his real name.

« What is this Bob? Aldo is a nice name. And besides, nice or not, it's yours. And I like it ».

THE YOUTH WITH THE BEAUTIFUL LASHES

For a long time now he has been called Aldo only at home, by his parents and his brothers. He has two brothers, but they are different from him, as he is fond of saying to them, even to Rolando, who is older than he is. Both are passionate hunters, inspired by their father, and they can't think of anything else or better to talk of than guns, traps, game, or their trade, which is house-painting. They don't smoke if it is necessary — as it often is, now that work is scarce — to give the dog the bran he needs; they spend the evening preparing cartridges, cleaning barrels and sights, and on Sunday, when the season is open, they leave the house while it is really still Saturday night, and he meets them as he is coming home, all of them in their high boots, dressed for the hunt. What does it matter to them that their regular clothes always need mending? They know that when their jackets and the seats of their trousers have become like spiderwebs, sooner or later there is a cast-off suit of Aldo's which, when they put it on, gives them the feeling of baptizing a Sunday suit. Not that Aldo gives them these clothes; he sells them at a friendly price, and for that matter, they are always good as new; on him, despite the wear of the office desk, suits last as if they were on a mannequin in a store.

He has an instinctive respect for his person, and his gestures are naturally controlled; even in squabbles, if he happens to get caught in one, he always comes out without a wrinkle. And with all this, he still remains a youth full of life, who doesn't spare himself in the course of his day, who at the gymnasium can give himself a workout on the rings, and before he went into military service and gave up his dream of meeting Jesse Owens, clocked 11: 1 in the hundred meters.

He's different, but he's very much attached to his people, and he wouldn't feel that he loved his family if he couldn't

213

criticize them and be indignant about each of their actions,
the most childish ones. They are a disorderly family, exactly
the kind of people he cannot bear, his very opposite, and one
day, when his mother was ill and they needed money, none
of them thought of the guns; instead he took the three suits
he had in the closet, his two pairs of shoes — those for dancing and the moccasins — and went to pawn them. And since
the sum wasn't enough, he took the cameo ring off his finger
and pushed it across the counter to the clerk. Then he came
home and said: « We're lucky. I found some penicillin that
wasn't expensive; let's hope it isn't made out of water ».

Now, after a year, putting aside so much a month, he
has come back into possession of all his things. He isn't mi-
serly, he knows how to budget, and his salary is sufficient
for him. And in this period of depression, neither his father
nor his brothers earns more than he does. So now the « chair-
warmer », the clerk, can look without humiliation at their
hands where the sweat is encrusted with splatterings of white-
wash and paint. The passion for hunting ends up wearing
out the edges of their shirts. On the other hand, from the
eighteen thousand lire that he gets in his envelope, he gives
half to his mother and the rest he dedicates to his elegance.
He is a sparing smoker, and the events of the day he can
learn from the radio or from the headlines posted at the
newsstands; his thirst for culture is more than quenched by
a weekly magazine; at times, since he is known not to be a
Fascist and since he recalls that he lives in Sanfrediano, he
buys the Communist daily and, as soon as he is across the
Arno, he folds it with the title-page on the inside. The movies, dancing (of which he is passionately fond), and his
other minor pleasures he pays for with his billiard game; he
could live off it, if he wanted to, but the profession doesn't
tempt him, in spite of his ability. There is a moral basis in
this destroyer of hearts; he never set foot, for example, in
the houses of prostitution. If a group of his frinds are headed
in that direction, he leaves them, and this attitude of his is
variously interpreted. Anyway, he says that he would feel

dirty if he had been there, that the brothel is a sore of society, a scandal, and above all, as far as he is concerned, there is also a principle of hygeine to be respected. At the same time, football and sport in general attract him less and less: on Sunday afternoons he prefers to go a little earlier to the district's dance hall, where the girls devour him with their eyes and line up to be invited by Bob to dance the boogie-woogie.

But if he is Bob in Sanfrediano, as soon as he has crossed the Ponte alla Carraia and started up via della Vigna, which leads to the center of the city, he finds himself suddenly reduced in stature, surrounded by the anonymous, become simply another good-looking boy, a Bob among Bobs, and not even the most striking of them. Thus as he is behind his clerk's window the impression he makes is of an entirely different kind, and the public's respect is equal to their impatience and their coarse language. He is an employee of the city, attached to the Ration Papers office, and he is a clerk who, because he is casual and smart, has been able to secure the Claims Window for himself. His colleagues respect him because they find him bright, always ready, and always on their side in matters that call for solidarity; and also the female fellow-workers, with whom he carries on a veiled and lofty courtship, which never exceeds the limits of the courtesy and adulation due to their sex. He neither gives nor asks, returns what he receives, an employee who will never advance very far, but will never lose his post, either. As soon as he has passed the front door of the building, its world belongs to him no more; he is well aware that his realm is Sanfrediano, his strength lies in his knowing enough not to try going beyond its boundaries. For that matter, he has no such desires; Sanfrediano is all his life, a hunting preserve all for him. He is a hunter different from the others in his family, he sets up his shooting-blinds elsewhere, and with the pool-cue or the bowling-ball in his hand, he sets an aim with an eye so sharp that his father and brothers would dream of having it for their gunsight. And if billiards procures him the admiration of his friends, and rounds out his budget, the girls represent his real sport, his art, and his religion.

He was still a boy when he had a first fiancee, then a second, a third, and from each of them he detached himself, in time, naturally, since the next one attracted him. « I made a mistake. You're not my type. I love her. Goodbye and thanks ». This had been his way of taking his leave, singular because it was inexplicable, and abrupt, perhaps the morning after the tenderest of conversations. He had wanted to be loyal, and his sincerity had always been misunderstood; he pictured himself as brutal, languid, sensitive, *extraordinary*, when he was probably no more than a boy obeying his own instincts, telling himself that he was about to meet his bride. And so, the poorly concealed sorrow, the confidences and the tears of the abandoned ones, were stored up like honey in the spirit of the girls of Sanfrediano, who took to spying as he passed, considering him as their young heart and their bright fantasy suggested to them. The legend of a neighborhood heart-breaker is born much in this way. And his athlete's excellence, also his supremacy as a fighter among those of his own age, his elegance and nonchalance, together with the splendor of his eyes (these gifts of nature, since they were rarely brightened by the light of intelligence) did the rest. Sanfrediano became for him a tree in bloom; he had only to cast his glance and stretch out his hand, and at his touch the hardest hulls opened and gave him their fruit. And he liked his role, and the game for him became a play where, repeating his part, he ended by assimilating and making his own the feelings of the character he was portraying. We will be seeing him at the test, this Don Giovanni of Sanfrediano, and he himself will tell us of what stuff he is made, at the appearance of *his* Commendatore.

Now, at his back, as he walked bold and proud through the streets of the quarter, with his suit impeccable, his hair and shoes one enormous glitter, already the remarks began to rise. It was the kind of murmuring that consolidates the dictator's position, while at the same time it begins to gnaw at his throne.

« The boy with the lovely lashes ».

« Everyone wants him, but nobody takes him ».

« Here he comes, the cock of the walk ».

« Look out, girls, the Grand Duke is passing by ».

And hence the name, which he had become proud of winning for himself, of the man who, on the screen, had kindled with passion and reduced in consumption the most beautiful, most talented, and most popular of actreeses. The girls never tired of going to see that film at the Orfeo Cinema in Piazza de' Nerli, where the poster was up for nine weeks, and the parents and the grandmothers went, reminded of La Traviata; all of Sanfrediano was moved, since for the them the prostitute redeemed by love remains the highest example of humanity, of poetry, and of edification. And as the grandmothers had sighed for Armando Duplessis, the person become a myth, the mothers in their turn had identified him with Rudolph Valentino and called their handsome men by the name of Valentino, so the young girls of Sanfrediano (every generation has its myth, progressively more inert and static as decadence requires) discovered in Robert Taylor their ideal of manhood. And Aldo Sernesi seemed Bob to them. And Bob he was.

« He's Bob », one said.

« They're twins ».

« They must have had the same mother ».

« Come on, Bob », shouted a loudmouth in the audience. « Laugh. Let's see your teth ».

The remark was like the slash of a razor, with the characteristic bite of Sanfrediano, and in the orchestra of the Orfeo Cinema there was a clamor of applause and dissension.

Anyway, from that time on, he smiled more often, and when the actor in a later film appeared with a moustache, the Bob of Sanfrediano also let a hesitant toothbrush grow over his lip.

« I love you, not him », Tosca went on, the first evening

they were out walking, an engaged couple, along the Arno.
« And besides, Bob is out of fashion now. If anything, you
ought to be called Tyrone. But you're Aldo, and that's that,
and from now on I'll scratch anyone that calls you Bob.
And, Aldo, if you really love me, you should cut off that strip
of anchovy over your mouth ».

GOOD WORK, BOB

She was leaning against the iron railing that protects
the apse of Cestello, in the corner far from the street-light,
and opposite them under the parapet, the Arno was swollen
and the dam filled the air with its noise. He put his arm
around her waist, and Tosca trusted herself to him, like something that folded, gently, and her lips had the taste of a
girl who is virginal and in bloom. Then she slipped from
his clutch, lifted her head, and held herself, her hands inside
the rails, a few steps away. He joined her, and felt that she
was panting, tenderly aroused. He smiled, master of himself,
Bob, whose kisses could turn a girl inside out.

This girl, who had blossomed during the war and had
been approached, in vain, by every boy in Sanfrediano. He
had looked at her a moment, in the days of the liberation,
and had said to her: « Wait for me ». Then he had let her
« stew », as he said, walking past her while she had the
plaits of straw in her hands and had blushed to be seen
seated so low and in such disorder. He had avoided her purposely at the dance hall, « to make her wait », and had seen
her answer him by offering herself, all red, to her dancing-
partner, proclaiming, openly and childishly, that it was her
defence; and then he had decided, the moment had come,
since Tosca no longer acted bold and smart, but looked at
him with the eyes of a little girl being punished, and with
a fire in those eyes that he knew he had been the one to
light.

He drew up close to her, caressed her, and said: « I know, you feel a kind of trembling... it's love ».

She shook her head, as if to chase away an evil thought or a strong emotion. « No, it's not that », she answered, « you were holding me so tight that you stopped up my mouth and nose, and I couldn't breathe ».

« You're still a baby », he said.

His voice was warm and tender, a man's and a master's.

« You're like a billiard; a single touch and you fall into the pocket... You'll see, without my love, beautiful as you are, you would have become just another ordinary woman, a Sanfredianina, like all of them... Didn't you feel like a queen while I was kissing you? »

She lifted her head and sought his hands, squeezed them, and her voice, on the contrary, betrayed the upheaval that she was trying not to show, and what she attempted to say, clear as it was within her, became more and more meaningless as she went on speaking.

« Perhaps, but now I understand. Like at billiards, you were playing before, but now the pocket is full. But not with me. I've seen you play, my brother used to take me, and with me the game is over, after me there won't be another round... you shouldn't act this way with me, Aldo, I don't like it, it makes me cry. This isn't the way... ».

And suddenly, as if her nature had rebelled against the fiction with which she was surrounding it, the words that she had wanted to disguise an amorous picture, came out homely and explicit from her lips, and her voice itself recovered its usual, high-spirited tone.

« Anyway, what is all this billiard talk? You mustn't act like a movie star with me, the way you did with the others. I don't want any smart talk. With me you have to be sincere. I weave chairs; I'm not a queen. At most I might feel that I was the Stakhanova of the straw-workers. But it isn't with speeches like this that you can get me under your spell ».

He wasn't surprised by her outburst, but only irritated,

he let go of her hands with a premeditated gesture, and seized her by the arms.

« Let's understand each other, little one », he said. « You see I was right when I said you were still a baby. You're what you look like, and first I'll have to teach you manners instead of how to kiss ».

She threw herself on his chest, not teasing any more, but humiliated, and she burst into tears.

« Come on », he said, « you'll get my suit dirty ». He wiped her tears with the handkerchief from his pocket, kissed her again, and said: « Aren't you ashamed? You act like a baby from the day-nursery ».

And still like a little child that comes out of school led by the hand, following the Arno and the walls of S. Rosa, all in shadow, high and immense like ancient bastions, she held her nose in the air, but looked down at the ground. And happy that his hand was holding hers, she insisted, but it was a way of surrendering and joking, a lover's impertinence:

« But tell me the truth, with Silvana and all the others, did you tell them that they were your little billiard ball? »

« No », he said, smiling and pleased with himself, at his joke: « I told them they were a bowling ball, and I was right. You're the billiard: little and hard, the way you are ».

« Watch out, then... if I hit your head, I could split it open ».

Then she said: « All of Sanfrediano knows by now that we are engaged. What shall I say to my mother if she asks me? »

« Tell her no ».

« And if my father asks ».

« All the more reason... and anyhow, it isn't so. Nobody at the bar or at the club has let me know that he knew, and unless you have some idea of spreading the news... You oughtn't to, because we should have plenty of time to get to know each other... Tonight was our first night together, but tomorrow we'll meet outside the gate and take a walk in the Cascine ».

« But what have you said to Silvana? She and I are friends, after all; I have to go see her and explain... ».

He stopped, lifted her face, putting his hand under the chin, so that the moon, perpendicular to the wall, illuminated it; there were cats that miaued, they too in love, and from the Arno there came an improvised song, accompanied by a guitar; and for this very reason there was greater silence around them, a great desert, animated by walls, moon, shadow, and songs.

« I don't want you to. I've talked to Silvana and have her convinced of how things are. We should talk just of you and me, think only of us and how much we love each other ».

He caressed her, and she spoke, her head down, her fingers torturing a button of his coat:

« I know, but I mean, what I mean is: it's to let me hold my head up, don't you understand? It's because I'm so crazy about you, and I'm afraid you could swallow me in one mouthful ».

Then he burst out laughing, and Tosca didn't take offense, but laughed along with him, at her own expression, and the sillier it seemed to her, the truer she felt it was, and she was happy.

A car turned in from the street along the river, swung wide around the curve, and turned sharply as if the driver had realized suddenly that the street ended and there was the wall ahead. The headlinghts caught the two lovers kissing; there were several people in the car, and they shouted, happily, ironically, in greeting. « Good work, Bob », loud and vulgar, it was the voice of a girl; then the car turned into the gate at via Pisana and disappeared.

« It was Mafalda », Tosca said. « She's lost every shred of self-respect. Now she rides around in men's cars even in Sanfrediano ».

« Yes », he commented, « she's given herself to the high life since I left her ».

Tosca was speechless, without the strength to react; his words had wounded her, not so much for the revelation they contained that Mafalda had been one of the « others », as for the indifference with which Bob had spoken, and the way he had turned to her, as if she, Tosca, were another man, a friend who shared his feats and his language. And she remembered how, less than a half-hour before, they had stopped at the railing of Cestello, he had said to her: « I love you and I'm sincere. The past is past. I've nothing to hide from you; I'm playing with my cards on the table ». And she thought: « Yes, your cards really are on the table », but she didn't say it. Her heart ached; she thought, while he was kissing her again, that her heart actually pained her, not just in a manner of speaking, but really, with a physical pain; and she thought that certain words, in reality, strike like a fist against the heart.

THERE'S ALWAYS A HUNCHBACK IN SANFREDIANO

Tosca's heart aches; therefore, it is easy to understand. Bob's, on the other hand — does he have one?

He was playing with cards that were marked, rather than on the table, but he didn't cheat. He knew the cards, that's all, he had learned them by heart, every possible combination. His working day revolved about the ancient and inexhaustible symbol of the skirt; when it becomes religion and hedonism, and in the man who plays around with it, there isn't even true and proper lasciviousness, but more a love of achievement and of the thought that guides it. He was a *cavalier servente* of the suburbs, who smothered with his good looks and his effrontery the ridiculous side of his role, arousing envy, passion, and bitterness. Every other emulation, or joy, or gain that life could offer him, he had now subordinated to this mission with which he felt himself charged and in which he realized himself, expending all his energies and faculties. Thus, any other action that he performed outside the circle of his loves, knowingly or not, he

performed simply to acquire a story that would be worthy
of him. He had been an athlete, and then a gymnast, and at
the last moment, he had made himself a partisan, for this:
another laurel on his handsome, youthful forehead. His imagination, like his ingenuity, was limited; it permitted him
neither to go deeper into the game, nor to vary it. His emotions sufficed for him as they were, all external, vanity and
superiority; and his conscience remained immobile amid the
intricate animation of his adventures, so that every time, he
could feel himself his own master, natural, sincere. He was
so now with Tosca, as he had been with the other girls, the
above-mentioned, whom he kept near him from time to time,
or distant, the subjects of his beauty and his ardor. Because,
though Tosca doesn't know it for the moment, Bob doesn't
abandon his girls decisively; he meets them still, with
greater or lesser frequency, and all of them remain bound
to him, they are faithful or unfaithful to him as he permits
it; but no one of them, not Silvana, nor those last ones that
preceded her, nor even Mafalda, who apparently has set out
on a different path, none of them has given up the idea that
she will be the one he will finally marry, the girl, that is,
who will at last succeed in putting the salt on the tail of
this peacock in Sanfrediano.

The truth is that Bob, himself the most convinced of his
power of seduction, had become understanding and long-
suffering; he allowed himself to be loved. Not he, but the
girls, did the courting and lured him on. He conceded himself, from time to time, according to the intensity of the call
and the constancy of her who was beseiging him. As the interest waned with time, or because a stronger call was urging
him on, he could not remove himself brutally from the old
relationship without causing in that heart a shock that would
almost be fatal. So he thought, and he realized that he was
unique, *extraordinary*, and irreplaceable, and that he hadn't
the right to deny, every now and then, the solace of a caress,
that drop of water that would nourish a youthfulness otherwise lost. He drew away, then, little by little, with tender-

ness and affectionate cynicism; and for that matter, his own personal nature required that he should always have « four or five girls near at hand ». And he was highly secret, conspiratory, and prudent in the course of his adventures; only when separation had become final did he begin to speak of the abandoned beauty, at the club, or where the occasion occurred, but always with care and circumspection, making using of allusions, anecdotes, and double meanings, often vulgar and always merciless, so that those who listened to him could easily recognize the unfortunate girl, but in such a way that he, « a gentleman of honor », was always in a position to deny, especially in front of the young men who had an interest in her, relatives or new fiances, the identification and defamation that resulted from his remarks. Thus his glory continued to hover, high and unreachable, in the sky of Sanfrediano; and since no girl had ever tried, as Silvana had been urged by her sister, « to change his face », that is proof, if nothing else, of the happy memory, or the gratitude, or of the nostalgia that Bob knew how to leave behind him in the hearts of his victims.

There was an undercurrent of fear in all this, undoubtedly, hypocrisy, and the unwillingness to face a situation fully, but there was also, let it be said, some authenticity on his part. He always loved the women who was near him, and only her, in the moment that he embraced her; but his day was starred with these exclusive moments, and gradually more of them, since by now Bob believed himself endowed with an immense reserve of affection that a single woman would be unable to focus and exhaust.

This chain of relationships with the intrigue, the lies, the demonstrations of affection that it required of him, and the populous presence of girls on whom he could exercise his personal charm, authority, and tyranny, permitted him to attain whatever life can offer that is perfect and desirable. Bob was a happy man, and not altogether unworthy of esteem, from the moment that he adjusted happiness to his own means; and he had been able to attain it, risking —

if not a great deal — at least something that was personal.
In any case, considered objectively, he was only a young man
a bit vain, adventurous within measure, who calculated the
limits of his own imprudence, a little Casanova of the suburbs, who lacked — besides genius and foolhardiness — the
original virtue of the great lover: the need and the desire
for full possession.

He, on the other hand, knew how to control himself.
A master of the tender ritual, but timorous at the same time
he was imaginative and bold in tender conversation, and the
girls always came completely intact and virginal from his
hands. And perhaps in the very fact that Bob never attempted to cross that threshhold of which he displayed himself
at the same time an expert and irresistible beseiger, each of
the girls saw a sign of respect that led her to believe that
she was really the chosen one, the one truly loved, so that
she could be patient, torturing herself jealously and helplessly, obeying him and waiting for him. Only one of them,
she whom he had made his mistress, she who could hope
more that the others that she deserved his choice, she was
the one, tormented by her secret, as we will learn, who
despaired the most, perhaps because she was the only one
who knew how really egoistic he was, how he exhausted his
sensuality in touching, in kissing, and in mere words, so that
he used his mistress simply to quench his sexual excitement,
and that special fidelity with which she was blessed was due
only to his meanness, if not also, finally, to his personal concept of neatness and hygeine.

He had to be the one then, Bob, to force them to their
knees, the girls of Sanfrediano.

But this is also an aspect of Sanfrediano, and it is something that is properly in the tradition, which has heights
and depths, like the seasons. And the girls of Sanfrediano
are their mothers' daughters.

In '21, the Hunchback, a Sanfredianino descendant of
Sanfredianini, hunchback though he was, had upset the entire district with his feats as a heart-breaker, and had mobil-

ized at the same time the entire Police Force with his feats as a safe-breaker. The police surrounded the quarter, placed armored cars and motor-cycles with machine-guns, and agents with loaded pistols at the mouth of every street: the Hunchback showed himself on a rooftop and urinated on the head of the Chief, who was directing the operation. In the meanwhile, from every alley and every house, the most virtuous women, the wisest and most honest wives, not only those who had been his mistress, came out and lined up together on the pavement, then they grabbed the legs of the policemen and the militia, so that the Hunchback could take the path over the rooftops to freedom.

« He was handsome », they say, « He was a hunchback, a thief, and the leader of a gang, but he was handsome ».

« He had a face like Christ in the Garden ».

« ...like Rudolph Valentino ».

And some years later, the same women, carrying in their wombs the very girls of Sanfrediano who are going crazy for Bob and are his slaves, their mothers and even their grandmothers threw boiling oil from the windows and the sinks torn from the walls, they loaded guns for their husbands, their fathers, and their sons, their men with red scarves, barricaded behind the cloth-stuffed windows and the carts of the ragman.

« We're made out of something special, here in Sanfrediano », they say.

« Tripe broth, with jasmine in it ».

Sanfrediano in reality is a tree, that flowers in an infinity of springtimes, and its girls are immortal as its stones are. Now, among the many who have run the same risk, five of them have been caught, more or less securely, in the same trap. But they wouldn't be what they are if, « before the game is over », they couldn't succeed in freeing themselves with their own hands.

A KISS AND A WORD

And it was Tosca who began, in her own part of the matter, to want to see things clearly. She was a girl « with her heart on her lips »; she thought of life as a series of events all explicable and explicit, and as soon as she tasted delusion and pain, her reaction was immediate: any contrariness or suspicion produced in her an unbearable suffering. « A kind of itch », as she said, « that has to be scratched right away ».

Now the fleas that Gina had put in her ear (these are Tosca's words and we are repeating them) aggravated the « itch ». She loved Bob — he was handsome, he had a job, and his kisses were enough to stun you — and she didn't want to share him with anybody, or to know that such a thing was being planned. She pulled the strips of straw over the frame of a chair, and they were Silvana's braids that she was pulling.

« Those braids! She's wearing her hair long, these moonlight nights... As sure as I'm alive, I'll cut that hair of hers off if she so much as... ».

God was in heaven listening, and He sent Gina along her way, making her catch the tram to save time. Tosca saw her at the window.

« Get off. I have to talk to you ».

« But I'm going to Legnaia. I'm going to decide about the house where I'll be living as a bride; my fiance is waiting for me ».

« He'll wait. Get off ».

Gina defended herself, the tram moved, and Tosca clutched the outside handle like a little boy playing. A passenger, a young man in coveralls, opened the door for her, and drew her in, holding her under the arm, as he said:

« There, I've helped you up; now do yourself proud in this fight ».

Gina had come on to the platform. « But she's a friend

of mine. It's just about some embroidery that we have to decide ».

« You've got the idea », Tosca said.

They got down at the next stop, and the workman renewed his impertinence: « A blond and a brunette; it would've been a real match, girls... Who knows if *he*'s worth it? »

The tram left again, ringing its bell and loaded with laughter. They were at the top of via San Giovanni, and under the shrine there was a lighted lamp and some flowers withered in the vases.

« You see that Madonna? » Tosca said, and she held her friend's arm. « You don't see her very clearly because she's faded, but she's there. Now, right here, you've got to tell me the whole truth, about Aldo and about Silvana, since I've been engaged to Aldo. Now, why do you say that she's got burning hands? »

Gina looked her in the face before she answered. « Aren't you getting a little excited? You'd think you were the one Bob had given up. This is something new ».

« There's nothing to worry about there », Tosca said, « and do me the favor of calling him Aldo when you speak to me... You know: I can't stand to hear my ears burning, when someone's talking about me behind my back ».

« And why don't you ask Silvana? »

« Certainly, I'll wait for her tonight when she gets out of work, but of course she won't be honest with me, and we'll end up hitting each other, and I won't know any more than I did before. But you must know everything she's planning to do ».

« I don't know, but she won't think of doing anything: what do you think she could do? She's such a slowpoke; she could drown in a glass of water... besides, with him, there's not much you can do — you'll learn that when he leaves you. You think you're going to set him on fire, but he can always shut your mouth with a kiss and a word ».

This Tosca didn't want to hear, but strangely, instead of

raging against her friend, she felt an unexpected dishearten-
ing, as she had a few evenings earlier, when Mafalda went
by in the car and Bob had said: « She's taken up the high
life since I left her ». And now, suddenly sharper, that first
sorrow of her life was renewed, in the thought that Bob could
be amusing himself with her, a word and a kiss, and then
leave her like the others, and she would be left with this love
that she felt for him, useless then « like a pot », she thought,
« with no place to cook ». She was silent, and suddenly her
eyes were wet. It was not yet a real sorrow, but rather a
presage, a feeling completely new, lacerating and hateful,
that comes before sorrow, the birth of jealousy, and it was
enough to bring her to life again.

Gina looked at her and the tears wetting her cheeks,
smiled again, and said: « If you want to straighten out things
with Silvana and want me there as a witness, I won't refuse ».

« Oh, no. That's a show you're going to miss. Aldo is
mine and I'm not sharing him with anyone, not even in
words; I'm not going to have him taken away from me. I'm
the one who took him away from the rest of you ».

« Hmf », Gina spluttered. » As far as I'm concerned,
there's not even a fingernail of his attached to *me* ».

This was an outright lie, since all of Bob was dear to
her, robbed her of her sleep and her reason, ·and now that
outburst had suddenly revealed her, but she managed to stop
and face the situation. Still her words had contained a meaning that Tosca didn't let slip by.

« What? How's that? What do you mean? » Tosca was
aroused, and the flames in her eyes quickly dried the tears.
« A fingernail now, but before that a kiss, a word... so you,
too, have been engaged to Bob, like Mafalda, like Silvana,
like me... ».

« Not at all. It was just a manner of speaking ».

« Swear it. Swear it here in front of the Madonna... say:
let me lose my eyesight ».

« Let me lose my eyesight ».

« Say it again, with more feeling ».

« Let me lose the power of seeing ».

« Say: let my hands become paralyzed ».

« Let my hands become paralyzed. Now are you satisfied? »

Now she had to bite her lips to keep playing her part, Gina, who probably loved Bob as none other ever had, who was planning to marry « to spite him », a spite that she was doing to herself. She swore, and at the same time mentally she repeated: « Madonna mia, forgive me, I'll go to confession, I'll light you a candle, I'm doing it because I love him ». And it seemed to her that to pit Tosca and Silvana one against the other was the next, and only way left her to clear the field of the two rivals, the most dangerous ones because the latest to whom Bob had become attached, and then she could lead him back to herself, he who never took her seriously when she said: « Watch out, I'm going to get married ».

« You'll get married when I say you can », he would answer. « I haven't decided yet that you won't be the very one I'll end up by picking... your hair is just like black silk — do you realize that's a new compliment? You know that it's just as if I had only you, I'm only faithful to you... isn't that a sign? »

« It's a sign, Bob, but it's a sign that's been going on for six years, and even since I was born, and you keep me in your hand like the two of diamonds, you just take me up when I'm needed; at times I'm even ashamed of my own hands, I'm so ashamed of what I've sunk to ».

Then Bob closed her mouth with a word and a kiss.

« You're my little billiard ball », he said, « that's what you are ».

In reality, she represented for Bob something irremediably different from what she would have wanted to be for him. She was his mistress and his friend.

And Tosca said, « All right, I'll come and get you if I think I need a witness ».

« *DO YOU KNOW THE BEAUTIFUL GINA?* »

« Children are the manna of the Lord », and as soon as they are born they become another hungry mouth to appease; the proverbs of the poor express the truth precisely because they contradict themselves, in Sanfrediano and wherever there are people who labor to make ends meet.

Bob was five years old when, in the same building, a little girl was born; he crammed himself with cake and candy and marsala on the occasion of her baptism, which was a good party, since she was the first child of a young couple who had saved some money from their little shop of drugs and dry-goods. The girl's mother took him on her knees, drew the cradle close, and said to him:

« Do you like her? Her hair is black like yours, and she has a lot of it for such a little baby. When she grows up, I'll make the two of you get married ».

« Certainly », Bob's mother said, « two of a kind ».

« If she grows up as fine as she was born, she'll be a credit to the song, and she'll drive the boys crazy ».

« *Do you know the beautiful Gina?* »

Her hair grew, became as soft as silk, and beneath it grew a girl whose features were a little common, in which she resembled her father, the mouth too big and the nostrils too wide for a girl, but the clear and beautiful eyes, the slim figure, softened her, and even more so her affectionate nature, which was of an innocence, for her years, even excessive in a girl of Sanfrediano. Bob ran into her on the stairs and in the street, pulled her hair, or clapped her unexpectedly on the back.

« Oh, you scared me ».

« That's nothing. Wait until I've married you. I'll eat up the dowry in the wink of an eye ».

She was growing up and Bob was to be her husband; it made her happy that he remembered she had been promised him, since he was the handsomest, neatest, and politest boy of their street and of the whole district. She was fourteen and the parties in her house had been many, gradually less elaborate, because her father fell ill, then died when her mother was still pregnant with the sixth child, the second son after the four girls, composing the family of which Gina was the oldest. The mother stayed behind the counter as long as she could, then for a week the store was shut, and finally it had to be sold, for nothing, a few thousand lire, and Gina had to leave high school just as she was beginning, to go to work in a dressmaking establishment, and then when she was eighteen and surer of herself, she left the workroom for the factory and became a cigar-wrapper, her mother having remembered in the meanwhile that she had a nurse's certificate.

It was a hard adolescence, full of sweat, typical of Sanfrediano, and she lived through it with resignation, even with fervor; now she had become a woman: she was slim, pleasing, what she had promised to become when she was still a baby, with a gentleness of manner that was no longer simply innocence, but was now her character and her chief virtue. And Bob was always her husband; she alone, of the relatives and friends who had been at her baptism, had nourished through the years the memory of that promise and that profecy — now more than it had been before — because they were engaged. This happened when she was sixteen, in the spring of '40 when he was already well along in his career as heartbreaker, and when his age-group was about to be drafted. But he was still being called Aldo, even if by that time he should have been called Bob.

« You don't mind that I don't have a dowry any more? »

« So much the better; then I can pull you hair without feeling guilty about it ».

And at once he told her what she meant to him. « You see, Gina, with you it's different. We grew up next door to each other, and to me you're like a boy who's my friend. With you there's no need for any foolishness. I know that, whatever comes into my head, I don't have to explain to you, because you understand by yourself. I married you the day you were born, from what they say, and in a way it's as if they were telling the truth. Now I see you've become a woman, and I like your looks. I've got a feeling that with you I can do what I want to, and it's all right with you. Isn't that so? »

It was a sincere but brutal way, however shameless, of declaring his love, certainly not what Gina might have dreamed was awaiting her, but she translated what Bob was saying into what her heart wanted to be said.

« Of course », she answered, « I'm in your hands; I always have been. I've never wanted anything else since I was old enough to think ».

Only later on would she understand what meaning his words had, and what truths they would come to reflect. She began to understand a bit later, when she gave herself to him — one evening, the evening of Ascension Day in that same May of 1940, on the great meadow of the Cascine, and there was a dinning of crickets, obsessive, in her memory, to accompany that eternal moment in which she seemed to lose consciousness, the sky falling into her eyes, loaded with stars, and Bob's breath, his embrace, was something immense, irresistible, trustworthy, that swallowed her — and then he failed to make his appearance at two dates. She had to wait for him at the door of their building to meet him and pretend to talk to him casually, because of the people, her mother and his, who were in the doorways, at the windows, to get a breath of fresh air.

« What's been keeping you busy? »

« A girl. I think you know her. Mafalda, the redhead ».

And when she sank back against the wall, annihilated, still hoping that he was joking, he asked her: « Aren't you feeling well? Wasn't this our agreement? There's no need for me to swear eternal love to you. You know you'll be the one I choose, sooner or later. But now I want to live my life, have some fun ».

« But I... » she began.

« That's right: you. It's as if I had already married you;

didn't I marry you as soon as you were born? », and he smiled at her, sure of himself and of what he was saying, « It isn't as if I did that with the others, you're enough for me; with them I just fool around ». And he went on: « That's the way a man who has any respect for himself ought to do! As far as I'm concerned, I'm perfectly honest: I come out and tell you, but another man, to the girl... that is, well, Ascension Day... he wouldn't tell her if he was having fun. You ought to consider yourself lucky ».

She fled up the stairs so as not to burst into tears and make a scene there in the middle of the street, after which everyone would have know, and Bob wanted to keep their engagement a secret. « If we make it official », he said, « we lose the freedom we have, and I, for the moment, don't intend to lose a speck of it », he had concluded, that very Ascension evening.

Then he went off to be a soldier and wrote her in care of General Delivery; he knew how to manage things, so he stayed in Italy, the war passed, and he came home to take up where he had left off. And when he wanted her — « like one off the street » she said to herself — as he went out in the morning, Bob walked down the stairs slowly, singing the song that had been theirs in the days when they were engaged, which now had acquired a shameful, infamous meaning, and « like one off the street », she repeated:

> Com'è bello far l'amore
> quando è sera

and he sang:

> Core a core co' una pupa
> ch'è sincera

and Gina knew that she should wait for him outside the Gate, and they would go to the storeroom where Bob's father and brothers, from whom he had lifted a key, kept their painting equipment, in the hours when Bob knew the others would be working someplace distant. And he was « her friend » and shamelessly told her all about himself and about the girls he had his eye on, if Gina questioned him about it. Now she asked him always, it seemed the only way she could see him sincere, « hers », when he confided in her, and swore to her every time that he loved only her, after all, possessed only her, even if he was wondering at the moment how to rid himself of some of the others to dedicate his time to the new one what was interesting him.

« That's just it: since I'm unfaithful to you with four or five at once, I'm really not unfaithful at all. They're the ones I'm being unfaithful to, when I'm with you ».

He was monstrous, and Gina understood him, she really saw Bob for what he was, « a poor thing » who took pleasure in putting her under his feet, who had to share his accomplishments with someone and couldn't with his male friends for fear that they might pay him back, some father or brother might get him with his back to the wall, and he, Bob, couldn't stand a taste of his own medicine; *he* had to be the one who abandoned his girls, and then he could boast with everyone, cause their names to be on everyone's lips. He was a coward, and she was no better, because she couldn't summon the strength to rid herself of him, and the baser she discovered him to be, the more she felt she loved him, and she gave herself to him « like one off the street », running to their dates, and only when he took her did she feel that he was hers and no one else's, coward that he was he respected the other girls finally. « As long as what's legal and what isn't », he said, « don't get mixed up, all the fathers that want to can come after me, I'll send them running with a good pair of slaps ». And Gina lay in his arms, and she seconded him, his complice and his victim, she felt that she was enjoying his successes with him, agreeing that Bice was more refined than Silvana, but neither of them could « lace the shoes » of Toschina, the latest ones to whom he remained faithful and whom he betrayed with her, in the storeroom outside the walls.

And suddenly she had seen the way to make Bob come to a decision. A rag merchant in via Camaldoli, whom she had always known, probably past forty (he said thirty-nine), but still young, pleasant, a little bald at the temples, had made some money just after the war selling scraps. «I have a million or so », he said, and he asked her to marry him. « I'm just the right age, more sensible than any kid, and you've always suited me; you're the only serious girl in Sanfrediano. And besides, if I get married — I don't say this to offend you — but at your house, all of you could breathe a little easier. I've already talked about this to your mother, and I know that she probably hasn't said anything to you because she doesn't want to influence you, but she would be happy about it ».

« You see, Bob », she said to him the next day, « mother knows about it, too; it's a piece of luck for us, and besides he doesn't seem so bad to me; he's a good-looking man ».

Bob laughed. « You'll get married when I give you my permission, when I've decided whether or not I'm going to marry you myself ».

And it was to speed up his decision, to bring him « at the door with rocks », to see whether or not Bob could do without her, that Gina had rushed matters so, and had set the date for the wedding. But at the same time she couldn't refuse his song; those were the only times she could see him and a word. And so her bridal house was already furnished, and the wedding was to take place within tyo weeks.

« Watch out, Bob. I really am going to get married ».

« Sure, sure, when the dome of the cathedral caves in. All right? »

MAFALDA, OR THE COACHMAN'S DAUGHTER

It was towards the end of September, on a pay day, when the spirit of a man is always ready to notice that the sky is wonderful and the girls are radiant. The sun had already risen, dissolving the last remains of mist at the river's horizon, and the sky was blue and immobile; Bob saw the top of the Bellosguardo cypresses surge up from the roofs, a perspective between the tiles and the sky. He admired himself again in the mirror, profile and full-face.

« You're all in order », his mother said, « the usual mannequin ».

His father and brothers had gone out.

« They have a job outside the city, perhaps they won't even be back for supper, because they have to finish it before tomorrow... this month things haven't been so bad », she added, « so if you want to keep out some more of your pay... »

« You're the best mamma in the world », Bob said, and kissed her on the forehead while he finished adjusting his tie.

Then he went down the stairs slowly, one step after another, and the world was his, he was singing. He stopped for a moment on the landing in front of Gina's door, still singing, and then he he was in the street.

Gina assured him that she would be there, coming to the window of the first floor, she asked: « What time is it, Bob? »

« Seven-thirty, beautiful ».

« That's good. This morning I thought I'd get to the factory after the siren, 'bye... What? »

« Nothing. I'm just glad to know that you get to you job on time ».

« Of course, these are the last days. After I'm married, I'll live like a lady. But I want to be on time and do my job right up to the end. I don't want to have anything to reproach myself with. Isn't that right? »

And she shut the window without waiting for his answer.

A little farther on, old Barcucci was sitting at the door of his place where he rented carts, with half a cigar between his lips and his crutch laid across his sound thigh and his stump, like a gun.

« Coming to the billiard game tonight, Bob? Those boys are waiting for you », he said, « you'll have to give them their return match ».

« Right. I'll bring all my month's pay with me ».

« Oh, there's no taking any money out of your pocket. You were born on a Sunday, lucky at games and lucky in love ».

« I know how to manage, Barcucci, that's the secret of my success ».

The old man spat out the cigar with his teeth; he was old Barcucci, who had seen the boys and girls of Sanfrediano grow up under his eyes and he could say it:

« Don't act any more Bob-like than necessary ».

Now via della Chiesa opened out long and straight in front of him, with banners of laundry at the windows and the population stirring already; the guests of the Public Dormitory were trooping out of the front door, suspicious, loaded with rags, looking around carefully as if to select the direction that would bring them a good day, and at once, an old woman, her face devastated and friendly, confronted Bob, who was passing near her, and held out her hand to beg. She had on a long yellowish dress, a kind of tunic, held in at the waist by a length of cord, and around her neck, down to her breast, a violet shawl, equally worn and discolored, like the tiny hat of black straw that rested on her stray locks of grey hair.

« You start work early », Bob said, « but I can't help you out ».

« That's all right », she said. « You're so beautiful that I'll be lucky today anyway, because you're the first person I've seen ».

He smile and dug two lire out of his pocket. « Here », he said, « for the compliment ».

« But it's the truth, and in my time I used to keep right up with the best of them. You're a real ray of sunshine ».

It was Bob, beginning one of his days, all of them lucky for him; a beggar woman had burst incense at his shrine, and on the other side of the bridge Bice was surely waiting for him. He went on, through the streets and alleys of Sanfrediano, following his usual path, like the little monarch he felt himself to be, convinced of the homage due him along his way, to which he replied with a close-mouthed smile, surly, a sparkling of his eyes, a wrinkling of his lips, a measured gesture of his hand, a greeting whose varying intensity marked his meanings, according to the detachment or the spontaneity that inspired him. And behind his back, the sighs, the exclamations, the wisecracks that accompany the Bobs of this world on their way, while they move lightly among the people, above and beyond the struggle, lovable, hateful, fatuous as dictators on horseback.

He turned as usual into via del Leone and raised his shoulders, if possible, even higher: in that stretch he might happen to meet Loretta, the one who most surely would be Tosca's successor, whom he was keeping in the meanwhile to « stew » in the fire of his glance. The garbage trucks were stopped in a line and blocked half of the street. Bob had to cross to the sidewalk opposite, where a little group of people were gathered about a man selling fried polenta — and now a few steps away, on his side of the street — he saw instead Mafalda.

She stood, leaning back, outside the door of the building where she lived, her arms folded, one foot raised against the wall, and she had on a light robe of blue silk that outlined her hips and gave her a careless, exciting appearance, the look of a girl still warm from her bed and naked under her robe. The thick, disorderly length of her naturally red hair, and her face without any makeup, where the freckles stood out against the pallor of the cheeks, accentuated the personal sensuality of her solid, working-girl's body.

« Good morning, your Highness », she said to him.

Bob wouldn't have wanted to stop. Mafalda didn't belong to him any longer; for some time now he had excluded her from the circle of his interests, and this showiness and shamelessness of hers bothered him. « Hello, beautiful ». He raised his hand to his forehead, imitating a salute and a bow, and made as if to go on.

But the girl, without moving, held him by an arm. « Do

you think I got up at this hour for nothing? I dragged my-self out of bed especially to say hello to you ».

« And I thank you very much, but I have to be going ».

« Ah ha », she snarled, « the ration tickets are waiting for you. For that matter, they aren't much good: how long has it been since there was a distribution of oil? »

He remembered that he was Bob and what the word Bob meant; he showed his teth, it was his beautiful smile, and at the same time looked her in the eyes severely: « It seems to me, baby, that you went to bed late and had a bad dream. Between you and me the account has been closed for quite a while ».

She let out a laugh, and the people around the polenta man turned to look.

« Closed? and when? why? Have we ever had any busi-ness dealings, you and I? »

And since Bob had started on his way again, this time she moved to catch up with him. But Bob knew his girls and knew how to avoid the noise that Mafalda seemed prepared to make.

« Don't shout, Faldina, you know that's the one way to finish my love for you ».

« I was wrong », she said, and she walked along beside him, and they were two friends talking.

« But you, look at the way you treat me. You don't show your face any more ».

« Then it should be pretty clear that I don't feel the need ».

She managed to control herself. He had a childish way of accusing the offended party and dropping her; she closed her lips and swallowed.

« It's not true that you're in a hurry », she said. « It's not eight o'clock yet, and you have to be at your office at nine. Come to my place for a minute and I'll fix you some coffee. I'm alone at home and we can talk. Now I can't walk along with you, in my robe like this. Come along, I have a thousand and one things I want to say to you ».

« And not one of them that might interest me ».

« Why did you leave me without any reason? »

They had reached piazza del Carmine, where he had gone on purpose, giving up his usual route, to turn into Borgo Stella, a brief, deserted side street, beyond the traffic and the quarter, where they could stop and remain, for the most part, unobserved by the few passers-by.

« Is this the first time that you've asked me that? Haven't I already answered you? »

« But am I the sort of girl you can just throw away? » she said, and her tone was now humble, pitiable, in contrast with the disorderly pride of her figure. And he was curt, the way he knew how to be, perhaps — though we wouldn't want to give a severe judgement of the case — because he knew he had nothing to fear, at least Mafalda had no one to support her, unless it was her father, the cabman, a drunkard, as old and exhausted as his horse.

« Am I the sort of girl who doesn't mean anything to you any more? » she repeated.

« Yes. Now you are. I don't like shoes that have been worn ».

At once she threw herself on him, and Bob had to hold her by the wrists, but he couldn't prevent her from shouting.

« Now, naturally, now yes, because I let myself be invited to supper by someone, and then I let myself go. But who was it who drove me to it? I hadn't ever been with anyone, and you could have had me, and you, you coward, thought I wanted to compromise you. Compromise you! to make you marry me. And who ever asked you to do such a thing? Who would expect you to marry a cabby's daughter, with her stockings torn and a desire for lovely things, the way I am? I'd have worked sweeping the streets if you'd asked me... yes, now I've got stockings, silk ones, all Sanfrediano knows it, you can't be compromised now... There are men with cars, landowners from the South, who get down on their knees until I say yes, and idiot that I am, with my mind always on him... it's impossible... the minute they see me, they all make passes at me, and the only one I really want treats me like dirt. Trying to make him jealous, to spite him, I licked the stones where he passed by, with his beautiful eyes on my mind, night and day. Was I blind, or what? Mister Lucky Break, Mister Moustache! Now he doesn't feel the need, he doesn't wear worn shoes, he has all he needs, new and beautiful, but who are they, where are they, who was that poor thing who was with you at the wall the other evening?... Now you're interested, aren't you? But now I'm the one who doesn't want you any more, go away... you're just a mannequin, you're made out of plaster, you coward... ».

They struggled, and he was afraid that a passerby, or someone from a window or from the garden, might intervene; he twisted her wrists and threw her against the iron gate. She bent and writhed in his hold, tried to bite the hands that held her immobile, and shouted, beyond herself, overcome.

« Look at me », she shouted suddenly, threw her head back, arched her body held by his hands; her hair fell in a mass of tangles, and from the robe that had come undone, her breasts appeared, naked and heaving. « Am I a girl you can just throw away? » she repeated.

« No. No », he said to her now, « you're the most beautiful of all, but get a hold of yourself ».

And as she gradually relaxed and her voice died down, he lifted her up and leaned her against the gate, helped her compose herself, as he held her. Now the girl's eyes were glassy, open and still, her chin trembled, and her hands were deathly and cold, until she began to cry, and came to life again, sobbing, her forehead on Bob's shoulder, as he caressed her hair, in silence, afraid of arousing her again, whatever he said.

A boy came by. He was running, but he stopped to load his slingshot with a stone to hit the birds on a tree in the garden, and so he saw them; he was from Sanfrediano and recognized them, stopped a moment to look, his head forward and his eyebrows raised. Then he said: « Say, Bob, are all your conquests girls like her? » and he ran off.

« That's how it is, Bob », she said, sadly, bitter against herself. « I've made a name for myself, and I'm ruining your reputation ».

He was disturbed still and prepared to be kind, comprehensive and, in his own way, sincere. « You're ruining yourself, not me. This way, what can I lose? »

« That's right », she said, « what can you lose? »

And soon she was herself again, tough, shameless; she set the locks of hair behind her ears, and more than anything else she was angry with herself for the show of weakness that she had made.

« What do I lose, myself, for that matter? By now... ».

She looked at him and tried to give her face an expression of scorn. She felt tired, heavy in every limb, and to keep this up was exhausting her.

« Why don't we », he said, « see each other? » and then, his voice lower, « tonight. You're not at all the sort of girl to throw away ».

« I can't. I already have a date... so good-bye, and forgive me, but you know how it is. My friends have taught me how to smoke a new kind of cigarette and sometimes, when I'm under the influence, the past comes back, things that are dead and buried, when my mind is fresh. Besides, as far as I'm concerned, as I said before, you disgust me ».

And she wanted to go on, hurling insults at that God of hers who looked at her and smiled, insolent and obstinate, for whom she had sacrificed herself in a special and, by now, rather extensive martyrdom. She knotted more tightly the belt of her robe and said:

« You want to know what my opinion of you is? I think you only like to fool around with women and do the sort of things we used to do when we were in elementary school, and as far as going to bed is concerned, I think that when it comes to the best part of the business, you have something missing ».

She turned her back to him and when she was a few steps away, without paying him any further attention — if he was still there he could hear her — she shouted to him: « Anyway, don't let it discourage you. You wouldn't be the first, you know ».

Bob was still there, unmoving. He shook his head, commiserating with her, the just victor who looks down at the dead body of the traitor at his feet. So he watched her go away, and as soon as she had reached the corner, he saw her cross the square at a run, and he imagined that she was running so that she would arrive home more quickly, where she could throw herself on her bed, shaken with sobs. Then he looked at his watch; et was eight-forty and only a few minutes were left him to spend with Bice, with whom he had had a date for three-quarters of an hour earlier. Who knows, he wondered, if Bice would still be waiting for him? Perhaps not, he decided, after three-quarters of an hour. Knowing that he had to be at his office at nine, Bice would have thought he had missed the date and would have gone away.

But Bob was already, evidently, a man about to be abandoned by his lucky star, if precisely in the one field where he could be called an expert, that is in the thoughts of girls, posing himself two questions in the space of a minute, he gave himself two answers, both wrong, Bice, in reality, was waiting for him; she would have waited until nightfall even. And Mafalda was by no means weeping on her bed, calling his name amid her tears; she had only begun to walk faster because she was in a hurry, feeling naturally a bit uneasy about being in her robe, among the few passersby, in the huge square she had to cross. As soon as she was past it and had reached the corner of via del Leone, she felt tired, undone, heavy, and she went into a bar and ordered a cognac. « I'll pay later », she said. And when the proprietress asked her is she wasn't feeling well, and how she felt, Mafalda answered: « Now I feel fine. I got rid of something that was on my stomach... I drink to the health of the unluckiest man on the face of the earth... He's the one that's in trouble », she explained, « he won't get any of his girls in trouble, no danger of that ».

BICE, CANDID AND CLEVER

In the little square on the other side of the bridge, Bice was setting on a bench beneath the statue of Goldoni, with her magazine of continued stories in her hand, her purse hung over her shoulder and held under her arm. She too was a girl nearing twenty, pale and blond, her lips slightly enlivened with lipstick; her face was that of an adolescent just bursting into bloom, whose virginal gifts of innocence and faith have yet to be disturbed by experience of the world and of the way things are. Her body, rather tall and slim, though well and explicitly formed, all her person, in appearance merely pretty and commonplace, won people over precisely because of the simplicity, the sweetness, and the casual modesty that inspired her and was so much a part of her that these qualities became singular and attractive. She was exactly what she seemed to be: quiet, credulous, optimistic, incapable of any violent feeling like a heroic ardor or a premeditated sacrifice, exquisitely feminine, limited and patient; yet this superficial, good-hearted and quick-witted way she had of looking at reality was her defense. She knew automatically how to fix her horizons; nothing that escaped her could give her any disappointment, since what escaped her didn't belong to her, but to the ranks of those dreams and fantasies with which she cradled her lazy imagination, without leaving her any anxiety or regret. Her naturalness and honesty were her moral strength, and hence authentic. She was a modest and cordial girl who enjoyed the inestimable gift of knowing herself, and in consequence — however narrow the space that education and culture occupied in her spirit — of knowing others, or of infallibly guessing their ineptitude or their loyalty; and she was wisely and sufficiently egoistic to remove and defend herself when the adventure of living, which she liked, called for any extra daring or presented any unknown quantities. For that matter, she knew that her future (in which she promised herself a husband, a house, some ease, and at least an escape from her salesgirl's counter) didn't depend on her; she couldn't be the one to solicit it, so she would have to experiment, choose, and not fool herself. She hadn't doubted for a moment that Bob would take up only a little of her life, but at the same time, she was taken with him, because he was elegant, he was handsome, in Sanfrediano a hundred girls would have envied her, and none of the other boys to whom she had been engaged knew how to kiss or to talk to her the way he did, with his tenderness and boldness, nobody else had his eyes or his smell. And she wasn't even pained by the fact that now, after the first months of their engagement, Bob was neglecting her; it was easy to understand: he was Bob, as beautiful as anyone could be, and she knew that she shouldn't sacrifice herself to him in an attempt to attract him; her future was certainly not going to be founded on him.

« I thought I wouldn't find you here », he said.

She had stood up, folding the magazine, and now she held out her hand.

« Patience is my chief virtue », she said, « but certainly, if I hadn't been on my vacation, I couldn't have waited for you. So you see, this week of holiday, even if it does come at the end of September, is good for something ».

Then she hinted: « I suppose your mother forgot to wake you up ».

He straightened his short, tight jacket, pulling it down over his hips.

« Hmm », he said, « I met someone ».

« Pretty? »

« No, just bothersome ».

« An old flame? » she guessed.

He had taken her arm. He said, « Don't ask me any more, because I'll just have to leave your curiosity unsatisfied... and hurry up, if you want to come with me ».

They walked faster, following the river to shorten the

way, and he said: « You ought to comb your hair straight back like that to show off that beautiful forehead of yours ».

She blushed. « Oh, you noticed it? » she exclaimed.

« And now, you say: oh, I just combed my hair like this without thinking about it... ».

« But I didn't. I fixed it this way on purpose to make you say what you said ».

« You're a love », he whispered, and touched her chin with his hand, a caress. « And when is your vacation over? » he asked.

« I see you've forgotten... I have two days still and... ».

« And I'd promised you that this afternoon, since I have Saturday afternoons off, we would go somewhere together ».

« And now you can't? » she said, stopping instinctively; he pushed her on by the arm, affectionately but energetically, because he was in a hurry.

« As a matter of fact, we'll have to put it off until tomorrow ».

« You can't. Why not? Oh well, you can't because you can't; by now I should be used to these whys that don't have any answers ».

As they were crossing the street at Ponte Vecchio, in the traffic, a car and a pushcart forced them to separate for a few steps, and now they were under the arch of the Archibusieri, together again, and he put his arm around her waist, pulled her to his side and looked at the watch on his wrist.

« I really have to run... but I don't want to leave you mad. Let's meet here when I come out, about one ».

« If I can », she said. « If I'm able to think of an excuse at home ».

She was a girl, and from Sanfrediano, so she wasn't lacking for excuses; and Bob, when he left the office at one, was more than ever pleased with himself that day, with his pay in his pocket, from which he could keep out more than usual; and Mafalda who sobbed on her bed; and Gina who wouldn't fail to keep their date and would threaten him with marriage to kindle his desire in a new way before she fell into his arms another time; and Tosca counting the hours and the minutes, one straw after another, her heart hurrying on the Cestello bell, which separated her from the evening, when they would meet at the entrance of the Cascine; and Bice who was already waiting at the corner of via de' Benci, keeping up appearances by pretending to look in a shopwindow. He came up to her, with these happy thoughts in his head, and smiled, moustached and content, but more to himself than to Bice, congratulating himself on being Bob and equal to his reputation. And he said to himself, tough, Sanfredianino in spite of everything: « Too bad I didn't make a date with Silvana, my little light-fingered seamstress; if I had fixed up something with her, this would be the day when they all pass in review, those still on active service, all my dear little billiards ».

« Where are we going at this time of day? » Bice asked.

« I thought we might have something to drink and a bit of pastry ».

« And then? »

« Then we can take a tram up to the viali and come back down on foot, taking our time, to Porta Romana, and then we'll be in Sanfrediano ».

« I've already eaten, but you'll get hungry in the meantime ».

« That depends on how we spend our time ».

And she, a wise girl who didn't like to make a promise that she wasn't willing to keep, even if it would have been pleasant to keep it, and crediting Bob with an intention that wasn't exactly his, said to him: « Then you'd better eat more than one pastry, to take the edge off your appetite ». And she said this without any malice in her words, but only an affectionate solicitude.

There, in the viali, with the trees that were turning yellow and a cricket, miraculous survivor, who sang in the field where they were resting, he was brilliant, tender, bold to the point of the illicit, but always within his special and cautious limits, and she was in turn joyful, aroused, confus-

ed, and constantly happy. Then they said goodbye, to meet
the next day — « maybe ». « Maybe? » — and the program
of his day was fulfilled as Bob had laid it out. Gina wept,
despaired, and told him it was « the last time ».

And Tosca came at her hour, at the entrance of the Cascine, but for a moment only, because she had a raging fever,
influenza, and she had already been crazy to take so much
quinine, hoping to send the fever down. But she could hardly
stand on her feet, and could only just say hello and goodbye
to him.

« I'm going to stay in bed all day », she said. « Let's
meet here tomorrow evening, at this same place ».

« All right », he said, « but you must promise to come
even if it should turn out to be pneumonia ».

« Don't worry. You'll see. Nothing could keep me away ».

She was different: wilful, sad, and excited, and he attributed it all to the fever and the quinine. He wanted to be
witty, and said:

« If you make me wait for you, watch out. Instead of
cutting off the moustache I have, I'll make it grow as long as
a Cossack's ».

« Don't joke all the time, Aldo », she said. « I love you
seriously, and I'll prove it to you, and you must prove it to
me, with the moustache or without ».

She signaled to the bus to stop, boarded it, without turning to wave from the platform.

And he went on his way. Now it as the billiard game
that was waiting for him.

A GAME, A FIGHT, AND A DIGRESSION
ON THE USE AND EFFECTS OF THE « FRONTINO »

« Shoot, Sultan », his opponent said to him.

Bob calculated the lay of the ball, the curve, and as he
manouvered his cue, he thought: « I do have a harem, after
all ». His girls, all of them together, came before his eyes,
the five of them that at present occupied him, counting Ma-

falda, who had returned to her place in the series through her own initiative; all of them were in line, like the balls of the game he was playing, and Tosca was in the center, more beautiful and more precious than the others, the little red ball. He smiled and made his shot, a good one, except that the red ball remained untouched, miraculous and proud on the vast green field of the table.

« Someone's resisting you, it seems », a voice said, among the onlookers.

« Just the opposite; she's the favorite », he said.

There was a gallery around them: Bob was exhibiting himself, and the wisecracks of which he was the object were in a tone of jesting admiration.

« Who is she? Do we know her? »

« You have to be the eunuch of the harem before you can have that information ».

« Nobody knows who they are, the ones that Bob is working on ».

« There's always a pair of pants behind the girl somewhere, eh, Bob? »

« Oh, I've always beaten my competition ».

« The friend that you unbutton your lip with is a lucky man », another one said.

« Why? Does Bob have a friend he confides in? He'd be just an ordinary man if he did; the women take up all of his time », the first one said.

He was a blond boy, an upholsterer, tall and thin, all eyes.

« Isn't that so, Bob? » he insisted.

« That's right, Gianfranco », he replied, chalking the end of his cue. « A woman makes a wonderful friend; there's more flavor to it ».

A big laugh went up, and his opponent in the game grew impatient.

« Come on. A little less talk. It's your turn ».

This time the shot was easy: his opponent's ball had stopped short of the line, and the red ball fell in with the others; but the shot was so easy that Bob overplayed it and instead of striking the center ball and finishing the game as he had meant to do, he barely grazed it, and sent his own ball into the pocket. Now, with these points lost, the game was in danger.

The upholsterer started up the chorus again. « The little ball's been unfaithful, Bob, but you'll forgive it; it's just another slut, and you're so generous ».

Bob dropped his cue, then caught it as the rubber-tipped end bouced on the floor, and at the same time, he looked at Gianfranco. Twice Bob had associated the image of Tosca with his game, and both times Gianfranco had commented on the outcome, as if he had been reading Bob's mind. Bob took a step and was in front of him. Gianfranco moved away from the wall, a head taller than Bob, his eyes were laughing.

« Looking for me? » he asked.

It was already a challenge, and Bob was forced to accept it. He said: « I wanted to remind you that the sluts, from first to last, have always had your family name ».

Swift and precise, Gianfranco's blow caught him between the nose and the mouth, and before Bob could react and put himself on guard, the two of them were separated. It was a mix-up, in Sanfrediano, and therefore, undoubtedly because of women. When calm was reestablished (the two adversaries were the only ones who hadn't been shouting), in the midst of the uproar, Barcucci, old, wise, and Sanfredianino, who before had been keeping score in the game, now assumed the right of directing the operations, and acted like the general and the judge that he was.

« Quiet », he imposed. « Now Gianfranco goes out first, then Bob. I think it might be best if they went outside the Walls ».

And looking around, at all of them and none of them, he explained: « They go out, and we'll wait for them here and drink over it ofterwards. We'll give them a half-hour for explanations or, if necessary, for a few punches... Nobody moves from here. And if somebody follows them, I'll break my crutch over his rear. And if he's a communist, I'll denounce him at the next cell meeting. It's clear enough that this is a private matter, and there's no reason to make it worse with a lot of talk. And besides these are two boys who don't need any help ».

Now Bob and Gianfranco walked along parallel to each other, a yard or so between them; and in spite of the threats of Barcucci, they were followed at a distance by a group of bold youths who weren't afraid of the old man's crutch, nor of the party discipline to which he had appealed; and they were for Gianfranco, naturally, his friends, though they were angry with him for not having told them about this poison that he had been nourishing.

« Are they fighting over Leda? »

« Or over Rossana? »

« Or Tina? »

they asked one another, all of the above-mentioned, as one said, goods that Bob had long since stopped hesitating over.

« It might be over Mafalda ».

« Which Mafalda? The redhead, the daughter of Panichi, the cabman? But I've been with her myself, and she goes with almost anyone these days; Gianfranco can't be fighting over her ».

« Could it be because of Luciana? » one suggested. « A while back I saw her and Bob dancing close together, closer than necessary, anyway ».

« Hey, Luciana is my cousin », another one shouted. « And they've already read the banns. I never heard of her having been with Bob. You'd better make it clear that you're wrong, or else tonight we'll make a night of it, and have a fight before they do, on the spot, without going outside the Walls ».

And that's what happened. So Bob and Gianfranco lacked onlookers.

It was eleven at night, in autumn; they turned the corner of via Sant'Onofrio, barely illuminated by an arc-light,

all the windows dark, and a wine-shop where, at the doorway and inside, there were a few men excited by the wine
and by their discussion. At the end of the street, where the
shadows were thickest, reflected by the row of lights that
follows the river, the ancient Tiratoio, the abandoned mill,
was even darker and more silent. The voices of the men
drinking reverberated in the air, which was windy and almost cold, full of cross-currents from the corner and from
the river. The two of them walked on the sidewalk; Gianfranco looked ahead, his arms at his sides with the fists
closed, like weapons already aimed. Bob had his eyes on
him, fearing a sudden attack; and as one step followed another, he felt his own irritation, instead of increasing, growing more languid; now he felt uneasy only because of the
wind and his lip which was swelling up, and the absurdity
of this silent march towards a battle, where he understood
less and less his participation. It was an event which hadn't
been included in the day's program, a « number » added at
the last minute, and it bothered him; he was tired, his house
was nearby, and he wished he were already in bed, his pyjamas on, his mouth cool from the toothpaste, reading the newspaper which would put him to sleep. It wasn't cowardice so
much as it was laziness; during the short walk, three or four
hundred yards, his thoughts turned quickly toward giving up.
Perhaps it was fear masquerading as common sense, but when
he spoke for the first time, he sounded more conciliatory
than resentful; it was a way of throwing in the sponge.

« Don't you think we're making fools of ourselves? »

Without stopping, Gianfranco said: « If you take back
what you said, and if that punch was enough for you. Otherwise, we only have a few yards left to go ».

« All right, I apologize. But you know it isn't because
I'm afraid. I'm the one who first taught you how to defend
yourself, when you were just a kid coming to the gym ».

« And now I've grown up. I'm only a couple years younger than you are, and I can give it to you; I've been wanting
to for a long time ».

They had arrived at the river; opposite them was the recess of the Walls, their battlefield.

« Now what? » Gianfranco said. « Are you sure you want to put your fists up? »

« Maybe, but first I'd like to know for whom and for what I'd have the honor of smashing you face in ».

« I've been wanting to give it to you for a long time », Gianfranco repeated.

And at last he blew up, took Bob by the lapels of his jacket, pushed him against the railing by the river, and shouted: « Silvana. Silvana. She's one you're not going to talk about, you bastard ».

« Oh, it's for Silvana. Well, listen ».

Gianfranco let him go, as if he had immediately regretted his action. He was a simple boy, sensitive and loyal, but proud; he was temperamental, but his instict, within limits, was subject to his will. Now he was angry with himself for having mentioned Silvana's name. She meant a great deal to him, even more — if possible — since she had rejected him, telling him abruptly and kindly that her heart was still beating for Bob « and only for him, whatever he may be, even if he's only amusing himself with me, neglecting me the way he does, taking me or leaving me; he's my first and my last — either Bob or nobody. » So it wasn't by speaking of Silvana that Gianfranco could humiliate Bob; he was revolted at hearing Bob even repeat her name. And if, at the beginning, he had hit Bob because of the insult at the game, now Gianfranco would like to take out his private rancor on Bob, who knew now the real reason was Silvana; though to Gianfranco, fighting meant descending to the other's level, fighting for Silvana as one Bob against another, and in any case, by doing so, he would offend her, Silvana.

Bob, taking his time, ran his hand over his lapels to smooth out the wrinkles and said: « You're young and so you don't know how to get along in the world. In matters like this, you talk things over before you start in with the punches, and then afterwards, you fight, if it's worth it. Now let's see if it's worth it. In the meanwhile we should get away from here or they'll come and find us and break up the discussion. Where do you want to go? »

« Wherever you want. By now you've wormed your way out of it. »

« That remains to be seen, too... who's gotten out of it, you or me. Let's go and sit on the steps of the Tiratoio; it's just a little bit further on, and we'd be out of the others' reach, » Bob said.

Now it was cowardice. But he was Bob still; there was a competitor in front of him and he couldn't hand him over a girl without discussing and struggling; he jilted, he didn't pass them on. Anyhow he understood that Gianfranco was the stronger, invincible; this was an obscure, but immediate impression, as if he were responsible for his actions, in some way, to this boy. Every so often Bob felt himself beaten at the outset, and his present state of mind could probably be connected with Gianfranco's actual position: a bold boy, hasty, idolized by all, especially now, after his feats as a partisan. More than that, seated now on the steps of the Tiratoio, as if in revenge for the blow he had received earlier at the game, Bob wanted to take the offensive, but he began with a blow that went wide of the mark and couldn't have left him more unprotected.

« First, understand this: I don't have any idea of letting Silvana get away from me, for any reason. And now, let's hear what you have to say; I can't imagine what it can be. Has there ever been anything between you and her? »

« No. But there shouldn't be between *you* and her, either. I know who you are. »

« What do you know? »

« More than you think, and more than the others think they know, » Gianfranco said.

It was a way of changing the subject from Silvana. And Gianfranco was a lover rejected by his beloved, who was looking for some truth that would make his rival suffer. It wasn't hard for him to find.

« I know, for example, very well that you never were a partisan. »

Bob leaped to his feet and stammered: « What?... I... but you're joking. »

« Sit down, greasy, » Gianfranco said, his voice insolent and vernacular; he had hit the mark and hammered in the first nail. He added: « Try and decide whether or not I have you in the palm of my hand. Have you forgotten about the certificate of recognition? I signed yours for you... You were seen out with your red scarf on when Sanfrediano was already liberated; and even so, for the little bit that there was left to do, you were always hiding God knows where; you were never around. Anyway, when they asked me about it, I gave a favorable opinion; we were friends and it was simply a matter of doing you a favor, and I knew that even if you hadn't been a partisan, at least you'd never been a Fascist. »

« Oh, no. Certainly not. No. »

« But as far as that goes, some of the Fascists were better than you are; those that paid with their lives and knew how to die properly. »

« I remember, by God, the ones that were shot in Piazza del Carmine. »

« Shut up. How can you look yourself in the face? »

« What do you mean? That I was afraid? That I was suffering when I saw them being shot? »

« You don't suffer for anything or anybody, you make others suffer... you aren't a Fascist, or a Communist, or a Demochristian; you've never been anything. Have you? Have you? Have ever been anything? »

« Of course. A partisan! »

Gianfranco laughed and said: « You're not so very wrong, after all. You know how many partisans there are like you? A lot more than there are real ones. »

« See, you admit it... and as for me, if I didn't have any recognition as a partisan, I deserved it as a patriot, someone who didn't take part in any of the shooting, perhaps; though a lot of them who didn't do the half of what I did... »

And as Bob was recovering himself and warming up, Gianfranco silenced him with a threat that could have intimidated only a guilty conscience.

« Did you ever think that I might take back my testimony? All I would have to do is say that I made a mistake, and then they would take back that patriot's card they gave you, and then, pretty boy, where would you hide your face when you went through Sanfrediano, with all the people as red as they are? »

Bob had a guilty conscience and was annihilated. He said, « It wouldn't be very good of you, if you did it, now that it's gone by... » It was a beseeching, from a man nailed to his cross, breathing his last sigh.

But Gianfranco wanted to consolidate his victory.

« And your women, » he insisted, « when they've learned that you're a coward, and all the district thinks you're one and will have stopped speaking to you, how will your women take that? »

Then Bob was himself. Suddenly, and almost surprisingly himself, he lashed out at Gianfranco, striking him on the forehead with the heel of his open hand, what in Sanfrediano they call a « frontino ». The thought of his declining in the esteem and the hearts of his girls, who were his life, had resuscitated him.

The frontino is a kindly slap, equal to a pat on the back, the substitute with a boy for a caress; and in opposite circumstances, it is the highest mark of scorn. In this case the frontino is used « not to get your hand dirty » with someone who is too low to be hit properly. And there is the so-called « interrogative » frontino, which is halfway between a compliment and an insult, and is an exquisitely plebian way of provoking a definitive feeling, in the reaction to it. The width of the gesture that accompanies the frontino, and the intensity of the smile of the man who gives it determine the various kinds, since as far as its force is concerned, whether it's the affectionate frontino or one of offense or pardon, the measure doesn't change. It is always a sharp, powerful slap, which shakes one's head, making it din, and clouding the brain, at the same time. In any case, there is nothing more appropriate than a frontino to resolve or change the course of a discussion, the discutant reaches the limit of tenderness, drama, or humiliation. But there is also a fourth occasion that demands the use of the frontino, and that is the one which applies to Bob, the man with his back to the wall, who is being punished or blackmailed out of proportion to his guilt, then, mortal and unspeakable, the frontino of desperation.

They were seated on the steps of the Tiratoio, where six centuries earlier the wool-makers of Sanfrediano had « pulled » the materials just dyed and washed; and at Bob's blow, Gianfranco's head bouced twice against the ancient stone of the building, as the billiard cue had done on the floor. At the same time, Bob got up and leaned over his friend, already helpful and conciliatory.

« Did I hurt you? » he asked.

« Not you. The building, » Gianfranco said.

And getting up at once, he found Bob again wide open, as he had been at the game, and he caught him with a fast right between the nose and the mouth. They were out in the open this time, and Bob couldn't and didn't want to refuse the fight, and in the silent darkness of the little square, they hit each other for a long time, silent, ferocious, falling, getting up again, both of them bloody, Sanfredianini who were punching each other. Until the group came up that had left the club, with Barcucci at its head, as fast as the young ones in spite of his crutch. In the course of their patrolling, with their loud comments, they had wakened the curiosity of all they met and had led them along, until at last they discovered the two fighters and forced them to shake hands.

And Gianfranco said: « I admit that maybe I brought

this punishment on myself. It's probably clear, I mean. I didn't think you were in such good form. »

Then, since they all wanted to know the reason for the argument, Gianfranco squeezed Bob's hand as if asking him to stick with the story, and said: « It was about a partisan action. Bob insisted that when we hunted out some 'blacks' that were shut up in a house, he was along with us, and it didn't seem to me that he was. In a lot of the other actions he was, but not in that one. »

« And now what's the decision? Was Bob there, or wasn't he? » someone asked.

Gianfranco laughed and said: « Well, if it turns out now, after the fight, that I'm the most banged up, it means that he was there. »

The crowd was thick around him: the cream of the district. It was a Saturday night, the end of the month, and everyone had in his pocket the rest of his pay, after the debts had been paid, those who had regular jobs, the rest was spent on films, coffee, the brothel and the tavern. Some applause rang out, and several comments were made, from this circle of outsiders.

« Fine! Even this time Bob landed on his feet. »

« And with what an opponent! »

« He's more of a partisan than we thought he was. »

« Especially since he was modest enough about it up till now. »

Now, as he heard these voices, the victory assumed for Bob an unexpected meaning. The fulness of the day that was hardly ended, and the happiness that he had attained in it had given him so much self-confidence that he had forgotten the physical and moral stature of his adversary; he had treated Gianfranco as he had when they were children, when his additional four years guaranteed him authority and supremacy. For a moment Bob thought how bold and how foolhardy he had been to provoke Gianfranco, first at the club and then on the Tiratoio steps — but a moment later, he was invaded by an exaggerated awareness of his own position, the comments of the people, the conciliating attitude of Gianfranco with its unsought admission — these all ended by persuading him that he had faced and won a decisive battle, that now he could squeeze Sanfrediano in his fist, according to his whim.

It had been, he thought, the great day of his life; unfortunately, it had rather been the beginning of his end.

BOB IS BOB, AND BARCUCCI IS HIS PROPHET

Who could face him, Bob, the next morning? He had brought low the hero of Sanfrediano, to whom even the stones bowed, and who, at twenty, enjoyed the privileges, the respect, and the glory of a veteran. The story had spread, in the course of the morning (it was Sunday), and they talked about it at the club, in the caffès, on the steps of the Carmine and of Cestello, the girls talked from one window to another, or in their doorways, with their best clothes on and their permanents just touched up. The comments were diverse and the interpretations varied, but at any rate the general opinion was upheld by the sticking-plaster on Gianfranco's eyebrow and the bandage around his eye, in contrast with the untouched face of Bob, freshly shaved and shining, with his lip just barely swollen. But on drawing closer to him, one realized that even though he had been revealed the stronger, even Bob had taken share of punishment, and that perhaps — who knows? — the marks on Gianfanco's face might be due only to some lucky and obvious blows, but not necessarily decisive ones in an objective list of the punches given and received. It was on this particular point that, at the club, at the billiard hall, and in the section meeting, Gianfranco's friends grew heated, since his manner of giving away the honors of the fight, his generosity and loyalty in admitting so promptly Bob's supremacy, were a part of his character, but at the same time they had been too fulsome and too hasty not to admit of some suspicion. Gianfranco had been fighting over a girl, that was clear, and he didn't

want to tell her name — and this, too, was to his credit —
but, in order to insure Bob's silence, he didn't have the right
to « mix the devil with the holy water » and acknowledge
publicly Bob's non-existent partisan activities. And then that
Bob, with a few lucky blows, had forced Gianfranco to show
himself with bruises and with adhesive plaster on his face
was, in addition to a sorrow for his friends, an offense to the
entire partisan movement, and hence a personal affront for
one and all.

« He'll see, » one said. « We weren't afraid of the Germans, and we won't be shut up by anyone like him. »

« By a little pipsqueak. »

« By a grease-ball. »

« A half-ass. »

« And let's face it », another said, « this Lord Bob is
beginning to smell a little. He comes to the billiard table and
takes our money, it seems that the Sanfrediano girls all belong to him, and if you go out with your girl, you have to
listen to things like: 'Let Bob teach you how to pick out
your ties, and how to wear your clothes, and how to comb
your hair, and how to hold your girl when you dance...' And
now, yesterday evening, in front of a whole bunch of outsiders, Gianfranco goes and says that Bob wasn't in that particular action, but in a lot of others, yes indeed. And we all
know — and until now this was the general opinion — that
Bob didn't do his duty until the very last minute, and who
knows even if he did it then, and how he did it... And how
are we going to get ourselves out of this situation? » he concluded.

Another, a tall, dark, good-looking boy, solidly built, with
wavy hair and a face that was almost smooth, his attitude
that of a wise and precociously spoiled adolescent, intervened
and said: « I'd suggest that we give him a lesson; we can
always figure out a way ».

Then it was Barcucci's turn to speak; he could always be
found with the boys, his crutch, his wit, and his common sense
always ready. « Halt », he said, « Let's summarize the situa-

tion. First of all, we can stop the idea of giving him a lesson before it starts. We all know where Fernando's proposal comes from and what he's getting at. I mean to say, that since Fernando aspires to the throne himself, all he would have to do is put Bob in a minority with the girls, and make himself more of a killer than Bob. We'll give Bob a lesson all right, when he's been properly warned, if he starts bragging about his partisan experiences; and as far as denying them with everybody, it won't be hard, you can leave that to me. But the real problem is something else: Bob got into a fight with Gianfranco and gave him some good punches, and Gianfranco afterwards, to maintain his position, went overboard in some of his statements. So he's the one we have to ask for an explanation. Gianfranco is responsible and has to make up for it. »

« All right », said the one who had spoken before, « but Bob, from now on, is nearer than ever to... » and he drew his finger across his throat.

« As for me », Fernando said, « I'd like to speak about something personal. The girls that I have — well, Bob dreams about them at night. They're, a certain kind of rocket that you can set off only in Sanfrediano, and for them Bob is nothing at all, and whenever he tried anything with them, he found himself walking home by himself in the dark... Besides... » he added, « who am I saying all this to? You all know as well as I do that, compared to me, Bob is just an amateur ».

« That's right », said Barcucci, « Bob's Bob, and you're Casanova ».

And this remark, with the laughter, the comments, and the slaps on the back that it aroused, was enough to reestablish the atmosphere of happines and confidence in which they waited for Gianfranco, the prelude to his rapid, convinced, and complete absolution; and it helped to send Bob still further along the wrong path, for the young men of Sanfrediano, who were waiting for the chance to show him...

But Bob in the meanwhile — who could restrain him?

Victor, everywhere heralded, he had returned home after midnight, at the hour when his father and brothers were keeping vigil about their hunters' blinds, and his mother was already asleep in her room. He was burning with thirst overheated, his head heavy and buzzing; three times, during the battle, Gianfranco's fiists had hit him on the temple, and only now was he aware of their force. Also his jaw suddenly woke up, and pained him if he moved his chin. He looked at himself in the mirror: his face was intact, and he smiled. Only his lower lip was a little swollen; it was nothing, he disinfected it and smeared it with vaseline before he went to bed. But he couldn't get to sleep. One by one, all the blows that Gianfranco had hammered over his body, found their echo, a little belated, but increasing as the time passed. Until his head seemed to be blowing up, it was burning, and he was sure that he had a fever.

He got up and poured some water into a basin, then added a few drops of cologne, and began to apply a damp handkerchief to his forehead. It was cooling, and he went on like that for some time, feeling that these afflictions were not entirely unpleasant, but rather like glorious wounds; he smiled to himself, content, wreathed with laurel, as he thought. Because Gianfranco wasn't just any boy of Sanfrediano, having been recognized the winner wasn't like beating just anybody — that he had done before, if rarely, for that matter — before he had stopped calling himself Aldo and, losing his boyish thoughtlessness, had begun to assume the conscious personality of Bob. And Bob wasn't very much disposed to giving punches, precisely because he was afraid of receiving them: he might be marked by them in some way, or undergo a humiliation which would have diminished him in the girls' eyes. The idea of being hit gave him the same uneasiness that he felt when he heard shots or had to watch, say, an operation. It was not exactly fear, it was sensitivity, a matter of nerves, if not of a gentle spirit. Everyone is made in his own way, he used to say to himself, and when the time came he had always been able to make the best of a situation. He didn't remind himself that there were certain situations he had always avoided, and only when against his will he had been involved in them, did he try to face them and resolve them. To tell the truth, they had always been resolved in his favor, but none of them before had been such as to call into play his whole personality, his fame, and his honor. Now this had happened, with Gianfranco, through what Gianfranco represented and the circumstance that ensued from this.

Bob, unconsciously but actively, understood all of this, and in his imagination he played with it, as he changed from time to time the cold cloth on his forehead, full of sweat, excitement, and visions. As he has beaten Gianfranco, now he could beat anyone. Gianfranco, if he should try again, or Joe Louis in person. At last Bob was a complete man, weaned from fear, with a history behind him, a partisan's, which included an undefined, but certainly conspicuous number of actions. And he was even capable of reliving those actions now, seeing himself with his Tommy-gun, his red scarf around his neck, here, there, in real places, hardy and proud, though the shots had no sound and the blood had no color, in the perspective of his memory.

By now he was delirious. And only delirium, the delirium particularly of a Bob, could have suggested to him the idea that, with a few punches and a treacherous frontino, he had acquired the virtues and merits of the adversary he had defeated, those merits of a temperament quite different from his own. And as far as that goes, if an outsider wanted to judge the extent to which Gianfranco had been defeated, he would only have to think of the cause of this delirium to make up his mind: Gianfranco's punches had quite evidently left Bob's face intact, but his face only.

But it was, above all, his face, physically, that Bob cared about; and his girls could look at it now and be proud of him. Now, it could be presumed, he would be much bolder in his sentimental affairs, and the threshhold which he had formerly forbidden himself he would now be less scrupulous about crossing: did there exist anyone in all of Sanfrediano who could get him with his back to the wall? A frontino, and that would be that, for anyone who tried. And Gina, if she wanted to, could get married; he would be generous: let her settle down in her new house in Legnaia in the arms of her ageing ragman, Bob was setting out for golder, rosier shores: Tosca, for example, and Silvana, for whom he had fought, and Bice « a treasure island », and still another who had come out recently, who in addition to her other qualities, had the name of an actress that Bob admired. « Loretta and Bob », he exclaimed, a child of Sanfrediano in spite of everything, « a pair of star attractions »; and for the last time, he changed the wet cloth on his forehead. The dawn had broken some time past, the sun had risen, the Cestello bell was ringing. His mother was busy in the kitchen, and Bob joined her there for breakfast.

The pain in his head had almost disappeared, and even if his body still ached slightly all over and his hands and forehead were on fire, his spirits were fresh; Bob felt himself in form, as never before. These were the results, and being an ex-athlete he should have known, of what boxers call the technical K. O., when a man continues to stay on his feet, a mere relic, and the clearness and decision of his actions are not normal, but mechanical, occasional, unthought out. And so Bob began his Sunday, and the counsels the night had brought him were stronger than ever. Groggy as he was, in a little while he would begin to put them into action. He started examining his lip, just barely swollen, and coyly, he found that it gave him a badge, the sign of the honor he had won for himself.

His mother had gone out to mass and to market, and he was still in front of the mirror, shaving, when the bell rang. He opened the door and found Gina. She shut the door behind her rapidly, timorously, and said:

« I don't think anybody saw me. Anyhow, I came to ask your mother for some salt, we'll say, I didn't know she was out. Instead, I was really watching from the window until she had turned the corner at via della Chiesa ».

He drew the razor over one cheek. « But do you really want some salt? Have you run out? » he asked.

« Does this seem to you a good time to joke, Bob? »

« Why? What's changed since yesterday? »

« I'll tell you what's changed. He wants me to go and spend the last week before the wedding in his family's house, so that I can make friends with his mother, and the two of us together can give the finishing touches to the house in Legnaia ».

« Well, go then », he said. « It doesn't hurt to have your mother-in-law on your side, and you won't be going very far away. Not more than fifty yards from here, as the crow flies ».

She came closer to him and took his arm, looking at him. He detached himself and said: « Don't make me lose time. This soap is getting dry ».

« But Bob », she said, holding on to the back of a chair, « do you understand what this means? The time has come when I'll have to tell him everything, that I don't want him, that I was kidding him along... Whatever he does then, I'll face it; he's crazy mad in love with me and could even kill me... But don't be afraid, even if I'm dying, I won't say why I did it, that I did it for you. And I don't even ask you for anything; what could I ask you for? It's the way it has to be, by now. I'm only sorry because it could have been a good thing for my family... All I want you to do is realize that this is the best proof I could give you that I really love you — if I haven't proved it enough already — and that I only want to be yours. I was a real Sanfrediano girl, as proud as the rest of them, and now I've become your dummy, your helper, and you couldn't have made me anything worse... ».

« Are you finished? » he asked.

« Yes, I know, it's natural for you. You were always sure it would turn out this way, that I wouldn't have the strength

to break away from you, and I knew it too, but I hoped...
now I don't hope for anything any more, now... ».

Bob interrupted her, his face half shaved and half soapy,
looking at her in the mirror where he was shaving and where
the figure of Gina was reflected, tall. He threw out his words:

« But there'might be another solution, did you ever think
of that? It would fix up everyone, you, me, him, your family,
your mother-in-law... ».

« What do you mean? » she asked, her eyes wide, her
heart aching. She managed to keep her voice normal; she
wanted to hear Bob say what she thought he was going to
say, what she hadn't wanted to believe him capable of saying.

He continued, in his off-hand, evasive way, making the
meaning still clearer: « You could perfectly well marry him.
That wouldn't make me give my father back the key to the
store-room... What I mean is, between you and me, everything could go on as before ».

It was a mistake. Bob was going to make others during
the day, but all of them could have been easily mended as
usual, if he hadn't made this capital error. He should never
have shown himself to Gina as she saw him now; also because
it was not his real self. His character was different; his cynicism and shamelessness were, after all, innocent. But now
he was the Bob of that special moment, he didn't stop to
think that his whole life depended on Gina and, losing her,
he lost everything, even his physical balance. He acted the
way he thought he could, he who now had the world at his
disposal, and « Sanfrediano for his doormat ».

Gina looked at his face in the mirror, the chin lifted
so that he could shave his throat; and this time words failed
her, she just stood there looking at him, and when he turned
and moved towards her, saying: « You're angry, I see, but
wouldn't that really be a solution? », she drew back, reached
the door, and flung out. Bob followed her to the stairs and
shouted: « I was joking. Can't you take a joke? »

He received no answer, went back in and finished shaving, making himself as handsome as he should be, and when

he went out into the street later, he met Gina's brother, the youngest one, whose name was Cesare like his father he had never known. Bob said to him: « Tell Gina she's crazy. Even if my mother wasn't there, she could have come back for the salt. I was just joking ».

But the child didn't seem to understand the errand, and instead asked: « Is it true that you made Gianfranco's face swell up last night? I'm sorry, you know; but you're a real killer ».

It was the first of the new and real laurels that Bob was gathering.

« What? Has the story gotten around already? »

« Did it happen or didn't it? » Cesarino said. « Up till now Gianfranco hadn't even taken anything from anybody ».

Bob was glowing like the sun on the windows of the nearby wineshop. He said: « How would you like a nice bag of roasted chestnuts? »

A little later, he went on his way, and it was the passage of a man borne along by the sun, one who needs only to turn over his cards to break the bank. Loretta met him as soon as he turned the corner of via del Leone. She was adolescent, sixteen, beautiful and from Sanfrediano, « a flower that's opened in the night and is wet with its first dew » — so she seemed to him, and he told her so, stopping her there, unlucky as he was, in the middle of the street, in front of everyone, almost directly opposite Mafalda's house.

« If I don't pick you now, when will I? »

She turned as red as a flame, looking all around, blinded by emotion, and pushing her hair behind her ear with one hand, she tried to appear calm and self-possessed.

« But, Bob, what do you mean? You're out of your mind... everyone can see us; my father is right there at the window ».

« Your father is fine where he is. When are we going to see each other? »

« We? What do you mean, we?... all right, Bob, all right. I'll be going dancing today ».

A swan was singing at that moment, but he, Bob, how could he hear it? He gathered these and many other laurels in the course of the morning; with one of them, he could have regained, very partially, the sympathy of the boys at the club — a sympathy which he had no idea he had lost, quite the contrary. This was when, after he had tried in vain to run into Silvana, he went to piazza de' Nerli to the bar for something to drink, and there at the door of the bar, practically under Tosca's window (she was no doubt in bed, nursing her influenza, and could probably hear him) in the midst of an interested and gossiping audience, he answered a notorious ex-Fascist who had questioned him:

« I didn't win and I didn't lose. We fought between ourselves, like fellow partisans and men of honor. Gianfranco hasn't changed because of what happened. He's still far, far above us all, especially you, and also me. Compared to him, what am I? »

It was a victor's generosity, a man sure of himself and of his future; and there were those present who understood this in its real meaning, and those who were more honest or less suspicious and cunning, who gave his words a meaning of pure gold. And Barcucci, among the latter, in spite of his white hair and his wisdom, since he wanted everything to be straightened out, waited for Bob about dinner time in front of his stand, and said:

« I know that this morning, in front of the bar there, you said some things that made sense. Good for you. But why didn't you come by the club? Are you afraid you have enemies there? On the contrary, after the way you acted last night and this morning, some of them who thought you were only good to chase skirts are beginning to change their minds ».

« I'm glad to learn that all of them have caught on. But really, I'm just the same, the same as I was yesterday and as I always have been. And I know that if we tried it again, Gianfranco could perfectly well send me to the hospital... I mean, perhaps I could send him there, too, in a manner of speaking... and I didn't come to the club this morning because », he laughed, with his tight-lipped, Bob-like smile, « precisely because I was chasing a skirt. And you know, Barcucci, I said to her: *come on,* and she didn't wait to say yes... a new one, Barcucci, the most beautiful one there is in Sanfrediano, the youngest of the beauties, and the most splendid... I'll let you guess who ».

« Go away, smart boy », Barcucci said, measuring his crutch, « For you the best one is always the latest one you're aiming at. But be careful that you aren't caught by one of them that can make your heart ache ».

« That one has still to be born », Bob said.

And Barcucci, just to be saying something, answered: « Who knows but what she may be already born and grown up, with her crutch aimed at you the way mine is. And maybe she'll give it to you right on the head ». As usual, he asked for a match, and then finished: « Because one of the two: either what they've always said about you and you've encouraged them to say is just borrowed glory, or else the girls of Sanfrediano — and I hate to admit it — aren't what they once were. They've swallowed their brains or something of the sort ».

« No, they haven't », Bob said. « I'm the one who's been making them pour their brains out, to suit me... this evening I'll come by the club, but this afternoon I'm going dancing; Sunday hasn't even begun yet. And tomorrow is another day, Barcucci. That's the way to live if you can work it ».

« While it lasts then », Barcucci answered, « good appetite ».

« What an appetite! » Bob said, « like a horse, a wolf, a lion! »

But it wasn't appetite, it was a fever he had, like a horse's as a matter of fact, and his mother realized it and suggested that he go to bed. She insisted so, that Bob nearly hurt her feelings, before he went off to the dance hall.

As he went out, on the landing of the first floor, he met Gina, who pretended that she had just opened the door that moment. Her face was done in, there was a hard look in her eyes that Bob didn't recognize, at least it didn't make him stop and think: in fact, she seemed to him a girl who was humiliated and was seeking forgiveness. With the world in the palm of his hand, Loretta at the dance hall, and Tosca when it was evening, punctual in spite of her influenza, Gina seemed more than ever his reserve ball, his most faithful.

« So », he said to her, « you managed to cook without any salt ».

She took another step below him, not turning around. « Do you still think the way you did this morning? » she asked.

He put his hands on her shoulders, weighing on her, and said, « Idiot, it was for your own good. As far as I'm concerned, to have you all to myself suits me fine ».

Gina freed herself and ran down the last steps hastily. At the doorway she let him pass and said: « I wouldn't have believed you could be so low. Really it's true what they say: a thousand years of good destroyed with a single curse. And you said it in time, thank God, to make me stop loving you before I could commit the final foolishness and refuse to marry a man that really loves me, even if he wasn't my first ». Then she said: « God, what a satisfaction it is! »

He looked at her, ironic, Bob; both of them were smiling because they were in the street where everyone could see them.

« Are you threatening me? » he said.

« More or less... a slim satisfaction, you're right, but... oh, don't start thinking of a tragedy in that little brain of yours; you don't deserve a real tragedy, it would be too much for you... but a nice little surprise somebody's fixing for you, and I think I'll help out ».

« Nobody alive », he repeated, « man or woman, can put Bob in the sack. And now, beautiful, take care of yourself. You're looking a little run down. Good-bye now ».

And he went off, unknowing, toward his fate. A few

aspirin, as his mother had suggested, a good sweat, would
have cleared up his ideas. But he was Bob, and Bob he wanted to be, so he lost his reputation, for always, and in what
a manner! It was enough for the sun to set and rise again
to send Bob, from Austerlitz, straight into Waterloo. They
were as strong as ever, the girls of Sanfrediano.

THE BEAUTIES' CONSPIRACY

Bob wasn't the only one who was feverish and suffered
with insomnia in those days and those nights. Not to his
knowledge, for reasons that were different from his though
they concerned him very much, all the girls that he thought
were his for the moment were awake and had a fever. Tosca,
Gina, Silvana, Bice, Loretta, and even Mafalda, each with
her own and different thoughts, were all alike in a common
and heartfelt purpose: that the time should pass quickly and
Sunday evening should come. He had to make up his mind,
the beautiful Bob: which one of them did he prefer? And
when the choice was made, then halt, the end of the enter-
prises of the young man with the beautiful lashes. Now the
dignity and the honor of the girls of Sanfrediano were at
stake.

Tosca was the one who wove the threads of the conspiracy, at first by chance, and then with a determination
that became more and more precise and with a mercilessness
that was a pure Sanfrediano quality. Assisted by luck, she
had been able to uncover all, or almost all, of the intrigue
that Bob kept going; one by one, she had confronted the
girls, she had joined them together, persuading them with
ease, by playing on their pride and their self-respect. Tosca
was sure that none of them would give then plan away and
tell Bob what was waiting for him, not so much because they
had all sworn, but because things were arranged in such a
way that each of them realized, apparently, that it was to
her advantage to make Bob face his responsibilities and
make him clarify publicly — that is, in the presence of all
of them — his feelings and the basis for his choice.

But gradually, as the facts became known, through the reciprocal and certainly partial confidences that the girls exchanged, as the hour of the trial drew nearer, the figure of Bob declined sharply in the heart of each one of them. And with greater or lesser resentment, offense, pain, with more or less disenchantment or nostalgia, already all the girls, as his secrets were exposed, were saying goodbye to him and preparing — whichever one was « elected » — to throw his choice right back at him. « Sanfrediano girls don't take anybody's left-overs », Silvana had already said. Bob could have had a thousand girls, and the last one would always have felt herself the only one, the winner; in fact, it was this pride that increased Bob's fascination and their love for him. But to discover themselves « all lined up together in his heart; or like a bag of peanuts in his pocket », as Tosca had said, or like « concubines », as Mafalda had added, offended them and freed them from their love. And so, just as Tosca's heart had stopped hurting when it should have been trembling, so in all of the girls, when they accepted the invitation to the « performance » and after their first perplexities and refusals they began to grow enthusiastic about its perfect success, there was this sense of bitterness, of separation, and fervent iconoclasm towards Bob. And Mafalda, more than any, who didn't doubt but what Bob would exclude her at the very start, had already removed herself, deluded, from the race, but was ready to kinde and encourage a noisy tempest. Hadn't it really been she, Mafalda, who secretly guided Tosca's actions, suggesting them to her and strengthening her, without seeming to, in her intention?

At first, as she had said to Gina, on Friday evening Tosca waited for Silvana at the exit of the workshop. They had been babies together, they knew each other thoroughly, and while Tosca was all enthusiasm, with « her heart on her lips », Silvana was thoughtful, with a nature that was inclined to shut into itself her own joys and troubles, enjoying and sharing those of other people; two characters, at any rate, both sincere, proud, and generous at once, and for all their apparent contrast, destined to comprehend each other, as in fact they had, having been intimate friends, until a short time before.

Tosca went up to her and said, « I know, I've behaved badly to you. It's nearly a month since I've got engaged to Aldo, and I've been avoiding you ».

Silvana wasn't looking at her friend, but at the horizon, where the river curved wide and full around the island. « Don't think I didn't imagine as much », she said, « I thought so... you asked about him too often ».

« I had a guilty conscience, and I was waiting for this moment, and now I've told you and I feel free again and I can have him all to myself. Besides, it isn't as if I took him away from you, he was the one who came to me, by himself, after he had talked to you frankly ».

Silvana drew away from the railing, against which she had been walking, and started across the street, to go away. Tosca as already raising her voice, shouting.

« I'm not used to making scenes », Silvana said. « And besides, I don't want anybody's left-overs ».

« And just who do you mean by left-overs? You'd be the one... What I mean is, what are you getting at? »

« You mean, what is Bob getting at. And it isn't true that he's left. We saw each other just last night ».

« When? »

« About this time ».

« Where? »

« None of your business ».

« It certainly is my business », Tosca said, her heart heavy, « Was it at the Cascine, by any chance? »

Silvana nodded; and they found themselves looking into each other's eyes, with the same anguish, and shame, and desolation.

« You might be telling the truth », Tosca admitted. « He did tell me yesterday evening that he had to go back to the office, a special occasion ».

Silvana smiled, to keep from bursting into tears, and to

maintain her hold on herself in this situation that was upsetting. « Keep calm », she said to Tosca, « we hadn't seen each other for nearly a week — all special occasions ».

And then, a little later, Tosca said: « Maybe he doesn't know how to leave you, without hurting you, or maybe he isn't sure yet which of the two of us he loves... he has to make up his mind, either you or me ».

« Or maybe », Silvana continued, in her tone that was both smiling and despairing, « he simply wants to act like Bob, with me and with you, as he did with all of them ».

« But he can't keep us lined up like this in his heart », Tosca said. « What are we, pieces of candy? Are we a package of dried chestnuts to keep in your pocket and chew one after the other? He has to make up his mind, and there's only one way. He can't go saying to you that he loves you and to me that he loves me, while the two of us, it seems, both love just one... He has to say in front of both of us which one it is that he really loves ».

« Oh no », Silvana repeated, because she felt she was the one that loved most and was loved least, and the idea of Bob's judgment frightened her. « I don't take anybody's leftovers. And besides, you can't do that sort of thing; we'd both seem ridiculous to him ».

« Whether you can do it or not, we'll do it. And if I seem ridiculous to him, it means that he doesn't love me... Sometimes I forget to set the votive light in front of the Madonna, so you can be sure I'll be able to forget him, too... and if he tries to act Bob... he'll wish he were just Aldo! He'll get a lesson that nobody'll be able to save him from. Of course », Tosca commented, « It wouldn't be easy for me ».

Then when her plan was already formulated, she said: « Let's wait before we start pulling each other's hair, let's sleep on the idea, and then meet tomorrow morning at eight-thirty and talk it over when we're a little calmer ».

They said good-bye, both of them sorrowful; and Silvana especially, with her proud and romantic nature, had been more deeply hurt by that conversation. Now that the reality had to be faced, Silvana felt herself helpless in front of it; and being, of all the girls, the one most prepared to understand and to sacrifice herself as she had explained honestly to Gianfranco, now that she was suffering still more for Bob, dreaming and deluded, she was the first to say good-bye to him in her heart. « I'll always love him », she thought, « but I don't want anybody's leavings, especially Tosca's, that loud-mouth... what kind of woman would I be anyway? I'd make all of Sanfrediano laugh if they came to know, and Bob himself, if he is just doing this to test me ». Tosca's feelings, on the other hand, were characteristically hers, animated and bellicose, as tough as she was, and she too was beautiful and hurt and in love, and more than ever determined to wrest from Bob a statement that would once and for all, as far as she was concerned « pour the wine out of the bottle ».

Saturday morning Tosca was on her feet as soon as it was daylight; she wouldn't wait until evening to meet Bob the entrance of the Cascine: she set herself to wait for him at the end of via del Leone, where he would have to pass before he crossed the bridge and went to work. There was a line of trucks blocking half of the street, and she stood in their shadow to avoid people as much as possible, with the conversations and greetings and the gossip that would result if they saw her waiting and then going off in Bob's company; in fact, she would walk ahead of him, as soon as he had seen her.

Bob was late, and Tosca was about to run to the head of the bridge, afraid that he might have taken a different route, when she saw him coming along with Mafalda. Tosca hid behind the trucks and then followed the two of them at a distance, among the people. So he hadn't left Mafalda after all, she thought, in spite of the life Mafalda was leading, they were still friends, and there she was in her bathrobe, accompanying him, after Bob had perhaps spent the night with her, Mafalda was his mistress. From the distance she saw them turn into Borgo Stella and stop, almost hidden, in the recess of a gateway. Then Tosca changed her direction and went to wait for Bob on the other side of the bridge, it was the next sure place in his path, and there she would confront him, and how she would confront him, after this second revelation!

After she had been waiting for him a few minutes, she looked around, and seated on the bench under Goldoni's monument, immersed in her magazine, there was Bice, who raised her head at this moment and smiled at Tosca. Tosca scarcely knew her, though she knew who Bice was and where she lived because at one time a sister of Bice's had been a straw-weaver before she had « evolved » into a typist. But she didn't know Bice well, who came from another part of Sanfrediano, as far away as via del Campuccio is from piazza de' Nerli — and it certainly wasn't for fear of Bice's gossiping that Tosca would give up her meeting with Bob as soon as he appeared on the bridge. In any event, she had to reply to the greeting; and then Bice got up and came over to her, unexpectedly friendly, and said:

« What are you doing? Something's happened to you, you seem a little upset... »

« Why? » Tosca said. « I'm here waiting for my mother; we have to go and get some chairs ». She became flustered (Tosca flustered!) and catching herself in time, changed the subject. « And you? What's new with you? Waiting for somebody?

« Somebody who isn't coming », Bice said, calmly and naturally.

It was a manner of speaking, a Sanfrediano proverb, and as Bice added: « I'm on my vacation, so I'm enjoying a bit of fresh air », already Tosca had stopped listening, in her excited state, she was constructing an idea of her own, using that sixth sense that is given women who are jealous and in love; she had acquired it through recent experience. It was nothing to go on, a vague suspicion, but gradually it became positive and assumed the certainty of a truth. Bice lived, as

Bob did, in via del Campuccio, and she was waiting for some-body who wasn't coming... « My mother isn't coming either, so I'm going on by myself », she said, « Good-bye ». She pretended to turn into via della Vigna and then came back, cautiously, and hid herself at the back of the monument, only a few steps away from Bice who had returned to her bench and her reading.

And so it was that Tosca had her third revelation. When she saw that Bob took Bice by the arm and, laughing, they turned to follow the river, Tosca wanted to run, follow them, and put it to him right then and there, making a scene, but her body refused to obey her, stayed motionless, leaning, broken, against the base of the monument, and she said to herself: « He's probably told her that she's his billiard ball or his bowling ball! » Then she remembered Silvana, and coming to life again immediately, running along the Borgo, she found her in front of her house. Tosca was worn out, now that her race was over, and emotion and scorn made her eyes shine; she was panting.

« Come on, come on », she said to Silvana, « there's news ».

Silvana was pale and withdrawn, her sleepless night over and her decision made. She interrupted, and began to walk away at the same time: « There's no use in your getting so excited. I leave the field to you... he'll have to be the one to come to me ».

Tosca was waving her hands, beyond herself, in an exalt-ation that was clearly rabid, her gestures heaving, not find-ing words, after the first ones with which she had struck Silvana; and Silvana became alarmed, took the other girl by the arm and drew her aside, beyond people's curiosity, in the alleyway of the Cestello. « Do you want a platform to speak from? » she asked. « Shame on you ».

Tosca broke into a hysterical laugh, which loosened her tongue and freed her alarm in loud vulgarity.

« We're there, my friend! We're beautiful little statues » and she pantomined the circling, childhood game:

> Lovely little statues
> Of silver and of gold
> I see a hundred
> One, two, and... three!

« This one is Tosca », she said, « and this one is the light-fingered Silvana, and this is Mafalda, yes, the redhead, the daughter of the cabman, and this one is Bice, who lives next door to him and works at the *Rinascente* department store, and then, and then... »

Suddenly she calmed down, became serious, grim, and precise: « Well, now we have to dig his eyes out », she said.

And she told it all, and then repeated: « As long as he took us one at a time, we could always believe that we were the last one and the real one, but now we know that it's just his profession, and for all we can tell, you and I, and God knows how many others are simply the 'special occasions' of Mafalda... and we wouldn't be worthy of Sanfrediano if we didn't skin him alive ».

Silvana was dumbfounded, still almost incredulous, and her hands trembled as she said, « It would be terrible of you to invent all this just to take Bob away... I've already told you that I don't want him any more, naturally, now that he isn't good for anything except the glue factory ». Then she sighed, adding, « This would have to happen this morning and make me late for work just when I have to begin a job that's the kind to wear your eyes out, and I need all the calm I can manage, and instead my hands are shaking... I look as if I had the palsy, see ».

« Make it stop », Tosca said. « If you listen to me, your hands will be needed for something else besides embroidery ».

They crossed piazza Piattellina and via del Leone to save time, since Silvana was late, and the trucks were still there in a long row, the morning rush was thicker now, even more people were crowded around the polenta man, and Mafalda was on her way home after she had had her cognac at the bar.

« There she is », Tosca said, « you see her, in her bathrobe, just the way I said... she's his regular work, and we're the special occasions! »

And she was Tosca: when Mafalda passed, lost in her own thoughts, Tosca spat on the ground in front of her, as a greeting.

Mafalda turned around and smiled: « Hello, Toschina », she said. « Eat something salty? »

It was a compliment, and since she had no reason to imagine a provocation, Mafalda thought of Tosca as a friend, a year or so younger, perhaps even two or three, though in spite of this, they had made their first communion together, along with Silvana, who was there now, too.

« It's for you to give Bob, from me », Tosca added, while Silvana was trying to drag her away, imploring: « She'll make us lose out completely ».

« I don't think so », Mafalda said, walking beside them, having caught on at once. She added: « So he's made a fool out of you too, that louse. Poor Toschina! » and she put her hand over the other's mouth. « Calm down », she said, « if we make a scandal, we'll only be playing his game ».

A little later, in the back room of the bar, deserted at that hour, Mafalda, who hadn't had to work too hard to lead them there and make them explain, said: « I swear on my mother's tomb — if that oath counts for anything any more — that I'm not his mistress... well, « she admitted, « I may have done a few things — all of Sanfrediano knows that by now — but with Bob, never ». And her eyes lighted up: « now the young man in question swore eternal love to me a little while ago, when Tosca was spying on us... you see, instead, that he's taking us all in, every last one of us, really being Bob. And Tosca is right, Silvana, it isn't just a matter of scratching his eyes out, we have to show him that the girls of Sanfrediano aren't asleep on their feet... I'll see to Bice, we went to school together, and we're still friends, even if we haven't seen much of each other lately... and since I know her, I'm a little surprised; she's an egoist and looks things square in the face. I don't see how she could have fallen ».

« With him! » Silvana couldn't keep herself from exclaiming, and it was already a regret, a farewell, overcome by her wrath and by the delusion that was growing in her now, too.

They had a meaning then, Tosca's words, on Saturday evening when she said to Bob that she would give him the proof of her love and would want the same from him. Pretending to have the fever in order to leave him in a hurry, and also because now being near him was unbearable and made her uneasy, Tosca boarded the bus and then got down at the stop near Borgognissanti: there waiting for her, with Mafalda and Silvana, was Bice too, who said the first word when the discussion was opened.

« It's a snare and I don't like it. I was with Bob today until three o'clock and I don't feel like sticking a dagger in his back this way. Why should we line ourselves up in front of him this way and say 'choose'? And as for myself, I don't have the least desire to be chosen... but you have to be stone blind not to see that Bob is Bob and so, all right, he chooses, he picks one of the four of us, and what then? The one he chooses will be the first one he's unfaithful to. We'll rid him of three of us, and for him that'll be so much to the good ».

« You talk like a female gigolo », Tosca bust out, suddenly calling her *tu*, in spite of their not being friends, « as if he were the Hunchback ». And then she added, « who, according to what people say, the more he was unfaithful, the more honored the women felt... Bob isn't the Hunchback, and besides we're another generation! »

They were far, but not too far, from Sanfrediano, walking slowly as they talked, along via Maggio, and when they had climbed the Sdrucciolo they entered piazza Pitti, with the palace in front of them, tall in the dusk, and struck in all its length by the moonlight. Bice bent her head slightly and looked at Tosca:

« You have to try hard, dear, to make me mad... I came here because Mafalda threatened to make God knows what kind of scene in front of my house, and also a little bit out of curiosity, to see you all face to face, you who say you love him so much. If I really felt that my life depended so much on Bob, in the midst of this discussion, I would feel I was drowning ».

This time it was Silvana who reacted, feeling that she was the one most touched by this remark, and in what she said there was all the confusion of the feelings that were hers then.

« Yes, fine. We're all... I don't know what. But he's shown that he considered us what we are now before we were... And he has to pay for it, he has to... »

« What are you doing here then? Spying? » said Tosca, coming face to face with Bice, masking a forceful threat in the calm that she maintained only with force.

Mafalda intervened, since the machine was in motion and she was too eager to see Bob run over by it. She said: « Girls, you're getting lost in ancient history... There are just two explanations, as old Barcucci says, either you don't have any blood in your veins, or else Bob appeals to you the way he is, that is, the way he's shown he is, the way Bice says she always knew he was, even if we didn't... If you like him like that, and you like being his slaves and sharing him with a lot of other slaves, I'm not with you... I haven't been able to eat a bite since this morning because of the anger and the pain he's given me ».

« Well, who has? » Tosca exclaimed.

« I have. And with a huge appetite », Bice said, « because I never had any illusions about Bob... but now », she added, « imagining it is one thing, and knowing it is another... from this minute on, Signor Bob will see me through the wrong end of a telescope, and I don't have to put myself on display for him... I've already made my choice, before he can make his. And for me, I've already given him his dismissal notice ».

Here Tosca broke in again, almost shouting: « Well then, are you or aren't you a Sanfrediano girl? You mean you don't want to throw the offense he's given you right back in his face? »

« He treated us like a harem ».

« All right, all right », Tosca continued, « But look out, Miss salesgirl, if you tell him about our little surprise, I'll tear your eyes out before I do his... And I forbid you to say where you work that you're from Sanfrediano ».

« Oh my », said Bice, « am I afraid ».

After another intervention by Mafalda and by Silvana, who was ready to leave because her face was so red with shame that she « didn't know where to hide it », Bice added:

« Of course, if there's going to be a real show, then I don't want to miss it... But let's make it a conspiracy and see that the show is perfect, because if I can put two and two together, and if I know Bob, can we be sure that we're the only concubines, as Mafalda puts it? »

« Why? » asked Tosca, « Won't we be enough to tear him apart, in the name of those we don't know about, too? »

Mafalda patted her tenderly on the shoulder.

Now, talking distractedly, they had climbed up the gravel square that the palace surveys, they stood in the moonlit shadow, and below, under the arc-lights, three young men drew near, then overtook the girls, beseiged them, casual, insistent, brilliant, invincible; and the girls had to be rude, tough, Sanfredianian, and almost take flight, to free themselves, running all the way back into the quarter to piazza del Carmine, where they stopped again, their backs against the long wall that we know, and when Mafalda then asked a question that required an answer, Tosca said:

« Well, we can't all wait for him, stopped dead in the middle of the street, especially not in Sanfrediano, nor outside of his office. Tomorrow evening, without his catching on, I'll lead him to the big meadow in the Cascine; we always end up going there. Do you know which place I mean? »

Of course they knew. Bob took all of his girls there when it was evening, and this coincidence (but it was more than that, a sign of his lack of imagination) angered even Bice, and aroused her first feeling of indignation. This was surely so, when she began to think: « Today he took me up on the viali, but because it was in the daytime, and during the day, the cascine are too close to Sanfrediano ». This is what she thought, but what she said was: « As if he were the only man alive, after all ».

« Those three who were bothering us just now, for example, were much more elegant and brighter than Bob, judging them at a glance anyway, especially the blond one... » said Mafalda, and she caught herself, so as not to reveal too much of her feelings and her real intentions.

« They were from another district », Bice insisted, « but even in our own neighborhood, in Sanfrediano that is, there are some boys that Bob can't set a candle to, with a position and a future that he would dream of having. There are ». She repeated.

Then, as if her conscience had given her a twinge, Silvana remembered the existence of Gianfranco, and she blushed, to herself, at the thought.

When the plan was concluded, the beauties said good-bye to one another, to meet again the next morning, and perfect it, make sure that nothing had changed while they waiting for the evening and the great test. And as Bice had divined, at least two beauties were missing in the conspiracy, the neophyte and the veteran, but Bob would take care of that, with his inconsiderate way of treating events and in those hours he would add the two to the chorus.

So, by the next morning, this much had changed: Bob was the order of the day in Sanfrediano, fighter and partisan, in addition to heartbreaker, things that no one had ever thought of him; and the girls had their first moments of fear, second thoughts, and the first signs of desertion. But it was enough for Mafalda to arrive with some unpublished news, last-minute information, to set the fire going again from the ashes, as the insult was renewed.

They had decided to meet in the Boboli gardens, in a side path behind the sundial, all of them beautiful, elegant and proud, in their Sunday clothes, their newly-made or just done over suits, their wool skirts for autumn, as the fashion and the season suggested, even if the temperature still didn't require them. And Mafalda arrived with Loretta, dragging her by the hand like an older sister, the younger one reluctant and cross.

« I was at my window and I saw His Lordiship starting his last official act... Now, speak up ».

Loretta changed into lofty pride her former expression of a schoolgirl caught being naughty, and said: « You're all biting your tongues off because Bob's told me how he feels, I know that. Because for him I'm just like a flower, and he likes me better than any of you. You want Bob to choose, do you? It's all right with me, but afterwards, you'll all have to look up to see me ».

« Anway », Tosca said, « you'll meet Bob this evening along with us. And this afternoon you don't go dancing ».

« That remains to be seen », said Loretta.

« I can see to that by myself », Mafalda said, « I'll lock you up ».

Then as the discussion went on, Tosca explained something that was bothering her: « If he should find out about it, he mustn't be able to tell all about it in his own way. Now that people are beginning to think more highly of him, Sanfrediano will believe what he wants it to; he's able to get us in the wrong and make us suffer the tortures of the damned... We need a witness, and I thought of Gina. She volunteered a few days ago, when it seemed to be just a matter between me and Silvana, and now, even more than before, I don't think she'll refuse. Gina lives in the same building with Aldo — I mean Bob — and she's a friend of his, and if need be, she can be his defense attorney, I'll talk to her about it as soon as we go back ».

Mafalda was against this idea of washing their « dirty linen » in the presence of outsiders, but otherwise Tosca's proposal met with general approval and was decided on. And the discussion started up again, thicker and thornier, until the ambush was defined in every detail, the girls were assigned their roles, and each one knew how she should behave in the great moment that was drawing near. Now

Mafalda had taken all the initiative, and concluded: « It's up to you, Toschina. You have to act just like the other times, so Bob won't have the slightest suspicion that you're hiding anything from him. He has to arrive at the meadow absolutely as innocent as a dove, and then we'll pluck him all together. We'll be hidden behind the pagoda, and to combine work with play, we'll start out early, and I'll make my father drive us. Tell Gina to be ready at eight, because my father's off duty then and won't say no, if I ask him as a favor. It'll be a lovely carriage ride, girls, before the party ».

And with Gina, who in her secret accepted the risk that her intervention involved, and with Loretta, tied all afternoon to Mafalda's skirt, the ranks of the Furies were complete. Because, at the right moment, Furies or Bacchantes they all became.

THE LYNCHING AND THE FINALE

It had been an unusual, stormy summer; and now the beginning of autumn was making amends for the beautiful season that had been missed. At evening, a light, spring-like breeze descended from the hills to ruffle the surface of the Arno, and the trees in the park just barely stirred. When the moon had risen, the Cascine gardens presented themselves silently, with their hollows, fields, and groves, for the couples of lovers; occasionally an adventurous cyclist wheeled past, singing, along the railing of the Hippodrome, or a rare automobile raced over the ring of the viali. Farthur on, toward the Indiano's delta, the shrubbery was thicker and the silence more profound, and the solitude more secret. Beyond the riding course, between the main avenue and the river, hidden all around by tall plane trees still full of lunar-yellow leaves, there extended, immense and unexpected, the Big Meadow. A long hedgerow, threaded through with barbed wire, followed the bank of the moat and, at the bottom, surrounded the field, connected with the gate that was the entrance. In the

center, a tree, centuries old, circled by a pathway, sustained
its magnificence, isolated and lonely, and at the slope of the
river, there was the ancient lodge of the Grand Dukes, in
the form of a pagoda, a hunting chalet where now the
gardeners stored their equipment. It was the only part of the
gardens that was closed at night; still, at one of the corners
the hedge bent over the moat, and it was easy to enter, if one
knew the way: it sufficed to hold the wire, with one hand,
up over one's head.

Bob knew the way; it was his secret passage, and the
great meadow was his heartbreaker's preserve. There he had
possessed Gina one Ascension evening, and there he had
performed the innocent feats with which he delighted and
bound to himself the girls of Sanfrediano. There, that evening, now weaned from his timidity, omnipotent and bluster-
ing, he thought of going further with Tosca, beyond the
threshhold that he had until now made his limit. The re-
verent, sullen welcome that he had received today at the
dance hall, and the glances, the ill-concealed proposals that
he had been the object of, more than before even, as he
danced with the girls, all of them desirous — this all seemed
to have set a kiss upon his gloriously swollen lip and had
finally led his state of well-being to the very limit of sense-
lessness. Now he was the greatest believer in the lion's skin
that chance had placed on the back of the domesticated,
perfumed little rabbit. And the sharp pains at his temple,
jaw, and ribs were reawakened in him by the excitement,
the light exertion of dancing, and the closeness of the atmosphere; his head started aching again as if a hornet had
made his nest there, preventing Bob from thinking and
wildly exasperating his arrogance. As he left the dance hall
to go to his appointment with Tosca, Bob made his decision
final, smiled at himself as he straightened his tie and
smoothed his hair in the mirror at the buffet, and thought:
« I want to fill Sanfrediano with my race. Who was this
Hunchback anyway? There shouldn't be a street in the
quarter without a child that looks like me ». And nothing

made him suspicious: the fact that he failed to meet Silvana, towards whom he was feeling particularly affectionate since he had fought for her, nor that Bice had failed to keep their date that morning (he had arrived quite late, and this time, dear, angry Bice hadn't waited), nor even the absence of Loretta from the dance hall: evidently his declaration had upset her to such a point that she didn't have the strength to come and meet him, but the next day he would pick her up like a little kitten all trembling with modesty and love; nor even the obscure, but insistent threat of Gina, whose heart he had wounded no doubt severely by his attitude, but it was a suffering that would do Gina good, make her understand how precious Bob's affection was, and the sacrifice and devotion that were his due.

Now Tosca was waiting for him, and her slim figure, in the red jumper that showed off the line of her breasts and the gold of her hair, was outlined and shining under the lighted street lamp at the beginning of the avenue. He grasped her shoulders, surprising her; she uttered a cry, turned abruptly and found herself in his arms, and Bob kissed her at once on the mouth. She tried to draw away from his demonstrative embrace; she was pale, cold, all quivering, and Bob struggled gently to overcome her recalcitrance. « You're more beautiful when you fight back », he whispered, « but you're mine, mine ».

« Not here, Aldo », she said, succeeding in breaking away from him, her voice betraying her emotion; and already he imagined her giving in, timorous and modest, on the still soft grass of the Big Meadow, behind the pagoda. And Tosca, he thought innocently, seemed to favor his plan, since she repeated:

« Not here where everyone can see us. Don't we want to go to our meadow this evening? I don't have the fever any more; I'm well again ».

He took her arm, caressed her hand, and they went into the darkness of the race course, where the intricacy of the foliage held off the light of the moon, and cast shadows like a fine rain.

288

« I couldn't have gone another day without seeing you », he said. « I'm the one who made you get well, through my own desire ».

Tosca was silent, and instinctively she began to walk faster. He felt her arm resisting him, and to him this uneasiness was pleasant, since it promised a struggle in which he was prepared to fight joyously, convinced that he would be the final winner. It was nine o'clock, the silence was all around them, broken only by the light rustle of the leaves and, far off, by the voice of the city that was extinguished in the complaint of the river, the merest echo, at their back, that added to the romance of the place. Bob spoke his last words as a seducer; they were poetic and silly, as his glory was dying out:

« I love you the way the moon loves the leaves ».

Now, in front of them there was a brief open space, beyond which lay the meadow, surrounded by a grove of trees. Tosca stopped, excited and determined, and said to him: « You still have time, Aldo ».

At that moment she was risking her pride, her first love so quickly and so meanly betrayed, and she was prepared to be unfaithful to her girl friends, if she could regain her illusions, if only in Bob's reply she could find — she didn't know what — some sign of a sincerity that would allow her to hope again. « Tell me », she went on, with no idea of how childish and meaningless her urgings sounded to Bob, « but be sincere, once and for all, in your life. Tell me... » she repeated, « do I mean something more to you than the others? Do think you could love me in a way different from them, a way that might become something real, real for you, too? »

« Don't be silly », he said, « You know it's as if the others had never existed. I only have you now, forever, and... »

But he didn't finish. Tosca, in silence, was already ahead of him, reaching the moat, she raised the wire with her hand, and when they were on the meadow at last, she began to run.

« Come on, Bob. Come on », she shouted. There was a

hysterical laughter in her voice, at once happy and lugub-
rious; her hair was moonlight, that ran and quivered in
the long meadow, in the direction of the pagoda. And still
Bob didn't suspect anything: it was an invitation, a child-
like outburst, a prelude to the joy that he would be able to
seize from her. He thought, in fact, that he would overtake
her, running, and throw her down on her back in the grass,
daze her with kisses and fold her thus, aroused and overcome,
in the ecstasy.

« Come on, Bob », she shouted, and her voice died out
as it ran over the field, without resonance, as if the trees
were holding it, or the moon. Before he could catch up with
her, Tosca had reached the pagoda and seated herself on the
step. A the same time, while the excitement and the impetus
of his running hurled Bob ahead still a few steps, from behind
the low building, into the moonlight, came the girls, and
Loretta's voice, as if a gag had been removed from her mouth
(instead it had been Mafalda's hand) shouted:

« They forced me to come, Bob, I'm not with them in
all this », and she was silent, burst into tears, and hid her
face in her arm, leaning against the wall of the pagoda.

Bob had stopped dead, a few yards away, paralzyed by
his surprise; his arms against his sides, he moved his gaze
over the girls who were arranged in front of him, from Tosca
on the step, to Gina who had also sat down there, and Silvana with her back against the door as if ready to leave,
and Bice, who took the sob-shaken Loretta into her arms.
It would be exact to say that Bob thought he was dreaming:
he saw them as they were, and his head felt more empty
than before, with the hornet that was buzzing inside it,
beating itself against his temples.

He couldn't believe he as dreaming: Mafalda came over
to him, her hands in the pocket of her tight coat, her hair
combed up on her head, everything seeming to underline the
boldness of her attitude, the provocation in her laugh. Laughing thus, she looked him over and then said:

« You didn't expect this, did you, handsome? A complete.

surprise. Well, here we are, a select little group of your conquests. We've come to ask you what you think of us, who's at the top and who's at the bottom. It looks as if you'll have to marry the one at the top, and you'll have to do without the others. Without them forever, that means. I hope you haven't been struck dumb; even the lucky girl wouldn't know what to do with a mute, I'm afraid ».

He seemed not to have heard, and kept looking beyond Mafalda's shoulder at the others, who remained motionless, seated, or standing, leaning against the wall of the pagoda. And now Loretta, who was consoling her own tears, lifted her head from Bice's shoulder, repeating: « I wanted to warn you, Bob, but it was like a kidnaping ».

At last poor Bob found his voice, and his first words were historic, those of a fallen hero: « And you, Gina, what are you doing here? You were the one who arranged this convention! »

« She... » Mafalda said, but then Tosca rose and came to her side, facing Bob, and interrupted:

« Gina has nothing to do with it. I'm the one, handsome, who uncovered your little secrets. We invited Gina along as a witness. And there's no use in your trying to change the subject, Bob, you'll have to give us all a convincing explanation ».

It was a different Tosca who was speaking, now without any illusions, but only offended, and also a little frightened, as — for that matter — each of them was. Now the reality of the situation was weighing upon them; the game had suddenly revealed itself to them, out of all proportion, beyond their powers to sustain it; and a shadow of fear, as if they were menaced by an inconceivable and yet imminent danger, diminished their hopeless aspirations in this waiting. In each of them there was repentance for what they had done so far, an uneasiness and a desire to resolve the stiuation as rapdily as possible. But it wasn't Bob's presence that gave them this feeling of embarassment; already his helpless reaction had completed their separation from him, they saw him as a mere mannequin against the moon. And yet, though fallen from their hearts, Bob represented now for all of them except Mafalda a burning reproof, a tangible one, which the girls didn't know how to remove, to make it disappear. And Gina suffered this anguish more than the rest: that afternoon when she had been taken into Tosca's confidence, she had gone to meet Bob and warn him, to line herself up on his side, as always, and for always, if he had wanted it, and he again had insulted and rejected her, repeated the horrid suggestion of that morning; and now that Gina found herself there, sorry that she had come, still his friend, she had hoped that finally Bob could reestablish himself in her eyes. Instead, here was Bob immediately descending to blackmail, ready to tell the other girls that she was his mistress, determined perhaps to destroy the only possible future that was left her: to be married and begin at last to live a life of her own.

But Bob — how vile was he, after all? A poor man struck by lightning in the midst of a meadow, with the moon beating down on his head, six enemies opposite him, he clutched blindly at the only one he knew to be in his power; threatening Gina, he had really meant to ask for her solidarity, which was necessary to him. And in the meanwhile, he began to recover a bit of his strength, as the very indecision and embarassment of the girls restored his confidence.

Gina had remained seated, her chin in her hands, and said: «Tosca explained it. They just wanted me as a witness. I'm here... »

« But on whose side? » Bob asked her. « With me or with them? » he insisted. And to emphasize a nonchalance he didn't feel, he lighted a cigarette.

« I suppose I'm on their side. Naturally », Gina said, « I'm a woman... »

« And if I said I knew how to upset it, your situation, I mean? If... »

But Mafalda interrupted him with her laughter. She, for one, was neither embarassed nor repentant, but only desirous of stirring up a dispute, in which Bob could be buried and she could have her revenge, and now the girls with their suddenly timid attitude, their tone of calm farewell, threatened to deprive her of just what she was waiting for.

« Don't try any short cuts, Bob », she said. « Here your old bag of tricks isn't of any use, nor your kisses, nor your little ways — the only things you're good for. We understand you. Leave Gina out of this, even if she has been under your power; we're glad then, because we can be sure she's on our side. Now she going to get married, and if you have any idea of blackmailing her... what'll we do to him, girls, if he tries it? »

It was little Loretta, her eyes dried and her curiosity suddenly awakened, who answered in the general silence, during which Tosca had gone back to her place beside Gina, whose hand she held, with Bice and Silvana at her sides.

« Bob isn't capable of such a thing. Bob is generous », Loretta said.

« He's only ridiculous », said Bice. It was the first time that she spoke, and her words had all the weight of a meditation. « What a delusion, Bob, dear! » she said. « I expected you to beat us up, one and all, and then I would still have been your friend. But instead, you only make me a little sorry ».

Silvana murmured something that Bob didn't understand.

« What did you say, Silvana? » he asked, stepping towards her instead of Bice, to whom he should have replied, but he sensed that Silvana was weaker and more confused.

« What did you say? » he repeated. « I still have time, don't I?, to beat you all up. Don't you think so? »

He insisted; it was a way of regaining the mastery of the situation and of isolating one of his adversaries. And since Silvana bowed her head and was silent, he imagined that she, like Gina, was on his side, and he said so:

« I had to give it to Gianfranco, all because of you, last night; I shouldn't have dirtied my hands... so now be good and quiet, and go on off to bed. March! »

Now he recalled his own feats as a fighter, the dignity

that they implied came back to sustain him, he felt himself strong again, Bob, the lion-tamer with the whip in his hand, and the girls at his feet. But only for a moment, and then Silvana burst out:

« Don't make yourself too important; it was just luck. Gianfranco can knock you out whenever he wants to, if he wants to. And be careful about offending me, because since this morning I've been engaged to him! So you can leave me out of this choosing that you have to do. Me, and maybe someone else, I think ».

And with the words that had been hers, Silvana's, Loretta said: « I don't take anybody's leftovers. And Bob, I believe I owe you an answer. It's no. And good night ».

But already, after Silvana's outburst, all of them were upon him at once, only Gina remained seated, absorbed. They surrounded him, Mafalda leading the revolt. All of them protested that they were the ones who didn't want him: how did he dare, little moustached thing that he was? And as far as fighting as concerned, unless he had a sister to fight with, he would have to do his punching in front of a mirror, on his own face, as Tosca said. The girls of Sanfrediano marched to the offensive, tough and lovely as their mothers had been, they stoned this would-be Hunchback, who had shown himself unworthy of their love, this low, inept traitor, who threatened them with a beating and then didn't give it. They were a circle around him, their hands in the air, their faces burning. Mafalda elbowed him and made him drop his cigarette.

He was Bob still, and his self-confidence, be it said to his credit, had not abandoned him yet again. On the contrary the shouts and the signs of revolt aroused his fury, which had broken out suddenly at the revelation of Silvana. He forcefully broke his way out of the circle, and stood still with a hand on his hip, indicating with the other hand the cigarette, its lighted tip shining in the grass. He turned to Mafalda and commanded:

« Pick it up. This minute ».

For a second the girls were speechless, and when Mafalda answered: « If that's the only one you have, you can forget it », Loretta bent over, picked up the cigarette, and gave it back to him.

At any rate, it was a little ground regained, and he thought it sufficient to begin the counter-attack; with his feet still firmly on the ground, he prepared to throw the field in disorder. *Bob Bob Bob* as he felt himself, he threw away the butt of the cigarette, put his hands on his hips, and said:

« And now, listen to me. You, Silvana, will get engaged to Gianfranco if I say you can; but first, all of you, I want you to know that I feel really sorry for you. I wouldn't choose not even the fingernail of the smallest of you. And as for any little surprises, I'll be fixing one up for you, in Sanfrediano. I'll see that everybody, first to last, is talking about you; and who'll be able to beny anything that I say? »

As he was speaking, the storm gathered, thicker than the moolight, over his head. The girls were still, unmoving, and he thought he had tamed them, imagined his words falling like anathemas upon their heads. In reality, that moment, which Bob thought was the prelude to surrender, was the moment when the girls were fitting the arrow to the bow.

Now he had got started, sure of himself, and he went on: « You won't find another repectable pair of pants, not even for their weight in gold. I'll fix you all up for good ». And he conceded: « Unless, of course, you want to be reasonable, and apologize, and then in time I'll be able to choose, when I feel like it ».

And with this, he had determined his own fate. But in his ignorance he wanted to go further, he wanted to load the gun himself. He pointed to Mafalda and said: « Naturally, you're excluded from now on. As you said to me yesterday morning, we never have had any business together, neither I... »

And now good-bye, Bob, good-bye! Mafalda fell on him like a thunderbolt with those fingernails which he had scorned a moment before, and after her, in one single leap, the fresh young frantic bodies of the other girls fell upon Bob, who had swayed under Mafalda's impact, and now was spread out on the ground, and they were on top of him, tearing him to pieces.

Loretta crawled on all fours out of the scrimmage and began to jump around them, clapping her hands, looking for an opening in the tangle wide enough for her foot, so that se could kick, though gently, like a child. But not the others, at any rate. And over the wild cries of Mafalda, of Tosca, Bice, and Silvana, over the moans and smothered curses of Bob, there was Loretta's hilarious, girlish commentary: « Now you'll learn, Bob. That'll teach you ».

And Gina, calmest of all perhaps because she was the most desperate, ran up then and beseeched them, weeping, but energetically untangling one arm from another, or leg from leg, a breast clutched in Bob's, closed fist, the solid and heavy breast of Mafalda. The struggle died down; ruffled and panting, the girls stopped for a breath, and Bob managed to get up, his beautiful suit all grass-stined and rumpled, blood dripping along one cheek from his swollen lip, which had now been broken open. Now Bob was finished; he was Aldo, and he fled. And in spite of everything, he was an ex-athlete, a runner, so that at once he was able to set a distance that opened the way to safety between himself and Mafalda, who followed holding her outraged breast, and Tosca, who came running after her.

But in his desperate running, he had headed straight for the tree, tall and solemn in the moonlight, so still running, he had to change his direction, he careened, one foot tangled with another, stumbled, and fell. Tosca and Mafalda were on him at once, and swiftly, while Tosca, biting and cursing, held him down, Mafalda took the belt of her coat and tied Bob's feet as tight as she could. Now Bob was immobilized, and Tosca, understanding her friend's manouver, took the belt that adorned her skirt and decisively handcuffed him, the poor thing.

It was a blind struggle, with no holds barred, until Bob

at last uttered a cry, lost his senses for a moment, and when he recovered himself for a moment as best he could, discovered his hands were tied. Mafalda gave him a careful punch, her fist closed, in the groin, and Bob had been struck the final blow.

So, no longer Bob, but a mere relic, he could react no further, and doubled over upon himself, moaning. The two girls rose, and then the others came up. And except for Gina, who would have freed him except for Mafalda's preventing it, all of them were breathless and excited, standing around him, deriding him. And as Bob continued to complain, to beg them to untie him, now destitute of every hope, of every shred of self-respect, Mafalda pushed Gina away, leaned over Bob and said, ironic and vulgar:

« Let's see now. Where do you hurt? »

He was all hunched up, aching, surrendered, and it was there that he hurt, he said like a child, begging them to free him, promising to keep his mouth shut, no one in Sanfrediano would ever know.

Gina had let herself go, weeping all her tears, lying not far away, with Bice standing over her, comforting her.

« Where does it hurt? » Mafalda repeated, kneeling astride him, her knees on the grass, unbuttoning his clothes.

And then his modesty was stronger than his pain. He fought back, tried to lie on his side, but Mafalda and his bonds nailed him flat.

« Now let's see if we can't make it go away, this pain that you say you have », Mafalda repeated, with a smothered laugh, ferocious now, in crossing that threshhold that Bob, in his way, had kept her from. And she succeeded; Bob was crouched over as far as he could, aching, beneath her, his pants undone, and then Mafalda clapped her hands over her head, and calling Tosca, Loretta, and Silvana, who instinctively had gone to join Bice with Gina, who now was striking her head on the ground in a crisis of despair, Mafalda cried — a mad and instinctive scream, as if at the discovery of gold:

« Girls, girls! I was right. It's the way I said. That's why the beautiful Bob only liked to play around. Look, girls, it's just a little toy! »

Her indignation was equal to her joy, both of them exorbitant, and possessed by these two feelings, as she knelt over Bob, he — who had no other defense — raised his head and at her, and Mafalda, in reply, gave him a frontino; Bob's head bounced twice on the grass of the meadow, which was not much to soften the final blow he had received. He lay back, the sky bright with moonlight fell over his eyes, and he closed them, stretched out his legs, unbuttoned, out of breath, barely murmuring, « you're disgusting », and then he was silent.

« Come on, girls! » she shouted; mad, shameless, she tormented Bob's spent body. « Don't act like little saints; here there's a mistake of nature for you to think about. Come and see what you would have gotten, after the choice! »

Curiosity drove them, the girls of Sanfrediano, and they looked. But all of them, including Bice, who had had other fiances before Bob and therefore should have been able to compare and understand, all of them were ready to attribute to their own inexperience the proofs of virility that Bob had given them, and to persuade themselves that the truth was what it seemed to be and what Mafalda, otherwise experienced and authoritative, suggested and insisted it was.

« What are you saying? »

« Really? »

« The shame of it! »

« Madonna mia! »

And Gina, who could have given them the lie and could have answered Mafalda's judgement with facts, lay on her face, a little bit distant, on the field of the famous Ascension evening, shaken with sobs, in a crisis which left her ignorant of the crime the others were committing, a crime also against her.

Anyway, Mafalda, now demonaically possessed, had yet to complete her infamy. She remembered that her father was waiting for them with the carriage; by now he was certainly drunk, more so that when they had come, and this was enough to make her decide on the final abomination. And, after all, she wasn't alone; she joined Tosca to her misdeed.

Tosca, that is, the most excitable. She, like Mafalda, perhaps even more so, was suffering a violent, uncontrollable physical upheaval in that moment; she looked at Bob, flat, bared, and she trembled, as the effort to keep from attacking him cost her painfully, exhausted her. Mafalda whispered her insane project in Tosca's ear, and Tosca nodded. They were two Furies, the virgin and the sinner, Alecto and Tesiphone, and the shook hands over the inert body of a sinless Orestes, squallid and tame, unworthy of his Areopagus.

While Bice, Silvana, and Loretta, each of them diversely confused and saddened, regretting the excess that they had reached, surrounded Gina, comforting her, Tosca and Mafalda dragged Bob to the edge of the meadow.

« We're going to freshen him up and then we'll be back », Mafalda shouted.

Instead, untying his feet, holding him by the arms, they led him out of the meadow and along the deserted avenue to the carriage. He was the mere relic of a man, full of afflictions, resentments, and pains in every part of his body, his mind finally gone after the impact of the frontino; he was a condemned man following his executioners, one at either side of him, carrying him on. When he was settled in the carriage, he had a moment of lucidity, and said: « Why are you tying my feet again? You're making a mistake; you should undo my hands ». But a fresh and definitive frontino from Mafalda sent him reeling against the iron of the turned-back top of the carriage and deprived him, this time completely, of his consciousness.

And they, the two girls, were now like two bandits, frightening and beautiful, the blonde and the redhead, their gaze freezing and the movements sure. Mafalda waked her father, who had fallen asleep on the opposite seat and suggested that he straighten the blanket on the horse's rump;

and old Panichi, stupefied by sleep and by wine, set about the job, when Mafalda, already on the box with the reins in her hand, drew them up, and the horse set out at his tired, hack's trot, still fast enough, however, to leave its master behind.

And so, unconscious, unbuttoned, a kind of *ecce homo*, lying crosswise on the straw seats, with the two unfortunate girls on the box making fun of him, Bob made his entrance into Sanfrediano. Only at the moment when they passed the gate, when the carriage already was leading behind it the people of via Pisana and via del Pignone, Tosca, as if the walls themselves had called her back to her senses, had jumped down to the ground and let herself be swallowed up up in the gabbling swarm that followed and surrounded the vehicle. It was ten or eleven o'clock on a Sunday evening, and the streets, the taverns, the caffes were still filled with people, the audience was coming out of the Orfeo cinema, and at the door of the club, waiting for him, Bob the billard-shark, the heartbreaker, and the partisan, there were Gian-franco, Barcucci, and their friends. And Mafalda, now madder and more demoniacal than ever, struck the whip over the horse's rump, cracked it in the air, and shouted:

« Look at him, Bob, the beautiful Bob! The girls of Sanfrediano are excommunicating him. And I'm the one to tell you about it! Go and marry them, and go to bed with them without a worry in the world. Bob hasn't touched a one of them. How could he? With what? »

Until, over the shouting, mercy triumphed, and common sense and shame. Bacucci hurried up on his crutch, accompanied by the boys, and they scattered the assembly, lifted down Mafalda and gave her those slaps that Bob had promised her and which now dissolved her tension into tears and convulsions. Bob as carried into the club, where he came to, straightened his clothes, and when he opened his mouth, the first thing he said was:

« It was all a lie! » Then he turned to Barcucci and said: « I'm still the same as I always was... »

« They certainly couldn't have picked a faster or a better way to get rid of their heart-ache », Barcucci answered. And he added, affectionately and paternally: « But you, well... what I mean is: of course, it's not your fault, it's a misfortune, but for God's sake, knowing the way it was, you had to go and make yourself Bob! »

And Fernando, reinforcing this, said: « Now you're going to need some friends in Sanfrediano, to get back into favor a bit ».

Many friends, if all of his girls were going to abandon him. Gina came back into the quarter just then, with Bice, Silvana, and Loretta, who were accompanying her. They were a group of Marys, already, informed of the turn of events, gathering the comments of the people, the laughter, the bitter wit of the Sanfredianini. And the women, the girls that Bob had excluded for some time from his circle, Leda, Tina, Rossana, and those others who until then had sighed for just one look from him, now grew savage as they talked of him, who until the evening before would have been placed on their highest pedestal. And none of them was a true Mary, all of them unfaithful, like Tosca, like Mafalda, they smiled, modestly, and their cheeks blushed purple.

« Go in! »

« Really? »

« Bob? »

« No. No. I don't want to hear it ».

And was he, Bob, so fallen from their hearts? Could nothing, not even the nostalgia for his kiss, for his words, raise some enthusiasm in them in his favor?

Bob was alone, shut in the washroom of the club, looking at his split lip, the scratches on his cheek, and big tears rose under the beautiful lashes. They were the tears of a man who is unarmed with the whole world against him, who knows that the truth is not enough to set things right again, when it is a truth that can hardly be posted on a hoarding.

On every wall in the quarter, from that evening, on Cesarino and his band of children wrote Bob's name and next to it a verb and an adjective that concerned him, and the girls of Sanfrediano without exception, *without exception*, read, as they walked by, what was written with chalk or coal over the walls of via di San Giovanni and via della Chiesa and del Leone, and they took turns congratulating one another that they had escaped *that*, thank God.

This was six months ago. Now the situation is a little better, or at least the gossip and the jokes are of a different kind: Bob and Mafalda are officially engaged; she has gone to work in a laundry, and has put her silk stockings away in a drawer. They will be married in the spring, which is natural, and Gina's marriage with her ragman represents, according to the Sanfrediano girls' ideas about matrimony and its seasons, an exception. Now the affairs of the heart, for everyone, are private again, but we can say this at any rate: Fernando has taken up the scepter to which he aspired. But they don't call him Bob or Fernando; they call him Tyrone. There always has to be a Hunchback in Sanfrediano, or otherwise how would the girls there torture their existence, what fun would there be in life before they ascend the altar? And this doesn't mean that all Bobs are Bob. On the contrary.

(translated by William Fense Weaver)

NOVEL 1917

BY

ALFONSO GATTO

To the white girls behind the panes
women singing in a river of moonlight
it seemed they heard a kiss's silence.
Below they laughed as they descended
from the terraces on sailors' arms.

My grandfather fell ill in his shirt
an enormous shirt made of wool.
He spoke no more, staring at that color
the grey of old prints and of soldiers.
His death arrived in a third-class carriage.
When at peace, he saw a whale
gurgling calmly on a sea of lead.

Like a woman, Roberto was singing,
he rang the tassel of his bath-robe,
playing, curtsying all by himself.
Maid and mistress, the flowers of success
he took all into his arms and was dead
as he wished, handsome to speak of, like
a girl with hair of gold.

All have left for the war
and the doctor who weaves his room
with the ancient odor of apples plays
in the afternoon always the trumpet of sleep.
As if he were giving his hand to all
to say good-bye and be left alone.

Now I seem to love him
and fail that sad smile of his
that he offers me, in the huge memory
of a family I believed to be dead.

Grandmother beats time with her shoe
buttoned over her white stocking.
Light and blind to her hair the wind
she believes she is seeing, and runs to the window
as if trying to fall in its arms.

In the green drinks bubbles the laughter
that rises and falls without knowing why.
And the families that enter, and the children
in laces and mourning for Mazzini.
Perhaps the loggia will set sail with the old
photographer that burns his Bengal light.

« Rain tonight, » grandfather says then,
his back to the family. On his head
descend the clouds that he dreams of,
on his moustache, a sweet, invisible weeping.
Over the great thoughts that he sees
the war runs through the countryside.
He does not withhold his greeting to those
who depart behind him, leaving him alone.

They will talk of me as of another
the great ladies, shut in the parlor,
they will blow a name in their ears
to laugh, exhausted. I recall
when, looking into Mamma's face,
I chose for her the gentle words
and the smell of the fields for the evening.

Elena runs through the rooms and comes
near my sick-bed and says:
« What do you look at all day long? »
She lays her head on the pillow, wishing
to see the sky as if with my eyes.
She speaks no more, but weeps, or if she laughs
flees, slamming the door on the woods.

She is the little widow of a dream,
the white veil covers her with black.
The war plants crosses in the garden
abandoned. Grandfather passes alone,
head in the clouds; he is heavy
as a coffin. He has watched me at length
as if he had listened to that thought
which is not mine, but born within me.

In a shining sultriness with shouts
they raise walls of silence and the gold
of the fields arouses cocks at the frenzy
of the sea. Then Roberto's song, the cry
of his, running in his bathrobe,
his sabre bared, cutting with the flowers
the swans, the cats, his beautiful head.
A shot, some blue smoke, and then, no more.
On the step of the sea he was found
dead with his singer's remains.

Grandfather leaves on a cart of clouds
I sleep next to him under a blanket.
We go towards November and oblivion.
Perhaps I have returned from silence
to remember those days made of feathers.
And you, o Grazia, who look at my past
of the mournful music that I was
accept in gift the organ, the voice
that I hear singing to me always death.

(translated by William Fense Weaver)

LOVE STORY

BY

GIORGIO BASSANI

> Enfin, des années entières s'étant passées,
> le temps et l'absence ralentirent sa douleur
> et éteignirent sa passion.
>
> LA PRINCESSE DE CLÈVES

I

As long as she lived, Deborah Abeti remembered the
short span of time that had preceded her baby's birth.
Every time that she thought of it, she was moved. Yet those
days had certainly not been filled with incident or excitement. She had lived for a month lying in bed at the end
of a corridor. From a window which gave on to the garden
of the maternity hospital, she used to look at the leaves
of a great magnolia, shining from the rain. It was April;
but already the weather was warm, and the window remained open all day long. Then, towards the end, she had lost
interest even in the magnolia leaves, so dark and polished.
Her pains came on her very late; she no longer thought or
felt in a normal way. She was reduced to being a swollen,
passive object (the calm surrounding her was equalled by
the calm she felt within) abandoned at the end of a hospital
corridor. She hardly ate anything, but the doctor because of
the heavy atmosphere which made it hard for her to breathe,
said that this was a good thing.

II

Then, after the birth, time began again to move on.
At the beginning, thinking of David (sometimes she
was hurt by the memory of his bored, discontented face; he

would hardly ever bother to answer her, but lay all day, stretched on the bed, reading French novels) Deborah went back to stay in the furnished room where she had lived with him the last six months. But then, by degrees, partly because the thought of the baby frightened her (she lacked milk, David never appeared, the little money she had was almost gone) she resigned herself to the idea of going home to her mother. And so, in the summer of that same year, Deborah Abeti had returned to the Via Salinguerra. She had seen again the winding, deserted alley, flanked by walls bristling with bits of glass; she had seen its wretched crumbling houses, and the grass pushing up between the cobblestones. And finally she had seen again the low, miserable room, with its dusty wooden floor and the two iron bedsteads side by side, where she had passed her early youth.

The floor of the room, which once perhaps had been a cellar or a coal-merchant's store, was not on the same level as the street, but a little lower. In spite of that, in order to reach it you had to climb an outside staircase and then go down an inside one. These stairs were like the two sides, hidden one from the other, of a triangle whose base was formed by the damp, dark entry on the one side and the equally damp dark room on the other, and whose apex was the landing and the door. This door, which on the side of the entrance opened onto a wall whose extent was lost in the darkness (the staircase, protected by a thin, rusty railing, went on up to the higher storeys), on the side of the room was almost at ceiling level. As soon as Deborah opened it, she saw from above her mother, who had raised her head from her sewing. There was no amazement in her eyes, only a keen enquiry. Deborah went slowly down the stairs, approached her, and at last bent to kiss her on the cheek. And the kiss was quietly returned, just as though Deborah had come in after an absence of a few hours.

Then came the question of the baptism. Deborah remembered how in the first days after the birth, while she was still in hospital, the thought of the baby's baptism had clashed in her mind, unexpectedly, violently, with the thought of David. David! After the interval of the last months of pregnancy, during which her indifference towards everything had gone on steadly increasing till it had reach- ed the complete insensibility of the last days, this had been the first time that she had gone back to remembering and suffering. Her love had been, and was, a love founded on self-distrust and devotion, a love that accepted all things and was ready to endure all things. For that reason and for that alone — she smiled bitterly — she had wanted to wait. But now, she added, why go on having scruples? What use was it? Finally she decided to confide in her mother.

« Are you mad? » the older woman exclaimed, crossing herself hurriedly.

Thereupon she began to talk. She talked (never had she been so unreserved, so ready) with a freedom and assu- rance that amazed her daughter. That same evening the baby, who had been given the name Ireneo, was taken to church. On the way there, the two women had hurried along, as though they felt themselves pursued. They came back, however, slowly, suddenly very tired, without exchanging a word.

The mother kept silence and Deborah too. Each was grateful to the other for the reserve which prevented them from dwelling on a time that had, for different reasons, been so grievous to them both. Their heads bent over their sewing, as they sat by the window, they kept one another company, they heartened each other. Between them, indeed, a strange, silent friendliness was born, a common desire for support which had no need of words for its expression. Both knew very well what was invoved. It was a pact which could only last in this way, if they avoided speaking of it.

But Deborah was always the stronger of the two. Some- times her mother could not resist the temptation to risk a joke, a veiled allusion. And if it happened, as it nearly always did, that the girl seemed not to understand it, not to resent it, the mother felt an impulse of tenderness that was truly maternal, something she had never felt for her before that time. Raising her head, she would look at her, spellbound. « Poor soul », she would say to herserlf, « how thin she has grown! » And yet it was in the very thinness of this face that she found herself, recognised herself at last. Deborah no longer resembled *him* and him alone. She no longer had anything of the deceitful sweetness which she had inherited twenty years before from her father, the mechanic from her mother's native village. « Men are all alike », « Man is a hunter »: it was in sententious or proverbial phrases like these, which she recalled indeed with a smile, that she sought relief and comfort. David, the son of well-to-do folk, of real 'big shots', was like *him*. In imagination she dressed him in her own man's blue overalls; she lent him his greasy, untidy hair, his thick lips, his lazy gestures. Men were all the same, all like this. The village community, too, which so many years ago, when she was found to be pregnant, had rejected her, chased her out, forced her to move to the city, gave by degrees its own cruel features to that other community, urban, bourgeois, which, having made use of her daughter, had then flung her away like an old shoe. Mother and daughter, she thought, they had suffered the same griefs, they had been worn by the same anxieties, suffered the same injustices No longer was there anything that could divide them. That was why their faces now looked alike. From these thoughts the old woman derived a strange happiness, a kind of fever took possession of her. One day she took her daughter by the hand and led her in front of the wardrobe mirror.

« Do you see, do you see? » she said in a stifled voice.

And for a long time they stood (no sound could be heard in the room but the hissing of the carbide lamp) looking in the tarnished glass at their faces side by side.

Naturally things did not always go so smoothly. Deborah was not always calm or ready to listen without answering back. One evening, for instance, the old woman set out to tell her own story. Towards the end, almost as her concluding words, she used a phrase that made Deborah start to her feet.

« If his parents had wished it », she had said with a sigh, « he would have married me ».

Stretched on the bed, her face hidden in her hands, Deborah silently repeated these words, heard again the sigh, so full of regret, that had accompanied them. She was not weeping; no. And when her mother hurried after her and bent over her, she could only show her a face dry of tears, an expression of contempt and boredom.

But on the whole her fits of impatience were rare (her mother was torn, at the sight of that impassive face, which betrayed no sign of anguished thoughts, between the contrary feelings of satisfaction and envy) and if they did assail her, it was suddenly, without warning, like squalls on a mild day. Once, hearing her mother call her by name, she turned round with a nasty laugh.

« Deborah! And why not Cunegonda, Genevieve? With the calendar to hand, you might have found something even better. ».

But the old woman did not reply. She smiled. The girl's outburst took her back to far-away things, which only she could understand. « Deborah » she repeated to herself several times. She thought of her man. She had come to stay in the town; and he, every Sunday, used to do sixty kilometers on his bicycle, thirty there and thirty back. He would sit there, where Deborah was sitting now. She seemed to see him still; with his overalls, his tousled hair... And then one night, on his way back to the village, he had been caught half way by a downpour of rain, and had developed pneumonia. From that time onwards she had never seen him again. Much later, he had gone to stay in a village in the Veneto, a mountain village, and there he had taken a wife and had had sons. If his parents had wished it, he would have married her. What did Deborah know about it, what could she understand? She alone could see herself reflected in her daughter and comprehend for both of them.

Sympathising with her daughter, understanding her, forgiving her; by these means she really felt herself a mother, for the first time in a position of superiority. For this reason above all else it had been quite easy not to reprove her for what she had done. Sometimes Deborah would stop working; her eyes would seek the window, her gaze be lost beyond the panes. And then it was with joy, a joy so complete that she did not notice its cruelty, that the old woman would begin to talk about David and the baby. No need to despair, she would say; the past was past, and since the child was there, one had to make the best of things. Besides, who knows? Wasn't he the son of a gentleman?

And really it was only thanks to this last phrase, which the mother had uttered thinking of something quite else, that Deborah suddenly recalled David vividly, saw again his long, sad, horse-like face. (No, she would never have gone to him; if she had seen, in the street, his great overcoat of sham blue fur appearing in the distance, or his raincoat pinched in at the waist; if David, passing by, had brushed her elbow; she would have walked straight on with her head bent down, certain not to be recognised...). She wouldn't have asked him for a penny, she wouldn't have bothered him. What could she have said or written? She remembered the week-old beard that he had let grow. How hot it had been in that room! He was always in bed, sweating, reading French novels.

Only after the old woman's cracked lips had widened in a happy smile (she would laugh at some memory or other, some dream, and Deborah's eyes, moving from the window, would dwell pityingly on her poor worn face), only then did she seem to regain tranquillity. After supper the two women would sit for a long time without clearing the things away, their elbows planted on the table, their chins cupped in their hands. The first to go to bed was always Deborah. But the other bed (the carbide lamp in the middle of the table spread a white, wavering light around), the bed next to the one where Deborah and the child were already sleeping, often remained untouched till far into the night.

III

Via Salinguerra is a tortuous street which starts from a wide, dusty clearing where long ago some buildings were demolished, and ends at the foot of the city's ramparts, at the edge of the countryside. Walking its length one has, particularly at the far end, the impression of being already beyond the confines of the city walls. This road, besides its appearance, has also the smell of certain countrified lanes the smell of dung, of ploughed fields, of stables. The very silence which dominates it has something pastoral about it; the church bells of F., heard from here towards evening, have a different, far-away sound. In fact, thought one is still within the perimeter of the city walls, one can say that the contryside does begin here, with the big market-gardens which lie beyond the red walls that flank the street on both sides — gardens of which few people in the city suspect the extent, though they know of their existence.

The lowing of cattle, the croaking of frogs, the smell of grass and hay, and in the evening the far-off ringing of the Angelus. The sounds and smells even reached down there where the two women, below ground, busied themselves sewing military stuffs for a tailoring establishment. They kept their heads bent over their work, and raised them only to exchange a word or two, or to look at the occasional passers-by; fugitive shadows that they could see looking up from below, shoes trailing over the cobbles, eyes indifferent, dazzled by the noonday light. Behind the women, at the top of the staircase, was a bell hung on a bracket in the recess over the door. A long cord, whose end emerged through a hole beside the street door, connected it with the outside. And this cord, which a puff of wind could shake with ease, seemed to ask to be pulled; it lent itself to violent jerking. Above the unpainted door (four boards roughly nailed together; on the protruding nail-heads the women used to hang odd garments and rags) every so often the bell to shake frantically to and fro. Although from outside one could only hear a mournful, distant sound, inside the room the silence was rent by a sudden shrill clangour. Every time, mother and daughter, seated by the window in their two shabby basket chairs, used to start violently and hurriedly turn round.

Now and then the old woman would lift her head and make as if to start a speech. She blinked her eyelids and coughed, but then, losing heart, let the phrase die away. She followed it up with a dry laugh, that was meant to be mysterious, charged with promise, but was merely painful. « If you liked, if you'd listen, what couldn't I tell you! ». In the laugh and the cough and the futile agitation there was this and something else besides; a longing to abandon reserve, together with a contemptuous pride and perhaps some last remnant of feminine vanity... And so, if Deborah did not welcome the suggestion (and she hardly ever did), her mother's senile need to talk, to fill the emptiness of their lives with something, resolved itself into a thick monotonous mumbling of the words she wanted to say but dared not pronunce — Deborah, Ireneo, David; and this, like a prayer, had power to calm her and bring her back to being the poor resigned old women which she fundamentally was. Then she used to think of Deborah in a different way; she thought that the girl was young, that she might yet get married. And when Oreste Benetti, who had a bookbinder's shop in the Via Salinguerra, began to visit them in the evenings after supper, she was perhaps the first to grasp that these visits were paid in her daughter's honour. She would go to and fro in the room, saying nothing. From her expression you would have judged her a goodnatured, discreet mother-in-law; yes, but one who had a proper notion of her own rights and the weight of her responsiblity.

Deborah kept the conversation going in a calm, subdued kind of way. She looked at the guest's big head, a head that seemed too heavy for the little seated body; she looked at his long gnarled hands, clasped on the table-cloth. As for the book-binder, he enjoyed reminding the two women of years gone by. He recalled Deborah whom he had known as a child, « so high ». She used to come into his shop, stand on tip-toe so that she could see over the counter and ask him to give her some snippets of coloured paper. He spoke to them both, he even seemed to take a certain amount of care to give his conversation an impersonal tone; but when he talked, his eyes turned much more often towards Deborah than towards her mother. It was in her face that he specially sought assent and attention; and she responded with a demure amiability, a composure of manner, from which he derived a pleasure he had never felt before. Without being conscious of it, she behaved in a way that was particularly pleasing to Benetti.

He was much shut up in himself, yet at the same time perpetually hunting after prestige. One of the few times that he addressed himself directly to the old woman was to remind her of the year in which she had come to live in the city. It had been a year, he remembered, of exceptional cold. The piles of dirty snow had remained at the sides of the streets until the end of April. The temperature had fallen so low that finally even the Po had frozen.

« Even the Po! I tell you, it was a real Siberia ».

He still seemed to see it, he said; the great frozen stretches. The waters had ceased to flow between the banks. He recalled the strange spectacle of the river, its banks covered with snow, and the river-side houses half buried under the snow. Towards evening the wagoners, who lived in the villages on the far side of the Po, used to come back from F. with their empty carts. They had transported tons of firewood to the city from the sawmills which worked in the woods on either shore. Some of them, perhaps for a bet, took their wagons across the vast icy expanse instead of across the iron bridge. They advanced slowly, a few yards ahead of their horses, holding the reins gathered in a bunch behind their backs. With the other hand they scattered sawdust, so that their clogs should not slip on the ice. Meanwhile they whistled, or let out guttural shouts. It was as good a way as any, added Oreste, of warming themselves and keeping up their own and their animals' courage.

Talking of the Po, he used the same respectful tone as when he spoke of persons or things pertaining to religion. Orphaned in childhood and brought up in a seminary, he had kept an almost filial veneration for the priests, for priests in general.

« I remember that during that famous winter », said he one evening, « poor Don Castelli used to take us almost every Saturday afternoon to look at the Po. As soon as we were outside the gate, we broke rank and each walked as he pleased and as God directed him. Fourteen kilometers on foot; it wasn't a mere turn round the garden. Don Castelli, poor chap, though he used to pant, was always in the forefront. He never wanted to take a tram, even for the return journey. He used to say that walking was good for the health and kept up the appetite. And he always kept me close to him », he added, looking with a smile at Deborah, winking his eye merrily, half facetious, half paternal. « He loved me like a father ».

« I was expecting the child », the old woman broke in at this point. « I felt lost in the city, I couldn't read or write, and if it hadn't been for her » — she nodded at Deborah — « I should have run away, back to the country. But what could I do? You know what country people are like, Oreste ».

« There was not another cold spell like that until 1917 » affirmed Oreste; and remained thoughtful. Then, with a sudden gleam in his eyes, « No », he corrected himself, « not at all. As far as I can tell, the cold in 1917 was much less intense. It was quite hot, where we were, on the Carso! Some things it's better to ascertain from people who got themselves reprieved from service — certain malingerers known to us all — » he emphasised these last words ironically — « who only saw the front on picture-postcards ».

Catching the allusion, the old woman stiffened. But then, thinking of her man who had been invalided and had never been through the war, she soon went back to weaving fancies about him, about herself, about all sorts of things that might or mightn't have been. If his relations had not opposed it, if he had not been ill, certainly he would have married her. In 1919 he had moved to a village in the upper Veneto, above Trento, where he had married. A wife and children. Who could say whether he remembered her. He too by this time must have grey hair; maybe he had even forgotten his own dialect.

« Wretch, wretch... » : while her face softened and grew tender, her lips never ceased to move. « Wretch, wretch, wretch », she repeated endlessly.

The old insult, after so many years, was transformed into a meaningless murmur, like the muttered prayer of a beguine.

Having established certain boundaries, Oreste could again show himself chivalrous, and could behave with delicacy, as indeed his nature inclined him to do. He was a self-made man and was proud of it. He had spent a sad boyhood, of which the only happy episodes that remained were the memories of those winter walks with his school-fellows. Then work had come, and his own craft. « We artisans », he would say, as though he were proclaiming a title of nobility. Deborah listened to him attentively. And he was pleased that she sat there before him, so silent, so composed, so ready to respond in a womanly way to his wishes.

He went on talking until late; he talked about everything, religion, history, prices, even politics. In the early days, Deborah, without ceasing to listen, would rock with her foot the cradle in which the baby was sleeping. Later, with the passing of the years (he grew up a delicate child; at about five he had a long illness which left him always in poor health and perhaps accounted for his rather undefined character) she got up now and again from her chair, went over to the cot, and stayed bent over the boy with her hand resting on his forehead.

IV

In the summer of 1928 (Deborah had just reached thirty) one evening when as usual they were all three sitting around the lamp, Benetti asked Deborah whether she would agree to marry him.

His question (he had spoken with great simplicity) had not been foreshadowed by any particular change of attitude. Even though vaguely expected, it had come out suddenly. Deborah looked at him. « Who knows how old he is », she thought, « perhaps forty-five, perhaps fifty, perhaps more... ». She seemed to be seeing him for the first time. Only now did she take note of those very dark, moist eyes, that high white forehead, framed by iron grey hair, cut short and stiff in a rather military style. Suddenly she was seized by a sense of embarassment. She wanted to say something and did not know what. In search of help, she turned towards her mother; but the sight of her mouth, twisted in a pathetic grimace, only increased her confusion.

« What's come over you? » she said to her in dialect. She felt her stomach heave with disgust, she was blind with anger.

Jumping to her feet, she ran up the inner staircase and went out, banging the door. From inside the room they could hear her going slowly step by step down the outside stairs, as though, overwhelmed, she were leaning on the railing. At last she reached the street, and at once raised her eyes to the sky. It was most beautifully starry. In the distance she could hear the music of a band. From the shutters of the little house opposite a thin gleam of electric light filtered through. Deborah leant her shoulders against the wall, she leant her whole back against it, and all the time looked up, at the sky full of stars. Beyond the wall she could hear Oreste's voice. He was talking quietly to her mother; his voice, the sound of his voice (she could not make out the words) persuaded her to calm down, invited her gently to come in again.

When she reappeared, she was a little pale, and that was all. Benetti and her mother, who all this time had not got up from their chairs, looked at her from below, while she came down the stairs, with the expression of those who await an answer. Deborah lightly shrugged her shoulders. What could she have said? She went and sat down again in her place; and that evening, and for that matter on the following evenings too, nobody mentioned the matter.

Actually Benetti soon made it clear that he was not cherishing excessive doubts about the import of the reply which Deborah had refused to make (as he thought, and let it be known that he thought) simply from timidity. As far as he was concerned, Deborah had already said yes, they were already engaged.

« One must be reasonable », he would say, « one must keep quiet and go straight ahead ».

As he said this, his contented expression contrasted with the sad, resigned tone of his voice. His goodness, his generosity (no slight thing; to fall in love with a girl who had had a child by a Jew!) filled him with pride. As regards David, though he let it be understood that he knew very well that he was the father of Ireneo, he always avoided speaking of him. He was a very devout Catholic, and his feeling for Deborah (and this, on the other hand, was evidence of the seriousness of his intentions) had always had something religious about it. A duty, a mission; he had always felt, from the very beginning, the need of feeling himself ready to forgive her, to absolve her from a great sin.

At bottom, he was not too sure of himself. No, he never mentioned David (he had the chivalry and the instinctive gentleness of certain soldiers); and if he tried to attach her to him by arguments which seemed to him greater than merely personal ones (twenty years difference between them; one must take that into account!) it was simply because he feared that Deborah might go back on a decision which he considered already taken. Certainly, in his discourses the idea of redemption through marriage was always implicit, suggested, never expressed in clear words. It was enough to allude now and again to Deborah's past, to her troubled, straying youth, to the necessity for redeeming it by a happier maturity, by a sober and serene life. That was what he would give her, what he offered her. « One must be reasonable, keep quiet and go straight ahead ». He alone, he had to convince her of it, was able to be her guide. The past was past; nevertheless, in order to be different, to be cured, one must think of it perpetually. Seated at the table, between the two women, he always led their thoughts back there where he knew his strength lay. Allusions, indications, nothing more. It was necessary that that story, which with the passage of time seemed ever more unreal and scandalous, should never be forgotten, even if it was not a good thing to speak of it.

But they were so on edge, their nerves were so tense, that a mere nothing sufficed to upset them. Afterwards they would be troubled for a while, they would give way to sulks.

Once, for instance, Oreste said that he really felt as if he were the father of Ireneo. He had let himself be carried away, he had gone a bit too far.

« What, aren't you my uncle Oreste? » exclaimed Ireneo, who was now eight years old and had got into the habit, every evening before going to bed, of getting his homework corrected by Oreste.

The book-binder turned with a start towards the boy. His confusion gave Deborah a very precise and gratifying sense of her own importance. While he hastened to reply, she and her mother exchanged rapid glances of understading.

For all that they were no longer young, and although they had known one another for so many years, theirs was a long engagement; and certainly if in the following winter the old woman had not suddenly died, it would have been longer still. However, after that famous evening, Oreste had been lavish with attentions and presents. Though he had given them to understand that after the wedding they would all three go to live in a new house (a little house outside the city gates, still in course of construction, for which he was negotiating) he installed electric light, he bought some furniture, a cast-iron cooking-range, a picture, kitchen utensils and so on. He was in love. If he married her, he was marrying her for love. He had never before thought about any woman. He lingered pleasurably over his actions and thoughts. He savoured them slowly, and derived from them a deep, self-centred happiness. He had known so many years of deprivation — all his youth, a great part of his maturity. He had every right to maintain that things should not be done in a hurry but that everything should proceed according to the proper rules.

He arrived every evening at the same time, at half past nine on the dot. The scene was always the same. A vigorous pull at the bell at the street door, steps which came up the stairs, his cheerful voice crying on the threshold « Good evening, ladies! ».

He came in humming between his teeth, but quickly checked himself, with a polite little cough. There were no variations over the years. And yet, in spite of that, if the bookbinder's arrival never failed to make the old woman catch her breath, if it always brought to her drawn lips the quick, indulgent smile of a go-between, Deborah no longer let herself be invaded by the sullen anger of days gone by. It was her turn now to think « Poor mother, how thin she grown, how she is ageing! » Soon, she felt, she would be gone for good.

Besides, so many years had gone by — she said to herself — everything was now so different, that when the rags hanging on the nails of the door shook slightly in response to the movements of the bell above them (the little clapper would go on trembling after the sound had ceased), it woke in her only a vague sense of comparison that grew continually fainter. The women had not even time to go towards the staircase to welcome their guest, they had not yet got up from their chairs, when there he was, up on the landing, his well-known voice singing the air from the *Barbiere*, « Buo-na se-ra, mi-e signo-re. »

Then the cough, and in came the cheerful little man with gray hair, the cheerfulness of the book-binder Oreste Benetti.

So many years had gone by, she herself had changed so much; why, even if she could, should she lose herself in recalling the past?

Certainly, when an equally vigorous ring at the bell had meant that David, huddled in his overcoat of sham blue fur, stamping his feet on the cobbles with impatience and cold, was waiting for her in the street (he had never wanted to come in, he had never wanted to know her mother); then it only took her a moment to dive into her coat, put on a touch of powder, adjust her hair in front of the glass. One moment; but that was long enough for her to see in the mirror, small and shining, with her hair drawn back on the nape of her neck (so that with the light behind her she looked almost bald), her mother's grey head appear and disappear.

« What do you want, what are you looking for? » she would shout. « Do you know what I've got to say to you? I've had enough of you and of this life. »

She would go out banging the door; David did not like to be kept waiting.

V

Still trembling, clutching his arm, she let herself be carried along. Usually they went up Via Salinguerra. When they had reached the end of the street and climbed on the ramparts (on one side could be seen the city lights, on the other the countryside stretched away, submerged in darkness) they would take that path which follows the line of the city walls, between a double row of sturdy trees, limes, oaks and chestnuts. They hurried along without exchanging a word. At that time David was intending to take his degree as soon as possible. He had had a reconciliation with his family (so that he could later on break with them on better terms, so he said) and therefore had got into the way of « being a little

careful, » to use his own words. Being careful meant not being
seen with her. It was necessary, she must realise that. He was
only doing it for the good of them both, not for any other
reason. Nobody would see them on that path, or in the cinema on the outskirts of the town towards which they were
making; nobody from the well-to-do circles in which his family moved. Besides, wasn't it more romantic like this? Love,
to be truly love, has need of these contrasts and subterfuges...

He had got into the way of being careful. For there had
been an earlier time (in the summer of the previous year)
when David did not bother at all about taking care. In those
days, in those really fabulous, really incredible days, (he took
her to the best cinemas, they would sit in full daylight in
the most central cafés) it really looked as though he meant
to break with his past. His studies, his friends, his family,
he *had* to finish with the lot of them (« I shall have nothing
left but you » he would sigh), he *had* to break with a life
which, as he said, simply made him sick. They would very
often spend the afternoons on the ramparts, lying in the grass
like a couple of gypsies. They slept with their arms round one
another where anyone could see them. Sometimes David would
get up and join a group of young men who were seated in
a circle playing some game of chance in the shade of a tree.
And while he, seated, lazily threw down the cards, she would
stand behind him, bending down now and again to give him
a word of advice. Standing behind him, almost protecting him,
watching over him... And the city was over there, not many
hundred yards away, sleeping in the sun under its red roofs
and behind its closed shutters.

They rarely went to the cinema in the evenings; often,
Deborah remembered, they went back to the ramparts. The
air was warm; pairs of lovers passed by whispering. And they
too, later on, waiting for a cooler breeze, would walk along
slowly. Now and again a grassy clearing would open beside
the path. The moon, mirrored there, made the cement benches (the few that were still empty) shine as though by their
own light, down there at the far end of the grass-patch. The

moon transfigured everything. Even the scraps of dirty paper, which by day you'd kick away, revealing filthy broods of flies, by night shone brightly, scattered here and there in the grass. The air was soft and scented; objects of all kinds became precious. Why, later, did everything change? The path, along which they hurried, was just the same, yet a few months, a change of season, had been enough to alter it from a friendly, welcoming place (the scene of their first and best love) into something hostile, even sinister. The mist, which was beginning to rise from the canals in the surrounding countryside, invaded the clearings, and transformed them into gulfs of darkness, frightening to look at; and the benches, clammy with damp, were quite deserted. And whereas in those days David, as they walked slowly, side by side, scarcely touched her; whereas he would turn to smile at her sadly, now and again, aware of her glance; now (so few months had sufficed to end his love for her!) now he held her tightly by the arm, he did not look at her, he hurried her along where she didn't want to go. Everything was changed, within and without; everything was finished. And if she had rebelled, if she had run away? Suddenly, as if in reply, the lights of the suburban cinema shone red and blue overhead. It was too late to resist. A warm, smoky cavern (pushed from behind, she slipped inside) opened before her with the slowness of a yawn.

But once inside, her nerves at once relaxed. The hall was long and low, not much wider than a corridor. Above the crammed auditorium, dotted with cigarettes, the buzzing of the projector brought her some kind of reassurance, she didn't know why. In spite of everything, she liked films. Usually they were lovely stories, beautiful romances. Poor girls, after many long adventures, would be given in marriage to the rich and charming gentleman, to the world-famous musician disguised as a student, to the incognito prince. In every case, virtue and beauty (beauty: but sometimes an ardent, faithful heart and a charming manner were able to compensate for certain shortcomings in face and figure) were offered as counterparts to the prestige of family and fortune, to superior education and social rank. Every so often she would glance at David. He had taken off his hat and coat. In the half-light she could see his long, thin neck, his sleepy, discontented profile, his wavy hair, shining with brilliantine. She put out a hand in search of his, and David let her. Sometimes he turned to answer her glance; he seemed peaceful, as if he too were in love. But then, roughly, he would push her hand away, draw himself away from her completely. « It's too hot, » she heard him puffing, « One can't breathe. »

Frightened, she did not insist. She turned her glance on the screen, and soon, fascinated by the film, she forgot everything. She even forgot David who, disappointed now at not feeling that hand with its swollen, chapped fingers searching for his (disappointed, indeed, at not being able to shake it off again) sat huddled in his seat as though he were afraid of being touched by her. With his suits tight at the waist, with his slow, detached gestures, David was up there on the screen, an angel, a god; and she, confused, in the auditorium, contented herself with looking at him, adoring him from afar. She was so absorbed by the film that later, as they left the cinema with the rest of the public, if David suggested taking her home by way of the path by the ramparts (his voice suddenly caressing –– « It will be a little longer, that way »), she shrank from him; the wakening was always so abrupt and bitter. The dreaded moment — and yet perhaps the moment obscurely wished for — was upon her. The inevitable step which, however she might fight against it in fancy, had nevertheless influenced the whole agonised undercurrent of her thoughts, the inevitable was upon her, she could not escape from it. She tried to find excuses (« I don't feel well »), she invented prohibitions (« Mother is expecting me in by midnight »), she pointed out obstacles (« It's cold, everything will be soaking... »): she tried every means of resistence. Outside the entrance to the cinema an old woman was puffing at a brazier, roasting chestnuts. « Don't you like hot chestnuts? » she asked him. At least let the square get clear of people, somebody might see them.

She tried not to yield, she tried to gain time. How much better it would have been, now that the mist was thickening, to walk slowly home. Nobody could have seen them, even if they had gone through the centre of the town, even if they had gone down the main street. It was getting so foggy that the globes of the street-lamps could scarcely be seen. They could have crossed the city (the mist lying on their lips, their eyelashes) as invisible to others as two ghosts. Because of the damp pavements, they'd have walked slowly, pressed close together like real lovers. David would have talked about himself, his studies, his plans for the future. He might even have talked about the film; he was so clever (though perhaps a little too harsh), so sharp in his judements... Or maybe they could have gone to some café and sat down there. David would have ordered two drinks, grappa for himself, anisette for her; and while they slowly sipped them, she would have felt happy. She'd have thought of nothing, except perhaps her bed and approaching sleep... To be able to trust David, to have no more need of his kisses in order to be sure of his love! But instead she yielded. And some soldiers, who had stayed smoking outside the entrance to the cinema, seeing them disappear in the direction of the ramparts, began to laugh, and went on to whistle and cat-call and shout bawdy jokes. It was no good walking faster. The soldiers' voices, which distance made shriller, followed her into the darkness, pierced her to the spine, made her shiver.

In the first dark place, in the first open clearing, she was thrown down on the grass. With her chin resting on his shoulder, her eyes staring, she let herself go.

Aftewards, she was the first to get up. And if at the last she had been seized by a sudden, harsh wish to struggle, (David never reacted; his long back twisted and then relaxed, exhausted) the fury which at a certain point induced her to shove him away from her gave place immediately after to a sort of fear. She hurried to adjust David's clothes even before her own. He seemed far away, by this time lost for ever. Already he was in a hurry to get rid of her; she could feel

it. But at the same time she realised that in David's impatience lay, more now than ever, the reason for this adoring
love of hers, which had no need of any other reward to keep
it alive. She had no cause to reproach either him or herself.
Hadn't she known all the time how the evening was going
to end? Everything had been only too clear, from the very
beginning. Yet she never had managed to resist, she never
had found the strength to say no.

They went on their way. If only David had said something, if he had taken the trouble to fill, somehow, the silence
that was estranging them more and more from one another!
But by now, cold and abstracted, he'd have said only nasty
things. Anything that had come from him, from then on,
would certainly only have wounded her. All the same, she
tried to make him talk; nothing could be worse than this
emptiness, this icy desert through which they were walking.

She tried some childish tricks. For instance, she would
ask « What is your mother called? » And when David did
not answer, she answered for him. « Teresa » she said, sepa-
rating the syllables in an affected, puerile way, Wasn't it
funny that she should ask him things like this, and that she
had to reply to herself? She was his little girl, his poor little
defenceless child. « And Marina, » she went on, « What is
your sister Marina called? » She burst out laughing. Then
she repeated « Ma-ri-na », with the exaggerated care of a little school-child who tries not to make a mistake.

He yawned and quickened his pace; yes, David was in
a hurry now to get rid of her. In spite of that, at that hour
of the evening, he liked to spin out long discourses about
exalted and poetic topics. He talked readily about himself,
he seemed inspired, even his voice changed. Its resonance and
the themes of his monologue harmonised oddly with the sense
of vague lightness which made them hurry along the frost-
hardened path. He told her about his relationship with a
society girl. He described her features — she was blonde,
with blue eyes and a delicate look; he boasted of her refined
tastes and sophisticated habits. Their meetings and encounters

(he would recount whole dialogues) always took place in the heart of wonderful forbidden worlds; a ball at the club, where he had seen her for the first time, a gala evening at the theatre, a meet of the fox-hounds. It was a difficult relationship, apparently opposed by both families (though mostly, as far as she could guess, by the girl's); a relationship, however, of mind and spirit, with which the senses had nothing to do — « that », which they had done just recently in the clearing, didn't come into it at all. It was a story, she thought, very like the film romances that she so much enjoyed.

They descended from the ramparts and entered Via Salinguerra. And though until this moment she had listened silently, almost breathlessly, when she realised from the outline of the houses and the lamp-posts that she was almost home, she felt a kind of fever come over her, a nervous disquiet. She felt small and unattractive, tiresome in her sudden vivacity. She hated the whole of herself; her shabby, ill-fitting coat, her mop of untidy hair (she needed to go to the hairdresser), her vulgar hands, deformed by hard work and chilblains. She had no illusions, she had seen herself in the glass. Made as she was, she *could* not be lucky, her fate was already determined. And then, more and more feverish and excitable, she would play the part of the old friend who is permitted to ask all sorts of questions and is able to give even the most risky advice. She took pleasure in concealing her true self, in disguising the reality of her feelings. Wasn't that, really, what David wanted? She had to behave herself as though there were nothing between them, as though nothing (far less the episode of half an hour ago) had ever happened. That was what he wanted from her. And wasn't this the price, after all, that she had to pay to make her love for David become beautiful, ideal and exciting, like David's love for the young lady at the club?

She felt pleasure and pain. David, incited, continued to talk. His words were light and cold, the words of someone whose desire is assuaged. The disgust which he felt when he looked at her hands clasped round his arm (« Cook's hands », he was thinking contemptuously, « why in the world doesn't she try to hide them a bit? ») made him more hasty and cruel. As soon as he had taken his degree, he would be off, (they reached the door, went into the entry, and she felt him removing himself, drawing away from their good-bye kiss). Maybe he would go to America, but alone. Alone, of course, because naturally he would never marry.

« The woman who loves me must have her head well screwed on. Clear agreements make long friendships. »

But wouldn't he marry the young lady he was so much in love with?

« No, certainly not; besides, it's not true that I am *so much* in love. And then, do you imagine, » he added emphatically, though with a shade of hesitation in his voice, « do you imagine that I could adapt myself to living for ever in this provincial hole! »

And in the darkness she agreed.

But occasionally (and she was sorry for it afterwards, in bed, when the ticking of the alarm-clock on the dresser and her mother's snoring made it impossible for her to sleep) occasionally she felt like laughing. She asked him « And what if I start a baby? »

She knew perfectly well that this question would force David to utter some absurdity or other. However, it prevented him from going away at once, it induced him to prolong his confused monologues for at least another five minutes. Certainly, David had never replied to the question except with absurdities, never to the very end. And yet — yet he had stayed on, a minute or two, a few minutes. Perhaps before going way he had kissed her. At bottom he had simply been a child, a spoilt child. If sometimes he could be rather horrid, it wasn't his fault, he wasn't aware of it.

VI

Who does not remember the winter of '29? To find a similar one you must go back to 1898, when the Po froze, or to 1917. So, at any rate, affirmed Oreste Benetti.

It began to snow towards Christmas, and it went on snowing and snowing till Twelfth Night. But the temperature was not yet fixed, far from it. In fact, just around Twelfth Night there was a brief interval of sunshine, of almost spring-like warmth, and the snow began to melt. From her bed the old woman listened to the sound of bicycles going through the slush. She had had to take to her bed at the first cold snap, because of influenza; and now, as well as a nasty cough, she was left with a slight oscillating fever. Besides, you could not rely on the weather. In the evening a sea of damp mist would creep in from the country, as heavy as rain. And when Oreste arrived, he was so drenched that he had to hang his overcoat up on the nails in the door as he came in.

He came down the stairs and seated himself as usual at one side of the table. The theme of his conversation was almost always Ireneo. In October, at the beginning of the school year, the boy had been admitted as a boarder at the seminary where Oreste Benetti had many connections; he had always been its trusted book-binder. He very often went there; he was now on his way back from it. Rather a slack pupil, rather unwilling, that was what he had been told about Ireneo by Don Bonora, the master who had succeeded his beloved Don Castelli. « But there is time, » remarked Oreste. « In Latin, the foundations are everything; and this Don Bonora... » He compressed his lips in a meaningful way. Then he went on to talk of the weather. He raised his eyes to the ceiling and cautiously sniffed the air. « We're not out of it yet, » he said, « the worst is yet to come. » Stretched out in bed, the old woman listened as usual without a murmur. She limited herself to wrinkling her forehead and smiling under the covers which she held right up to her mouth.

As usual, Oreste was right. The worst spell of cold was yet to come. In fact, at the beginning of the third week of January, the sky was again covered with clouds, the temperature fell, and together with a furious north wind an extraordinary snowfall attacked the city. Wind and snow; it was something unknown. In some points, where there had been

sweeping gusts, the snow was three or four foot deep. People
in the streets had to walk in Indian file along narrow trenches
which men with shovels, engaged by the municipality, did
their best to keep clear. On the ramparts skiers appeared in
complete alpine outfits; ski-ing contests were eventually organised, and Via Salinguerra, usually so deserted and silent,
became on this occasion full of movement and colour. Attracted by the novelty of the spectacle on the ramparts, the
whole city passed along this street.

Suddenly, with the return of the snow and the cold,
the condition of the old woman became more serious. Outside
the window-panes, through which the daylight now filtered so
dimly that electricity had to be used nearly all day, the snow
could be seen whirling down, thick and fast, on the caked
mud in the street. The doctor spoke of pneumonia and, given
the general condition and the age of the sick woman, there
was little or no hope.

The old woman lay listening. The city was on holiday.
Via Salinguerra resounded with cheerful shouts, hurrying footsteps, the sound of cars and motor-horns... What was happening? But all the sounds and voices came to her as though
from a great distance.

« I can't hear well, » she complained, « I can't hear any
longer. »

« It's snowing, » replied Deborah slowly, seated beside
the bed. « That's why you think so. »

The room was full of people. Behind the priest and the
server — Oreste had not forgotten to send for them — there
was a little group of the poor women of the neighbourhood.
The priest left, but they stayed behind. With black shawls
over their heads, fingering their rosaries and now and then
putting their handkerchiefs to their eyes, they were gathered
under the window where for so many years Deborah and
her mother had sewed military garments. Oreste, standing in
the middle of the room, between the group of women and the
bed, in the dim half-light, kept his hands folded; his lips
moved rapidly and steadily.

But it wasn't because of the snow that all the sounds came from so far away, as if muffled in cottonwool. The old woman laughed to herself; she knew better. Useless to lie to her. « The worst is yet to come, » Oreste had said. But this time Oreste was wrong. She would be gone before the worst occurred. She was right this time. As for Deborah, she would get married. What is better than marriage? — And as she died, her mouth, tensed by the strain of the death-rattle, began to tremble at the corners with a smile that tried to appear, and perhaps finally was, a smile of happiness.

Suddenly Oreste moved, came forward, bent over the bed-head. The old woman's open eyes were sightless; she had stopped breathing. Light and precise, his hands were lowered over her eyes; he drew down the eyelids, he crossed her arms over her breast. His quickness, his neatness (his hand was now adjusting the blankets) fascinated Deborah. Then he withdrew, and went back to the middle of the room.

Deborah did not stir. She stayed by herself beside the bed, gazing at the waxen profile of her mother. She looked at every feature with a stubborn, almost eager, attention, feeling herself meanwhile invested by a strange sense of freedom. For so many years they had worked together, under the window, avoiding looking at one another. Now it was different. The closed eyelids, the nose seen in profile, the lips half opened in that vague, absurdly happy smile; everything in the face of the dead woman seemed to her new and surprising, yet at the same time as if rediscovered. Meanwhile something, an old knot of rancour and reserve (if she wept, she wept for that) was loosening itself in her breast.

She raised her face from her hands.

« I should like to be alone. You too, Oreste, you too go away. »

« Yes, dear, yes, dear... »

There was a new coldness, an air of command, in her reddened eyes and in her voice. Oreste had never seen her like this. It was with a shade of submissiveness, almost of fear, that he detached his eyes from hers. The neighbours were already on their way up the stairs. The last of the group, he too reached the landing and finally closed the door behind him.

Sitting by the side of the bed, with her elbow planted on the coverlet and her cheek leaning on her hand, Deborah remained alone. She thought of her mother, of herself, of their story. And little by little her imagination carried her into another room very much like the one she was in now; the room where, at the beginning of a long-ago spring, she had gone to live with David. As here, there were two beds side by side, a wash-basin in a corner, a tarnished mirror, a chest of drawers. The only difference (apart from the weather; under the roof, as the summer approached, the heat had become stifling) was in the window; here low, on the level of the street; there high, opening over a view of roofs, the countryside, and in the distance the hills of B. Otherwise it was just the same, a repetition. She saw herself beside another bed, with her elbow planted on the coverlet and her cheek leaning on her hand, intently keeping watch during those long summer afternoons, over another body, the body of David. He was sleeping. But his breathing was so slow, his long jaw so pale under the beard of many days' growth, that sometimes, seized by anguish, she would shake him by the arm. « What is it? » he would mutter, half waking. He moved around in the bed, (a novel dropped to the floor with a thud), the back of his pyjamas looked soaked with sweat; he fell asleep again.

The room, she remembered, was on the top floor of a big tenement house, once a barracks. One day, during the period which now seemed to her immensely distant, almost lost, David had proposed that she should go and stay there with him. He had decided, he said, to make a definite break with his family, and to begin a new life. Why had he wanted to force things to that point? She had never understood; always, from the very first, it had been hard for her to understand what he was thinking, or to forsee what he would do. However, she had asked no questions, she had not hesitated for a minute. She went out one evening with David and she did not come back; that was all. A few days later she let her mother know where she was. She had had no reply. But at that time, who thought about tomorrow? Even David did not seem to think of it. The word « why » rose in her mind much later when, after the birth of the baby, she had gone back to live in that room, and the solitude had terrified her. From the window, very high up — more a dorner than a window (the idea of living in an attic had pleased David at first, it seemed to amuse him) she could see a long way off, beyond the black mass of the trees in the park, beyond the farthest roofs of the city. From over there, from the country-side, came the darkness which soon was to fill to room. « Why, why...? » The baby lying on the bed began to cry. She moved away from the window-sill, sat on the bed and gave him her breast. Then she lay down beside him. And so sleep came, with the dark and the monotonous croaking of frogs. Only then, not before (pregnancy had been for her a period outside time, which she remembered as one remembers a dream) had she understood that everything was truly finished.

But David, she persisted, who was he, what did he want? She had never asked him, she had never understood. He was reading law (a superannuated student, behind-hand with his exams and degree; he spent the afternoons sprawled on his bed, reading a little, sleeping a little) and he was living with her. « What does your husband do? » she was asked by the wife of one of the hospital attendants, who lived with their four children on the floor below. « He is out of work; but soon he is going into the sugar refinery » she had answered. Wasn't that what he had told her? David had only to talk — how he could talk! Then everything became easy, possible, credible. Marriage? A pure formality. Besides, if she set so much store by it, next year at the latest they would get everything regularised at the registry office. By that time, who knows, his parents... She would become his wife — « my missus » he would add smiling. In the mean time, it was just as though she really were.

The park, where there was an ice-cream kiosk, was not more than a hundred yards from the tenement house. In the evenings after supper they would go downstairs. They held hands; and at every step of those interminable stairs (four families on each floor; beyond the walls, the sounds of gramophones, voices, crockery...) she felt David's boredom and weariness growing. But beyond the dark foliage of the park trees, the acetylene lamp of the ice-cream kiosk shone in the distance, bright like a tiny light-house beam. Seeing it, they hurried towards it. And it had been on one of these evenings, while they were walking towards this point of brightness, that she had plucked up courage to tell him about her condition. « You know, I really think I'm going to have a baby », or something like that. For she had to tell him. David did not seem supprised, he made no reply. « Lemon or chocolate? » he had asked her kindly, when they came to a stop in front of the high zinc counter. While he sipped his ice (he always chose a mixture of vanilla and whipped cream) he looked at her from head to foot, sadly. She, as usual, had chosen chocolate. But that evening, one of the last, she had not managed to get to the end of her ice. « Don't you think it's unbearably hot? » said David suddenly. « At Cortina, in the evenings, one has to put on a pull-over ». His family had gone up to Cortina at the beginning of July. They were staying in the Hotel Faloria, a huge place as big as a castle, in the middle of a wood of firs and larches...

« Who was David, what did he want? Why, why...? » The question found no answer; it never would find one. Besides, it was late. Someone, perhaps Oreste, was knocking on the window. One must get up, go and let him in.

VII

In fact it was Oreste.

When he had closed the door behind him and rejoined the group of neighbours who had stayed talking on the threshold of the street-door, Oreste took part in the women's gossip until, a good half hour later, they had all dispersed. Left alone, he began to pace up and down in front of the house, not knowing what saint to turn to. Two contrary feelings were warring in him, two feeling necessarily opposed. On the one hand he felt urged to go away at least for an hour or two, to hurry and shut up his shop and to look after everything which the old woman's death, alas, entailed; she had got worse so suddenly that nobody, not even he, had had either the heart or the time, in the last two days, to prepare for the worst. But Deborah was alone, and the thought of her was enough to detain him. Several times, stooping down, he had tried to look into the room through the dirty window. He had distinguished, beside the white shape of the bed, a little figure, black and bent. During all that time, then, Deborah had not moved. « What is she doing? » he muttered from time to time, with affectionate impatience, like a husband already. The first shades of evening were falling; it had stopped snowing, but the cold was biting. Around him, through the windows of the houses, he could see the lighted interiors, kitchens and living-rooms. Something definite had to be done, and quickly. At last, after he had stooped down once more to peer into the room and, because of the darkness, had seen nothing, he decided to tap on the windowpanes with his knuckles. Then he stood listening, his heart pounding. And no sooner did he seem to hear Deborah's step on the inner stair than he quickly went through the entry was already on the landing by the time that she opened the door.

Immediately, at the first glance, he realised that he had regained the upper hand. With her back leaning against the door-post, Deborah looked at him silently, losing her eyes in his. Everything in her attitude asked for protection.

« Good God, you can't spend all night like this », he said, beneath his breath but almost roughly.

Then, without raising his voice or going beyond the threshold, he began to expound his plan. He must run off and close his shop and couldn't be back (there were some other little things to see to) for about two hours. Before he went, however, he would drop in on one of the neighbours, a Mrs Bedini, who had already offered to come in, to ask her to do so. « What for? Gracious, to keep you company, to have a bite of supper with you ». Well, anyway, he added at once, seeing that Deborah at the word « supper » began to shake her head in disagreement, anyway old Mrs. Bedini had better come, if only to pray with her. « So mind you don't close the door » he added smiling. As for the rest, she was not to worry about anything. He was ready and willing. « Trust me », he said, touching her arm. Anyway, he repeated, he would be back at nine at the latest; all right?

And when he had pressed her hand, he ran down the stairs and disappeared.

Oreste was right, but the old woman was no longer there to observe it. The thin, pink light which next morning made its way with difficulty through the ice-encrusted panes (Deborah was lying on the bed next to her mother's, Mrs Bedini was drowsing in an armchair, while Oreste, who had prayed all night long, was standing by the window, looking at the weather) was a light which came from a distant sun, lost in a pale, misty, blue sky, a sun that gave no heat. Since the evening of the previous day, when the snow stopped, the temperature had fallen rapidly. By now, Oreste reckoned — while he blew gently on his numbed fingers, the collar of his coat turned up round the back of his head, with its short bushy grey hair — at this moment the thermomenter must be indicating ten, fifteen, perhaps twenty degrees below zero. That, he foresaw, would stabilize the weather. For a long time, for all January and perhaps a good part of February, there would be even sharper frosts. They would have an exceptional winter, during which the canals and the rivers of the region would be frozen, and the drinking-water pipes would burst; the winter would be comparable only to that of 1898...

The funeral took place in the late afternoon of the following day. Behind the third-class hearse, which slid along over the trodden snow, Oreste walked alone, except for the priest. On his advice (advice given in such a fatherly, protective tone that it seemed to have the weight of an already taken decision) Deborah stayed at home. As far as he was concerned, favourite old pupil of Don Castelli, veteran soldier of the Carso, the intense cold renewed his energy, miraculously restored the lack of his many lost hours of sleep. The wheels of the hearse, high and narrow, lifted clods of snow which, before they got to the top of the circuit, fell noiselessly back, scarcely dusting the spokes and springs. He walked with his eyes fastened on the tracks made in the snow by the wheels, looking at the little landslides of snow which the iron wheels made all along the way; and meanwhile his pace, which he instinctively regulated by that of the priest, gave his bearing something of that cheerful alacrity of a good trooper which he had had when a young man.

It was already night when he came back. And instead of tapping on the window, as in the past few days, he preferred to announce himself by the accustomed ring at the bell. Deborah was standing at the foot of the stairs, waiting for him. During his absence she must have slept. Her face, which earlier had borne signs of profound weariness, now looked fresh and rested. Certainly she had changed her clothes. He sat in his old place, by the lamp. From there, while Deborah busied herself about the stove, he watched her with satisfied contentment, with the gratitude which came into his eyes whenever he thought he detected in a word or gesture of hers the wish and desire to please him.

« For tonight », he said, « Mrs Bedini will come and sleep with you. I must drop in there later. Tomorrow I will go and talk to Don Bonora, to see if he will let the boy come home to sleep, at any rate for the time being. Later on we shall see ».

It was he, now, who disposed of her future.

After supper (they sat opposite one another as they had done almost every evening for all these years) their conversa-

tion turned to her mother. Oreste talked at length about her
life and her good qualities, with much kindness and much
tact. He went on to describe the place in the church-yard
where she would be laid tomorrow. It was a most beautiful
place, he assured her, a place fit for the gentry. Did she remember that covered walk, built recently in red brick, which
described a great curve from the Certosa almost to the ramparts? Well, her mother was to be buried under that. (« Buried, poor thing, the earth will scarcely touch her ») A most
beautiful place, he repeated, open to the south, so that the
sun warmed it from dawn to evening as in a greenhouse.

« Of course », he added after a pause, « tombs are dear » :
but immediately, as if to forestall any possible ambiguity in
the phrase, he made it clear that Deborah was not to worry
about that. « In all these years of work, I've been able, thank
God, to put aside a little ». And since she had given him
reason to hope (...here he felt a moments's uncertainty) ...since
she had led him to believe ...seeing that, he thought, it
would have pleased her poor mother... « In short, what is
mine is thine » he said, looking her steadily in the eye and
using for the first time *tu* instead of *voi*.

As he spoke he leant forward gently over her chair, not
without gallantry. Then he rose, and hurriedly taking his
leave assured Deborah (there were so many things they had
to talk about) that he would come back to see her on the following morning.

VIII

« We have so many things to talk about » : every time
he took leave of her Oreste would either affirm this explicitly or at least imply it silently with his serious, kind eyes.

Actually, the one to talk was always he. When he was
not dealing with memories (his boyhood spent in the Seminary, the war on the Carso furnished him with his usual themes) there would be long discourses on religion, with particular reference to the duties of the clergy to society and the

relations between the papacy and the state. His patriotism, after the Conciliation in February of that year, overflowed freely in expressions of sentimental tenderness, just like a lover's whose desire has been granted. The Papacy and the State, each, in its sphere, must be free but in agnement. In support of this proposition he quoted passages from the Bible, the Gospels, and Dante, in which his dream of perfect concord and universal harmony found the support of authority. Even human history seemed finally to be sobering down. Perhaps, with the spring that was just beginning, the age of peace and joy would be initiated; the mythical golden age would be renewed. His eyes, while he spoke of these things, shone with exaltation. The little house outside the city-gates (almost every evening, when he had shut up shop, he used to bicycle over to see how the work was getting on) would not be ready before May. He had never taken Deborah with him to show it her. It was to remain a surprise to the last. She knew the place, of course. It was on the opposite side of the city, in the neighbourhood of the station, in an area entirely given up to new buildings. Each little house had a plot of its own land round it, where vegetables or fruit could be grown. And meanwhile, as the work progressed, he **would argue** with the mason, because a newly white washed wall showed patches of damp; or with the carpenter because a lock didn't work; or with the foreman because, thanks to the bad organisation of the undertaking, the date of handing over had been set back a month. Each discourse finished like this, with the concrete image of a happiness long dreamed of, but already in sight, already within grasp, from which he was separated by a steadily diminishing space of time. In May, at the latest, they would be married.

As for Deborah, she tried to support her fiancé with all the good will and the wish to share that she could command. No longer, of course, could she exchange with her mother, at the appropriate moment, the knowing smile that often rose to her lips; but by degrees she learnt, effortlessly, to do without this. The ardour which shone in Oreste's eyes was

so sincere; the world created by his fancy was so warm, so
kindly, so welcoming, that she gave herself up to it willingly,
or anyway without protest. All the light and all the warmth
came from him. She merely let herself be illuminated and
warmed, like an extinct planet that continues to live on the
life that is shed on it by its parent sun. The golden age, the
happiness which Oreste's eyes and words promised her, she
didn't believe in the depths of her heart that she would ever
see them or that they were possible on this earth. However,
although she could not delude herself, although she was conscious of the damage which time and grief had wrought in
her, she nevertheless realised confusedly that her only reason for existing was now linked with these fancies to which
she clung with so many secret reservations, with these dreams,
« Still dreams », she thought, « at my age, with a son who
is already a big boy! » What arguments, besides, could
she have set against Oreste's? If the strength that came from
the reflection of his limitless faith had failed her, what could
she have put in its place? Perhaps — and she smiled — memories of the past? He was her superior in everything. All
her other thoughts were formed slowly, with difficulty; but
this expressed a real, precise fact, whose truth she never
doubted, not even in the depths of her consciousness. The
conviction of her own inferiority always filled her with pleasure and peace.

May came. During the last days Oreste's haste became
anxious, anguished. Deborah would say to him, smiling, « If
I didn't know you so well, I should say that you'd become
another man. You have waited so many years, a week more
won't be such a disaster ». Actually he had not changed at
all, as none knew better than she. She knew everything about
him. She knew very well that the reason of his sudden impatience, apparently so out of keeping with his character, was
the same that had induced him to wait for so long, contenting himself for years with a promise that had never been
formulated in words, accepting every kind of delay. Then as
now, far stronger than any possible egotism, the dominating

feeling in Oreste was that of a man who dares not hope for too great a happiness, of which he feels himself unworthy. For that reason he wanted the marriage to be celebrated with the greatest solemnity; immediately after the words of consent and the blessing, the organ burst into Mendelssohn's wedding march. Marriage represented the crowning, late and difficult, of his whole life; it was a destination beyond which it was futile, perhaps impious, to direct one's gaze. After it they would walk together, protected by divine providence.

The years that followed were in fact tranquil and happy ones; years of work and, if not of actual riches, of confortable prosperity. There were no more winters like the winter of '29; certainly Oreste never saw any such, for he died soon, in the spring of '38. Towards the end of every autumn, he used to stand for a long time by the window, studying the weather. He thought that in this new house, where nothing was wanting, where there was even a central heating plant, no winter could ever worry him again, however bitter it might be. The future smiled on him. After marriage, Deborah at once conformed to his pious practices, and had got into the way of going frequently to church. She had grown plumper and better looking. The thin girl, sharpened by anxiety, whom he had known so many years ago, when he had first come to pay his regular evening calls in a certain house in Via Salinguerra, was transformed by time into a fine, quiet woman, a little bit fat, with that plumpness that is so becoming to pious women. All this, even this tardy beauty of his wife — for which, between seriousness and jest, he took a little credit — showed that the Lord had blessed their union.

IX

« He was happy » Deborah sometimes said to herself.

But immediately, as though an inner echo distorted it, her voice became interrogative, twisted itself into a question full of doubt and sad suspicion. « Would he have been happy? ».

Only now, now that he was no more than a memory, did she know that he would not, that something would always have been lacking. For years, for all the years of their married life, he had wanted a son, a son of his own, and she had not been able to give him one.

How much he must have struggled, to keep her from realising this, to keep himself from realising it! Every time that Deborah thought of this, she called to mind the loving care, more than fatherly, which he had always taken of Ireneo, though his tenderness was not reciprocated. When the boy was thirteen, just out of the Seminary, he had taken him into his shop and had prepared a little bench specially for him, between the threading machine and the glass door. He had wanted to teach him his own craft; and she seemed to see him still (sometimes in the evening, after Benediction, she used to go on foot to the binder's shop) behind his counter, his zealous eyes fixed on his pupil, who was distracted by the least thing that came from outside, from the big square outside the shop. She seemed still to see and hear him; with his big, vigorous trunk (disproportionate to the size of his limbs) perched on the stool behind the counter, and his knotted hands (on the left gleamed the wedding ring) which, even when his eyes were elsewhere (lifted with his voice to greet someone coming in), never for a moment ceased to work. How much he must have suffered, seeing that, not content with all that he had done and was doing for the boy, he had wanted him, at a certain point, to take his name! The significance, the true meaning of all his actions became clear only now, when he had gone for ever. He had always tried to deny himself, to stifle within himself a different need, a different desire.

And yet, she was sure of it, he had never despaired. In the most secret recesses of his spirit, he must have always been sure that Deborah, one day or another, would come to him with the great news. Before long, without any doubt, she would have given him a son who was really his own, a son who would not have grown up with the precocious,

343

silent, unmotivated sadness of this fifteen year old boy. Ireneo had developed with an intelligence that was not very
bright; a tall, thin boy, with the long jaw of a sad horse.
Though Oreste had given him his name, his honourable
name of an honest though unpretentious artisan; though he
was teaching him his craft as he would have taught it to
the son of his own body; in spite of all this the boy had
never wanted to call him anything but « Uncle Oreste ». Only
with the birth of a son could Oreste have said that he had
not been deceived when, in February 1929, he had predicted
the return of the golden age. Without this... But death,
snatching him unexpectedly, had quenched, with his life, any
seed of despair.

These were the only shadows, thought Deborah, the only
worries that had troubled the serenity of their life.

(translated by Margaret Bottrall)

POEMS

BY

ANTONIO RINALDI

POEM

« Here my mother smiled ». Aloud
I repeat the words, and in the brief
room that still is hers
I picture the weeping, the faces
turned to stone, and the white
linen of all the dead
upon the beloved image
extended without a shudder.

In the summer morning
gathered into the shade
and a flaming silence,
my thought is clear,
like a happy song
over still roads,
the madness is clear
that whispers absurdly again, while a breath
of wind, barely audible, crosses
the sill and a grumble
of life overturns me.

And, out in the sun, I deny
that I am cruel;

         yet

in the day a mourning ended,
and my step is unsure
in the light that shines:
senses the waiting shade
my discordant consciousness.

PRAYER

With evening
eyes fell into their lids,
swallows into the nest.

And here from the late day
a cry retells me
that all looks in darkness
that I too have fallen.

Fallen like the flower
in the womb of the sad grass
to sleep with the sun,

let the air alone watch over us,
let it conquer us, this solitary life
of heaven that holds every sorrow.

IDYLL

The tear on the eyelash
once withheld and spent
is slowly reborn and rises
together with it a name
never known, the name
incessant and unique
that set my throat afire.
What other word ever
is to be said of me?   Evening
resembles me and the face
of the night I do not fear
now that, filled and green
with the last light, the womb
of the leaves hesitates, now that an edge
of sky gathers me.

(translated by William Fense Weaver)

POEMS FOR A PRINT-COLLECTOR

BY

ROBERTO ROVERSI

RACHELE

The torrent flies like a maddened bee
and the children laugh on the bridge.
The priest drowses in the sun:
his face is burned
like the Calvaries in ancient abbeys;
a cockrel slowly reclines into sleep
his wing falls wearily, he closes his eyes.
Paolo near the window
whistles, carving the wood,
Osso watches a spider's web
beautiful, full of tales, against the flame.
Diletta, apple-flower,
her head bent, lightly sleeps.
The others, in the tender green of the hills,
hunt the marmots, fat and torpid:
in their damp holes the beasts laden
with an ageless slumber
appear slowly
but a snare shines in the sun,
tightened for the kill.
The partridges, in ermine mantles,
transfix the calm.
Thin as a twisted poplar

Rachele looks at the clouds, the birds,
in the marvelous desert
she hears the distant voice of her sons
and the wan breath of sleeping Diletta.
Still in the doorway,
nailed there like a holy picture
— her eyes are two blazing poppies —
the woman waits and to her own time returns.

The quivering girls wait for their friend:
Rachele the bride, Rachele dressed in white
— the cloth is rough but her heart is a crystal.
The friends wait, the girls,
until she comes down the wooden steps,
her face aflame, her glance a fugitive.
They ring the bells:
she looks, tired and laughing,
she gives them all her hand,
today she is happy — the holiday of her life —
she has seen herself in the mirror,
she has washed her body in warmed water.
Rachele! Rachele! the doors open,
every window invites her.
Today they will dine in the square
and dance on the cobblestones,
the men fatigued by the wine,
the girls all red, their hearts malicious.
Tomorrow the men will go off to the border
— and the women to pray
against avalanche, the torments, the ravines;
now her friends accompany Rachele
— the cloth is rough but her heart is a crystal.
Let another draw the water: she is happy in the sun
like the hay beside the house,
eating her white, white bread,
light as the first son's cheek,

she will drink the glowing, bubbling wine
and the men will sing of her love.
Tomorrow all will be ended
and death will be possible once more!
They ring the bells at length;
Rachele! Rachele! every door is opened
every window invites her.
The girls are singing, thinking of their day,
the youths envy the night its sacrifice
and the man his tender prey.
In the heart desire glows afresh.

They dug him the pit
stone after stone, pick upon pick,
with sweat and long exertion.
When years had fled, one next the other
— the leaves in the plain were stupendously yellow —
the man came down, rigid, among the rocks:
death had stripped him and divided him
and a malevolent wind had dried him up
at the boundary of his house.
As they had rung in festival
the bells on the wedding day
as hard and merciless now
was the clang of the saddened bronze.
They set him in the grave without tears or pain
but in the sunset's silence, when nature,
memoryless, delays to gaze at its prodigy:
and without lament, since all know
that each good or evil has its time
and its reason.
The children by their mother, stiff and surprised:
Osso is watching a vagrant cloud
that marks with shadow his father's transfixed face.
With a few fistfuls of earth he was covered
his face blinded and his hand imprisoned,

then like a herd of lambs
full of sleep and stupefied
the little ones returned in the evening
to the usual walls, the accustomed rest.
But in the night-time silence
the man's deep snoring was silent!
She freezes
at the memory of that night, eternal.

Thus Rachele
digs each day her niche for eternity
like water that cuts rock and sculps it
to open the way under the arch of the sky.
And she counts her children when they leave at morning
and come back at evening, because her chicks
are gentle and trembling at their work.
— Carlo, at your milking, look out
for the horns of the impatient cow! —
If Rachele waits at the doorsill
it seems to her that someone must leave
and no one ever return,
that the boys must go down into France
and the daughters to the plains
and she stay alone
like a cypress set on the bank of a ditch.
Let one, at least, stay to close her eyes
the day of her final labor!
But if she shouts now, the children answer;
Osso running among the rocks, slips
and gets up crying,
Diletta wakes, looks about in confusion,
Carlo arrives, laughing, with the milk,
Osso grows calm.
On the mountain
slowly the evening spreads its silence.

THE TAPESTRY

The river turns red as the sun is born,
the nightingale rests; only the low sparrow
hunts in the furrow, but a shout frightens him.
Blinded falcons, with hard, shaggy talons
fly, their scent avid at the call
of the trembling prey:
the moan is vain, seized
the bird bends his head, and the falcon returns.
The proud horses drink at the castle's fountain;
the serving boys shout
at a hunchback on the stair: « O dwarf!
Deformed half-man! You'll wear out your back! »
and he hurls himself at them with terrible gibes.
In the dusty tapestry shines
the great banquet table,
the fruit rests in salvers engraved
by a patient artist,
the men laugh, their mouths crammed full;
rosy-glazed, quartered lambs
dissolve in the odor of bay and rosemary.
In silence the king is fed. Terrible
is old age — God! — worse than death.
His neck is wrinkled like a snake in August,
he clasps his paining hand
on the bow that he once bent hardily,
his voice is deeper than the sound of a cask,
no wind can equal him.
The gentle queen sits at his side
and her body seems the foam
that lightly pursues itself upon the sea;
the king observes her, seeks her hand
but she turns to ice
as if a serpent had touched her,
foul vision!

Some of the knights shout a toast
and greedily gulp down their wine, others laugh
and whisper maliciously to their neighbors.
The king rises: the immense shadow splatters
black on the wall; the queen rises
white in her dress of snow;
the men abandon their cups,
the candles tremble exhausted,
the deserted table
is like the sea after a tempest.

AFTERNOON

Suddenly the ball goes flying
beyond the hedge and the field,
beyond the gate of the neighboring villa;
fallen into the garden
red with soft, sweet-smelling peaches.
Gioietta runs swiftly, shouting,
and her dress swells like a sail
fresh in the wind. And the girls meanwhile:
one lies in the hay, one snorts
reddened by play, one has her face
lined with sweat and over her lip
the slow, avid drops descend;
another with worn-out eyes
leans against a trunk, offering
her neck to the shade that drinks her in.
And here, Gioietta returns with the ball
and peaches, apples, and pears in her skirt
which she offers like a goblet.
Each of them seizes a fruit and she too
bites with her white talons
a fruit that breaks open,
fearful, bitten, and the juice
runs to her chin in a flaming river.

353

Then the sky darkens;
but the weary girls
do not see the clouds
that hasten from the distant hills,
while the wind bristles and lifts
the hair that is already disordered;
the tender flowers are shaken in the fields.
The swift rain falls
and the motionless girls,
some lost in thought, others smiling,
throw down the fruit and, awe-stricken, gaze
at the unfolding boughs, the leaves
that are suddenly dark. A peasant runs by,
an awkward black pig is pursued
by a barefoot boy over the field;
above the thunder-claps they hear
the thuds of closing windows...
At some sudden summons
the girls, with happy cries,
under the rain, run and disappear.

(translated by William Fense Weaver)

THE HOUSE IS MOVING

BY

GUGLIELMO PETRONI

PART ONE

I

« Yes, yes, there's a man! » said the woman with the black shawl.

« He must have been killed by the blast ».

The Hotel *Aquila d'Oro* had not crumbled onto itself like most of the other buildings in the square, but by one of those frequent chances had merely lost its facade, showing part of its hundred-and-fifty-eight rooms in rows one above the other like cubbyholes in a cupboard. The first light of day, which had come suddenly as happens on beautiful days in summer, lit up their now naked interiors, so that in each room one could see what had happened and what was left. Among the few people who were on the spot, along with the firemen and first aid teams, a group had collected in the part of the square still clear of fresh debris. Its participants were now speaking of the bombing, of what was left in the neighborhood, of what was no longer, and of the dead — who were few, because the district had been almost completely abandoned by its inhabitants. The words of the woman with the black shawl made everyone turn towards a room on the second floor. Of those which were visible it was the least damaged: inside almost everything was in its place, not even a chair was upturned; only a porcelain washstand, evidently previously fixed to the no longer existing wall, hung into space, swaying imperceptibly, attached to a piece of lead piping. The rising sun shone almost gayly on that porcelain suspended above the dust and desolation all around. On the bed in the room which was still intact someone seemed to be stretched out quietly sleeping.

« But he's moving! » several people said suddenly, « he's alive! »

In fact from the bedclothes still covered with plaster two arms appeared; after the arms, a young man's head was seen to rise from the pillow. Finally the sleeper, waking up in that room so open to the winds and to indiscreet glances, sat up in bed.

The casual spectators, who had grown in number, stood silently, astounded, as if they were present at a resurrection; whereas the man waking up in the middle of so much ruin looked around without seeming excessively worried. At a certain point his glance met that of the people standing in the square, who were quite overcome by the spectacle, the banality of which, in the circumstances, was turning into something of a firacle. The man, after, making a sort of embarassed smile, perhaps a little annoyed, but polite, and a gesture which might have meant: — you see the kind of world we live in? — prepared to think about his own business. He got out of bed, carefully avoiding stepping on the plaster which was scattered around the floor, and approached his clothes which were hung on the back of a chair.

« He's in pajamas » said a woman, breaking the silence into which those present had fallen.

« Now he's going to get dressed ».

« That was a close one! »

« His brain can't be where it ought to be ».

« He must have been frightened; the others all ran at the first alarm » said someone who seemed well informed. « Who knows why he stayed? Apart from the staff there may have been barely ten guests, almost all of them officers ».

« He cannot have heard the siren ».

At this last remark, made very seriously by a youth with flattened cheeks the colour of white wood, there were a few smiles, certanly the first smiles in the area since the destruction.

While those present, released from their momentary stupor, exchanged impressions in low voices, as one does in the presence of the dead, the man in the room had actually begun to dress, carefully hiding his bare legs behind the jacket hung from the back of the chair. As soon as he had finished he collected the few things scattered round the room and bundled them haphazardly into a suitcase which stood open on the table; he then opened the door, but was seen to retreat in a hurry, the passage evidently being blocked in that direction. Next he went cautiously towards the edge of the floor which ended abruptly, and without addressing anyone in particular of those who were watching him from below, still astounded by the unusual spectacle, he asked:

« Who can help me get down from here? »

His voice sounded warm and rounded as it came through the air, a nice voice, entirely devoid of cordiality. Those present consulted among themselves; then someone ran off behind the debris to where picks could be heard at work. A few minutes passed during which the young man stood up there in the same position in which he had said the last words, as if suddenly petrified by the horror all around him, by the danger he had run, by the tragedy of the mute and contorted things which from up there he could see much better than anyone else. He looked as if he had been hit by a sort of retarded fear; and those who were watching him waited in the most careful silence. Actually, Ugo had stopped because he had been struck and annoyed by the sudden thought that there might no longer be a train to take him home: — I may have to go a long way on foot, or at best find a cart — but he was unable to finish the thought as many voices from the ruined square recalled him to the dead landscape around him. In that fresh and enormous tomb he had the sensation of many corpses buried beneath many bricks, and of much twisted steel. — The dead are silent — he thought. But the end of a fireman's ladder was stretching towards him like a tentacle; he watched the contraption with a certain amount of trepidation as it approached, and had the desire to step back. — Look what I have to do — he muttered to himself, annoyed. From below two firemen were inviting him to descend by gesturing and shouting up instructions. Evidently Ugo was not going to get out of it too easily alone; perhaps he was one of those people afraid of empty spaces.

The operation was rather long and tiring, but at last he found himself on firm ground with his suitcase standing beside him. For a moment his grey velvety glance met that of a dozen persons; he turned his eyes on them with lips tight and firm, and after that glance, no one asked anything. Bending down to pick up his bag he remembered something and turned to the man who had practically carried him down, saying:

« Thank you, you were most efficient ». From his pocket he removed some money which everyone scanned with his eyes, then handed it to the fireman. « If you think... ».

« Thank you » said the man quickly stretching out his hand.

« Thank *you*. May I? I'm Ugo Gattegna ». He shook the man's hand, then, with a hard monotonous step, walked off towards the largest rent in the debris, leaving those present once more overcome with their sadness.

After a few hundred yards Ugo found himself in front of a plain, patched here and there with vast cultivated fields, under a clear sky colored by the last pale red of dawn. Larks skimmed the fields, and two large clouds filled a stretch of calm horizon.

II

Cesira raised her arms to heaven when she saw Ugo appear at the end of the slope in front of the Big House. Down there, far away, entering the gate, small as an insect, Ugo bent his shoulders to face the steep drive lined with cypress trees which led straight up to the front door of the house. Cesira came to meet him, grabbed his bag, and after a short, barely whispered greeting, walked behind him, unconsciously imitating his gait with its hard monotonous step. « I was worried about you » she said after a while « It's three days I've been waiting at the door. After the news I heard from down there I didn't know what to think! »

Ugo shrugged without answering. — There's really no way of opening his mouth — thought the woman; but she immediately realized it was a useless thought and said:

« Besides, now that you're here it's all right ».

« Yes, it's all right, Cesira » Ugo answered as he crossed the hall of the house whose walls were hung with two enormous antique mirrors in gilded frames on which ivy leaves were carved.

— These Gattegnas — Cesira murmured imperceptibly to herself; it was one of the habitual exclamations which had come to underlie her whole way of reasoning, dating back forty years: these incomprehensible people; all the same, big, heavy, silent, with the shoulders of domesticated oxen.

Without the least change in their set gait, they crossed a large room furnished with old things, not without taste, and impressed with the stratified elegance of more than one generation, then took the staircase with its light wrought-iron banister, which still showed signs of ancient white paint and gilding where the little cross bars were joined, and which led to the floor above. Without the least hesitation, both bending their backs as if about to climb a mountain, they burst into Ugo's darkned bedroom.

« Shall I open the window? »

« No, I'm going to bed ».

« Goodness knows you must be tired; you may have had to come on foot? »

« I'll call you when I wake. Thank you, Cesira ».

« Have a good sleep ». The woman closed the door, slowly went back down the stairs with an agile youthful step, despite her age. The kitchen was large. In the middle stood a huge table. To one side were two great cupboards between which was squeezed an old armchair with a soiled damask back. Cesira picked up her rosary from one of the arms of the imposing chair, thew herself into it, and leant back her head.

In that armchair she had spent perhaps not less than half her life. The other half she had spent running after the Gattegnas, of which the only one left was the last and purest example.

She had started sitting there as a young girl, almost a child, from the day she had been called to the Big House from her family of peasants to become the personal maid of the lady of the house, Ugo's mother, who was Piedmontese. How she had been envied for it, how many comments she had received from the other peasant families who also had girls her own age!

Yet for her, a few years had been enough to form quite a different opinion of her good fortune. Rather intelligent, too much taken to seeing to the bottom of things, with that openess of spirit which is common to the peasants of Tuscany, she had quite well understood what this new position, aquired through the preference of the Gattegnas, really meant for her.

In the village a short speech she had once made to one of her suitors was often repeated. Pretty, gifted with a certain natural fineness, she had sometimes been courted quite implacably; and her old suitors, now all grandfathers, had for years repeated the phrase without really understanding what she had meant by the words. The man to whom she had made the speech had courted her furiously, had followed her with incredible stubbornness, until she decided to speak to him at greater length than usual and get rid of him definitely with the words which remained fixed in his memory, and which he repeated for years. She had said to him: « Willingly would I like to be able to say yes, Ottavio; but it is now nine years that I have been in that house and I have had to learn many things; I am no longer what I used to be. Those who want me can no longer give me what I need, and those whom I might accept do not dream of looking at me, even by chance ».

From then on Cesira became even more reserved and intractable; though no one knew that for many days she spent several hours, the ones which were free from her usual duties, crying silently in her room beside the kitchen. During that period the elders of the Gattegna family died, then in the next fifteen years Ugo's parents also died, so that she remained alone with the young master; for, with the diminution of the family, the servants had also grown fewer, ending up with herself alone.

Besides, she had always devoted herself to Ugo since he was born. From the moment he had begun to mouth the first few words she had been asked to address him in the formal manner, and she had accepted the request without dreaming of finding it inconvenient, so lacking was she in the susceptibilities of her fellow peasants with whom she had discussed the matter and who were astonished at such a mode of addressing a child who could barely walk.

Her mother, on one of the rare occasions when she had met her in the vinyard, had said to her:

« Aren't you ashamed of addressing a child that way? »

« Never mind, mother, these are things you cannot understand » Cesira had answered brusquely.

It was now many years that she and Ugo lived alone; she had supported him during his first steps and followed him closely throughout his existence, except for the period of his studies in the city; but never had a word passed between her and that last of the Gattegnas which might have built a bridge of cordiality in their relationship, yet there existed between them a silent and profound solidarity under which it was quite impossible to discover the slightest shadow of sentiment. Cesira was intelligent.

III

Cesira knew that Ugo would not awaken till morning and did not expect his call. Outside, a faint light still framed the black woods as she began to lay the table for her supper, placing the china and beautiful silver, devoid of adornment except for the Gattegna G, on a small Flanders cloth at one corner of the table. She prepared the small square with the same attention as always, stopping to see if everything was disposed in its regular order. In a few minutes she had finished her modest cold meal, replaced everything, and returned to her armchair.

When she had come to the house as a young girl she had sat in that armchair as a game, and to watch the other servants; then it had become a habit, and now that she was, alone, growing old, with long hours of idleness and waiting in her days — a necessity. Her major periods of idleness had begun at the time when Ugo had left the Big House to frequent the university.

— The same year Ugo went to the city —. Thinking about it the woman shook her head with a movement which was followed by a slight smile of commiseration for herself, now mechanically repeated every evening for many years as she found herself engulfed, always at the same hour, in the only thoughts which completely occupied her mind. She could still smile at herself even though the smile, like the memories, had for some time become one of her monotonous habits. Her mind ran over the past, methodically fixing upon recurrent images. Yes, it was she who had raised him, always followed him as he grew up, as he became what he now was, as rigid as his mother had been, big and reserved like all the Gattegna.

And Cesira would turn, always as if by accident, to the time when Ugo was a child, to the time when she used to put him to bed, then wake him in the morning when the air began to warm. Then, after reciting a few prayers, Cesira would pick up her rosary from the arm of the chair and go to bed.

Before lying down she would accomplish a reasonably laborious *toilette*. It was more or less the same as the one she had helped Ugo's mother with for many years; for, like all northeners, she knew how to use cosmetics with a natural wisdom.

During this operation which she accomplished meticulously but without the slightest touch of feminine coquetry, her thoughts would follow the usual course: now she would remember Ugo's mother who had died the very first year Ugo had left the village to finish his studies in the city. It had been Cesira who had recalled him with a telegram, and who the next day had waited for him at the door of the Big House till she could see him enter the gate from the main road. Running towards him she had grabbed his bag and followed him, as usual imitating his hard monotonous step. That time he'd been the first one to speak:

« So she's dying » he'd said.

« I'm afraid so » she'd answered.

« Yes, she's dying », the boy had concluded, going up to his mother's room where his father and a few others had been for some time with the doctor.

Later, while her aunt had stayed to watch the body, father and son had silently gone down to the drawing room with that same gait which looked as if it were going to take them who knows where. Sitting by the round table they had stared at the floor. An hour later the father had said: « She's dead ».

The son had assented, nodding his head, and another long pause of those silent Gattegnas, one of the silences which fell like lead, accompanied them through the night. Thus she had found them in the morning. Seeing them with their eyes fixed on an indefinite spot between the floor and the main wall of the room, she had the clear sensation that the air was saturated with the powerful and silent workings of their lonely minds. « But who knows », Cesira had then concluded to herself, « if they really thought about the dead one ».

The dead woman was different; she had gone through her life with body erect and lips tight; from the height of her rigidity, which really quite suited her, she had given new order to the house, the same order which now, though there were only two left in it, continued like a perfect mechanism which once set in motion proceeds indefinitely.

When, at Ugo's birth, she was taken with labor, even before the doctor and the midwife had arrived, she had called Cesira and said to her:

« Listen, always be near me; all women cry unpleasantly when they give birth to their children and I do not want to do so. Stay right by me and squeeze my hand if I cry ». And Ugo was born while his mother, rigidly silent, never once uttered a sound. She bit her upper lip and was mute; her body showed the spasm by jerking, but from her mouth not a sound issued, until, exhausted, she fell back as the child's voice was heard above the others.

IV

Cesira always awakens at the same hour, prepares breakfast for the young master, then sits in her armchair with her rosary in her fingers. Outside, beyond the rows of vines, at that time of day the woods are no longer black, but a wide brown strip which divides the red earth from the silky white sky. She begins to pray; but her usual memories, almost identical each day, begin to assail her with a strange implacable method; the lives of the Gattegnas live again in her, pulsing through her veins, and the sight of the vast kitchen table (which in the morning is quite cleared, but will not remain so for a good part of the rest of the day) brings back the image of the master, of Ugo's father, who died stretched out on it. He had been brought back on the shoulders of a group of peasants who had laid him there, his stomach ripped open by the tread of a tractor which had crushed him when a raised piece of ground had given away as he supervised the work. He was still alive, with his eyes open, but no longer spoke. The peasants lined up along the kitchen walls with their arms hanging down, hat in hand, and Ugo came down from upstairs in his blue striped pajamas.

The son had leaned across the face of his father; for a long time they looked into each other's eyes, their identical mouths, forcefully impressed on solid faces, moved rhythmically but neither pronounced a single word. She had stayed to one side and saw the man die under the fixed and obstinate gaze of the son, who watched him silently with violence in his eyes.

He died before the doctor and the priest could reach him, and she had to think of everything for the funeral; Ugo never said a word, did not go to sleep, and the next day followed the coffin with the peasants and the neighbouring landowners; he did not answer the greetings of those present, stood to one side, and at the cemetery took her arm motioning her to stay until everyone had gone. Once alone they too went out; Ugo drew the black gate after them and stayed for a moment looking back, with his hands against the wrought iron. It was a cemetery of only a few square meters enclosed by a high wall covered at several points by evergreen creepers; in among the grass which grew tall and undisturbed one could see a few marble slabs, as well as terracotta ones with nothing but a number on them. On one side stood the Gattegna chapel; it was a small plastered construction, simple, with a modest and severe architectural motif of grey stone; on the main beam above the door a large G was carved in stone which had once been gilded and which still retained a few flakes of gold that sparkled in the sunlight. There was a great silence and Ugo said his first words in two days:

« How beautiful it is here ».

Then, until they were home, he said nothing, walking slowly beside her, and only when they were on the doorstep to the kitchen did he add:

« Now, Cesira, you and I, here... it's two nights I haven't slept; I'm going to bed; good night ».

« Good night ».

Ugo had recently given up his studies; he had come in one night without warning, and said to his father:

« I'm not going back, I'm giving up my studies ».

« Never mind, don't let it worry you ».

« I'll stay here in the country ».

« If you like, but try not to shut yourself up completely ».

« This summer I'll have three friends of mine come for a few weeks ».

« Very well ».

And in fact that summer two young men and a girl arrived. Often, during those days Ugo's two friends Gianni and Rafaele would say to their host, trying to make much of it:

« We don't understand; you were the best of us all, you had taken to studying with such enthusiasm ».

« Never mind » Ugo would invariably answer, putting an end to the conversation; and so the other three would speak gayly together while Ugo for the most part remained silently listening. Sometimes he'd take the girl by the arm and say:

« Luisa, come out with me ».

She would follow him docilely; they would go for a walk along the path by the woods, he with his monotonous hard gait, she with almost the step of a child. From up there you could see the plain alive, full of houses, lined with roads which linked the clusters of villages, stretching a network of light lines on the green and red of the earth. The railway cut across the whole plain with a straight dark line that occasionally disappeared in the uneven terrain from which at certain hours vast purple shadows stretched out like faded spots of ink; in the warm afternoons the shallow valleys often held the vapours of the earth making zones that were bathed in a yellowish atmosphere; the heavy smoke from a faraway glassworks ran with the wind. Here and there fires from burning dog-grass would be lit; and during the season the rumble of tractors could be heard, or during the harvest the crackling of threshers.

Up there the two of them would stop to look. Ugo would not speak as he showed her the landscape. Lifting a hand and indicating a point, he'd motion her to listen to the sound that drifted up to them, muffled by space; Luisa understood, assenting, and thanking him with a rapid glance which disclosed all the whites of her large, intelligent eyes.

A shining canal ran towards the horizon like a chromed steel nail pointed at the sky.

« It's like a cut in the earth » Luisa once said to Ugo, who assented with a slight movement of the head. Then, as if going on with a speech she had kept silent until then, she said suddenly:

« Without you, we are no longer the same, the three of us ». She was refering to their life as students, to the years she had passed with him and Rafaele and Gianni in close intimacy. They had really felt the loss of him; Ugo had been a friend whom it had been hard for them to get used to, but who had eventually occupied a large part of their existence. His very silence, at first a difficulty, had finally tied them more profoundly, attracted them towards the secret of that closed heart, of that mind in which they suspected a complex and exhausting work. But one day he had left them all and returned to the country.

« Are you happy up here, alone? » the girl asked again.

« I don't know ».

They were silent, and Ugo indicated with his hand a great flock of birds which obscured a point in the sky.

« It's impossible to imagine what you think ».

« Sometimes I think: — You fool! — then I no longer

think of anything. Sometimes I listen to the churning of my mind, but I try not to pay much attention to it ».

« The boys are fond of you and they too are very sorry you left off your studies », said Luisa encouraged by his long sentence: « I am a woman and can be misunderstood; but you are a man of few prejudices, you are intelligent and can certainly judge me in the right way ».

« Yes ».

« I have always thought that you had important capacities, I have always believed you capable of important things and even today I'm of the same opinion; I think, I don't know, that few have been able to understand you ».

« Yes? » said Ugo looking at her coldly. Luisa lowered her head and they were both silent. They were seated on the grass, an automobile slid along the asphalt of the main road and Ugo followed it with his eyes until it disappeared. In the silence that followed the voice of the peasants could be heard, and even at a distance the open vowels which were typical of the region could be recognized, while the rest of the words seemed to die in space before reaching them there. Luisa had remained with her head down, and when Ugo turned absentmindedly towards her he saw two long clear tears on her cheeks; for a while he sat watching her in silence, then informed her:

« You're crying ».

Luisa did not answer; Ugo thought of other things, and several minutes passed, then all of a sudden without turning towards her he said:

« A cup of Cesira's coffee will certainly do us good », and he got up to return to the Big House.

V

A brief sound of the electric bell took Cesira from her fleeting memories; she got up, took the tray with breakfast, and went up the two flights of stairs which led to the floor above with the aglity of a young girl. Ugo's room was in darkness.

« Good morning ».

« *Brava* Cesira » and he waited for the woman to unfasten the blinds before opening his eyes. Every morning when he'd finished his breakfast Ugo would lean his head against the pillow for a few minutes thinking that there was something all around him which seemed never to end, — it never will end — he said in fact. Then, that morning, for a while, the image of the two previous days stood before him; he was present at the devastated city quarter: — there must have been many dead — he thought; then concluded: — the dead do not speak — and quickly got out of bed as if he had several things to do.

His bedroom was incredibly filled with small objects, placed a little everywhere; furniture and shelves were littered with tiny objects which every morning, as soon as he was up, Ugo would go over as if to make sure they were all present, looking at them, cleaning them of dust, and quite often examining some of them at length as if he were seeing them for the first time. There were gold watches of great value and others quite worthless, little statues of metal, of ivory or plaster, little boxes overflowing with stones of all colours, crystals, cups, silver trinkets and rings with stones of considerable value, tobacco-boxes and little glass balls with coloured fillaments inside, a few butterflys in glass trays, and many things whose original purpose could no longer be discovered. Every morning Ugo would pass a couple of hours looking at these objects which for years had been placed around in a certain way. He loved all these small things, knew that the loss of just one of them would make him frantic, and noting this slavery, every morning would become angry with himself: — stupid! — he would think; but nevertheless there was the hollow joy of violently possessing these objects.

He would then dress with care, and about noon go down to the drawing room. The great room, clean and severe, had

remained unchanged since he had learnt to know it; the
main wall consisted of a great glass window, from which,
through old curtains yellowed by time, the garden could be
seen in deep shadow, thick with greenery and trees. On a
small table there was always a pile of letters and papers; it
was the weekly mail which invariably accumulated there by
the armchair in which Ugo usually sat. He never touched the
letters, nor the papers to which he continued to subscribe;
only on Saturday, a little after midday, Baccelli, the administrator of the Gattegna lands and interests, would arrive.
Each time the poor man would try to speak to the young
master, repeating the attempt from year to year without ever
losing hope that one day he'd succeed, but invariably ending
up by taking the mail and going to the kitchen to relieve his
feelings on Cesira. He'd stand in the middle of the room,
his legs apart, his courduroy jacket undone, looking at the
woman who paid no attention to him, saying:

« I'd like to know who'll listen to me in this house. Everything could go beautifully but no one takes the least interest,
and all the responsibility is on my shoulders. Whose are the
lands, are they mine or his? One day I'll give up the whole
thing, fed up ». Then he would notice that not even the
woman was listening, would lose his patience, pull out some
money, count it, and place it on the corner of the table.
Then Cesira would rouse herself: only in that moment was
it possible to see in her a little of her peasant origins: in
her approach to the money, in counting it, there was still
much of that distrust and devotion which is common to
peasants.

« It's right ».

« It's right, it's right! I know it's right, let's hope it'll
always be right » Baccelli would answer with anger, going
towards the door to leave; then he'd remember, take out
the mail from his pocket and look at each envelope one by
one, keeping those which had to do with the administration
of the land and very often coming back to lay on the table
those which were addressed to Gattegna:

« I don't know what to do with these ».

Ugo never reads the few letters which are addressed to him. On Saturdays, along with his soup they reappear at the table, and at most, while he eats, he glances at the envelopes, tilting his head between one mouthful and the next, sometimes going so far as to turn them over to see if the sender's name is on the back; but he leaves them on the tablecloth, and in the end they go back to a drawer where others have been sleeping, intact, for years.

Every day, as soon as he gets up from lunch, the second half of the day stretches out before him: an unavoidably uncomfortable thought. In the morning there are no hesitations: his objects, his *toilette*, waiting for lunch keep him thoroughly occupied; but the afternoon is different. In the afternoon he starts by walking up and down in the drawing room, passing near the papers which are laid on the table, still neatly folded, trying to read the visible headlines, without worrying if he only sees half of them; the sentences and words which pass beneath his eyes usually lead him to make some observation to himself in a low voice; and when the main headline, as happens almost every day, begins: « The Heroic Batt... » or « The Iron Speech of... » he feels no need to know how the sentence continues on the other side of the fold; the adjectives are even too much for him as he repeats them mentally: « The iron, the iron... What kind of an adjective, what kind of taste! » — And all this sometimes manages to keep him busy for a whole hour. But eventually he decides to go outside, opens the glass door and goes out among the little pebbled lanes of the garden, immediately disappearing behind the high, illkept, thick hedges. He likes the sound of his footsteps on the pebbles, just as he gets a slight shiver of pleasure from the vibration of the glass panes each time he opens the door. Ugo often goes as far as the main gate, without ever going beyond the boundary which separates his property from the asphalt of the main road. Here he usually stops for a long time; but now that so many military convoys disturb the quiet of the countryside he is almost always obliged to turn brusquely as soon as he has reached the boundary and go back up towards the Big House. This is perhaps the fullest moment of his afternoon, as the sight of the drive with its hundred framing cypress trees is for him an image in which the greater part of his life is reflected, he feels something of his youth reflower in it. The air begins to colour; the sun, which by now almost touches the hills, seeps through the rows of cypress trees, between each trunk, creating blocks of voilet space in which insects are visible even from the distance. When Ugo goes down to the main gate he does so largely in order to find this spectacle before him when he turns to go back. Then a great calm fills his heart, and he feels the need to go up to his room, near his objects; he runs to sit at his desk where the books are laid out which he often reads at this hour, small patches at a time; or, if he does not wish to read, he extracts a few small square sheets of paper from a drawer and lazily scribbles on them with a pencil; after an hour some of them are filled with words such as: « *Spiroteca, graminacea, perdifiato, sebacea, pannocchia, porcella, procella, pinella, crivella, taverna, sesamo, apriti, saluta, militare, scorpione, fiore, morte, sognare, sorte...* ». Others contained broken phrases without definite meaning: « *Like a feeling issueing from a statue* » or: « *He will come, he will not come, what difference does it make. Certainly, everyone, come, came, will come, will come without doubt* ». At other times true and proper reflections would appear on these scraps of paper, piling up in the drawers of his desk, reflections he was unaware of making and which he would only see as they appeared on the paper from the point of his pencil.

VI

Towards the end of August, after innumerable weeks during which the sun had shown itself obstinately resplendent and implacable, on the last Saturday of the month it rained very hard; along the whole glass front of the drawing room water poured thickly and noisily, and Ugo felt well, he was satisfied; for too long when he had opened his eyes in the morning he had seen, through the window Cesira would open, the clear blue air and that bright polished sun; and it had come to fill him with sadness and annoyance. But now that it was raining he had brought down his volumes on comparative anatomy, his university texts, and was carried away by his reading, unmoved by the trembling of the house as a sharp bolt of lightning struck the woods: in fact a quiet joy had posessed him, languidly rocked by the noisy shaking of the whole glass front which at times seemed about to break.

At noon Baccelli arrived, hesitating in the doorway because he was dripping with rain.

« Come in Baccelli » said Ugo when he saw him standing in the door: « At last it's raining today ».

Baccelli, encouraged by the unusual extra sentence, came in and even before being near him began to speak hesitantly in the hope of being listened to for once.

« You like the rain? So do I, even if it has reduced me to this state, because it's good for the fields ». He was silent for a moment, wavering:

« Listen Mr. Ugo, I have something to ask you, you must really decide to speak to me every now and then, otherwise I won't know which Saint to turn to ».

Ugo shook his hands violently, with the evident intention of interrupting the man's speech.

« It's raining today. Take the mail and be calm ».

The administrator, knowing he had nothing to add, that any attempt would be useless, took the mail and went ont to the kitchen in a foul humour.

« He doesn't understand a thing » he said coming in; but Cesira's cold, indifferent gaze cut the words on his lips; he left the money and went over to the door to examine the mail.

« I don't know what to do with this ». He placed an en-

velope on the table and went out, disappearing under the
heavy rain.

With the first course the letter came back to Ugo by his
napkin; Ugo looked at it rapidly and began to eat, glanced
at it several times without touching it and finally began to
think of something else. But as he was about to get up he
turned it over looking for the address of the sender which
by law now had to appear on every letter; he read it: Rafaele Rachini, Via Roma 11, Bologna. He lit a cigarette
without showing any signs of having noticed what he'd read,
sat quietly smoking for a quarter of an hour then went and
sat down in his armchair. When Cesira was clearing the table
and about to put the letter with the others, he said: « Cesira,
I'll read that letter ».

« You'll read it? »

« Yes, give it to me ».

Taking it in his hand, he placed it delicately on the edge
of the chair, and when the woman had finally gone, stopped
smoking, opened his eyes, and began to unglue the envelope,
trying not to break it: at last he read carefully.

« *Dear Ugo,*

*How long without news of you. Gianni and I have
written to you twice, then gave it up because you didn't even
deign to answer, to give us a precious answer. But by now
we know you well enough and have borne you no rancour.
But this time we insist on an answer; so* coraggio!

*Many years have passed but we have never forgotten you;
now and then we have spoken of you, always as the dearest
of our friends. We hope that this time you will decide to
consider our modest handwriting, especially as in recent times
so many extraordinary things have happened to make a real
hell of our lives. An answer from you is essential; and for
Gianni, of the greatest importance. There is no need for me
to describe all the events which brought us both to Bologna;
Gianni and I have always been together during these years*

of war and have lived as fate commanded; Luisa is in a small town in northern Italy where she teaches school. She too has always remembered you, and when she writes the first thing she does is ask news of you.

It is absolutely essential for Gianni to have a change of air, he must find a healthier place and get away from me; he needs a quiet little place in which to be away from everything and everyone for a little while; but where can one find a quiet little place nowadays? We thought of you, of your house, of your land, and your dear hospitality. At first Gianni opposed me, but given the circumstances and with my insistance he finally decided and authorized me to write to you about it.

So I repeat hurriedly that it is absolutely necessary to find Gianni a quiet place, and it is necessary for you to answer, that you do not keep us in suspense, because we cannot wait and it would be an ugly thing on your part, even if you did it out of indifference. He will give you little or no trouble; we have always been very modest in our ways and quite undemanding, as you know, but now we have learnt to live on even less, much less than the little we used to; so you need not worry. The important thing is for you to answer, even negatively if you have reasons for not accepting; but quickly, quickly, please! We think of you affectionately.

Your Rafaele ».

Ugo remained without moving, his head leaning against the back of the chair, listening to the rain which had resumed with violence.

An hour passed, and at last, without changing position, he called Cesira. The woman appeared on the threshould:

« Cesira, I must write a letter ».

« A letter? Very well ».

« A letter for Bologna ».

« I understand ».

« Well ».

« Well? »

« Well, I'll have to write it ».

« Yes ».

« I will need some things ».

« Certainly; in your bedroom? »

« Yes ».

« I'll take care of it ».

« Fine ».

« On your desk? »

« That's right, Cesira ».

« Ink and all the rest » said the woman going off almost running.

Ugo listened to Cesira's footsteps and when he understood that everything was ready, climbed the stairs with studied slowness. In his room he sat at the desk examining all that the woman had prepared; he looked at the inkstand and pen, two strange objects in his room, especially where his eyes had so often rested for long periods on nothing but friendly and accustomed things; he looked at the new objects with distrust, but at last, arranging some paper in front of him, he dipped his pen, kept his hand for a long time poised in the air, then threw himself at the paper and began to write rapidly. He filled three thick pages, was about to start a fourth when he stopped, took the written pages, tore them into four pieces, then into eight, then into sixteen, and called Cesira.

« Do me a favour ».

« Yes ».

« Take this envelope. There's an address on the back. Go to the post office, or send someone; all that is necessary is that a telegram be sent with my signature, a telegram saying: « Let Gianni Come ».

« Let Gianni come ». The woman repeated, running down the stairs. A little while later she went out into the rain protected by a great umbrella of green waxed cloth.

VII

To say that Ugo forgot things would not be exact. Memories of recent and far away events sometimes occupied him the whole day, or rather, not entirely, but in tracts, intermittently. There were lacunae in his memories, empty spaces into which he fell and rapidly climbed out, only to tie up the images in sudden ways, like jerks: but at a certain point he would become bored, shake his broad shoulders as if to unload a weight, lift his forehead high, and so manage to feel free again of the tangle of things which had passed, stronger to face the interminable hours of his days. In fact, despite appearances, he faced time, which seemed so slow to him, by bending his back to it like a labourer who must daily submit to heavy work; but his was not boredom, he violently refused the vague thought that sometimes appeared in his mind of considering himself a bored individual, he was too healthy, too physically strong; his health almost depressed him, it kept his shiny brown face, which was constantly shaved, taut and firm. Even in his heart he could not accept himself as bored, and, though in fact he knew that he was bored, completely so, the idea made him shy with himself and he would narrow his eyes to consider things with greater ease; actually his inertia did not come from an aversion towards work, and he quite often had the sensation of being thrown into some frantic work from which he came out as exhausted as a peasant during the torrid days of harvesting wheat. But what was it that possessed him so profoundly as he passed his days in his armchair or on one of the sofas of the Big House? It was rare for Ugo to ask himself such questions but occasionally in his idleness even these questions flashed through his mind, such thoughts appeared, such sensations — for it would be better not to label as thoughts all that took place in Ugo.

It is years since Ugo has thought; Ugo feels everything he imagines; forms of life, ideas, and even the simplest daily manifestations of his lonely existence are not ideas; he feels all the things that cross his mind as if he lived them; in fact he is convinced of having accumulated in his being a profound experience of life, a vast and tiring experience which has already broken the charm of everything. He is convinced of having lived everything, whereas, except for the few secret experiences of a rich and fortunate boy, except for the few secret excursions of a youth, still unsure, on the verge of independence, his existence is bare.

Furthermore Ugo has the sensation of knowing things and people even before he has heard of them or approached them. At the end of the day he often notices that everything he has seen which seemed new, all the small and less small events which have taken place in those hours, both near and around him, were in fact already known to him before they happened, that he had been expecting them to take place, as in fact they did; but all this leaves him quite indifferent.

Ugo greatly despises the majority of men's actions, and a large part of their words annoy him, though he does not despise his neighbour, even at times believing himself to have a certain devotion towards others; but living with others is quite impossible for him. As a student, when he lived in the city, he never rode on trams or buses, only going on foot or in taxis, not because contact with others annoyed him, but largely because he was obliged to put his hand on some support still warm from another hand, and an unrestrainable repulsion would shake him throughout, making his stomach contract in rebellious spasms.

Ugo did not forget things, he did not forget other people, but his memories were not merely recollections: all of a sudden a face would assail him, a past event, an endearing image which he would posess violently till it was consumed in a short time. He had in fact found himself remembering Gianni; and a conclusion was born from it which he repeated to himself — I live like a beast —; but a second later he had shaken his shoulders and gone down towards the main road, stopped at the threshold of the gate, and then turned slowly back, thinking of other things and especially looking up at his cypresses one by one. A few peasants greeted him as he passed, and he removed his straw hat looking at them without flicking an eyelid. He would always take off his hat when the peasants greeted him, and they would look down and then conclude among themselves that he must be a good devil, that young master of theirs.

« *Un soir, l'ame du vin chantait dans les bouteilles* » : the verse had come into his head as he'd turned his eyes for an instant and seen the rows of vines; and then « *...Je sais combien il faut, sur la colline en flamme* ». It was one of the books he had not read for years. Behind him on the road a military convoy passed, then the sound of a car stopping right in front of the gate, but Ugo did not turn; someone was following him, catching up with him. There were two officers; they greeted him, and once more he took off his hat. The peasants had gone back to their work, but were stealthily watching the newcomers with great attention.

« Good morning: we'd like something to drink, some wine if possible ». Their Italian was rather devoid of grace.

« Wine? Yes » Ugo had answered, starting to walk again. One of the officers said:

« Here we are in an oasis. You wouldn't know there was a war on ».

« War » Ugo said with difficulty.

« A heaven on earth, but the war has destroyed even better ones ».

Ugo walked on. At the front door he let the strangers go ahead and asked Cesira, who had appeared from the other side, to fetch some wine. After looking around for a long time one of the men in uniform felt it his duty to say:

« You must excuse us, but around here there are no shops, and we, who live as soldiers, sometimes do things which we normally wouldn't think of doing ».

Ugo did not answer, but sat down pointing to two chairs.

« An old house ».

« Old house » said Ugo.

« To think that for you, for all the people in these parts, a wine like this is normal! Ah; a real heaven on earth ».

Ugo remembered the lines which had crossed his mind a little earlier and forgot about the soldiers.

« These are hard times, but they'll pass » said one of them conciliatingly. Ugo felt he should answer somehow, then was quiet.

« We still have three hundred kilometeres to go ».

« That's a lot » said Ugo.

The officers stood up and saluted with little bows and mechanical jerks of the head.

« Thank you, good evening ».

« Good evening, gentlemen ».

The two men went out and were no sooner gone than Cesira came in to collect the glasses; as she went out she said:

« I was frightened ».

Ugo looked at her without answering.

« It's because you don't hear all that they say, otherwise you'd understand one can well be frightened » the woman added without waiting for an answer.

« Quite » said Ugo.

At that moment someone knocked on the window frame, which shook all over; Ugo turned.

« There's a man » said Cesira « how could he have got in from that side? »

« See who it is » said Ugo annoyed. A second later he felt two hands on his shoulders:

« Ugo, it's Gianni ».

Ugo turned slowly and looked his friend in the face.

« I'm Gianni! » and to put an end to that cold questioning stare he embraced him tightly. « You haven't changed a bit. I'm glad to see you again ».

« I'm glad too », said Ugo with exasperating slowness, then for a second still stared at the young man who stood before him with a smile which was about to become embarrassed: « I almost didn't recognize you ».

« Do you find me changed? »

« Yes, you're different, but you're still Gianni ».

« I've been outside quite a while, but I saw those people; what did they want? Do they often come? »

« No ».

« I didn't come up by the main road because I remembered the path behind the hill, then I climbed over the garden gate by the woods; it was a good thing; that way I missed them ».

« It's prettier that way », said Ugo, « but sit down, you must be tired ».

« They've gone away, haven't they? »

« Who? »

« Who! The men in uniform ».

« You must be tired, in a little while we'll dine, then I'll have your room made ready ».

« My God how little you've changed! You'll be that way for ever ».

« How did you travel? »

« By various means. You know, today one travels as one can ».

« I know ». Ugo then remembered a little of his journey, the devastated city, and forgot his friend. Gianni sat in front of him and never stopped watching him, with a smile of satisfaction on his simple open young face; then said:

« Aren't you going to say anything? »

« What do you want me to say? »

« Well, aren't you going to ask me anything, after so long ».

« How are you? »

« I'm well, good Heavens! Years don't seem to pass for you » and so saying he laughed with sincerity.

« They pass, they pass », Ugo answered.

« At least tell me if you're pleased to see me. I'm terribly afraid of bothering you, I didn't want to, but Rafaele... ».

« He did the right thing, and naturally, I'm pleased to

see you. Though you needn't make me say so; however, you're at home ».

« Your home! » said Gianni pointing his finger at his friend with a warm smile.

VIII

Now the mysterious silence of the house was no longer; it no longer seeped, soft and vast; but no one other than Ugo could have noticed it; in the morning he managed to hear his guest's footsteps in a room far from his, though still on the same floor; he could hear a door open almost silently, the imperceptible noise of an object being placed on a piece of furniture; in fact from early morning he heard the presence of his friend; and though he had not yet asked himself the reason, he could not find anything in it the least disagreeable; rather it seemed to him that the vague feeling of the other's presence helped him even better to isolate his old habits and make his own time run in its accustomed changeless tracks. In the morning he would stay in bed even more immobile than usual, and almost did not feel content until some tiny indication, which no one else would have noticed, confirmed Gianni's presence in the house; then one of his usual phrases would cross his mind, or perhaps it would pass before his eyes like the sudden flight of an insect; — I live like an animal —, it was an instant, because immediately afterwards he would take pleasure in repeating it over and over to himself, finally concluding: — I know nothing, nothing at all —, and this seemed useful to him to decide to get out of bed. Then, as always, he would approach his objects: no one could have said what all of it meant to him; but while contemplating those myriads of tiny things time passed indifferently for him; all of it satisfied him like an accomplished universe which had the power of annulling any other presence, while that sort of demon of possession grew giant-like in his heart, filling his body and soul.

As a discreet guest, Gianni had never entered the room, knowing his friend well enough, and, letting himself be guided, even when it was not possible to behave logically, by a certain instinct which permitted him to sense what was possible with Ugo, and what would be an irreparable mistake because a mistake without reason, without any logic with which to classify it or make it comprehensible. Gianni believed himself to be entirely out of Ugo's life, at least for the greater part of the day, and would never have imagined that instead he was present to him most of the time.

When they would meet in the living room, smoking before lunch, Gianni who would sit in front of his friend and always end up by pointing to the pile of mail which accumulated in the same place till Baccelli came on Saturdays, and say:

« Aren't you going to read them? »

« Not I » Ugo would answer.

« Why? »

« You may take the paper if you like; but do these things without my having to tell you ». Gianni would then read the paper, and Ugo, sitting in front of him, would be able to see the whole headline which up till then he had almost always only seen part of. Every morning now he found them in front of him and felt obliged to let his eyes run over them with horror; all those words, almost always written in too large print, made him uneasy and nervous especially when they rang with the usual tenor's timbre, conventional and pretentious. In the long run Ugo was pained and would say to Gianni:

« Stop it ».

« Why? »

« Some of the words are insufferable ».

« But if you never read them ».

« I can see them from here ».

« They certainly make for bad blood ».

« You too? » Ugo would ask, barely hinting a half smile. Gianni did not understand, but would fold the paper and they'd sit silently in front of each other until Cesira came in with the soup. When they were together that way without knowing what to say, Gianni would break into a well-meaning smile with a certain uneasiness, but only meeting the cold caress of his friend's grey velvety glance, he would turn his head towards the window through which the trees in the garden could be seen.

And the days passed. On Saturday Baccelli would arrive, take the mail, and go to the kitchen to complain to Cesira; otherwise there was nothing new all week.

With the passing of time Gianni was beginning to feel tired and nervous. Often he would stay away most of the day, walking alone on the hills, being careful not to go too near the main road on which long military convoys passed almost daily.

At times Ugo would feel the presence of his guest more strongly, and the silence would grow tighter around him; the other man's presence would become a familiar shadow which could move through the stillness of his own world without violating it. But Gianni was really a discreet guest: he would never have thought that under the circumstances his simple habits could have acquired such a subtle power of control; in fact he was surprised to find himself provided with a special instinctive way of analysing his own movements, endowing him with a sort of hypersensitivity which could be applied to the most common and insignificant of his own gestures. His days were spontaneously impressed with the presence and the unexpressed needs of Ugo's life, and he ended up, without realizing it, by being a little like him, by impressing his own being with that of his friends.

Meanwhile all around them something was gradually changing; it was known that especially there on the plains a hollow persistant unrest had insinuated itself among the people; the rumble of military convoys heading South had become continuous, incessantly disturbing the quiet of the fields. The peasants on the hillside often turned their eyes towards the horizon as if expecting something, as if beyond the area they could embrace with their eyes, some dark spirit were hovering which was capable of suddenly making itself known and a worry to their existence.

Gianni would wait for the paper with ever more impatience, and when it arrived would go outside the house to read it. Then one morning he said to Ugo:

« It's terrible how time passes slowly up here; I'm sorry Ugo, one lives in perfect peace with you, but at certain times peace becomes a worry; I can tell you because I know how many things can worry one nowadays ».

« Peace, peace; well!... » Ugo answered.

« But you've never asked me anything; is it possible you cannot realise that many things are happening now? »

« What would you want me to ask you? » Ugo answered. Then after thinking for a moment, added: « Listen, it's as if you were in your own home, if there's anything you need, tell me. I know that all the rest exists, I know it quite well, but let it go ».

« I have nothing to ask of you Ugo. Here I have much more than I need; and then, do you really think it's possible for each of us to know, when the cards are down, even approximately what we really need? Perhaps things that everyone needs, things which we don't even know ».

IX

And two more months passed; Gianni was becoming sadder, but made an effort to remain placid and impassive, imitating Ugo. He now spent many hours of his day observing the military convoys which slowly and monotonously slid past on the asphalt; since the military traffic had become more intense the continuous vibration of the air, the incessant rumbling of the engines, seemed to make the inhabitants more nervous: there was a certain unrest all round which Gianni could notice from listening to the conversation of the peasants as he crossed the surrounding hills, bored as he was, and taken with the general nervousness which no one, with the possible exception of Ugo, could avoid.

Occasionally, even though it was off the main road, some soldiers would come up to the Big House; then it was up to Cesira to handle them, offering them wine, as the two young men would respectively retire to their own rooms on the floor above.

The soldiers were feared by all, and it seemed as if the world were being filled with them. The more their number increased the greater the general fear and constraint became; and the peasants greeted them with cold smiles and broad gestures of courtesy. Even in that stubborn, isolated countryside disquieting news had begun to circulate; collective apprehension spread like the wind, and the presence of the soldiers recalled and enlivened in everyone the memory of the most recent tales which reached them, especially from the city, greatly diminishing the desire for incredulity with which the peasants obstinately sought to defend themselves.

Even Cesira occasionally seemed to have something to say when she entered Ugo's room, but she always came out without speaking. Ugo noticed it, all he needed were a few imperceptible attitudes on her part to understand her intentions; but he believed he already knew everything she wanted to tell him, and in any case, almost the same instant he happened to notice these things, he'd forget them and his mind would wander on its own.

Finally Cesira had decided to speak, and stopping in the middle of his room with a plate in her hand she said:

« Master Ugo ».

« Cesira? »

« I hear so many things being said; here we are quiet enough, but the people of the plains tell such stories ». Ugo was silent, but Cesira, convinced he was listening, went on: « No one knows what will happen, but it certainly won't be anything good; many people are already taking their things away to safety, don't you think we ought to... ».

« Eh! » said Ugo getting up and going out to walk on

the pebbled lanes of his garden. For some days he had been observing Gianni more closely, who, noticing it, was thinking — He wants to tell me something —.

In fact, meeting him under the garden pergola, and encouraged by his expression which was unintentionally one of questioning, Ugo asked:

« You have only that suit, haven't you? »

« Yes, and it's certainly not in a very good state ». As a matter of fact Gianni was rather down at the heel, his pants and the sleeves of his jacket were raveled in spite of his trimming them every morning with Cesira's nail scissors, even getting up early sometimes to try to patch the material with strands of thread.

« Come with me ».

« Into your room? » asked Gianni, who, despite his curiosity, had never tried to get into Ugo's room, certain that he would have encountered his annoyance if he had done so.

« Yes ».

Actually, to anyone who had not been in it, Ugo's room presented the singular spectacle of a teeming mass of minute, vivid, colored objects placed in a strange manner, pullulating all over the place. One did not know where to look, and a thousand details beckoned simultaneously. Gianni stood still in the middle of the room like a child shown into a room with a Christmas tree. But Ugo called him peremptorily.

« Come over here ».

Gianni did so meekly.

« Let's look for a suit, I have so many it annoys me to see them ».

« No, no, never mind » Gianni managed to say convinced of the uselessness of his weak protestation. « By now I've got used to this one ».

But Ugo looked at him sharply, breaking off his words; and there was nothing more to add. From his wardrobe Ugo brought out a suit and some clothing, which he placed on his friend's arm, who let him do so muttering a timid thank you almost to himself, to which Ugo was not listening.

387

He finished by saying that he hoped some day...

« What do you hope, forget it, now go out and put it all on; I think it will fit you reasonably well ».

« It was high time » Cesira said to herself a little later when Gianni appeared at lunch in his new outfit. « High time » she repeated to herself with satisfaction.

« Cesira, tomorrow morning prepare the trap » Ugo said unexpectedly as the woman was clearing the table. For a moment Cesira was surprised.

« But it hasn't been out for years ».

« Hitch it up, it will go fine, all it needs is a dusting and some oil to the wheels. Signor Gianni and I need to go into town ».

X

« So we're really going? » Gianni asked the next morning when, still in bed, he saw Ugo come into his room, almost ready to leave, his felt hat on his head.

« You should have been ready by now, instead you're still sleeping ».

« But you never said another word last night and I didn't know ». But he started to dress hurriedly. From outside came the sound of the bells on the horse which was already hitched to the trap.

« There's a coat on the chair because it's cold out now ».

Outside the plain was hidden by the mist and from the road a continuous rumble of passing cars could be heard. At the gate they had to wait for an interminable convoy to pass before they could go out on the road. It was cold; for a long time they watched the trucks and warlike contraptions go by with frozen soldiers nestling on them, some of whom lazily stared at the elegant trap whose passage they blocked. Then the convoy ended and they set off towards the main town.

« Where are we going? » asked Gianni.

« To town. It's more than a year since I've been there ».

« But Cesira told me you made a trip before I arrived ».

« Yes, but not to the County seat, I went elsewhere. For some years I had wanted to see again certain things in a gallery, but I hadn't thought that now they were all closed, and I made the trip for nothing ».

« What an idea, nowadays. You ran into a bombing, she told me ».

Ugo did not answer, he held the reins in his gloved hands, the same color as his raincoat, and looked straight ahead. Gianni sat staring at his friend's profile; a face which rarely bore an expression even slightly different from the one he was watching at that moment: always equally immutable, even if on rare occasions a faint shadow of feeling seemed to want to cross it. — Always the same fixed coolness — thought Gianni, imagining there still to be, under the appearances, a hidden churning of mute and massive ideas, of undefinable sensations and imprisoned images.

Gianni was feeling well; he watched that unapproachable face whose beauty seemed of stone, and, as he began to feel its attraction — the same attraction which had once brought them together and made them friends — a nervous irritation seized him to think he had never been able to get close to, or discover, a moment of abandon in this being. Even now he felt the weight of the months he had passed with him, only it was as if he had been alone; or was it Ugo who had been alone? Ugo who was really enclosed in an inaccessible solitude, an isolation which could have been odious if it hadn't been for a strange quality, hard to define, which flooded the spirit of the rare persons who had managed to approach him.

« Well », he said aloud.

The horse was trotting with an almost mechanical pace towards the County seat, the old city. More than once during the journey Gianni had asked himself why Ugo had decided on the jaunt. At this thought his heart was suddenly inflamed by a violent resentment: — But can it be possible, can it be possible — he thought — that with this man not only must one never understand anything, but one must end up by obeying him, by doing what he wishes without even having an explanation! — And at the end of these thoughts he asked in an unintentionally loud and irritated voice:

« Listen, can one at least know why we are going to town? »

Ugo turned towards him slowly, looking at him with a slight interrogation in his eyes, waited a moment, then answered:

« I don't know, I felt the desire to ».

« But what will we do there? »

« We'll call on some relatives of mine, at my house, then we'll go around; it's years since I've put foot in my house, now I feel I'd like to ».

« Have you relatives here? »

« Yes ».

And again they were silent; the road became wider, covered by thick plane trees, and ever more densely lined with houses, old peasant houses and little bourgeois villas.

« Let's at least try to be careful » said Gianni as the ancient city gates appeared at the end of the road. « You know, I think it might have been better if I hadn't come with you. Not for me, but I wouldn't want to get you into trouble ».

Ugo answered with a sharp gesture, obliging him to be quiet, then said:

« Don't worry about anything, here I am known to everyone ».

« Yes, but I've never told you about myself, perhaps I should have forced you to listen to me once at least ».

« There would have been no need for it, and then you wouldn't have succeded » Ugo answered, surprising Gianni with the joking tone with which he said the last words. After a while Ugo went on: « I don't want to know anything, nothing, understand? I already know too many things » and this time he was almost hard. He sunk deeper into the collar of his raincoat though the early morning chill had been dispelled by the sun which was stretching bolder shadows on the asphalt outlining the silhouettes of roofs and tree trunks.

They crossed the few streets of the town and entered a maze of small lanes winding between old houses and grey palaces. Every now and then Gianni felt angry again at having to follow his friend without knowing what they were about, without being able to ask where they were going and what they would do; at last, still resentfully, he asked:

« Why can't you let me know where you're taking me; is it possible that you can never feel the need to say what you want to do, or what you think? It makes one really angry ».

« Eh! » said Ugo, and Gianni could not tell whether it was meant for him or for the horse that was just then stopping in front of an old palazzo, grey and rather depressing.

« We're stopping here » said Ugo pointing to the dark stone entrance. Gianni turned to see better; on the keystone of the arch, which was the only untouched architectural detail of the old construction, obviously embellished in several successive eras, the name « Gattegna » was carved.

« Is that you » asked Gianni.

« No, no, that's my family, sometime back ».

« Naturally, that's what I meant. But who's there now? »

« It's rented to several families; but the main floor is still mine, and some relatives of mine live there ».

The horse was tied to the grille of a first floor window.

They went up the staircase, large and dark, which here and there maintained the structure of an ancient and outdated architectural severity, and which now seemed rather dirty. On the first landing Ugo rang, and an old woman with large slippers came to open, asking suspiciously:

« Who do you want? »

« I'm Ugo Gattegna ».

The old woman opened her eyes which were buried into the wrinkles of her face and stood for a while opening and closing her mouth, then cried out, making an echo down the stairway:

« The young master! » and ran off.

« Let's go in » said Ugo annoyed, starting to take off his coat. After a moment the old woman came back:

« Come in, come in; only the young lady is home ».

« The young lady? »

« Miss Adele. I'll open your rooms, but it's years now since anyone's been in them: what'll we do, what'll we do! » Then she stopped to watch Ugo with her mouth open and again a shrill cry echoed against the vast ceilings of the house:

« Oh, oh, the young master, oh, oh! »

Ugo said: « My friend and I will sleep here tonight ».

« Oh, oh! » the old woman went on.

Just then a young girl with a striped dress came into the hall, tall and very young; in the darkened room she stood in front of the window but it was impossible to see the lineaments of her face around which her very blonde hair, against the light, made a halo.

« I'm Adele » she said without moving, her voice that of a grown woman, with a firm, cordial timbre. Ugo turned slowly and observed her for a long time, in silence, quite unworried.

« I'm Adele! » she repeated insistently.

« I'm sorry. I'm Ugo Gattegna ».

« I know that quite well, I am Adele » and as Ugo seemed to be waiting for further explanation she went on without annoyance: « Adele Briganti of course, no? »

« You » said Ugo « But weren't you small? »

The girl laughed quickly, and stretched out her hand.

« How could I still be small; I too have the right to grow, no? If one were to come around a little more often ». It was obvious that she was avoiding the use of either the « you » or the « thou ».

« This is my friend Gianni, Gianni Ricci ».

The girl's face, large and well-built despite the light skin common to blondes, had a high forehead, perhaps a little too high, curving at the chin towards a long and rather narrow neck. She was wearing a simple little dress of white linen with brick colored stripes, and her movements suited her studiedly easy air. She was wearing Turkish slippers with a red pompon.

« Well Ugo, what kind of surprise is this? If you'd warned us we could have prepared your rooms, the house is in disorder ». Then, evidently making an effort, she decidedly went ahead with the « thou »: « So you really have remembered your house; we'd begun to think you'd quite forgotten our existence; we've often thought it was time we called on you, as you won't even answer our letters ».

« Where's your father? »

« He's gone out with mother, but they'll be here for lunch. Of course you'll stay with us ».

« No. Now we'll take care of the horse, then we'll find some place to eat ».

« You'll stay here; besides it's quite impossible to find a place to eat nowadays ».

« We'll stay here then, if Gianni doesn't mind ».

« I don't know; you know better than I ».

« Today we'll stay here ». Ugo smiled broadly, and Gianni watched him with surprise.

When they were outside, Gianni said:

« That's a nice girl; who is she? »

« She's my cousin ».

Then they went for a walk through the town, and during the whole time Ugo's only words were:

« Soldiers, soldiers, all one sees is soldiers ».

« It's the same thing everywhere » Gianni answered.

XI

The Gattegna's old town house did not have any special history; it was a smallish old palace dating from a few centuries earlier; in fact, it was obviously a much older building than appeared at first sight, as certain architectural elements still had definite renaissance characteristics. The Gattegnas had remodeled it at various times, and every remodeling dated from one of the fortunate periods in their commerce which had once made their name well known almost everywhere. Now it appeared to be a neglected old building with a few worn indications of gentility; the two top floors had been turned into flats for rent, the ground floor housed a notary's office and a dentist's; the main floor was still the Gattegna's; up till about ten years earlier they had lived there most of the year, especially in winter, then the Gattegnas had slowly lost the habit of the city, especially when the Big House had been done over and enlarged by Ugo's mother; and the country house became even more definitely their residence when a tram line was built which made a speedy link between the country and the County seat.

The large house, made up of great rooms, dark corridors, and beautifully vaulted ceillings, had begun to show signs of being abandoned after the family had almost definitely settled in the country; it was then decided to give part of the house to Ugo's father's sister who had married Rosano Briganti. The agreement on that occasion, as with all things, had been established by Ugo's mother: the relatives were to live in the house with the understanding that they keep it up for the the Gattegnas for whenever they chose to be in town, even if only for a few days.

Ugo's aunt, a pretty fair example of the Gattegna family, tall and of few words, had been happy to live in her father's house, where, especially after Ugo's birth, she had stayed almost entirely with her new family. Ugo's main memories of the house were of the brief stays during his first exams. He also remembered having met his cousin, who, as a young girl, almost a baby, had watched him without smiling. Since his first year at the university he had never set foot in it again, even on the rare occasions when he passed through town. During all these years his uncle, feeling some scruple, had written, giving news of the house, and asking after Ugo's

life, inviting him to come in from the country; but these
letters had ended up, almost all sealed, in the same old
drawer. Although there was no great distance between the
city and the Big House, and with the tram one could get
there in less than an hour, his aunt's family had never taken
the trouble to go out there, party because they thought it
up to the nephew to give some sign of life, and party out
of inertia, as their relations with the Gattegnas had always
been good, but utterly lacking in effusion.

« He's a fine one! » Adele's father would sometimes say
when they spoke of Ugo in the family.

« Just like his father and his grandfather; my father
and brother were just like him; Adele's mother would say,
and then add »; but Ugo outdoes them in everything: he's a
real living prototype of the Gattegnas. « He even has a bit of
his mother. In some ways he's like her; she had a lot of tone,
and was terribly monotonous in her habits ».

This was all Adele knew about her cousin. That
morning seeing him so big, so elegant, yet cold and indifferent with that strange gaze which escaped or counfounded
one, not that she considered herself a girl who could easily
be confounded, it had had the effect on her of meeting some
stranger who, for some reason, seems immediately familiar
and friendly. Then she had thought: — We're cousins, aren't
we? — And concluded to herself: — I could have quite
easily addressed him with the « thou » immediately, silly
girl! — And then she had shaken her light hair with a
gesture of annoyance.

Even her mother and father had been a little perplexed
when they heard Ugo had arrived; it was his house all right,
and they had often written to him to make up his mind and
come back to take care of his interests in the city; but by
now they had got used to thinking about it from time to time
as an accomplished duty. His sudden unexpected visit had
almost put them out; then the three of them, with the maid,
set to work to put a little order in the rooms that had been
closed for so long.

« We'll fix his rooms, and he can do exactly as he pleases. You were quite right to invite him to lunch, Adele, and the friend too, of course. Does that bear really have a friend? I'm curious to see him; what sort of friend is he? »

« Uhm, I didn't see him ».

« You didn't see him! »

And now, after the first impression, the rare novelty had broken the grey monotony of the enormous lonely house, without resources at that time, and had given them a certain gaity which pleased them.

« You might at least have answered some of our letters » Adele's father said benevolently when they were all seated at the table. He was a tall man with large eyes and a lot of hair, always dressed in black, and with high starched collars, or perhaps they were celluloid, which forced him to keep his neck horribly straight above minutely speckled grey ties, invariably adorned with a pearl stickpin. Ugo did not notice the words were being addressed to him and continued eating while the others stopped to watch him. His aunt shook her head with a smile, and the others were silent.

« Ugo » said Signor Rosano, this time in such a way as to oblige him to listen, « I'm pleased to see you; but you should think of us more often ».

« I live in the country » Ugo answered this time.

« It's barely an hour away ».

« I hadn't seen you for a long time ».

« But we've written to you many times. Now there's no tram. Ah this war! For us it's almost impossible to move nowadays, but you have a horse; it would do you good too ».

« Yes, the letters... » Ugo answered vaguely; and this time it was Gianni who could not refrain from a smile and a significant gesture of the hand.

« You're not from round here » Ugo's aunt asked Gianni.

« I'm from Bologna ».

« You must have had a terrible journey ».

« Yes, very bad. It was frightful ».

« What times we live in! » Rosano exclaimed.

« Yes, they're bad times all right, but I'm afraid there'll be worse ones coming ».

« Why? » asked Adele.

« Why? Well, because you haven't an idea of what bad times really are ».

« But how could anything be worse than this! » said Rosano.

« Don't you think the war could come right here into this part of the country? »

« You really think so, we're already quite uncomfortable ».

« Why shouldn't it; can we really fortell? Haven't you seen how all the previsions made by those who have our affairs in hand have recently turned out to be throughly wrong; how could ours possibly be right; we have so few elements with which to judge how things are really going ».

« And if the war were to reach us here, what would we do, father? » Adele asked.

« How do I know. Thank heaven we've been spared so far, and the country is peaceful here ».

« Don't rely too much on that peacefulness. Compared to other places we're really in a peaceful spot. Here no one can imagine what happens in certain parts of the country, and what life has become in certain cities ».

« I know, I know » said Mr. Rosano, « I have friends who come from the big cities and I've heard of incredible things, of frightful tales. Here it's different, and sometimes I ask myself if I should really believe all the things one hears around ».

« I can assure you that what is known is less bad than some of the things that actually happen. Few people can realize it, too few; I'd say it would be better for everyone to be in the middle of some of these horrors. Believe me, people round here haven't suffered enough yet ».

« Luckily » said Ugo's aunt.

« Dear lady, sometimes what seems to be good fortune may turn out to be a real and true calamity, it depends on one's point of view. In fact it is unfortunate that there are places in which one cannot realize all that's going on nowadays ».

At his point Ugo's aunt looked at her husband and daughter with an expression which, to them, might have meant that she'd finally discovered how the boy could be a friend of Ugo's.

« You're a sort of idealist, but life is a different thing » said Rosano in the tone of a man who knows many things.

« Here people suffer too little if not at all » Gianni went on « because the privations you put up with in these parts are the simplest of the normal sacrifices imposed by war. Here one suffers too little, that's why one doesn't understand all one should, I can assure you ».

At these words, Ugo, who had given no sign of life up till then, stirred himself and answered his friend:

« One always suffers to the extent of one's capacity; we all suffer, who can say he does not suffer? »

« Ugo, you live much on yourself ».

Just then they stood up, and after having a cup of coffee with the others, Ugo and Gianni went to their rooms. They were old rooms with lacquered wooden beds, a few carpets, and pictures on the walls for the most part depicting religious subjects.

From the windows one could see into a garden, entirely closed off by the four storey building, a green square made up of ancient trees, thick hedges, and shadows. The static green, closed in by the walls of the house, bathed in deep silence, attracted the two young men who leaned their elbows on the windowsills, each one trying to penetrate with his eyes the thick foliage through which the four columns of ancient portico could be seen.

« Why did we come to town? » Gianni asked once more, trying to find an explanation for Ugo's sudden decision, so foreign to his habits.

« No reason. I suddenly thought about your boredom, trying to understand what you think about; but don't worry, here we run no risks ».

« What risk should I run? »

« Well, I don't suppose I know much about what's going on, but even I can often understand a situation ».

« Thank you Ugo. I too have noticed that during the time I spent with you in the country I no longer thought of anything, in fact I'd forgotten many people and many things that are important to me ».

« It means that being alone for a while has done you good and rested you, I think you badly needed rest. I'm glad you could take it here, with me ».

Gianni was especially struck by this last sentence; it was the first time since he'd arrived that Ugo had said anything of the sort to him in a familiar and even affectionate tone, and he was pleased and even a little moved by it.

« I knew it ».

Gianni hoped that that particular moment wouldn't fade; he had the impression that for some special reason Ugo had inadvertently raised an edge of the strange cloak that always hid his heart.

« This is a beautiful garden » Gianni said after a while, only to be able to go on speaking; he wanted to keep the conversation alive as long as possible, and perhaps for that very reason, he didn't quite know what to say. But Ugo was entirely taken up with the brief spectacle offered by that window which opened onto a closed and forgotten world far from the presence of men despite its being in the center of the house as well as in the heart of a city.

« It is beautiful » Ugo answered. « I can remember being here, looking at this buried and forgotten patch of green, when I was a boy, especially when they left me here for a while before exams.

« You never did go to public school, did you? »

« No, when I was a small boy I had a teacher at home, and my mother followed my studies with great care ».

« I'm not sure it was best ».

« Best? It was a horror! » He said the word « horror » almost with emphasis, and once more Gianni had to control himself so as not to show his astonishment.

« How could it have been pleasant? » Ugo went on after a pause: « After all nothing is pleasant. Boredom is at the bottom of everything, and even if everything had been different, boredom would still be there now, I believe ».

« It might have been different, though ».

« Perhaps. You know, in those days I'd sometimes get up from bed to see the peasant children on the road all bundled up on their way to school, with their satchels round their necks. I was always awake: in the silence of the early hours of a winter morning their voices would float up from the main road, then I'd get out of bed and watch them passing down there far away; alone, in twos, in sixes or more, chatting together, sometimes throwing stones as they walked; then I'd go back to bed and wait for Cesira to wake me ».

Gianni assented with his head to show he was listening carefully.

« Later I too would throw stones in the garden; but my mother would say: — no stones —. Yes stones, I'd think, than after a while, yes stones, no stones: then I'd think — no stones, no stones, you fool! — and I'd have loved to throw one in the air ».

« Well, the other boys had their troubles and worries too, I assure you ». With these words Gianni wanted to lighten the pain which, after watching that face for many days, he could see vibrating under the bronzed skin, the velvety grey eyes.

« Other interests, other interests. They'd say to me: you must understand. And unfortunately I always understood, damnably well ».

« You should have gone to the end of your studies at the University, Ugo. I think it would have done you a lot of good ».

« Did you hear the noise my uncle makes when he eats? »

« No, I didn't notice ».

« I did, and if I were to tell you that it pains me, that I feel upset by it, what would you say? I don't put up with much in other people; I'm no good at doing things if they need to be done in close proximity with others; too many things nauseate me, make me sick at the stomach; and if I hadn't had you three when I was studying, I think I would have only lasted a few months instead of years ».

« Luisa and Rafaele were and still are very good friends to you ».

« I remember them, now and then ».

« They wanted to help you in those days, but you're so difficult to understand ».

« You might as well say impossible, after all I know that there really isn't and wasn't anything to understand ».

Gianni almost felt uncomfortable, it was the first time he'd seen Ugo go off his own fixed track, and although it was one of his greatest desires, although he had always sought for any tiny abandon in Ugo, now he felt perplexed. So he said:

« If you did it for me, I'm grateful; but if you'd preferred, we could have stayed in the country, I assure you I like the life there with you, and am happy ».

« I did it for you, but now it's different; still I'm glad I did it ».

« Will we stay here long? »

« I don't think so, not later than all of tomorrow ».

« Are you pleased to have found a place that reminds you of certain moments of your childhood?

« Oh, its not that any more, there are new things, new people ».

« Ah » said Gianni, but he hadn't understood. Then he went on: « everything's changed, nowadays everything goes so fast ».

« Things change for everyone. My cousin, for instance. I'd never noticed her before ».

« But if you didn't even look at her! She seems to be a nice clever girl to me ».

Gianni saw his friend's face cloud over, saw his eyes staring back at him as they had done before. Moving away from the window, Ugo said:

« Let's go out, let's go for a walk in town ».

In the night a great inhuman scream filled the sky, embraced the whole city savagely, died out rapidly, started again, was silent, repeated, was finally silent. Immediately after it those who were awake could hear a rustling muffled by the barred windows, in the next house, in the apartment above, in the palace across the way. The whole city, bestirred and oppressed, could be heard waking out of its sleep. Almost every night now it was the same; sometimes the alarm would awaken and shock the citizens several times in a night, though nothing had ever happened and there was little to fear. The peaceful little provincial city, even though it lay on the route of the night fliers, going heaven knows where to carry their sad messages, did not represent a plausible target for their purposes. Yet perhaps in no other place did the impassioned wail of the siren bring such intense dismay, such compact fear. Every new alarm seemed to make the pacific provincials even less accustomed to its inevitability: the whole city would wake up, leap sleepily to its feet, and run, ragged and without reason, or control, into the lurid cellars of the century-old palaces, crouch in the mouldy smell of centuries of dampness, in the deep silence of despair, or be caught up in the frenzied madness of hysterical fear which raised strange and upsetting moans and out cries. Children would be born prematurely, and old men die of heart attacks shuttling down the dark stairs in the arms of their families; insurmountable shynesses, heirs to a tradition nourished in the sacristy for centuries, fell away under the insufficient protection of silk pajamas and old night gowns so worn they were ready to fall into pieces at the slightest strain or false move.

Why is it that in certain small cities in the provinces, especially among those which in terms of the war are most protected by their own insignificance and more respected than others by the discomforts of the times why is it that terror and despair should reach levels which bear no relation to the silent, almost indifferent resignation of other cities where almost every morning the dead can be counted in hundreds if not in thousands? It is hard to say, and whoever does not know the excitable spirit of our small provincial cities, whoever does not know how stories and bits of news which come from far away, where things have really happened and been faced, grow and are spread in the minds of people.

Ugo had not wakened, or rather had not opened his eyes, he had stayed quite still and perceived quite clearly the dark antlike movement of frightened humanity deprived by fear of centuries reserve; but he had not wanted to wake completely. Gianni however had wakened all of a sudden, had tried to turn on the light, but the current had been switched off as during all alerts; from where he lay he had heard someone rush out of the house, then had listened to Ugo's regular breathing. Finally, unable to go back to sleep, he had lit a cigarette. At the noise of the match scraping aganist the box Ugo had not immediately realized what was happening; then he too began to look for a cigarette.

« Are you awake? Did you hear the alarm? »

Ugo could not remember, though he knew quite well there had been an alarm, and after lighting a cigarette he asked:

« Do you think Adele has gone down to the cellar? »

« I thought I heard the others run down in a hurry » said Gianni, thinking to himself that Ugo's preoccupation was rather unusual.

« What nonsense » said Ugo « you've no idea how all of this annoys me ».

« Why? I didn't think it had bothered you much, you didn't even wake up ».

« No, no, it's not that; but all this fear, this nervousness which comes over people who want to save themselves at all costs, goodness knows from what. Above all I can't bear the disorderliness that it all brings about ».

« Well Ugo, it's not so difficult to understand, and it seems quite logical; after all this fear is quite natural, no? »

« Perhaps, but it's in rather bad taste ».

They were silent, smoking. Gianni still wanted to talk, would have liked to ask: — bad taste? — but said nothing and felt happy being near him, having the sensation of being able, if only slightly, to take part in the others feelings.

Then Ugo went back to sleep, and Gianni was left sitting up in bed, listening. He could hear the regular breathing of his companion; and then the desert all around them in that immense silence. And he thought about himself: it was time he did so; he had remembered nothing of his recent past. The scream was heard again, then little by little the noise of those who were coming up from underground, going back to bed. As he stretched out to go back to sleep the light went on and he saw Ugo asleep in his bed; his face in repose had a relaxation he had not yet known, as if it were carved in stone. Again he felt an intense pleasure being near this man who was always strong, always the same, capable of keeping everything to himself, of loading on his own shoulders the weight of his own life; then Gianni turned off the light and went to sleep filled with a physical well-being which almost made him shiver.

XII

« *Tient'a su! tient'a su!* » This reminder of Pascoli would pursue Ugo every time he heard an axe fall in the woods. Since dawn that morning he had been listening to the sound of the axe echoing through the woods with a persistance which would have been exasperating if Ugo had not liked it and

listened to it with satisfaction. *Tient'a su*: these three words
kept coming back to his mind with frightening monotony,
and he listened to them multiply themselves into infinity. In
the afternoon when work in the woods was resumed he began
to realize that never in all the past years had he heard such
intense work in the woods, and said to himself: — it sounds
as if they want to destroy it — then he started to think of
other things, for during those days there was something that
came back insistently; ever since he and Gianni had come
back from the city he had isolated himself more and more,
taken with the desire to organize and make sense of something which kept coming back to his mind as if some doubt
were assailing him; but then he would end up by forgetting
it and think of something else. Now the continuous felling
that came from the woods attracted him more and more, it
seemed too vast, it gave him the impression the whole wood
was being attacked by an army of rodents, and the sound
which reached the house thickly and harmoniously no longer
pleased him; it began to produce a certain discomfort. At
last he went to the kitchen, crossed it almost rapidly, and
stood in the doorway from which he could look down on the
profile of the woods; from there the brisk sound of the axes
seemed to multiply and repeat itself in an infinite echo; it
looked as if Ugo were listening, but in fact he was thinking
of something else; the kitchen door was an almost novel
point of view for him, he could have counted in his mind the
number of times he had chanced to look out at his land from
up there, and although the view differed only slightly from
the one from his bedroom window, the few yards difference
were enough to make it all seem new, all invaded by the clear
sensations of memories of his pale far away childhood.

As he stood on the doorstep his thoughts were suddenly
interrupted by the characteristic sound of a tree falling;
part of the profile of the woods beneath his eyes began to
waver, the highest and most majestic boughs of an oak which
rose a few yards above the other leaves began to sway, moved the branches all around for quite a distance in a disquie-

ting wave, then suddenly fell forward, modifying the contours of the hill which for a while were bathed in a sort of
golden dust. Ugo breathed deeply and stood for a long time
with his eyes wide staring down there, still incredulous of
what he had seen.

« It isn't possible, it isn't possible », he started to mutter
to himself. Cesira turned at the sound of his voice.

« Cesira! »

« I'm here », the woman answered.

« Good », said Ugo, his voice once more monotonous and
calm. « Send for Baccelli immediately ».

— Call Baccelli — Cesira stood for a moment watching
the young man, then, after, having deduced by herself, with
that spontaneous instinct which guided her in matters with
the master, that he must be quite upset, she hurried to tell
a peasant to have Baccelli come.

Baccelli was almost perturbed by the call; for more than
ten years he had hoped for something of the sort, had wanted
Ugo to show some sort of interest in him, in the land, in his
work which he not unjustly considered misunderstood or
little known by his taciturn landowner. The irritation which
always seized him in the face of Ugo's disinterestedness had
become a habit, there was by now a motif of pride and satisfaction in it, for, without meaning to, Baccelli had come to
feel that he alone was the driving force of such a vast and
complex pattern of interests.

However, out of habit, he had always waited for, and
insisted on, some sort of a sign of interest from his landlord;
and now that for the first time he was receiving such a sign
when he least expected it he was surprised at himself, for,
as he walked up to the Big House where his long awaited
desire was about to be fulfilled, instead of feeling satisfied, he
was irritated and forced to admit that after all the call was
annoying him.

Ugo was sitting in his armchair looking at the newspaper Gianni held in his hands, running over the headlines

which appeared on it. *Cruel Defeat Of Enemy Fleet* was written in enormous unwieldy letters, but his mind was full of the hammering that came from the woods; every now and then one could hear another crash and another of the century old trees, which he knew one by one, would come down, cut off at the base; but he remained impassive, though he had to admit an acute pain even more pronounced than the one engendered by the tiresome adjectives of the headlines on the paper before his eyes.

When Baccelli came in he barely moved his head; but said nothing.

Gianni took his eyes off the paper, looked at them both, then went back to reading.

« Did you call for me, Master Ugo ».

« Yes, I saw one of the large trees in the woods being felled; what's going on? »

Baccelli rolled his eyes, not understanding a word of what Ugo meant by this; — now why is he thinking of trees? — he wondered. Then answered:

« I'm having quite a number cut, there's a huge demand and I've made a very good contract, you've no idea how advantageous; we're taking in more with this than we do with a usual whole year's income; there's a firm carrying out some building that pays us well, very well ».

« But what has got into your head, Baccelli? »

« What do you mean! What's come into my head. I'm serving the interests of the administration, aren't I? »

« Yes, yes, but... » said Ugo. Baccelli however interrupted him:

« Just think that with this one deal we put the whole property back on its feet, we can go on with all the work we had to suspend at the beginning of the war; costs have risen so much, and with this deal our economy is reorganized to a very surprising advantage ». Now Baccelli was happy. It was the first time he had been able to explain to the young master how he was handling the administration of his lands, and once started, there were very many things he wanted to say.

« Never mind Baccelli » said Ugo cutting his speach off sharply with an abrupt gesture which the administrator knew all too well: « I only wanted to be sure my impression was quite correct; it isn't a matter of the usual annual cutting, this time they're cutting down the whole wood, they're thinning out the old trees and that I don't want; besides, I've no desire to make good deals ».

The little man's breath was taken; for a while he could not speak, and the veins on his head were seen to grow; at last, very slowly, he managed to take hold of himself and began to speak in a forcedly calm and courteous tone:

« Listen, Master Ugo. This time you must let me speak all the way through or I'll end up by losing my mind and not understand a thing ». Ugo smiled as he watched him, and pointed to a chair saying:

« Sit down, Baccelli ».

« Yes, yes, thank you, that's better, thank you ». He was silent a moment, readjusted himself completely and started again, confident of his argument, with the tone of one who wishes to finish a question:

« I really don't know what you think, and, without offending, I must say that you do not have — and quite rightly how could you — any experience with matters pertaining to the land and to business. Nowadays wood has risen in price to the limits; its an immense fortune to own a wood such as ours; so far we have only just managed to avoid the inconveniences of the war, and if I were to tell you of all the foresight I've had to employ with all this requisitioning, this enforced harvesting, and other devilries which have developed these days, it would take a whole day ».

« I can imagine, I can imagine ».

« So with all these things it wasn't as if our administration were in one of its better moments; but luckily our land is blessed by God, it must be said; I know of some properties that are completely going to pieces. That we should have had a chance such as this is a matter to interest you too, no? You even more that me, don't you think? » Seeing that he was getting no answer, he proceded: « We have to thank Providence that I was one of the first to make a contract with this firm for a large quantity of wood from large trees; its a real fortune, and if I hadn't done it I'd feel guilty towards you, I wouldn't have been doing my duty, don't you think? »

« There's no doubt about that, Baccelli; I have great admiration for your work, for your competence and scrupulousness, I appreciate your work much more than may appear: I've been wanting to tell you so for some time, but I've never found the way in which to speak of it. But this time the trees are not to be touched, I don't want to see the wood reduced, emptied; never mind, Baccelli, don't let it worry you; the blame isn't yours. So have them stop the cutting as soon as you can; and what is done is done ».

This time Baccelli really didn't know what or how to think, he couldn't understand what could have happened, nor was he even convinced that Ugo's was a real and proper order. He thought for a while but his brain was confused, there was something about the whole thing that made him quite incapable of reasoning; but this time too he managed to calm himself and realize the situation; he knew his man and knew there was little he could do.

Then, after making a great effort at concentration, he believed he had found a decisive argument with which to oppose the absurdity of the landlord:

« But I have a contract with the firm that is carrying out fortifications on the Apuan Alps, down there, luckily quite far away; you see, our trees are being used for the war! In fact, you must believe me, I asked a lot of well informed people in town, it's a good deal and we're lucky; but you don't realize that things might change from one moment to the next, and then they'd not only come and get this wood but they wouldn't even say good day, and we couldn't breathe a word. Now at least I have a good contract in my hands ».

Gianni had stopped reading and was following the discussion. Ugo, who so far had been listening absentmindedly hoping Baccelli would finish quickly, lifted his head, was silent for a moment, then said very slowly:

« I hadn't thought of that, but I might have guessed it. In that case Baccelli, the whole affair annoys me even more, and I'll thank you to see that not another tree is felled beyond the ones that have unfortunately already been killed ».

« But it means millions, understand! millions! millions! » the little man desperately spelled out. But even that word, which he perhaps thought magical, had very little effect on Ugo who smiled and said to him benevolently:

« Go on, Baccelli, run along and don't worry».

« But don't you realize! let me explain: do you know who we have to deal with? Those people could even force us, make us give them everything they need, then never even pay us: but now I have a contract! »

« For the moment they can unfortunately find another hundred people who will take your place; so there's not too much to worry about », said Gianni. « Then we're rather out of the way ». And lastly, after having thought for a moment, he added, turning to Ugo: « Don't let them have the trees, don't let them have them ».

Baccelli had turned pale, and Ugo, who had noticed it, said to him nicely:

« Go on, Baccelli, and thank you, thank you for everything, you really are a friend. Goodbye ».

Baccelli went out hurriedly, his head low, oppressed by a boundless sadness and disturbed to the roots of his soul.

« I think you did well », said Gianni as soon as they were alone; but was immediately quiet, intimidated by the cold caress of that velvety grey glance.

XIII

In her own way Cesira never took long to size up situations; and as far as the Gattegnas were concerned she had a sure instinct. It was not difficult for her to have a precise sensation about what was going on inside her young master on occasions such as these, and this time too she had only needed what she'd heard, along with the disconnected phrases which Baccelli had uttered on his way through the kitchen, pale and upset, full of resentment yet inevitably bent to the will of Ugo. Even though Cesira had not quite been able to explain to herself all the sensations which had induced Ugo to refuse the cutting of the trees in the wood, she could run through the various feelings inside of her which had led the young man to refuse abruptly; now she too had stopped on the threshold of the kitchen to look out at the wood, that wall of shadow down there beyond the rows of vines, those beautiful old trees, that greenery in which the autumn wind whispered and moaned... « And to make fortifications! Bah » she had finally said to herself feeling that with that there was no longer any mystery in all that had happened during the afternoon.

But Cesira could also take account of many things which Ugo never would have known; in fact it was not long before she came to hear of the resentment raised among the day laborers who had been called to fell the trees, who had seen the earnings they had counted on disappear, and all because of a whim of the young master, as they saw it. Then there were those who said that master Ugo must not be quite right in the head; others who said that the gentry thinks in ways that one can never understand: and of this last remark she even felt quite proud. Others, however, had said that in order to give up that kind of a deal Ugo must have been led by goodness knows what secret plans for even greater profits, claiming there could be no other explanation. But there were also a few who let it be known they know much more, who, rather quietly went about saying that Ugo had forbidden the felling because it was intended for fortifications: « he's against them, mark my words » they'd repeat; only these remarks aroused a certain apprehension in the woman, who, sitting in her armchair, in the midst of her usual memories, thought back to these comments. Naturally, as always, she had been careful to keep out of the conversations, and once they were over would invariably think of Ugo, and that old feeling of security she enjoyel whenever she thought of a Gattegna would come back, and so she would feel reassured on this last episode too.

Ugo had always loved the woods. As a child, during the hours that were permitted, he'd be placed on the lawn where Cesira could watch him without leaving the kitchen and hear him say:

« The wood is pretty, isn't it, Cesira? »

« Of course it's pretty », she'd answer.

But the child was bored with always being left alone on the lawn and would somentimes gesture to the peasant children who would come to look at him from behind the vine leaves, keeping a proper distance; at his gestures however, they'd run away as if caught in some mischief.

« Why can't they stay with me? » the child would ask her.

« Because it's not done ».

« Is it really not done? »

« Of course not. Why don't you play with your ball ».

« But I'm bored with the ball ».

« Then play with your gun ».

« It's boring, too ».

« But you have so many nice things ».

« They're all no good ».

« Be a good boy; after a while I'll fix your lunch ». And the child would sit for hours playing on the grass looking towards the woods. Then his mother would come, and he'd say:

« I'd like to go in the wood ».

« Not in the woods, there are vipers and it's damp », his mother would answer.

« But the wood is pretty », the boy would answer.

XIV

When evening falls on the countryside the peasant families leave the fields, come down from the hills, and their shadows lengthen across the furrows and the cart tracks; a greyness stretches across the plain which has the reflections of mother-of-pearl, the uneven patches in the terrain disappear, and all one sees is an expanse of violet, an opaque shadow which blends sharply with a sky suddenly turned azure and strangely deep, the last ray of sun eclipsing rapidly after having stretched up as far as the mountains and overflowed onto the houses of men. While the women and children go home, many of the peasants go down as far as the main road; as soon as they set foot on the asphalt, coming from the various paths, they set off towards the general store, walking along the tram tracks where grass has now started to grow, no tram having been seen since the war. The store is set a little back from the road among the fields to make room for the double track where the trams which used to come from opposite direction could safely cross each other. The store has two barred windows under which are two long benches made of stone; between them is the door, covered by colored reed matting. As soon as the change from day to night begins, the light is turned on in the store, many peasants of differing ages collect there, some seated on benches, some squatting on the ground with their backs to the walls or the stable doors, some standing around. The younger ones play restlessly, putting their hands round each other's necks as if they were still not exhausted from a day's work in the fields, trying to throw each other on the ground with muffled curses and laughter: « Will you stop that! » the elder ones say from time to time without expecting to be obeyed. All these men with their beards longer or shorter depending on how near they are to Saturday, their pants loosely supported by leather belts derived from outworn harnesses, almost always speak to each other in grave tones even when they are saying the most awful gossip, occasionally commenting on the headlines of a sort of bulletin tacked to the front door near the foodstuffs, tobacco, and rare copies of the local daily. But it is no longer the time for bicycle races and almost all the football games have been suppressed; so few of them buy one; it's enough to read the headlines for the war news, a few words of the large print mouthed out by someone is enough to start long comments on the war to which many add a few observations derived from letters sent from relatives scattered here and there in the strangest corners of the earth fighting a war too big too imagine. It is then that from time to time someone chances to turn up, who has influence in the neighborhood, and it is he who speaks: with agile movements of the hands, with sudden jerks and broad gestures of their arms, they attempt to explain the strategy of the battles in the North and of the battles in the South to the most attentive listeners: « You see, the war isn't something one can explain so simply; do you really think it matters so much to lose or gain a little ground? War today is something quite different, sometimes we don't even vaguely know what's decisive, there are new weapons, of which for the moment we know nothing, which will completely change matters. So it's not up to us to judge, there are those who are thinking about such things, and how we will win; then when we've won there won't be any more talk of war for centuries and centuries because we will dictate the law to the whole world! »

« Right! » cry the peasants, « so long as there are no more wars ».

And the strategist, putting his black hat on, goes back to his circiut where he has much to do and to say. Before carrying on with their conversation the peasants wait for him to be well out of the way, beyond the bend in the road, meanwhile each one thinking of the words he has heard, repeating them mentally with much distrust; besides they are distrustful by nature, and every time that kind of person leaves after speaking they discover that when people who count come to speak to them they listen and believe them, but that no sooner have they turned their backs than a flood of doubts assails them, and each one, for his own benefit, begins to make gestures of incredulity and contempt.

« But goodness knows how things really stand ».

« Anyhow Gattegna didn't want to sell the wood ».

« I'd been called to cut wood, and I've lost several days work ».

« Well ».

And in all those 'wells' repeated and left that way in the air like so many doubts suspended above their heads, the good nature and simplicity of these people, who know of nothing but their own work, is revealed without encumbrance or subtleties to those who can understand and recognize it:

« I wonder why he wouldn't sell the timber? » one of the younger ones asks, trying for the hundredth time to hitch his trousers under his belt from which they will soon slip down, once more showing the hem of his underclothes.

« How can one know what got into his head? Meantime we lost several days work ».

« I think », said a man with a handlebar moustache « he's hoping to make more profit; everything is going up ».

« It's hardly the moment to wait! The steward was saying today that right now the deal was assured, but that soon no one knows how things will go. It's no time to play ».

Standing amongst the others was a young man who had said nothing so far, but had quietly been smoking and listening carefully to everyone, with a skeptical look on his face; he was a really imposing young man with a flat face onto which his nose, eyes and mouth had been forcefully flattened; beside him stood a thin young man in a jacket, with a little pointed moustache and a great tuft of black hair like a mane. For a while they continued to listen to the chatter of the others, then the big one, with a voice that was worthy of his stature, said:

« You haven't understood a thing ».

« I suppose you understand it all », someone answered.

« Some things you'll never understand, that I can assure you ».

« He certainly can » said the small man.

« That's right, Pietrone understands everything, there's no doubt about it », someone said with contempt.

Pietrone made a gesture with which he intended to send them all to the devil, when suddenly, as always happened, at the very same moment almost everyone got up to go home, including the owner of the store: « Goodnight, all », and he began to put the shutters on the door.

« What did you understand? » Faldella asked his friend Pietrone.

« I've understood that Gattegna is against them, that he doesn't want to give his timber because it would be used for fortifications, want to bet? »

« Do you really think he's against them too? »

« Everyone likes millions, and he's turned them down. That kind of people never understands anything much, even less than these, but when they do understand, they know what to do much better than anyone else, and they're even capable of losing on their own business ».

« Then you think Gattegna understands? »

« Yes, I think so ».

« Then you ought to tell your friend ».

« We'll see about that; but first I'd like to talk to him ».

« To Gattegna? »

« Naturally ».

« And how will you do it? »

« I'll think about that, good night ».

« Good night ».

They had reached a cross road and left each other.

Pietrone was well known throughout the neighboring countryside; he was one of those peasants occasionally found in those parts who have devoted little of their energy to the fields and who prefer to save it for the almost daily bicycle ride into town, or from one village to the next; of those who know every tavern in the neighborhood and in the County seat, who have developed a sort of compromise mentality between that of a tramp and a peasant; who are ready to organize a poaching expedition with exceptional skill, a deal of any sort, a fray or a supper in the country taverns. He had even been in jail as a result of a fight; but that he would laugh about. In public places he was always ready to fight without wasting time, and in some places when he would come in with his inseparable Faldella and a friend gathered here or there, many would look down or pay their bills and leave hurriedly. The peasants don't like his type, but generally fear them a good deal, and even when they speak badly of them make a point of being their friends, even searching them out to flatter them. Pietrone was fairly well known in town, at least in the market neighborhood; everywhere he had friends of all sorts and people often used him to solve some knotty problem or to find someone ready to handle the most disparate deals. In fact he was one of those types in whom a strange, disorderly rebellion without reason has taken hold, but extremely tenacious and resentful of everything because of the love for a violent and confused independence.

Faldella was a sort of protegé of his, of quite a different kind; almost constantly following Pietrone, ready to help him in any undertaking. He was the son of well-to-do farmers, had inherited his father's lands, but instead of going to work as everyone else in the family had always done, he had had others work it, above all preferring to use it as a guarantee against all sorts of debts and stupid intrigues by virtue of which each year his property diminished and was on the way to complete extinction.

For some time Pietrone had been friendly with a group of new acquaintances he had met in a tavern in town: after long talks with them Pietrone would explain to his friend:

417

« They are against these talkers, these rotten people ».
Or would say: « one day these people will be worth more
than the police, don't you worry » then they would both feel
happy, and they would get the vague impression by following
these new friends that they were doing something which
could be done with a clear conscience; this last phrase being
also Pietrone's.

XV

After the interruption of the felling of the trees in the
woods, Ugo had developed the habit of going there in the
afternoons.   Quite often, after having forgotten something
to which he had been much attached, some tiny indication
would bring him back to it and he would feel doubly attracted to it by the long period of forgetfulness, making it the
principal object of his interest for an indefinite period. Now
not a day passed that he did not go to the woods; sometimes
he would touch Gianni's arm, who would immediately understand and follow him quietly, he too almost as silent now
as any authentic Gattegna.

It was in fact a century old wood full of glens and impassable thickets, almost entirely made up of huge trees which
often framed the countryside with all the romantic force of
a large oak, with all the sentiment which the Italian umbrella pine can give to a stretch of land; as a child he had
counted the largest and most spectacular trees one by one,
and several of them were known to the family almost as
real people, there were even some which in recent genera-
tions had acquired special names which were spoken of by
the Gattegnas with pride. Gianni and Ugo no longer needed
to exchange many words; at times a few monosyllables were
enough to convey a whole speech; only when they would
run across the stump of a freshly cut tree Ugo would occasionally say:

« That one I knew ».

Then they would go on walking for hours until they

tacitly decided to go home; and the young Gattegna, waiting for it to be time for supper, would go up to his room to look at his things or write a few of his tiny notes.

A rainy day interrupted their walks, and Ugo announced that the next day they would once more go into town.

With the hood of the trap raised to avoid the dampness, the two young men set off at dawn. By now Gianni would follow his friend, sometimes profoundly annoyed, sometimes happy with that life, with the monotony of the countryside which he was beginning to love. The only time in which he could feel his old passions awaken and let himself fall into bitter thoughts was when the morning paper arrived with the mail; he would read it from cover to cover, sometimes re reading it, and would then bury himself in calculations through which he tried to discover, by using the news in his own way, how the war was going and how things might really be.

That morning the road was deserted. The horse trotted through the mist and dampness of a drizzle which seemed to be suspended in the air, whilst they sat tucked up under the hood with a red and black striped steamer-rug over their knees. The silence around them was pleasant and neither of them felt the need to speak.

A kilometer from town, where the asphalt, dark and shiny with humidity, ran in a straight line all the way to first outlying houses, they were both shaken by a shouted order:

« Stop! Halt! »

Ugo drew the horse up and waited, without leaning forward to see who had challenged them. A moment later two militiamen's faces appeared on either side of the trap, well shaved and protected by hooded capes of grey-green material, their guns casually pointed towards the inside of the trap:

« Where are you going? »

« Into town », Ugo answered.

« Have you your papers? »

« I am Ugo Gattegna » and so saying he pulled out his

wallet. One of the militiamen stuck his head in the trap to see better, then said to the other one:

« Gattegna, yes, yes, that's all right, I know who he is ».

« And the other one? »

« My name is Stefano Nicolai » Gianni answered precipitously, pulling out a wallet and showing an identity card.

« He's a friend of mine and he lives with me », added Ugo. The two militiamen casually examined the card and motioned them on.

« I'm sorry », said Gianni.

« Oh! » said Ugo.

« I hadn't told you... » Gianni went on; but Ugo interrupted him:

« It doesn't matter. What terrible people one has to put up with! »

« I'm sorry », said Gianni again.

« Don't worry, I'm well known round here and my name is a good sort of passport ».

They entered the city. At the gates and in the streets there were many soldiers, but no one else bothered the small carriage which proceded at a slow gait towards the Gattegna town house. Before reaching it Gianni again felt the need to ask:

« But do you realize why I... ».

« Oh », Ugo said once more.

« I ought at least to explain ».

« Never mind ».

As soon as the old woman had run off to announce them, Ugo's aunt appeared in the hall. A quick glance at her solid profile, at her mouth which was pressed like graphite into her face, was enough to put her down as a good example of a Gattegna; but in her movements, her way of doing things, she clearly showed the influence of a different sort of life, even if a certain parsimony of words on her part did not need to be discussed in order to be exactly catalogued.

« Well, if it isn't my own nephew », she said, trying to be particularly cordial.

« We felt like a change ».

« Excellent, excellent ».

Then Rosano arrived.

« Always by surprise, but at least one sees you from time to time. Good, good, good; go right to your rooms and we'll see you at lunch ».

Waiting for lunch, the two friends went to their usual window.

« We didn't see Adele », said Ugo.

« She must not be home ».

A little while later Adele came to see them to tell them lunch was ready, and turning to Ugo, added:

« How much stuff you brought, it's a real fortune; nowaday's one can't find anything in the city. It's not a matter of money, some days one doesn't know what to do to prepare a meal ». In fact Ugo had noticed a large hamper which Cesira had had put in the back of the trap before they started.

« I can't understand why you had to choose today to come into town, it isn't very prudent; everyone's shut indoors since yesterday », said Rosano as soon as they'd sat down to lunch.

« What's happened? » asked Ugo.

« Well, there was a lot of shooting last night, and yesterday soldiers were stopping everyone in the streets, arresting several people; it's a real tower of Babel ».

« That's why they stopped us on the road ».

« Yes, yes » said Ugo. Then after a little added: « I heard it mentioned yesterday, so I decided to come ».

« What! » said Adele « that's more like a reason for staying quietly up there ».

« It's not the moment to expose oneself, on days like this », said Rosano.

« Well ».

They started to eat in silence and Gianni began to notice that Adele's father made more noise than the others with his mouth, that he often needed to run his tongue along the back of his teeth, and Gianni was surprised to feel a certain uneasiness almost verging on disgust; how many other similar people had he sat next to without ever having noticed such a thing, and yet now, if he hadn't made an effort, the distaste would have become insufferable. A tacit feeling of rebellion overcame him, almost a fury against himself, against the man who was happily eating, and even more against Ugo, whom he could see on the other side of the table, most certainly in the prey of that same sort of obsession. Then Gianni calmed down and almost smiled to himself: — what nonsense! — he thought.

That night Ugo wouldn't make up his mind to turn off the light, smoking one cigarette after the other, observing Gianni almost as if he were expecting something from him. Gianni on the other hand was thinking of the day they'd been through, remembering the nonchalance and lack of surprise with which Ugo had faced the militiamen, and his lack of amazement at the false name he had given when he handed over the identity card with which he had so often been able to save himself in the difficult life of the last two years. Ugo had acted as if he had known it all beforehand: was it perhaps a rapid and instinctive gift for facing up to situations? Or had he realized everything in a way that had escaped Gianni? Perhaps there were more things in that head than appeared; but it was difficult to understand. He had not spoken to anyone of his recent past, and as for talking to Ugo about it, that had been quite impossible; and even if he had tried to do so more boldly, he was sure he would have provoked nothing but annoyance and impatience. Meeting his friend's glance as he smoked, he twice smiled, and the silence became almost painful, heavier, until Gianni, if only to break it, felt the need to say:

« I wouldn't want to get you in trouble ».

« There's no danger, Gianni: you're the one who's likely to have trouble. But don't worry. I was thinking of something else. I'm not bothering you, am I? »

« No, I'd like you to talk ».

« Don't you think I ought to suggest to these people to

come up to the Big House if things get more complicated in town? »

« It would certainly be a good deed ».

« They're the only relatives I have. Why don't you tell them? »

« Really, I don't think it's up to me ».

« No, you tell them, tomorrow, whenever you get the chance. Good night ».

« Good night ».

That night the sirens again raised their voice above the city, and all around the terror increased. But the two friends stayed in bed and perhaps slept almost uninterruptedly.

The next day after lunch Gianni was left alone chatting with Adele's parents to find a way to tell them what Ugo had asked him.

« May I come to your rooms? » Adele asked Ugo, who was moving off alone.

« Why not? »

They sat down in two armchairs and Ugo lit a cigarette, but Adele did not smoke; instead she watched her cousin not without a certain infantile curiosity. She had wanted to follow him, thinking she could get him to talk a little; his silence and indifference, though she knew them from before, had struck her. She had never thought of her cousin, but now that she'd met him, she was trying to understand him in her own way; but evidently she was not very good at judging others.

« It's not easy, you know, to talk to you », she said.

« I know Adele, I know. And I'm sorry ».

« One doesn't know what to think about you. Am I boring you? »

« No, but I think you'll be bored if you stay here ».

« I hope not ».

« Gianni is a boy who knows how to talk, and needs to; up there with me I think he leads a pretty dull life ».

« And if I really wanted to talk to you? »

Ugo raised his eyes towards hers and his grey glance made her a little uneasy.

« Yet you look like an easygoing man, not without gifts. I've never met such a difficult companion. Aren't you afraid of being disliked? »

« No ».

« You're none too polite ».

« You're right, forgive me, I'm not a good companion ».

« You may be wrong there ».

« Perhaps, yes, perhaps ».

« To tell the truth I sometimes have the impression you're putting it on, trying to make people think the world annoys you ».

« It's not always that way, Adele ».

« But everything has its limits, and you often go beyond any bounds ».

« I don't see myself the way you do ».

« Perhaps you're a little hypocritical, maybe very much so ».

Ugo was feeling persecuted. With his habitual gestures, with his normal behaviour, he had always managed to cut off any tiresome conversation; but this time he soon had to recognized that his usual methods would be of no use. Meanwhile Adele went on:

« Yes, yes, you must be used to doing what you like without thinking of other people, aren't you? »

« Right ».

« Yes, just as it whips through your head, no? »

« Whips? »

« Whips. As it goes through your head ».

« What goes through my head? »

« Oh! I tell you you could even annoy a Carthusian monk; but I'm staying right here to talk, and if you don't want me you'll have to chase me away ».

« I won't chase you away; I like seeing you ».

« You even know how to pay compliments! »

« I won't chase you away, but try not to torment me ».

« You're as hard as a rock! And as stubborn », said the girl, almost as if she were speaking about herself. « And weighty; yet if one were to push you onto a steep road you'd roll even faster than others ».

« I don't know what you're saying. A literary metaphor, no doubt ».

Ugo was silent, continuing to stare at her calmly.

« You must think me pretty stupid ».

« I don't think of such things ».

« I don't think, I don't believe, I don't know! » the girl repeated irritatedly trying to imitate his cadence.

Ugo was looking towards the window as if he had not heard her, instead he had heard her but was thinking of something else. The girl was getting even more annoyed, not even thinking she might be a nuisance; and in that moment she realised that Ugo had perhaps completely forgotten her. She then had the leisure to observe him for a while, as he did not show any signs of noticing her, and her face, which had so far borne an expression of affected impertinence, became suddenly serious. As she arched her eyebrows two deep commas appeared at the corners of her mouth.

« But you might not be very well » she said seriously, without noticing the infantile air she was taking: « Perhaps, Ugo, you should do something; change your way of life. But it's not so easy nowadays... ».

« What about nowadays? » Ugo asked.

Adele got up, her feelings hurt, realizing he had not heard anything of what she had said except for the last four words.

« How can you not pay attention to anyone else? You're not the only one in the world, are you? You could at least do it for the sake of that tiny bit of politeness we're all obliged to use towards each other ».

« Be patient, don't get angry. You see, I was watching the top of that cypress tree which seen from here rises quite a bit above the roof, whereas when I was taking my exams it was still a good bit lower ».

« But there aren't only things, there are people, don't you think? I'd always heard it said, even when I didn't know you, that nobody interests you. Luckily mother has very little of the Gattegnas and I'm more like father than mother; I haven't acquired anything from the Gattegnas, and, I can tell you: I'm very pleased I didn't ».

« It's quite a bit of luck, you're right », said Ugo who wanted to appease the girl's anger.

« So it's true; it's all a sense of uneasiness with you ».

« Why not, life isn't easy, do you find it easy living in this world? »

« If you mean nowadays, no ».

Ugo was now looking straight at her and there was almost resentment in his manner; he stared at her fixedly, enveloping her with the velvety greyness of his eyes: the girl, after sustaining his look with a frown that was also a little comic, lowered her eyes turned her head, and missed the smile of satisfaction with which Ugo was watching her.

« You said nowadays, but it was not by chance that you said it ».

« At our age it doesn't take much to understand that we live in a cursed period ».

« Why? »

« Because we're denied the things which could make us happy, make us enjoy our youth, make us feel that it isn't just passing away for nothing, that it isn't all useless ».

« At our age. But you're still a girl, you've got time! »

« Yes, and I suppose you're old. You see, you don't even have the right idea of yourself ».

« Perhaps ».

At this point Ugo decided to interrupt the conversation, no matter how, as it was seriously beginnig to annoy him, and also, for some reason, to worry him; but it was a different annoyance from usual, largely because he felt violently irritated with himself. Then the others appeared in the doorway.

« Here they are », said Rosano. He was dusting a bottle of wine which he held in his hand.

« If we won't know what to eat, there's quite a bit left to drink. The cellar's still full. Come on Ugo, let's have a glass, it's wine from your property ».

« Thank you ».

« You must be a man who drinks heavily; I hadn't thought of that before », said the girl suddenly. Gianni started to laugh, explaining that Ugo never drank more than the most normal of human beings. The mother, however, looked at her daughter a little worried and asked:

« What sort of talk is that? It's hardly appropriate ».

« I've been talking to Ugo and I wanted to see how he's made », Adele said candidly.

Ugo who had remained seated whithout speaking, felt something fill him with dismay. He would have liked to get up and run away, but realized it would be a little ridiculous, and stayed where he was. Finally he felt himself blushing: at first he was surprised; it hadn't happened to him since he was a child; then he became furious with himself, trying to appear indifferent, but although it was his most usual attitude he felt embarrassed and lost; he had a suspicion the others could follow all these sensations on his face, and remained with his eyes turned towards a vague part of the wall ahead of him. Actually no one was watching him, but even if they had looked into his face, nothing or very little was transpiring of what to him seemed extremely obvious. Adele had started to chatter, her voice banal and petulant, and to Ugo it seemed suddenly insufferable and insignificant.

Rosano sat down next to him and said:

« I want to thank you; we had recently been looking around, as many of our friends, many families in town, have had to arrange for a place in the country. Some have even transported their most important belongings out of the city. We were thinking of it, but we didn't dare turn to you; we've seen so little of you during the last few years that we've almost lost contact, yet we're really the only relatives you have.

427

It was high time, and we're grateful to you, aren't we, Georgia? We didn't know which way to turn if we'd had to leave the city, but now we feel better; however I don't think it will be necessary, I think all these worries are exaggerated and all these precautions excessive; but if everyone's doing it, we'd best think about it too ».

« Now you know where you can take refuge in case of necessity », said Ugo in a sharp tone, devoid of cordiality; so much so that Rosano was struck by it and said no more.

PART TWO

I

Only in this countryside inhabited by taciturn people whose spirit is alive and fertile can certain phenomena reach such proportions; yet, at the same time, outwardly, they do not lead to the confusion one would normally think. Just as a field of wheat is bent and disordered on a summer's evening when the sky is overcast and the air dark and clear, just as the stalks are ruffled and contorted almost without adding sound to the rustling of the wind, so in the hearts of lonely men any frightening news, or the announcement of inevitable disaster begins to struggle and take on gigantic forms; but the silence remains. Whoever does not know the country thoroughly cannot really understand how such uneasiness spread collectively and is nourished like embers beneath the ashes, how it flares up suddenly, striking at everyone, entering every heart, where it remains for a long time if not for ever closed within each individual.

It wasn't the news built on air, the invented fears, but the aspect such things took when being passed from mouth to mouth, from village to village, even including the lesser cities, that would have most disconcerted a stranger. Stories were told of fabulous and far-off events which, if one wished to, one could check on in the daily papers and understand without too much effort or phantasy. But they were nevertheless spoken of as phantastic happenings which one could only believe with difficulty; and as a result they would become even more deeply impressed in the peasants' minds, always caught in some dobt, and accepted with ease as a sad reality. The war was by now moving North and might even have turned up there; but with all their good will it was not easy for them to believe it; they would speak of it as something possible, but were all the more terrified of it in proportion to the need to rebel at the thought of its being a real possibility.

What was even more inexplicable was the fact that they felt the need to search out and inform themselves through indirect chanels, more especially through those to whom they had never given much weight; everyone felt the need to listen to those whose information they eventually accepted, but with their accustomed mistrust. They needed to search for light among the very same men they considered least apt to be believed; of them they would ask questions, would listen to their complicated reasoning, urging them to speak at greater length and as clearly as possible, desiring their most dispassionate opinions, then would go away shaking their heads as if they were still incredulous about what might happen, and, in fact, were perhaps really incredulous, but were also more impressed with what they had heard than if they had really had the power to believe it completely.

Nevertheless, each in his own way began to make his own calculations, testing the ground to find out the other's intentions: but it would happen that those who were asked would in turn ask; those from whom some counsel could be expected because they were reputed the smartest were actually seeking counsel themselves, so that for the moment they all passed from not knowing which way to turn, to a state of absolute incredulity, from incredulity to terror, from terror to hope, and their souls were in prey of a terrible tempest which each one hid from himself.

The countryside was uneasy. They worried about their

gold; the peasants in those parts always possess a nice little bundle of gold trinkets, heavy and unwieldy, passed on from father to son, added to at each wedding, at each first communion. In their minds the men were already looking for safe hidingplaces, and their money too, of which they now possessed more since the city had turned directly to them for food, had become a source of infinite worry and strange thoughts.

At the store, whereas they were all agreed that what he said was nothing but lies, that it was useless to listen to him: — He's even been in jail, think of that! — they still tried to listen with sharp ears to what Pietrone chose to tell them.

« All you think about is hiding your belongings, instead it's yourselves you'll have to hide ».

« Yourselves », Faldella would repeat.

« And why should we hide? What have we got to do with it? »

« Because retreating soldiers will be hunting you and the beasts in your stables more than your belongings and your money ».

« More after men than money », Faldella would say.

« Nonsense! » the peasants would answer annoyed, yet without being able to hide their anxiety.

« Nonsense? You'll see if Pietrone invents things. You think I say these things just to gossip? Well, I say them to do you a favor, because it's the truth, because one of these days we'll all have to come to an understanding ».

« And the women? » someone asked.

« Ah, women. I don't know about women, I'll tell you in a few days; but think of your animals now, those are the ones to put in a safe place ».

« Put the animals in safety », Faldella would repeat from behind Pietrone's shoulders.

« What do you know more than we do? »

« I know, I know, my friends; but you just do as you please ».

As the discussion became more animated, certain questions began to make way against infinite reticences; at about

that time one of the men who counted most in the neighborhood would turn up on the main road, and, as if by common accord, an enormous silence would follow. Faldella
would draw even closer to Pietrone and even they would stay,
though they were evidently becoming nervous and beset with
worries. The others, who were almost all on their feet for the
discussion, would sit back down on the ground or the benches.

« Good evening, gossipers », the newcomer would say.
« And what were you talking about? »

« Ehm... ehm... »

« Have you lost your tongues? Don't let yourselves be
worked up by too many speeches, there are people around
who are too fond of gossiping, but it won't last long. Only
we know how things really are, if you want information come
to us. We can now say that better times are on the way,
and soon, sooner than you imagine, you will know how the
war is really going, and who's going to win. Don't be foolish,
there are those who know what they're doing, and are doing
it for you and for us ». After going on for a long time in
this vein they would conclude: « and when we have won, the
first to feel the benefits will be us, understand, just us » and
they would then disappear where they came from.

« Goodnight », Pietrone would then say, the first to go
off in the opposite direction, followed by his shadow.

« Are you going? Wait for me ».

« No, I'll see you in a few days ».

« In a few days », Faldella would say.

The peasants would sit around for a moment still absorbed
in their thoughts, then almost all together would go off silently, while the eldest would utter an exclamation towards the
sky which in no way encouraged the others. The night would
swallow these shirtless men; while all around the lights of the
houses thinned out as the shutters were closed. « Good night ».

II

Of the timber that had not been turned over from the Gattegna property no one spoke any more; everyone had forgotten the episode except for Baccelli, who had lost his peace of mind in renouncing a really exceptional profit, in which he too would have participated, albeit on a smaller scale, and he now went around, cursing in his heart the incomprehensible strangeness of the last Gattegna.

Pietrone too had not forgotten, and for more than a week had been thinking of a way of making use of the episode to speak to Gattegna. It was very difficult for him to establish relations with the owner of the Big House; he knew no one who had actually exchanged a few words with him; but Pietrone had that fixed idea in his head and was slowly formulating a plan to bring it to fulfillment.

When, after a few days, he presented himself at the kitchen door of the Big House, he was received with cold amazement and undisguised resentment by Cesira who stared at him with hostility.

« Excuse me, may I come in? »

Cesira went on looking at him; she too like everyone else knew Pietrone a little, and though she had never had any contact with him, many times she had seen him around the countryside or at the store, and his visit seemed rather strange.

« What do you want, Pietrone? »

Pietrone, with his cap in hand, came into the kitchen almost timidly; but sure of his broad voice, made no preamble:

« I would like to speak to Signor Ugo, just a few words, but it's something important. His refusal to allow the cutting of timber in his wood has been badly received by certain people, he might find himself in trouble ».

« What trouble? »

« They say he's against; and with those people, with people who think that way, there's no joking, especially now-adays ».

Cesira would never have been able to admit that the Gat-tegnas could find someone who could cause them trouble, but at such hints she too felt disturbed.

« I don't know anything », she said, « but its all a lot of gossip. How could master Ugo want to listen to such foolish-ness? »

« But you tell him I need to speak to him ».

« You? »

« Yes, me ».

« He hasn't come down yet. If you really want me to tell him, come back this afternoon ».

After lunch Cesira briefly informed them that a certain man of the neighborhood wanted to speak to the master, and went on out without waiting for an answer; then, a little while later, she came back to say that the man had come back.

« Who, Cesira? »

« That Pietrone ».

« Who is he? »

« I don't know him ».

« And he really wants to speak to me? » said Ugo, look-ing questioningly at Gianni.

« But if he wants to speak to you, have him come in », said Gianni.

« If he really wants to speak to me, let him in ».

Pietrone came in with his cap in hand, walking with care-ful steps and a smile which revealed tiny closely set teeth absolutely out of proportion with either his enormous body of the big rustic face on which the smile seemed almost sin-ister, if not a little funny.

Ugo did not know him, did not remember ever having seen him, but realizing he was a peasant, made a pleasant gesture for him to come nearer.

« Excuse me for coming in here, but I wanted to warn you of something which I must say to you privately ».

433

« Go right ahead, my friend can stay and listen ».

« I wanted to say... You know, I listen to many different kinds of people, and the other day, the man who is bossing the neighborhood because he can do so now, at least for the time being, was speaking of you down at the store, saying you had forbidden the cutting of timber because it was to be used for fortifications. You know, I can say it to you frankly, I don't think the same way they do, and so I thought it might be best if I came and told you; these are ugly times, and those people are more dangerous than one thinks, they're capable of anything if they single out a person ».

Ugo was listening without answering and Pietrone found himself stuck in the middle of the room.

« Sit down ».

« Thank you ».

« You might like a glass of wine ».

« Yes », said Pietrone.

« And as for what you're heard, don't let it worry you ». There was a moment's silence, then the man went on:

« It's always better to be careful, to be ready ».

« Ready? »

« Yes, yes ».

« Thank you, thank you » said Ugo, and the conversation for him would have ended there if Gianni hadn't wanted to know a little more.

« You, Signor... »

« Pietro, my name is Pietro, Pietrone ».

« You did very well, Signor Pietro » but just then he was seized by a doubt, mistrusted the man, and so, instead of going on, added: « they say so many foolish things, so much gossip; but I don't think Signor Gattegna has anything to worry about, though thanks all the same for the warning ».

« But those are terrible people ».

Ugo was already thinking of something else. Happy that Gianni had relieved him of the problem, he had not grasped the meaning of the last words, but drew a deep breath when he heard Gianni say:

« I'll see Pietro out, you don't mind? »

« On the contrary, you'll do me a favor. Goodbye, Pietro, thank you for your trouble ».

Pietro made a sort of half bow, Ugo shook his hand, then heard them both going out, and leaned his head on the back of the armchair.

Gianni saw the man to the gate, walking slowly and talking till they were near the main road where they said goodbye.

On the road Faldella was waiting for Pietrone.

« What did he say? »

« He speaks very little, but there's a friend of his, the one that came out with me, he seems to have understood quite well; he asked me many things and told me to come back to see him when I had news from the city. I think he's experienced in these matters ».

« You'd better be careful, you never can tell ».

« I have a good nose, and I do things right ».

« But what do you want from them now? »

« If they open up they can be useful to us; then Gattegna doesn't mean anyone any harm, and he's not dangerous. If they open up I can tell people in town that we have important people with us in this area, understand? »

« Of course, I understand ».

« Besides my friend said we've got to be on the lookout nowadays because we've no time to lose ».

« There's no time to lose, of course ».

Coming back in Gianni sat down in front of Ugo, then asked him:

« Are you sure you have nothing to fear? This man seemed sincere, and nowadays in these matters one can't really joke ».

« He was certainly sincere » said Ugo.

« It'll be better not to be too trusting, which is another good reason ».

« For what? »

« For being careful ».

« Careful, why? »

435

« Well, just leave it to me ».

« Yes, yes, you do whatever you think best ».

III

During the next weeks Gianni met Pietrone several times: Ugo who had seen them together never asked anything. Throughout the countryside reigned a silent dismay; the road was again filled with soldiers, and convoys passed almost uninterruptedly. At night the almost incessant rumble of their engines rose to the hilltop like a great trembling; at times Ugo would go to the window and watch their movement for a long time, and Gianni who would be near him would say:

« You see? »

« Soon it won't be wise to stay here any longer », Gianni would answer him.

For the last few days the paper had not arrived because the mail had ceased to function. The war was approaching, and the peasants were uneasy and mistrustful, the women watched everything with suspicion, the men had prepared sacks full of disparate objects and some had secretly buried their money and gold. Gianni often met Pietrone who brought him news he judged to be from a fairly reliable source.

In that uncertain and uneasy atmosphere only two creatures remained estranged and impassive, Cesira and Ugo; the two of them continued to lead their usual existence, each one occasionally observing that subterranean agitation, would stop to watch the incessant coming and going of cars on the main road, then seemed to forget everything the minute they were back in the room. In fact Ugo forgot everything he saw during those days the minute he took his eyes from it, he managed willfully and without any effort to forget the spectacle of war which was continuously growing; in her heart Cesira would try to do likewise, but her uneasiness would not have been stilled if she hadn't had the possibility of feeling the young Gattegna near her.

On the other hand Gianni had become more prudent, he would stay away from the road which was teeming with soldiers, and had already warned Ugo that he should take more precautions so as not to be caught unprepared in case of necessity.

« But no, but why? » Ugo would answer.

« I'm sure that at some point I will have to leave this house and you too won't be able to stay here, not even Cesira; beyond the hills the mountains could be a safe place for the time needed, and I know that up there we'll be among safe people ».

«But why leave here? »

« Haven't you eyes? Can't you see what's happening? Don't you realize that very soon we may find ourselves in the middle of the war? Then I can assure I know one should not take what's going to happen too lightly ».

Ugo would not answer; only once while Gianni was almost forcefully trying to inform him that the soldiers were retreating, taking livestock and men with them, he asked:

« Do you think they will take things too? »

« Of course they will, try to understand me, try to listen to what's being said and put your faith in me ».

« Then I'll hide them » said Ugo.

After that day Ugo ordered Cesira to put all the moveable objects in his room into various trunks — the gold, the trinkets; then he called for Baccelli to have him hide the trunks on the other side of the hill; Baccelli, who for days had been doing nothing else, who was busy having the livestock and the most expensive farm equipment removed, and who had organized a sort of temporary village in one of the Gattegna's woods in the mountains, barely answered his master, had the stuff loaded on the first cart that was leaving for the mountains, and went off preoccupied with the direction of operations like a general preparing for battle.

In the city there was no less confusion, by now soldiers were everywhere, many command posts had been sent there, and whoever could leave his house and seek refuge in the country was doing so as fast as possible. Ugo's relatives were also caught up in the collective panic, and in one day decided to go to the Big House taking with them their most essential and precious belongings. They arrived on top of a hired cart which managed to reach the Big House by making a wide detour through the hills, across country lanes and fields, as one could no longer travel on the main roads. Military convoys were now moving from South to North.

All day long Ugo would stay in his room, bared of all his things, in a foul mood; he felt as if he were in a strange place, and would continually walk up and down repeating to himself: — what nonsense! — He would only calm down by leaning on the windowsill and watching the long line of military vehicles.

When he heard his relatives had arrived he went downstairs; they all sat down in the living room and Rosano said:

« Here we are pretty well out of the way, it's a thoroughfare, let's hope we won't be bothered, but there's really nowhere safe any more ».

« What do you think of it, Ugo? » Adele asked.

« Nothing ».

« But doesn't it all worry you? »

« Yes, yes ».

« In town one hears tales that seem impossible, they say the soldiers drag all the men off with them, they kill, take the livestock, steal, that they shoot; then they say that they... »

« That's enough, father », said Adele; then asked: « and is your friend still here? »

« Yes, he's up on the hills, but later he'll be here ».

Then Ugo and Adele went out for a while, climbed as far as the edge of the woods from which they could see the main road, crawling with cars the sound of their engines making the air throb. Otherwise the plain seemed deserted; there wasn't a thread of smoke, not a sign of life.

« I'm glad you came », said Ugo; but in his heart he wasn't sure that he was.

« Really? » said the girl with enthusiasm: « everyone's leaving the city ».

« Let's get away from here », said Ugo.

« Wherever you like ».

They went down the slope towards a group of peasant houses behind which the land fell away in large terraces, cultivated and scattered with olive trees; here and there were lettuce patches, rows of vines, everything squared off in the regular series of steps with loving and meticulous care. The two young people walked on, up and down, losing themselves in tiny paths cut into the high hills; and enclosed by hedges and brambles; every now and then a large tree would rise towards the sky with its black shadow balancing the countryside which sloped towards the plain.

« One feels one's losing one's balance up here on this terrain which slopes to one side », said Adele. Ugo was silent, though struck by the sentence; it seemed a particularly curious observation and he tried to discover why he thought so; but he only felt the sensation that in those words of Adele's there was something to do with him personally; as if one of his shoulders were lower than the other, as if one of his arms weighed more than the other; he tried to think of something else on the subject, but apart from these sensations he could find nothing that interested him: he then remembered the girl who was next to him, and looking at her, said:

« What a strange remark of yours ».

« Which one? » asked Adele who was no longer thinking of her last words.

« The slope of the landscape ».

« It's just an idea, I live in the city and everything there is always on one level, there aren't any slopes ». Ugo stopped in the middle of the path, slowly turned his shoulders, stood in front of the girl as if he wanted to block her way and looked into her eyes. Adele tried to withstand that hard yet caressing, velvety grey, glance looking back into those eyes with their eyebrows straight as a ruler, then lowered her head, shaking her hair which fell onto her shoulders almost white against the light; she raised her head again, willfully sought out her cousin's eyes and started to smile with an expression that meant to be sure of herself but which betrayed a touch of nervousness; in fact the man with the big shoulders who seemed to have rooted himself in the path like a tree, like an insurmountable obstacle, was giving her a sense of subjection, almost of fear. She tried to accomplish her slow and skillful smile: but Ugo's face reflected, as it never had before, his immobility so difficult to understand; and his mouth, so strongly carved above the large powerful chin, might have given the impression of something entirely devoid of life, cut out of stone. Adele tried to finish her smile naturally, then asked:

« Do you want to stop here? » and as Ugo would not answer, all of a sudden she turned and ran off towards home; after barely ten steps she stopped, made a conciliatory gesture with her arm, stood for a moment watching Ugo still motionless in the middle of the road, then definitely fled, her hair blowing in the wind.

Ugo stood and watched her till she had disappeared; then, he too, with his hard, monotonous step, started off towards the Big House.

Before reaching the villa Adele ran into Gianni.

« Where are you running? »

« Home », she said, slowing down to a walk beside him.

« Have you been for a walk? I'd heard you'd arrived ».

« Yes, I went out with Ugo, but he stayed back there ».

« Did you leave him alone? »

The girl laughed happily, then said:

« I felt like running away so I left him there in the middle of the path ».

« Ah! So you stand people up! »

« No, but with Ugo one never knows what to do ».

« It's difficult, one's never quite sure ».

« And where are you back from? »

« I made a little tour round here; the countryside is agitated! a sort of subterranean collective fear, everyone's expecting something, and they're not far wrong; listen? » He was silent a moment and the echo of the rumble of thousands of motors on the road reached them like a cascading waterfall, like a monotonous mechanical wail.

« One doesn't know where to go to be safe, but I feel easier here than in the city ».

« Yes, this is a thoroughfare, it won't last long here, but there'll be a moment when it will be wise not to fool ourselves, and get out ».

« And how can we do it? »

« All we need do is go off towards the mountains Don't worry, there are more ways out than you imagine, and many preparations have already been made for us all. The hardest thing, I think, will be to make your cousin understand all this, as he will not listen to reason; I'm sure he understands things as well as we do; but he won't hear of it; perhaps he's resentful, something like contempt, but then who knows what he's thinking in that head? »

« Who knows? Who knows? »

« There's no point trying to guess with Ugo, yet I'm sure there must be a way of understanding him; there ought to be the right kind of key for him too ».

« Right, you couldn't have said it better! We must find the right kind of key ».

« Yes, but now it's only important to convince him to worry a little more about what's going to happen ».

In fact that evening Gianni tried with much skill to make a long speach to Ugo; he told him with great precision, assuring him of its exactness, of the horrors and dangers that would develop the moment the centre of warface passed where they were; and it would pass there, as the new holding point at the front was down, near the Apuan Alps. Rosano tried to throw doubt on everything Gianni said that was most worrying, but finally concluded that he had prepared himself as best he could, that he and his wife and daughter had a knapsack ready with which to make off at the slightest alarm. Seeing that only Ugo was not taking part in the discussion, Gianni then said:

« You too will have to make up your mind, Ugo ».

« Make up my mind? »

« Certainly, there won't be much choice, you won't want to stay here, isolated in the middle of a war? »

« But no one will hurt me, I don't even notice other people or what goes on around me, and being alone most certainly will not bother me ».

« But what kind of reasoning is that? » said Adele's mother, who usually listened in silence.

« I don't think reasoning helps very much; however, in such sircumstances its absolutely useless », said Ugo.

« If you won't make up your mind, at the last minute we'll drag you after us by the ear », said Adele.

« Never mind, we'll see ». And with that Ugo had nothing more to add.

The next day when Cesira came into his room Ugo said to her:

« You'd best prepare yourself to leave the house if there is any danger, Cesira ».

« Everyone's talking of going away, most of the men who are still around are going to the mountains today. What a business! »

« Then prepare yourself, too ».

« Will you be coming? »

« No, no, Cesira ».

« Then I'll stay here, master Ugo ». And she went back down to the kitchen.

IV

The next day Ugo went out with his cousin, and this time too the girl came home alone preceding him by almost an hour. When Ugo came in it was time to sit down to supper, but he did not take his place, remaining standing.

« Aren't you sitting down, Ugo? » Adele asked.

« No ».

« Why not? » asked Adele's mother.

« Because I don't want to eat ».

« Aren't you feeling well? » Gianni asked worriedly.

« On the contrary, but excuse me, I'm going upstairs ». And he went up to his room.

When Cesira came in with the soup she immediately asked after the master, putting a plate at his place.

« He doesn't want to eat tonight ».

Cesira, without even noticing it, stopped tending to the guests, stood thinking for a while, then said as if to herself.

« It isn't possible ».

« Why not? »

« Please excuse me a moment ». And without waiting for an answer she was heard climbing the stairs with surprising speed.

Ugo was standing at the window. From the plain came the noise of cars, even more cumbersome that usual: the air was black and tepid, the sky full of stars.

« Master Ugo », said the woman.

« What is it Cesira? »

« They told me you didn't want to eat ».

« It's true ».

« But that's never happened ».

« Don't worry Cesira; besides, I have a few biscuits here ».

« Aren't you well ».

« Very well ». And for Ugo the words marked the end of the brief conversation; Cesira knew it well, and did not need to experiment to know that Ugo wouldn't have answered her further. Cesira went back down the stairs in a bad mood and gruffily served the others. Besides, no one wanted to talk, and as soon as they got up from the table each one went to his room.

During the night, slowly and indistinctly, mixed with the rumble of the engines which gave no peace, a sort of autumnal voice, which seemed to come from underground, out of space, began to be heard. Only Ugo was immediately able to notice that new note in the midst of the clatter that filled the countryside, that new voice which was added to the already familiar rumble of trucks; only he could hear it, because he was awake. He had stayed at the window to listen to the ever more frantic rumble, and to look out into space. It seemed as if the fields were shaking, as if a tireless wave were rolling across the plain, and he had stayed there without thinking of anything; two or three times he had been attracted and become less vague at the sound of a horn-owl drifting down from the woods, and had cut himself off from the rumbling as if to defend the last shred of silence of the hills and fields which had always ruled the nights from up there. For a few minutes there had also been a nightingale; Ugo had listened to it too, but then had smiled and said to himself: — You fool! — Had listened with aching heart, and then repeated angrily — You fool! — But the incessant thundering which had appeared on the plain seemed to make rapid flights through the air, advancing along the horizon, broadening in the distance.

The dawn came, and the sun appeared slowly, re-emerging inexorably to continue eternally on its route, or at least it seemed inexorable to Ugo who, still standing at the window, was waiting for it hostilely. When the dawn came Ugo felt frighteningly empty, and started to search the very core of his entrails. He was searching for that powerful and domineering activity which he did not realise was so much a part of his hermit's soul and so much a necessity to his health; that twisting of things within him was perhaps the struggle of his spirit perennially nailed to his muscles, a prisoner of his nerves which were constantly taut, despite appearances.

There was no sign of life from the peasant houses, although the sun was already skimming the treetops; not a door was open, not a cart or a beast in the fields, not a thread of smoke at that time when every house would always send up a black column into the sky. By the first light of the sun the road seemed crammed, the shiny tape of asphalt was completely hidden by a flow of indistinct things which moved monotonously up it, like a row of ants, like dense germinating liquid. And the other voice on the horizon would not cease, in fact it was growing stronger as if to dominate the deafening sound of the motors. Only then did Ugo listen to it and take it into consideration, only at that moment did he understand, stopping his thoughts for a moment on that thunder which was invading all space and said to himself: — It's the cannon. —

Almost at the same instant the door of his room opened; Gianni came in pyjamas and said excitedly:

« Did you hear? »

« Yes. Good morning ».

« It's the cannon! »

« Yes, It's the cannon! » Adele's father could be heard shouting from below.

« It's the cannon! »

As Gianni went over to the window by his friend, something moved among the rows of vines.

« Some one's coming! »

They were silent and eventually saw Pietrone and Faldella come out into the open, looking around cautiously before exposing themselves. They spoke together pointing at the house, but before they could make up their minds Gianni called to them. They approached, making signs not to shout, and when they were under the window, said:

« Come down quickly; you must hurry ».

It was time to leave the house. It would have been wiser to have left it at night; all around them the peasants had gone over the hills during the night or the previous evening; patrols had been searching the plains, had set fire to a few houses, killed an unknown number of people; now they had been seen at the foot of the hills, and they might not hesitate to come up as far as the first houses on the slopes. There was nothing to do but take the path towards the woods slipping out of the back of the house through the garden. « Three kilometers from here we will find others who are waiting for us, but we must hurry » with these words the two men had finished their excited recital.

Coming back, Gianni did not have much to explain, as Adele and her parents were already in the living room with their knapsacks ready. Gianni too was ready in a moment, but there was no sign of Ugo.

« Leave by the back of the house, wait for me near the coal shed, in a while I'll be there with Ugo and Cesira ».

« If you don't come too, I'll come back, understand, Ugo? » Adele had yelled up as she went out with her parents. Then Ugo appeared on the landing of the staircase and greeted the girl with a vague gesture of his hand which could have even been meant as a sign of assurance.

« You go along, go along » Gianni kept repeating as he joined Ugo.

« Ugo, I can't make a long speach, there's no time for discussion, no one must remain here, it would be madness, come away with us ».

« No, Gianni. What could happen here? You must go, because you, have reasons for being out of the way; for you, you know, it's different ».

« But now it isn't a question of that ».

« Go along ».

« But don't be absurd! »

« Go along ».

« No », said Gianni angrily.

« Run along. They're waiting for you ».

On the hillock below, on the threshing floor of the nearest peasant house, something was moving; the two friends watched carefully; there were soldiers, then two more came out from behind the wall carrying their guns in their hands and looking about circumspectly.

« Armed soldiers », said Ugo.

« Yes », said Gianni, paling. « Ugo, come with me, I beg you ».

Just then Cesira appeared in the doorway. Gianni turned to her: « We must run, in a few minutes they'll be here! »

But Cesira was not listening, she was looking at the untonched bed; all of a sudden, raising her arms she cried:

« My God, master Ugo, but you haven't been to sleep! » and she stood questioningly frowning in the middle of the room; meanwhile Ugo was trying to push Gianni towards the stairs:

« Go on. I tell you, go on ». Gianni held back; outside a few shots were heard in the distance, then Gianni began to move backwards down the stairs pleading with Ugo:

« Please, please ».

« Look after Adele! » Ugo shouted after Gianni as he went out of the garden door and ran towards the woods without really knowing what he was doing.

Left alone, Ugo stepped back from the window, leaving it half closed, and sat down at his desk; then, noticing Cesira, said to her:

« Sit down Cesira and stay with me a while ». Then suddenly he turned and looked at her:

« But you must run. What are you doing here? You must go with the others, run! »

« What are you thinking of! » said Cesira in a tone of reproof.

<h1 style="text-align:center">V</h1>

On the plain, at three different spots, there was something burning, the black smoke of the fires rose straight towards the sky in the still air; there wasn't a breath of wind.

Cesira had closed all the windows in the house; only the one in Ugo's bedroom was left open a crack, and though from outside it looked barred like all the others, Ugo could look out every now and then at the main road and the plain below. Occasionally groups of soldiers could be seen here and there on the hill, coming right up to the first rows of vines to rest and eat the sour grapes, some had gone close to the woods but had stopped at a safe distance, watching the denser parts and making wide detours. By now the infernal noise of the road merely served to accentuate the stillness all around; the countryside was deserted.

Ugo felt curiously well, almost happy; rarely had he experienced such complete relaxation. At the thought of being so isolated from everything and everyone he felt filled with a profound sence of peacefulness; Cesira would spend an hour or so in his room sitting on a chair by the door, as still as an inanimate object, also quite happy. They felt they'd now reached a state they had longed for for years and nothing of what took place outside those four walls bothered them in the least, though they could now quite clearly understand it.

At first, when he looked at the woman who had stayed with him, she too quite undisturbed, he had thought: — What an egoist! — Then he had said to her:

« I was wrong in not forcing you to go, and now it's impossible ».

« But no, what are you thinking of, Master Ugo ».

« But it's dangerous ».

« Do you think so? » the woman had said.

« Cesira, perhaps you don't realize, I should have made you understand that here... »

« Don't worry; I understand quite well ».

And silence had once more fallen between them in the room filled with the vibrations which came from the bottom of the hill, the cannon now reaching them roundly and regularly, always nearer.

When Cesira had seen him sit down at his desk and scribble on his bits of paper she had thought with satisfaction: — Master Ugo is happy. But how could he manage without me? Who would have cooked for him? — at this thought she was reminded of something and went downstairs to the kitchen to prepare some lunch.

« Be careful », Ugo had warned her. « From outside, the house must look empty ».

« Certainly ».

The whole day passed that way, Ugo stayed quietly in his room getting up every now and then from his chair to look through the crack in the blinds: now, though the road was still crawling with vehicles as if their diabolical passing would never end, a lot of soldiers on foot could also be seen scouring the countryside, especially in the plains, in silent circumspect patrols, rarely coming up onto the hills.

Cesira installed herself in Gianni's room on the first floor, near Ugo's room, in order to be ready for any eventuality, but perhaps even more so as not to feel completely alone as she did downstairs in the barred house surrounded by the insidious rumbling which had submerged the deserted countryside. Ugo had never needed so little attention from the woman; he had not felt so peaceful for a long time, and was even looking forward to the days which were still to be passed in that situation with an intense joy which seemed to prickle under his skin; there was also an undefinable sadness in all of this, and also a great uncertainty as to the reality of the wealth of joy that possessed him; but his thoughts about even the immediate future were nothing but fleeting flashes, whereas he would live every instant that passed and sink back into it, as if it were all eternity.

Evening came slowly that day; from time to time though separate and near, gutteral voices were added to the noise of the road, sometimes clearly enough to distinguish shreds of conversation when groups of soldiers would stray from the road towards the first heights of the hill. There was also the sound of rifles being fired, and an occasional violent explosion; then, before the night had definitely smothered all those men with their noise in a blanket of darkness, the cannon was heard nearby: it was no longer a steady thunder, but the bursts were separate from each other, punctuated by pauses, after which they would return with a splitting crash, or a deep heavy rumbling.

Ugo finished his supper, and seeing the time, said to the woman:

« It's still early, stay with me a while ».

« Thank you, master Ugo ».

« Why thank me? »

And they both sat in the dark; he in his armchair by the desk, she on a chair by the door, as still as could be. In that silence the windowpanes would shake from time to time, and the night air made a door on the ground floor squeak on its hinges.

« I'll go down and close it ».

« Leave it, it will keep us company ».

Cesira was not of the same opinion, but tried to convince herself that just then, the low squeaking was a friendly voice, and quite soon she succeded.

« If it bothers you », said Ugo.

« No, I'll close it before I go to bed ».

In the darkness which came very suddenly they noticed each other's presence. Cesira had started to recite her prayers in her mind, for her rosary was still on the chair in the kitchen. Ugo was silent; steps were heard outside, then voices; there must have been soldiers right by the vineyard, on the edge of the clearing in front of the kitchen; for a while they could clearly hear the brief foreign words, then nothing. If they could have seen each other they would have seen that they were sitting quite still, holding their breath, but without the least worry showing on their faces.

« They're all around the house », said Cesira.

VI

Ugo

It you're frightened, stay here.

Cesira

I'm not frightened.

Ugo

That's right. What have we to be frightened of; since we won't leave anything, we can't be afraid of losing anything. And yet these last few days I've wondered if I were entirely lacking in something. But doubts don't help; one shouldn't have them.

Cesira

I never have doubts.

Ugo

About what?

Cesira

About another life.

Ugo

Another life? Let's hope not, this one's quite enough.

Cesira

I don't think one should talk that way.

Ugo

Who told you so?

Cesira

Well, no one.

Ugo

One has to have ties, someone must want us, then perhaps... But I'm all here, complete and finished. Here for me everything starts and ends every instant, in the very same moment:

I am nothing but myself, aren't I, Cesira?

Cesira

If you say so.

Ugo

That's right, I have to say it, no one else can say it, or not say it. Everyone else has so much to think about.

Cesira

It's better not to think of anything.

Ugo

That's right, as if we were nothing, and yet when all is said and done I am something; even I know and remember some faces; but actually there's only me, no one but me.

Cesira

Aren't you feeling well, master Ugo?

Ugo

I wish I weren't, if only for once; but this health of mine twists and turns inside me like a caged beast protesting and roaring without anyone to hear it; I, however, quite often hear it. It's disgusting! But there's nothing I can do. How I wish I could! I can know all about any of my gestures, curl up inside myself, but it's not enough; there must be something I don't quite understand, some far away, vast guilt mirrored in me who am blameless, who know nothing. But at last tonight I feel tired, my head feels heavy.

Cesira

You're tired! of course, you didn't sleep last night, your bed's still untonched.

Ugo

I'm tired because one cannot hold one's self up, damn it up and compress it for eternity; the time comes when something slips past, wants to escape from constrictions, and tie up with, search out other people, forget one's own being. Perhaps I should have somehow been able to understand that one gets out of one's own life if one has the courage to enter into others'.

Cesira

You've studied, and you know what you say.

Ugo

Instead I don't know. What have I ever studied? I know nothing but what has always been in here, always been imprisoned, forever held in with violence, and with no way out.

Cesira

Master Ugo, if you'll listen to me, you'll go to bed, you must be very tired, and I'm afraid you're not feeling well.

Ugo

To be really exhausted to the point of needing someone else to handle one's body and one's soul, that might be the way out.

Cesira

For whatever you need, I'm always here, you know that, master Ugo.

Ugo

Poor Cesira, always there, always ready to help the Gattegnas, this breed which has spawned me into the world as a rare plant which can vegetate on its natural strength, when all the time there is this spirit that works hard and struggles within it. I should not have been spawned, but cultivated, learnt the job of making an existence for myself.

Cesira

It must be very late.

Ugo

It will always be later, Cesira. But what nonsense, what a way of speaking! It must be this solitude which affects us, Cesira. Let's go to bed.

Cesira

Do you need anything?

Ugo

No, nothing... But what a way to talk, what nonsense! I don't need anything Cesira, good night.

Cesira

Well, good night then.

Cesira went to her room in the dark, feeling the wall to find the door. She undressed almost weeping, oppressed by a pain she could not account for; a sort of boundless sadness oppressed and engulfed her. She ended up by undressing hurriedly and throwing herself face down on the bed to drown a fit of sobbing which was shaking her thin body. Silent tears overcame her, enclosing her in the most utter despair, which stayed with her throughout the night. She did not know the reason for her tears, she had never dreamt that one day the master would speak to her at length; and, as she cried, she repeated mechanically: « My God, my God, forgive me! »

Meanwhile Ugo, after a few minutes, was peacefully sleeping, the room filled with the even breathing of a strong, healthy man.

VII

In the morning Ugo woke up at the usual time and even before hearing the monotonous rumble which for so many days had come up from the road, he realized that the cannon had noticeably approached.

Cesira was already up.

« Prepare me a blue suit and a white shirt ».

« Do you wish to go out? »

Ugo smiled:

« Do you think it possible? »

« How stupid of me! » said the woman.

« It really wouldn't be possible », said Ugo going over to the window. Tanks were still passing, but only a fraction of the ones that had passed in the last few days; the asphalt again looked up at the sky, and the men who walked passed in single file, their guns on their shoulders, had greatly increased in number, sagging with fatigue, oppressed by the weight of complicated weapons. Now and then a group would stop for a while on the grass.

Ugo took an hour and a half dressing carefully, then went down to the living room, but even with the curtains drawn it still felt too open; so he went to sit in a special little study right next to it in which it was perhaps a year since he had set foot; it was a sort of little library with a desk between two beatiful armchairs. Even with the doors shut, the windowpanes rattled occasionally; but when he would stop to listen he could hear the desert all around him growing.

Ugo was feeling well that morning, he had slept through the night, and now, as they did during the the best days of his solitude, the old books which covered the walls of the little room attracted him violently, passionately. He began

to look them over. It was not an easy job for him to, read
the series of labels, for each one carried with it, in the speed
of time, all kinds of sensations which Ugo was capable of
enjoying and understanding in all their subtleties, as if instead of an instant he had devoted an hour to each. But in
front of the title of a three volume work he stopped; he
knew it quite well, but when it passed under his eyes he
thought: — this one today —. He put the books near his
chair and began to read:

    « Mamma, como dolore de morte,
    « me pare forte lo planto che fai!
    « Eo vedo, Mamma, che si in core afflitta... »

    The three lines in the book removed him from all other
sensation, and the first part of the day passed quickly; in
the afternoon Ugo had prepared to pass the time the same
way, but that day Cesira was extremely sensitive to what was
going on outside; she seemed to be drawn taut, listening to
every tiny sound which came from outdoors; in fact, at a
certain moment, she went into the little, room, approached
the closed window and said: « Listen ».

    Ugo unwillingly looked up from his reading, closed the
book with his finger as a bookmark and started to listen.
Steps could be heard, a group of men was walking near the
house; it wasn't the first time in those days, but now the
steps resounded within a few feet of the house, and although
someone was speaking in a low voice, the foreign words could
easily be heard.

    « Don't worry », said Ugo. « They're the last ones by
now ». And he went back to reading.

    The men passed right under the window, their steps
dying out round the corner of the house where they stopped
in front of the main door. Ugo went on reading, but was in
fact listening despite himself, while Cesira leaned against
the wall, her face quite white.

    Not two minutes passed before the whole house was
shakes by an explosion which made the walls and the furniture rattle; Cesira put her hand to her mouth. Another

explosion just like the first caused a creaking; it was the front door which was beginning to give.

« They're breaking down the door » said Cesira.

« Then we'd better open it ».

« No! »

« Oh yes. Otherwise in a while they'll come in anyhow. Come with me».

They stopped in front of the door which was already showing some light under the impact of new blows.

« Ask who it is », said Ugo.

« Who is it? » asked Cesira, suddenly calm.

The blows stopped; there was a moment's silence, then an uncertain voice said:

« Is somebody there? »

Another voice ordered:

« Open up ».

Ugo approached and opened the door. He had to move out of the way as five dirty soldiers rushed in, their faces dark with many days' beard, their weapons pointed towards the entrance as they stood in a row. A moment later an officer came in; he was tall and thin with two deep lines on his forehead. He looked around, then said to Ugo:

« Are you Italian? »

« Naturally ».

Then he made a sign to the men and to Ugo indicating for them to move back in the house. They all went into the living room; Ugo led the way followed by Cesira who seemed to have recovered her calmness, and who would not take her eyes off her master.

« You may go on back to the kitchen », Ugo said to Cesira. The woman started to obey him, but the other man interjected:

« No », then asked: « is there anyone else in the house? »

« No ».

The officer sat down after ordering some of the soldiers to search all the rooms, and Ugo too sat down. The two remaining soldiers stood in front of him with their guns

pointed, watching the officer to see if they should allow him
to sit.

« How did you happen to stay here, all around there is
no one, all the other houses have been abandoned ».

Ugo did not answer at once, he was already suffering
from an enormous desire not to say anthing; just a few words
would mean so much energy that for the first time it could
be seen from his face.

« I'm in my own house ».

« There's no one anywhere around, and you stay here
hiding, why? »

« I'm not hiding, I'm in my own house, and I haven't
the slightest idea what other people are doing ».

« But in a short while the others will be here, if only for
the time being ».

Ugo shrugged and looked the officer in the eye without
answering. The officer seemed to be taking on a more familiar expression and was watching him as if he were paying
a call and making polite conversation.

« No one », said a soldier, coming down from upstairs.
Two more came back from the kitchen and the cellar holding
a good number of dusty bottles. The officer pretended not
to notice.

« We must go, sir », he said turning to Ugo.

« Whenever you choose », Ugo answered.

« But you will have to come with us, you don't seem to
have understood », said the officer with an almost pleasant
smile.

« No, I haven't understood ».

The officer's smile vanished immediately.

« It won't take you long ».

Ugo's lips were seen to narrow slowly, start a light pressure on each other until the outline, usually large and
clearcut, appeared like a purple slit on his face. Cesira who
had hardly noticed anything, so busy was she observing her
master's face, shuddered at the sight, and began to look at
him pleadingly, opened her mouth to say something, but said

457

not a word; and Ugo did not see her because he was not thinking of her.

« Come on ».

Ugo got up, went behind the armchair, leaned his arms on its back and calmly began to watch the man who was giving him such imperious commands. Cesira kept her eyes riveted to him, but Ugo, instead of looking that way, went on watching the officer with a calmness only broken by his spasmodically tightening lips.

« I wouldn't try to resist », said the officer cordially. Ugo continued to watch him. For a while they stood facing each other, Ugo with his hands on the back of the armchair, the soldier unsure of himself. At last the officer made an impatient gesture, but Ugo stayed where he was with his candid grey eyes on that face whose irreparably sealed mouth, betrayed its only program.

« Then take him. We cannot waste time, we don't really have very much », said the officer to his soldiers in the language Ugo knew well enough to understand.

Two men came nearer to take his arms, but with a movement which had every appearance of being quite natural, Ugo straightened himself and they were both thrown more than a yard. Then the two soldiers, with the help of a third, started to approach again, but Ugo, with the same ease he could handle a small object, lifted the heavy armchair into the air, without the least strain, ready to hurl it at the nearest one.

There was nothing but a small sharp click, short and absurd, like the cracking of a piece of furniture when the season changes. Ugo fell, and the armchair rolled away from him, upsetting a small table. Outside, two or three simultaneous explosions, together with many others further away, shook the air. The officer gave a quick order and the soldiers started for the door with the bottles of vintage wines in their hands, while the last one, just before going out, detached a painting from the wall and went off with it under his arm.

From the open door one could see the countryside barely touched by the rose light of the sun which was already setting close to the horizon; far away a column of smoke bisected the view which was framed by the doorway. One could now hear the cannon bursts, near and far, enclosed in short pauses of heightened silence.

VIII

Instead of losing her head Cesira felt herself stiffen into a cold, normal calmness; the moment the soldiers moved off without even bothering about her, she rushed to Ugo to find out the seriousness of what had happened. At the same time Ugo had managed with difficulty to turn over and stretch out on the floor. He remained in that position with his eyes towards the ceiling, without saying a word: seeing him move, even before taking care of him, Cesira ran to close the door, but could only push it to, as the sides no longer fitted; then she knelt by Ugo.

« Can you say something? »

« What do you want me to say? »

« You can't stay here ».

« I don't think I can move, right now ».

Then the woman collected all the cushions in the room, and with skillful movements, trying to move her master as little as possible, as he himself could to nothing to help her, improvised a sort of couch underneath him which was not too uncomfortable. Finally she uncovered the young man's stomach, where his jacket was pierced, and bared a small dark hole on the skin a single drop of blood.

« It doesn't seem serious, to look at ».

« What people they are », said Ugo, but in making a slight movement he paled rapidly and tightened his lips. The woman was worried by only one thought: not to lose her calm; and this preoccupation so absorbed her that she couldn't yet think. It had grown dark and she ran to light a kerosene lamp, putting it on a nearby chair and going back to look at the wound. Ugo kept his eyes closed; his breathing was even, and his forehead cut by a deep line which was new to his face, always firm and unruffled.

« How do you feel? »

The woman gave him some water to drink, then tried to bind the wound, which was still not bleeding, with a little gauze. Now she too was pale, her hands had begun to tremble, and at a certain point she fell forward with her head on the edge of a pillow, lying there, fainted. Outside it was quiet, instead of the noise and explosions of a few hours before there was absolute stillness all around the house, throughout the contryside and the plains.

When Cesira came to, she stayed for a long time in that uncomfortable position, unable to move. She searched her memory, saw the yellow light of the lamp throw longer shadows on the floor, and, for an instant, the image took her back to a life forgotten some forty years, she seemed to see the house she was born in, the familiar light of the evenings of her childhood; but she had not yet properly formulated the impression when she felt herself being dragged back to something more impelling; it was then that she remembered, not without difficulty, all that had happened, and came back to reality violently, with an image which overlapped the confusion of her thoughts. She moved, and one of Ugo's hands which was resting on her hair fell to the cushion; she lifted her head and looked into his face, met his velvety grey eyes staring right back at her and both of them smiled.

She thought of running out to call someone, opened the window, but the darkness and silence, compact and infinite, reminded her of their situation; they were alone now, still alone, far from everyone, from friends and enemies. The cool air of the evening seeped in, Ugo turned his head and speaking with difficulty, muttered:

« Leave it open, it's good ».

« How are you feeling? Tell me how you're feeling, tell me something ».

« Stay near me ».

« Don't worry », and she sat down beside him on the edge of the upturned armchair, her eyes fixed on that face, so large and well known to her; but Ugo did not move, only occasionally rolling his eyes without moving his head; his face had become quite white, accentuating the look in his eyes, a little dampened but profounder than usual.

Cesira had to make an effort because the more she realized she had it to herself, the more the silence all around her depressed her and the more she became impassively involved with her one preoccupation — that of doing her duty and not losing her head, of remaining vigilant and wakeful. The night passed slowly, suspended in a boundless stillness.

Then a slow mother-of-pearl caress moved across the floor beneath the drawn blinds, the lamplight turned red, slowly becoming a melancholy faded yellow spot in a pale ray of sunshine; but the silence was the same as at night.

Cesira would not have thought of moving if she had not been startled and frightened by Ugo's voice which asked her:

« Would you draw the curtains? »

She ran without thinking and pulled the cord with such violence that it broke off in her hand. Beyond the window-paning the trees of the garden appeared, and behind them the dark stretch of woods with the sky above it, already white, almost pressing against the glass with its color of cotton wool.

« Thank you ».

« Tell me how you're feeling ».

« I don't know, I've never felt this way before. Stay with me ».

« There's nothing left outside, the plain and the country-side are deserted, a few houses are burning », said Cesira after going out into the kitchen.

« Someone may even come back today ».

« Oh! » and with this exclamation the woman kneeled down by Ugo.

« Shall I look at your wound? »

« Leave it alone, it'll stay right there, and there's nothing we can do about it; if I don't move I don't feel it ».

Several things had collected on the floor, a few coffee-cups, bottles of liquor, a plate with some useless medicaments. Ugo was very thirsty and every now and then drank water and a sip of strong liquor.

Cesira had set the armchair straight and sat down in it, praying with her rosary in her hands.

« Don't pray now, please », said Ugo; and Cesira stopped.

« Cesira ».

« Yes ».

« We should talk, I'd like to talk a little ».

« Yes, yes », the woman answered quickly; but felt filled with a sort of dismay she could barely disguise. Ugo's eyes had become red at the edges and his lips had a trembling which would last for a moment, but which did not escape the woman: Ugo was now burning with a violent fever and would occasionally smile briefly.

IX

UGO

It isn't always easy to talk, to know what one wants to say. All night, so many thoughts, so many thoughts and so many empty spaces Cesira, do you understand? It's good for us to speak a little, you will know how to listen, you too have never been happy.

CESIRA

Perhaps; I don't know, but it doesn't matter.

UGO

It doesn't matter because it's pointless; one is even born happy when possible.

CESIRA

Don't tire yourself, master Ugo.

UGO

It isn't tiring, I can't move at all, I just feel I'm burning.

CESIRA

It's the fever.

UGO

Whatever it is, it doesn't matter. I would like to remember all the people I know, apart from you, Cesira; there's a great confusion in my head. Besides, perhaps I don't know anyone; I don't know anyone, do I, Cesira?

CESIRA

Oh, yes...

UGO

I must think of Rafaele, Luisa, you remember Luisa? Then there's Baccelli, we mustn't forget him. Don't forget anyone, Cesira, keep everyone in mind understand? We must remember Adele too.

CESIRA

Oh, yes.

UGO

And don't forget I have many things to do, that I have several things to say. Keep it all in mind.

CESIRA

Don't worry, how are you feeling?

UGO

Don't you think the house is moving?

CESIRA

No, what are you saying! It's the fever.

UGO

There's someone who wants to come in; let him in.... No, no! Send them away... I must go out now, help me, I must go down there.

CESIRA

But you can't move; no, be still! What's come into your mind! Be still, for heaven's sake.

UGO

They don't want to come to me, I know, they don't really love me. Cesira, nobody loves me, I tell you.

CESIRA

For heaven's sake, you're feverish.

UGO

God, how many people! But no one will listen to me, no one can hear what I'm saying; you too,, Cesira, aren't listening, and you're quite right not to do so. I'm alone, I'm so alone.

CESIRA

Yes, there is no one, really no one; but I'm here, I'm here, master Ugo.

UGO

That's right, we're alone, you say it too. How really alone we are! Have a little drink.

CESIRA

Is it you who wants a drink?

UGO

The house is moving.

After this last phrase Ugo closed his eyes and immediately dropped off. Cesira bent over him; for a long time she listened to his light irregular breathing, watched his closed eyes which were wet with a few tears, wet with a silent unconscious crying. Cesira could not remember if she had seen him cry as a small child, but searching her memory she was seized by a doubt which had not yet crossed her mind; it struck her that her master might die right there, but repeated to herself: « No, it couldn't be possible ».

Then Cesira got up and mechanically set about doing odd jobs to which she was accustomed, looking into the living room from time to time at the wounded man who continued to sleep, the sat down beside him again. Several hours passed, then, suddenly, steps were heard outside. Again there were people walking stealthily behind the house, while on the main road one started to hear the noise of a few vehicles. Cesira ran to the middle of the living room and stared at the entrance in terror; through the hall she could see the door move, someone was slowly pushing, and it was opening.   Three black faces, three pairs of white eyes set in ebony faces stared back at her; a smile flashed across the teeth of three mouths, and it was almost a greeting. Cesira screamed and brought her hands to her mouth. At her scream Ugo woke up. The Negroes came in, looked around as they crossed the room, barely glanced at the man on the floor, asked something which Cesira could not understand, then went out into the rows of vines.

« What's happening? » asked Ugo.

« Negroes ».

« What Negroes? »

« They came in and went out ».

« I know, don't worry ».

« How are you feeling? »

« Perhaps a little better ».

« There are people on the road again, I could go see if there's someone who will help us... ».

« Not yet, Cesira. I think it would be useless now; then I need you near me ».

CESIRA

I'm here.

UGO

There's something on my mind, I want to think about it but I can't. When was I ever capable of thinking? Never, was I Cesira?

CESIRA

I couldn't know, master Ugo.

UGO

No, no, one can't really know, one can't really know anything.

CESIRA

I'm afraid you'll tire yourself.

UGO

It's of no importance, that doesn't count. Do you remember, Cesira, how long time used to be for us? Now instead it runs, flies, it passes us vertiginously and we cannot see it. But our time has been long.

CESIRA

What time?

UGO

Oh, all of it, all of our time. When I was a child the days stretched out before my eyes like a dark passage which never ends. I would look at the other children.

CESIRA

You were very quiet.

UGO

It isn't easy to know what a child can do. I've never know what a child could do. There were too many things which gave me a stomach ache just to think about. But now it's time to think of the others: do you remember?

CESIRA

I thought we had spoken of them this morning.

UGO

As if I really knew someone, as if someone remembered me. There isn't even any pleasure thinking of some things when they aren't even true.

466

CESIRA

What things?

UGO

Yes, because they are real. However, if I think, some shadow remains; a life has even been made of mine; it will be a poor life, but it has existed, and that's already a lot. If one looks carefully, when I wanted to, I always managed to be liked; but it was all coquetry. At the end I thought seriously; perhaps just one sentence would have been enough and I would have immediately been answered: — with all my soul! But I never said anything; too many things I knew too damned well before they happened, perhaps for that reason I did not search them out. But it has no importance.

CESIRA

Master Ugo, you are certainly right, but I'm a poor woman, and now I'm very upset. We can't stay here this way; now I'm going out to look for someone to help us, I'll find someone, I'm sure, who can help me.

UGO

Not yet, wait. You can write, can't you?

CESIRA

Well, more or less.

UGO

Then take a piece of paper and a pencil. You mustn't make any mistake, and remember everything.

CESIRA

Do you want to write to someone?

UGO

Try to write everything I say, as best you can.

And with her doubtful handwriting Cesira slowly transcribed the words that Ugo gave her. For her it was an exceptional effort; she had never written anything, except, occasionally, a few notes which read: *Lectric lite, beens, prise of telegram*. Ugo dictated to her slowly, trying to adapt himself to her powers of transcription. Cesira, all wrapped up in her effort to be exact, understood nothing of what the master was making her write, and when at a certain point Adele's children were mentioned, in order to confirm what he was thinking, Ugo said:

« She will have them, I tell you she'll have them ».

« What? » Cesira asked, lifting her eyes from the paper.

« Oh, nothing, nothing; write a little more, we've almost finished ».

After half an hour Cesira's effort finished.

« Gianni will see that this is understood », said Ugo. « Now you had better hand me the paper so I can sign it, I know that's the way it's done ».

Cesira helped him, vaguely beginning to understand what it was the master had dictated to her.

« Don't let anyone read this paper before showing it to Signor Gianni, if I don't see him ».

« But of course you'll see him », the woman protested energetically, touching his face with her hand and looking at him with a sweet smile.

« Of course I will », Ugo answered « but now I'm really tired ». His forehead was cold and damp, his lips almost black, and his eyes had grown darker, almost sunk into their sockets.

X

At last Cesira decided to go out. It seemed as if the landscape had been flooded with soldiers. They were everywhere; the plain seethed with them, on the hills they were coming out all over the place. Most of them were dark-skinned or altogether black. The first white face Cesira saw she approached; no one paid any attention to her.

« I need a doctor, there's a man dying ». But he didn't understand, looked at her a moment, shook his head; and it was the same with her next attempts. Then the woman went back to the house, frightened by those people, and even more by the thought of her young master up there alone on the floor of the living room. She had barely returned when Faldella and Pietrone followed her in, a gun on their shoulders, frightening her.

« Don't be afraid, it's us ».

Seeing Ugo stretched out on the improvised bed on the floor Pietrone let out a rough exclamation, and Ugo, who seemed no longer able to hear anything, had a slight expression of pain cross his face; perhaps this last perception of the world of the others' helped him move away more happily from all he was leaving.

« What shall we do? » the two men asked each other.

For some time Ugo had not spoken, and the light in his eyes seemed extinguished.

« A nice round hole in his stomach », said Faldella. And they stood there without knowing what to do.

« Signor Gianni will be along in a while. He'll know what to do all right, he's a fast one ».

« He shouldn't be long now », said Faldella.

« He'll be very upset; he was worried; he could only think of his friend. What I say is, how can one be so obstinate, what did you have to stay here for, all alone? »

« We stayed in our own house, minding our own business », Cesira answered Pietrone abruptly, momentarily resuming her old tone of voice.

« If only he could speak », said Pietrone.

Cesira had again leaned over her master and forgotten about the men. Ugo's breath was as light as a child's, and the woman stayed listening to it for a long time, dreaming: it was as if it were yesterday.

When Gianni arrived along with Adele and her aunt and uncle, the silent Gattegna no longer had anything to add to the few sentences he had spoken throughout his obscure existence.

In the bedroom where Ugo had been carried, the newcomers found not only Cesira and the two men, but a couple of doctors in shorts with effeminate white legs.

« If he had been helped in time it wouldn't have been too difficult to save him, but now there's nothing to do ».

In fact, a few minutes later, Ugo closed his lids even more tightly, and without anyone noticing it, passed away slowly, in silence, alone.

XI

The peasants were once more coming down towards the foothills and the plain, pushing the ox-carts ahead of them which they had hidden in the woods or in the farms high up in the mountains, their horses loaded down with sacks and useless household equipment. Baccelli came too, at the head of a caravan of carts on which he had loaded all the most useful equipment of the Gattegna properties. There were also many armed men from other regions, tanned by the sun and with broken boots.

The Negroes had all moved north in a hurry to reach the slopes of the Apuan Alps; the whole countryside was now filled with thousands and thousands of young men in shorts, smiling and friendly, demanding and rough, all furnished with small, fast cars.

The village churchbell was heard again after many days of silence; tolling for the dead. The first peals had barely gone out across the plain when an improvised coffin made out of a few nailed planks was seen to appear from the Big House, and Ugo's body wound its way down the paths of the hill on the shoulders of four peasants. Behind walked Adele, her aunt and uncle, Cesira, and Baccelli, all in silence; then came a long line of men and women, and slightly to one side, Gianni. The new soldiers who were moving through the area watched the sad and disconnected funeral procession with curiosity, stopped for a moment, surprised, then went on their way.

The bell contiued its melancholy pealing.

And there again was that small square patch, enclosed by four bare walls half covered with creepers, that unadorned chapel on which the Gattegna « G » was carved with its three antique flakes of gold still shining like pupils enriched by a century of sunlight, made perennially serene by the constant gaze of a corner of the world really inaccessible to the worries of men.

The churchbell was silent and everyone went home.

Ugo's relatives, with Cesira and Baccelli, went back to the Big House; everyone was held by a different sadness, which cut differently and more or less deeply into their hearts, to last for different periods of time.

In the house Cesira waited for a moment when no one was noticing her, to go and sit in her armchair; only then, after all those days, did she pick up the thread of her thoughts which spontaneously turned from the present to the past.

She had not cried, except for that night three days earlier, and now she still didn't cry, but was thinking, remembering.

In the sitting room Rosano broke the silence; Gianni and Baccelli were also there, Baccelli a little to one side, not knowing what to think.

« This shouldn't have happened ».

« Be still, father ».

« He was the last of the family ».

« Quiet, mother ».

Then Cesira came back with the piece of paper which Ugo had had her write; she handed it to Gianni and went back to the kitchen. Gianni started to read it, read it again without saying a word and passed it on to Baccelli, then Adele's parents read it and Rosano said:

« What a way of writing! » Then added: « now it must

all be made legal, and that is up to you it seems, Gianni ».

Gianni looked at him with contempt.

« I really don't know what's come into you, father ».

« There are some names I don't know », Adele's father went on addressing Gianni.

« I know them », said Gianni coldly, « Try to think of something else, at least for the moment ».

« We'll see to it later, of course », said Baccelli with compunction and very excited; he had also seen his name on the paper and had been overwhelmed by the size of the fortune which came to him, but was also honest and simple enough already to feel the pleasure.

He greeted everyone respectfully, then went off muttering that he would come back in due course to speak with Signor Gianni.

« We should be going too, goodness knows what's happening in town, it would be better to try to get there as soon as possible to see what's happening to the house », said Rosano addressing the women.

« How will we get there? » asked Adele.

« Let's stand on the road, maybe we'll get a ride ».

On the road they did not have to wait long. As they stood wide-eyed watching the myriads of cars and other vehicles of all sorts which were headed towards the city, two blond boys in shorts stopped a small car, looked at Adele with big happy smiles, and motioned her to get in.

« Yes, yes, those too », they answered laughingly, pointing at her parents; and all three nestling on that strange speedy box, they set off. The two blond soldiers kept turning and making friendly gestures to Adele who ended up by smiling, quite pleased.

XII

Gianni and Cesira were left alone. Cesira seemed suddenly aged, showing her real age, walking bent over. Towards evening she started to set the table for Gianni.

Gianni, left alone, had gone up to his friend's bedroom, had leaned against the windowsill and watched the noisy passage of the new army without thinking of anything. Then he had started walking up and down the room, and each of the objects that was still there attracted his attention for a long time. On the desk he saw a few notes on which Ugo used to write with a pencil; in fact something was written on them; he started to look at them as he had done with the objects, but not touching them, not even moving them slightly, contenting himself with deciphering what he could see on the topmost one: *...nothing to resolve, no problems. To know how to wait is the most difficult task, no one knows how to do it; but there is an end even for those who don't know how to wait. Toil, patience, toil, toi, to.*

He stayed for a moment thinking, then went down and sitting at the table asked Cesira:

« Didn't Signor Ugo say anything during the last few days, Cesira? »

« I don't know. He spoke, but I'm uneducated, Signor Gianni ».

« And the paper you wrote? »

« He dictated it to me, he was already quite sick; I don't know how to write, but I put down every word he said without skipping any ».

« I saw it, Cesira. You were very succesful ».

« I did the best I could ».

« He thought of everyone, did you see? »

« Everyone he knew ».

« What a strange man ».

« He wasn't strange, he was a Gattegna ».

« Now you can take a rest, you can retire peacefully to the house which is left you in the will ».

« Oh, no » said Cesira with violence. « I will stay here ».

« But the house will belong to Signorina Adele if she marries ».

« Well then », said the woman after a long pause, « I will stay here and serve Miss Adele ».

« But you could have a better life ».

« A better life, me? ...a better life... » And she raised a finger to the sky with a solemn gesture which intimidated Gianni.

Now the silence in the house drew down around Gianni almost like a friendly caress, and at times he almost had the desire to turn, as if there were someone near him. — Inside of me there will always be something of that man — he thought — even if I didn't want it there —. And this filled him with sadness and peacefulness both at the same time.

(translated by Peter Tompkins)

NOTES ON CONTRIBUTORS

GIORGIO BASSANI, though born in Bologna March 4, 1916, has always lived in Ferrara till 1943, and now lives in Rome. He has published: *Storie dei poveri amanti* (1946), *Te lucis ante* (1948), *Storia d'amore* (1948) and a few essays. He won one of the « Premi Roma » for 1950 with a small volume of poetry which will soon be published by Mondadori. He is associate-editor of « Botteghe Oscure ».

ATTILIO BERTOLUCCI was born in San Lazzaro (Parma) November 18, 1911. He has published two volumes of poetry: *Sirio* (1929), *Fuochi in novembre* (1934). Two more will appear shortly: *La capanna indiana* (short poem) and *L'egoista* (verses). He is also responsible for several translations such as D. H. Lawrence's *Studies in American classic literature,* Balzac's *La fille aux yeux d'or,* and Ernest Hemingway's *Green Hills of Africa.* He lives in Parma where he edits a series of modern Italian and Foreign poets.

GIORGIO CAPRONI, born in Leghorn January 7, 1912, has lived for a long time in Genova; he now teaches in Rome. As a journalist he contributes to several newspapers and periodicals. His works include: *Come un'allegoria* (1936), *Ballo a Fontanigorda* (1938), *Finzioni* (1940), *Giorni aperti* (1941), and *Cronistoria* (1943).

GIUSEPPE DESSÍ was born in Cagliari August 7, 1909. He has taught in various cities in Italy and is now Director of Studies in Ravenna. He has published: *La sposa in città* (1939), *San Silvano* (1939), *Michele Boschino* (1942), *Racconti vecchi e nuovi* (1945), *Storia del principe Lui* (1949). A long story of his will appear in no. 6 of « Botteghe Oscure ».

FRANCO FORTINI (pseudonym for Franco Lattes) was born in Florence, September 10, 1917. A graduate in Law and Letters, he was editor of « Il Politecnico » from 1945 to 1947. He has translated Eluard, Gide, Brecht, Kierkegaard, Doeblin, and has published a volume of poetry *Foglio di via* (1947) as well as a novel *Agonia di Natale* (1948).

ALFONSO GATTO, born in Salerno july 17, 1909, now spends his time between Como and Milan. He was one of the more influential writers of « Ermetismo ». He was active in the forces of liberation. His main works are *Isola* (1932), *Morto ai paesi* (1937), *Poesie* (3rd edition 1943), *La sposa bambina* (prose writings 1943), *Amore della vita* (1944), *Il duello* (1945), *Il capo sulla neve* (1946), *Nuove poesie* (1950).

TOMMASO LANDOLFI was born in Pico (Frosinone), August 9, 1908. He has lived most of his life in Florence, taking a very active part in the Florentine review « Letteratura ». He has published: *Dialogo dei massimi sistemi* (1937), *La pietra lunare* (1939), *Il mar delle blatte* (1939), *La spada* (1943), *Le due zittelle* (1947), *Racconto d'autunno* (1948).

JOYCE LUSSU SALVADORI was born in Florence, May 8, 1912. She took an active part in the underground and the struggle for liberation. A journalist, she now contributes articles on politics, as well as short stories and poetry, to various papers and periodicals. She has published *Liriche* (1938), which was favorably rewiewed by Benedetto Croce in « La Critica », and *Fronti e frontiere* (1945).

GUGLIELMO PETRONI, born in Lucca, November 30, 1911, lives in Rome. During the resistance he was jailed by the Nazis. He has published: *Versi e memoria* (1935), *Personaggi d'elezione* (1937), *Il mondo è una prigione* (1948), *La casa si muove* (1949).

VASCO PRATOLINI was born in Florence, October 19, 1913. He has published *Il tappeto verde* (1941), *Via de' Magazzini* (1942), *Le amiche* (1943), *Il quartiere* (1945), *Cronaca familiare* (1947), *Cronache di poveri amanti* (1947), *Mestiere di vagabondo* (1947), *Un eroe del nostro tempo* (1949).

ANTONIO RINALDI born in Potenza (Lucania), July 5, 1914, has almost always lived in Bologna, and more recently in Ferrara, where he teaches. He has published *La valletta* (1938), *La notte* (1949). This last volume of poems won the « Renato Serra » prize in 1947.

ROBERTO ROVERSI was born January 28, 1923, in Bologna, where he now lives. He has published two short collections of poems in small limited editions.

MARIO SOLDATI was born in Turin, November 17, 1906. He lives in Rome, directing movies and writing. He has published *Salmace* (1929), *America primo amore* (1935), *La verità sul caso Motta* (1941), *L'amico gesuita* (1943), *Fuga in Italia* (1947), and has been an art critic as well.